Applications in Basic Marketing
Clippings from the Popular Business Press

1995-1996 Edition

William D. Perreault, Jr.
University of North Carolina

and

E. Jerome McCarthy
Michigan State University

IRWIN

Chicago • Bogotá • Boston • Buenos Aires • Caracas
London • Madrid • Mexico City • Sydney • Toronto

Printed in the United States of America.

ISBN 0-256-18834-3

1 2 3 4 5 6 7 8 9 0 P 2 1 0 9 8 7 6 5

Preface

This is the sixth annual edition of *Applications in Basic Marketing*. We developed this set of marketing "clippings" from popular business publications to accompany our texts—*Basic Marketing* and *Essentials of Marketing*. All of these clippings report interesting case studies and current issues that relate to topics covered in our texts and in the first marketing course. We will continue to publish a new edition of this book *every year*. That means that we can include the most current and interesting clippings. Each new copy of our texts will come shrink-wrapped with a free copy of the newest (annual) edition of this book. However, it can also be ordered from the publisher separately for use in other courses or with other texts.

Our objective is for this book to provide a flexible and helpful set of teaching and learning materials. We have included clippings (articles) on a wide variety of topics. The clippings deal with consumer products and business products, goods and services, new developments in marketing as well as traditional issues, and large well-known companies as well as new, small ones. They cover important issues related to marketing strategy planning for both domestic and global markets. The readings can be used for independent study, as a basis for class assignments, or as a focus of in-class discussions. Some instructors might want to assign all of the clippings, but we have provided an ample selection so that it is easy to focus on a subset which are especially relevant to specific learning/teaching objectives. A separate set of teaching notes discusses points related to each article. We have put special emphasis on selecting short, highly readable articles—ones which can be read and understood in 10 or 15 minutes—so that they can be used in combination with other readings and assignments for the course. For example, they might be used in combination with assignments from *Basic Marketing*, exercises from the *Learning Aid for use with Basic Marketing*, or *The Marketing Game!* micro-computer strategy simulation.

All of the articles are reproduced here in basically the same style and format as they originally appeared. This gives the reader a better sense of the popular business publications from which they are drawn, and stimulates an interest in ongoing learning beyond the time frame for a specific course.

We have added this component to our complete set of Professional Learning Units Systems (our **P.L.U.S.**) to provide even more alternatives for effective teaching and learning in the first marketing course. It has been an interesting job to research and select the readings for this new book, and we hope that readers find it of true value in developing a better understanding of the opportunities and challenges of marketing in our contemporary society.

William D. Perreault, Jr. and E. Jerome McCarthy

Acknowledgments

We would like to thank all of the publications that have granted us permission to reprint the articles in this book. Similarly, we value and appreciate the work and skill of the many writers who prepared the original materials.

Linda G. Davis played an important role in this project. She helped us research thousands of different publications to sort down to the final set, and she also contributed many fine ideas on how best to organize the selections that appear here.

The ideas for this book evolve from and build on previous editions of *Readings and Cases in Basic Marketing*. John F. Grashof and Andrew A. Brogowicz were coauthors of that book. We gratefully recognize the expertise and creativity that they shared over the years on that project. Their fine ideas carry forward here and have had a profound effect on our thinking in selecting articles that will meet the needs of marketing instructors and students alike.

We would also like to thank the many marketing professors and students whose input have helped shape the concept of this book. Their ideas—shared in personal conversations, in focus group interviews, and in responses to marketing research surveys—helped us to clearly define the needs that this book should meet.

Finally, we would like to thank the people at Richard D. Irwin, our publisher, who have helped turn this idea into a reality. We are grateful for their commitment to making these materials widely available.

W.D.P. and E.J.M.

Contents

Marketing's Role in the Global Economy and in the Firm

1 How to Get Closer to Customers, 2
2 Capitalism Going through Growing Pains, 5
3 Japan's Imports Rise, and U.S. Companies Are Gaining New Sales, 8
4 Uruguay Talks Settle Key Issues, 11
5 Clean-Air Deadlines Pull "Clunker" Vehicles into Inspection Lines, 13
6 Fortress Academia Sells Security, 15
7 Banks Profit by Sweet-Talking Overdue Payers, 17
8 Down-to-Earth Ads Are Aimed at Those Thinking of Heaven, 18
9 Indiglo Watch Lights Up Better Times for Timex, 19

Finding Target Market Opportunities

10 U.S. Mission Goes beyond Video Games, 22
11 Back to School with Binney & Smith's Crayola, 24
12 Bikers Give Ski Resorts Summertime Lift, 26
13 Photography Companies Focus on Niches, 28
14 Waterbed Makers Target Younger, Groovier Snoozers, 29
15 Targeting the New Professional Woman (♀ x $ = ?), 31
16 Vacationing Families Head Downtown to Welcoming Arms of Business Hotels, 35
17 Snack Time? Give Me My Cereal Bowl!, 36

Evaluating Opportunities in the Changing Marketing Environment

18 Ambulance Companies Fight Municipalities for Emergency Market, 39
19 Revolution in Store for Record Shops, 41
20 It's a Mail Thing: Electronic Messaging Gets a Rating—Ex, 43
21 Clinton's Regulators Zero In on Companies with Renewed Fervor, 44
22 Movable Feasts: More People Dine and Drive, 47
23 Kellogg Reports Brisk Cereal Sales in India, 49

Getting Information for Marketing Decisions

24 Old Market Research Tricks No Match for New Technology, 51
25 A Potent New Tool for Selling—Database Marketing, 53
26 Focus Groups Meeting in Cyberspace, 57
27 They Know Where You Live—And How You Buy, 58
28 Rivals Duel Bitterly for Job of Supplying Market Information, 60
29 Data Gap, 62

Buyer Behavior

30 Population Growing at a Furious Rate, 66
31 Marketers Pay Attention! Ethnics Comprise 25% of the U.S., 68
32 High-Tech Marketers Try to Attract Women Without Causing Offense, 70
33 Class in America, 71
34 HBA Companies Are Making Hay with a Little Horse Sense, 74

35 War Stories from the Sandbox: What Kids Say, 75

36 Big Accounting Firms, Striving to Cut Costs, Irritate Small Clients, 79

37 How Not to Buy 300,000 Personal Computers, 81

38 On-Line Service Offers Fast Lane to Small Businesses, 83

39 To Sell in Japan, Just Keep Trying, 84

Product

40 The Ticket to Ride: Smart Cards, 86

41 New Lessons in Customer Service, 88

42 Chinese Flagrantly Copy Trademarks of Foreigners, 89

43 Double Entendre: The Life and the Life of Pepsi Max, 91

44 Attack of the Fighting Brands, 92

45 The Mystique of the Brand: Jarred, Bagged, Boxed, Canned, 93

46 Officials Say "Check It Out" for Better Diet, 95

47 Anatomy of a Fad: How Clear Products Were Hot and Then Suddenly Were Not, 96

48 Their Appeal Could Run For the Long Hall, 98

49 Gillette Succeeds as Others Fail by Reinventing Itself, 100

50 Detergent Wars Bubble Over in Europe, 101

51 Flops: Too Many New Products Fail, 103

Place

52 QVC Draws Wares from Everywhere, 108

53 Contact-Lens Sellers Just Don't See Eye-to-Eye, 110

54 Banks Bag Big Profits with Supermarket Branches, 112

55 Allen-Edmonds Shoe Tries "Just-in-Time" Production, 114

56 High Tech Puts Them Back on Track, 116

57 Can Europe Deliver? 118

58 Firm Takes Season Rush in Stride, 121

59 Japan Begins to Open the Door to Foreigners, a Little, 123

60 Warehouse-Club War Leaves Few Standing, and They are Bruised, 125

61 It's Getting Crowded On Line, 127

62 Marketers Shouldn't Give Up on Wholesalers Just Yet, 129

Promotion

63 Cow-ering from Dairy Products: Lactose Intolerance Marketing, 131

64 First Advertorials; Now Advernewscasts, 134

65 The Internet Snares More Businesses, 135

66 Looking for Mr Plumber, 137

67 The Death and Rebirth of the Salesman, 138

68 In Japan's Car Market, Big Three Face Rivals Who Go Door-to-Door, 142

69 A Satellite TV System Is Quickly Moving Asia into the Global Village, 144

70 Avon Calling, by Fax, Phone and Infomercial, 146

71 Minorities Play the Hero in More TV Ads as Clients Discover Multicultural Sells, 148

72 Hiring the Right Exec Tough in E. Europe, 149

73 From Witches to Anorexics, Critical Eyes Scrutinize Ads for Political Correctness, 151

Price

74 How to Escape a Price War, 153

75 Remaking of a Legend, 157

76 Discount War Can Be Confusing, 160

77 Global Money Trends Rattle Shop Windows in Heartland America, 162

78 Drug Firms' Lobbying to Defuse Criticism by Clintons Pays Off, 164

79 Now, the Tables Are Turning: U.S. Firms Face Dumping Claims Abroad, 167

80 Retail Giant's Loss May Hurt Consumers, 168

81 Frugal Public Forces Firms to Hold Line, 170

82 Final Final Sale! Stores Unload Buyers' Errors, 172

83 Stuck! How Companies Cope When They Can't Raise Prices, 173

Marketing Strategies: Planning, Implementation, and Control

84 Policies Are High-Risk, Not Practices, 178

85 Looking Chipper? You Bet, 180

86 How H-P Used Tactics of the Japanese to Beat Them at Their Game, 182

87 Total Customer Service, 185

88 "Do Call Us": More Companies Install 1-800 Phone Lines, 191

89 Quality Woes Are Spreading Like A Rash, 193

90 Quality: How to Make It Pay, 195

91 Saturn "Homecoming": Publicity Stunt, or Triumph of Relationship Marketing? 199

Ethical Marketing in a Consumer-Oriented World: Appraisal and Challenges

92 The Global Village Finally Arrives, 201

93 Managing by Values, 203

94 Rating Game Is Serious at Buyers' Guide, 207

95 Unjustified Returns Plague Electronics Makers, 209

96 Libraries of Killers Often Include a Book or Two from Paladin, 211

97 Chlorine-Free Paper Is Clean But Unpopular, 213

Marketing's Role in the Global Economy and in the Firm

HOW TO GET CLOSER TO YOUR CUSTOMERS

Often, you don't need huge budgets for effective marketing

BY CHRISTOPHER POWER

They were two of marketing's greatest entrepreneurs. In 1916, Clarence Saunders of Memphis opened a small grocery store—the forerunner of today's Piggly Wiggly—where shoppers, not clerks, picked up items themselves and took them to the cash register. In 1930, Michael Cullen of Long Island added a twist: He turned a parking garage into a spacious supermarket that offered unprecedented variety. To spur demand, Cullen took out big newspaper advertisements to promote name brands such as Ivory soap and Maxwell House coffee. The mass-marketing revolution in America was born—and retailers and brand-name manufacturers were to profit immensely.

Skip forward six decades. Retailers of every stripe are under intense pressure. Merchants and developers have doubled the amount of store space in the U.S. over the past 12 years, even as Americans' real income has barely grown. Giant chains such as Wal-Mart Stores Inc. dominate this glutted market and push their own store brands. Increasingly, established marketers such as Procter & Gamble Co. and Philip Morris Cos. vie for consumers who have often concluded that the only difference between brands is price. Private-label and discount cigarettes, for example, now account for 37% of industry sales, up from almost zero 12 years ago.

If classic mass-marketing no longer packs the same punch, what's a company to do? Marketers are starting to answer than question the way Karl A. Steigerwald does: "We have to go back to being small shopkeepers," says the marketing director of Spiegel Inc. Steigerwald obviously doesn't mean tearing down supermarkets. In some ways, the task is more daunting than that: Steigerwald thinks marketers should travel the painful road back to developing relationships with customers who are now grossly overloaded with product choices.

That means thinking small and acting entrepreneurial--whether you're a giant such as Spiegel, PepsiCo, or 3M, or an up-and-comer such as Manco, a duct-tape maker, or Health Valley Foods, a New Age food marketer. It also means stepping back from the old tactics of 30-second commercials, product line extensions, and massive promotions, and thinking instead of new ways to appeal to consumers. Companies both big and small can accomplish this through technology that uses vast new data bases to plumb people's buying habits. Or they may devise promotional strategies that make a marketing campaign especially memorable--and create a tighter bond with the consumers. The idea, whether big or small, is to recapture the drive and originality of Saunders and Cullen.

If those marketers were alive today, they might already have latched onto data-base marketing. That's what Pizza Hut, PepsiCo Inc.'s $3.6 billion fast-food unit, has been doing. This year it is spending an estimated $20 million on this strategy, which involves creating electronic profiles of some 9 million customers who have gotten deliveries of its pizza. Built from phone orders since the company began home delivery in 1984, the data base can track pizza-gobbling habits across the country. As a result, says marketing chief Robert Perkins, "you can target the relevant message to the right consumer." As a direct marketer for the Republican Party in the 1980s, he pioneered data-base methods that reaped millions in contributions. Now, his goal at Pizza Hut is "returning marketing to the 19th century," a time when merchants knew their customers by name.

He can't do that exactly. But in promotions this summer, his office sent out coupons that matched the tastes of the addressees: Lovers of Neapolitan-style pizza got offers for those, not for thick-crust pizza. Consumers who had been willing to try new foods got a mailing for Bigfoot, a giant-pizza innovation. Customers who had not ordered in a while got deeper discounts than others. Very precise—and very successful: Analysts expect third-quarter Pizza Hut earnings to rise 25%.

At Spiegel, Karl Steigerwald is thinking 19th century, too. In fact, catalog-merchandise buyers at the $2.2 billion marketer are now nicknamed "shopkeepers." That title reflects the changes Spiegel made in order to rebuild its earnings, which declined 77% between 1989 and 1991. Spiegel executives decided that the company's big catalog hand to act like a small, customer-friendly one. To achieve that, Steigerwald told buyers for his book to assume they were creating their own specialty catalogs. Their offerings would then be displayed more distinctly inside the old catalog, somewhat like boutiques in a mall.

Liberated, the buyers surveyed customers to devise "shops" for women who wanted romantic apparel, or for customers who wanted cheaper prices. They also set up a system to track sales

(cont.)

by item to make sure the new catalogs-inside-the-catalog reached their intended customers. The result: some 20 catalogs folded inside the big book, and a 12% sales gain last year, as well as a 32% jump in operating income.

Spiegel and Pizza Hut are both giants that have used their ample finances to get closer to customers. But small marketers need not despair. They can use sophisticated technology too. And they can use nimbler marketing strategies to outwit bigger rivals.

Jack Kahl knows about taking on giants. The chief executive of Manco Inc. in Westlake, Ohio, has transformed his maker of duct tape and packaging from a $4 million company in 1977 to an $85 million enterprise this year. In giant chains such as Wal-Mart and Kmart, Manco now leads the market for tape with about a 40% share, up from almost zero in 1979.

His secret: Ignore the conventional wisdom, which says you can't do much with a ho-hum commodity product, especially when you're facing big, well-entrenched competitors. Kahl noticed that customers often called duct tape "duck tape." Why not create a duck mascot and inject some humor in the marketing? "I said: 'If I can make this work, we'll have a brand name,'" recalls Kahl. Soon, a goofy yellow duck was festooning Manco's packaging and in-store displays. Consumer recognition—and sales—took off.

Manco would probably be just a flash in the pan, though, if Kahl had not followed the fun and games with serious legwork. He courted Wal-Mart, offering special computer-based inventory control that dramatically raises efficiency. He also competes with 3M and others on price, cutting costs to retailers by up to 20%. Lacking funds for massive ad campaigns, Kahl sends out 32,000 greeting cards four times a year to buyers and managers at stores he supplies. Retailers also get his newsletter, which prints insights from everyone from Socrates to Thomas Edison. The store managers clearly remember him—and back his products against mighty competitors.

Kahl created a new identity for a tired product. Likewise, W. L. Gore & Associates, the maker of Gore-Tex fabrics, created a new product in a tired category, dental floss. Then, instead of advertising massively, Gore used niche marketing and data-base technology to create customer enthusiasm.

The company's technicians applied their lessons in creating strong fibers to make a superslick floss. The product, called Glide, doesn't snap, slash gums,

NARROWING THE GAP

HOW BIG MARKETERS CAN ACT AS DEFTLY AS SMALL COMPANIES...

TAP THE DATA BASE
Use purchase data to customize incentives and direct-mail based on demographics, location, product preference, and price.

HIRE FROM SMALLER RIVALS
They excel at "guerrilla marketing"—using local promotions to get close to customers and break through advertising clutter.

HELP YOUR RETAILER
Creating store-specific marketing programs —as Dannon does for retailers selling its yogurt—will win retailer loyalty, differentiate your product, and build local sales.

...AND SMALL MARKETERS CAN OUTWIT THE GIANTS

FIND THE MISSED OPPORTUNITIES
Small marketers can often focus on a relatively neglected product—such as duct tape or dental floss—and take share from a bigger player or increase sales in a tired category.

APPLY THE PERSONAL TOUCH
Smaller marketers can get a big payoff when top executives pay personal attention to customers' letters, retailers' queries, and sales staff's suggestions.

EMBRACE TECHNOLOGY
The cost of data base technology is dropping, making direct-mail marketing a viable tactic for small marketers with tight budgets.

or shred between the teeth. Well and good, but how to take on floss giants Johnson & Johnson and Gillette Co.'s Oral-B division? John Spencer, the Gore manager responsible for Glide, went for word of mouth in his launch last year. Six months before he hit drugstores, he sent samples to dentists for them to hand out free to patients. "The response was incredible," Spencer says.

Because patients liked the floss, many dentists started buying it. To capture customer names for future product launches, Gore at first sold Glide to the public only through an 800 number. In some instances, enthusiasts ordered cases by phone. As a result, Glide had a wide reputation and a core of dedicated users before it hit the stores.

Health Valley Foods, an Irwindale (Calif.) maker of health cereals, soups, and snacks, has been as clever as Gore at outflanking big companies by using technology and niche marketing. Started back in 1970, the company at first sold just to health-food stores. It ignored supermarkets but even so was able to build an unusually loyal following.

It developed a bond with consumers in several ways: The founder, George Mateljan, often answered letters of complaint and inquiry himself, and consumers were able to get friendly advice on healthy eating by calling an 800 number. The names all went on a mailing list for special promotions on Health Valley's growing roster of products. Soon, Health Valley had enough customer loyalty to move into supermarkets, a remarkable achievement for an independent operating in a mass-consumption category such as cereal. Since 1989, its sales have doubled, to more than $100 million.

Glide and Health Valley Foods are both rising brands breaking into the crowded marketplace. Dannon, an established brand, is trying something else. By sharing research with retailers and tailoring marketing to individual chains, it increased sales 9% through late August vs. 7% for yogurt overall.

But it's possible, even without deep pockets, to revive a brand that has lost out. Take Soho Beverages Inc., which Tom Cox, a former manager at PepsiCo, bought with a partner from liquor marketer Seagram Co. after Seagram had acquired Soho and failed to make it thrive. The tiny brand, once a healthy niche product in New York and a few other places up and down the

(cont.)

East Coast, languished inside Seagram because its sales force was unused to selling to delis.

By contrast, Cox has managed to boost sales 50%--from a small base--in the first eight months of 1993. Furthermore, he has done this on a shoestring budget that doesn't allow for such strategies as national data-base marketing. "We collect our data by hand," he says. He hired Korean- and Arabic-speaking college students and had his people walk into practically every delicatessen in Manhattan in order to reacquaint owners with the brand, spot consumption trends, and take orders. To create a new connection with consumers, he sponsored local designated-driver programs--and offered motorists free Soho Soda in the bargain. "It's guerrilla marketing," says Cox.

It's also a lesson in not giving up. The U.S. may not be virgin territory for marketers now, as it as back in the days of Clarence Saunders and Michael Cullen. Many consumers, however, still thirst for the new. Even more, they like to feel that they're being listened to. That may be a yearning the shopkeepers of old satisfied best--and one that still holds the secret for marketing success.

With Zachary Schiller in Cleveland

Capitalism Going Through Growing Pains

by James Cox
USA TODAY

BUDAPEST, Hungary--After all the talk about initiative, empowerment and customer service, the final frontier for employees at the Budapest Marriott is, strangely, fun. They don't seem to be having any. And that bothers General Manager Michael Keskin, an American. He says he's resigned to it for now. "They've learned so much, but they can't seem to learn how to have fun on the job."

Keskin's predicament--if it even amounts to one--could have been astonishing five years ago. Western experts, given their first look at the wreckage left by the collapse of communism, issued bleak assessments of eastern European workers. It would be at least a generation, they said, before a western-style work ethic flowered and the countries developed true market economies. Fun would have to wait.

The experts, it turns out, were both wrong and right. Since the fall of the Berlin Wall--five years ago Wednesday-- eastern Europe is a place of rapid-fire change and maddening intransigence. Former East bloc counties--Poland, the Czech Republic, Hungary, Slovakia, Romania and Bulgaria--are lurching forward in fits and starts, experiencing quiet successes and spectacular failures.

From Poland to Romania, entrepreneurship is flourishing, yet thousands of huge, inefficient companies remain in government hands. Stock exchanges and mutual funds are blooming, but many business basics--such as phones and banking services--are in short supply. The newly homeless beg outside modern offices housing new millionaires. Younger workers get raves from western employers, but their parents have been written off as undesirables whose bad work habits are too deeply ingrained.

WHERE THEY STAND

Economic slides appear to be over

For most of the northern countries-- Poland, the Czech Republic and Hungary--the economic growth appear over. Poland's economy pulled out of its downward spiral in 1992. Last year, it enjoyed the most robust growth in Europe--4%. Polish growth is expected to leap 4.3% this year and near 5% in 1995.

"Poland is ready to bust loose and really become a booming economy," says Stephen O'Connor, co-publisher of the *Budapest Business Journal.*

The Czech Republic experienced a 1% decline in gross domestic product last year; it expects 2% to 3% growth this year. Hungary's GDP fell 2% last year; it should rise 1% this year — the first increase since 1989.

Slovakia and the southern countries of Romania and Bulgaria have been laggards. But even in troubled Romania, there are signs of life: Exports — mainly metal products, minerals and textiles — are up 46% this year.

Regionwide, the private sector accounts for more than half of economic output, ranging from highs of 65% in the Czech Republic and 55% in Poland and Hungary to a low of 35% in Romania.

Economic reform efforts have produced five years of high inflation and high unemployment, but both seem to have stabilized, if not declined.

SERVICE VS. INDUSTRY

Small business is overshadowed

Outsiders looking at the privatization of state-run enterprises have focused on big manufacturing operations. But the engine of growth across eastern Europe has been the service sector.

Retailers and other service businesses were first to be privatized because they employed fewer workers and had minimal capital needs.

In Romania, for instance, 60% of the retail sector is in private hands, vs. only 2% of the industrial sector.

Thousands of small eastern European entrepreneurs are working for themselves for the first time in their lives. They've transformed the streets of their cities and towns by opening clothing stores, restaurants, bars, gas stations, hotels, hair salons, taxi companies, newsstands, butcher shops, consumer-electronics stores, produce stands, galleries, pharmacies, coin-operated laundries, travel agencies and auto-repair garages.

Still, troubles at big industrial companies have overshadowed small-business successes.

Czech newspapers, for example, have doggedly followed the failure of a U.S.-led management team to reverse the fortunes of Tatra, a giant Czech truck manufacturer.

Yet they've paid scant attention to the country's vibrant tourism industry, which brought in $1.4 billion last year — 4.5% of Czech GDP.

Small businesses are working miracles, says Poland's Zbigniew Niemczycki (nem-CHIT-skee) — who has witnessed the dramatic changes since starting one of Poland's largest conglomerates in the early 1980s — one of his country's wealthiest individuals.

"The biggest change in this country is that if you drive around, you'll see every gas station with a small cafe-bar, you go to a store and you can buy anything you'd get in the West, you go to a restaurant and people are smiling and serving. It's all become part of normal life," he says.

LIVING STANDARDS

Inflation still rages

Statistics paint a grim picture. Persistent double-digit inflation, only now being tamed, has eaten away at buying power. Real wages have fallen throughout the region. In Bulgaria, for instance, though real wages grew 7% in 1992, they fell 25% in 1991 and 11% in 1993; Slovakian real wages skidded 25% in 1991 and nearly 8% in the last year, says PlanEcon, a research firm specializing in eastern Europe.

The United Nations Children's Fund recently blamed the economic changes under way since 1989 for triggering "a deterioration of unparalleled proportions in human welfare" throughout most of the region. UNICEF cited rising malnutrition, alcoholism, disease, stress and crime.

But not all the news is bad. For one thing the statistics on wages and buying power ignore the region's vast and booming gray market economy: Millions of eastern Europeans haul in unreported income from construction jobs, fixing cars, peddling cigarettes, driving unregistered cabs or translating for western business people.

More importantly, there is strong evidence the free market is helping create a vibrant middle class hungry for consumer goods. There are 770,000 households on the waiting list for telephones in Hungary — incredible in a country of only 10.3 million people. Satellite dishes cling to apartment balconies and farmhouse roofs. Executives carry cellular phones in their briefcases. And flimsy Trabants, Skodas, Ladas and Yugos are now outnumbered by Fiats, Volkswagens, Opels, Fords and Mercedes on many eastern European roads and boulevards.

Niemczycki, whose company wants to build houses and duplexes in American-style subdivisions, predicts an explosion in housing construction.

"Poland has a housing shortage of at least two million units," he says. "People are stacked on top of one another — children, parents and grandparents living in small apartments together."

The importance of the emerging middle class goes beyond consumerism, says Keith Crane, research director at PlanEcon. "There's a huge group of talented people who had been knocked down, pushed around and beat up by the old system," Crane says.

"They're the ones who are creating new companies, pushing a rapid turnaround in

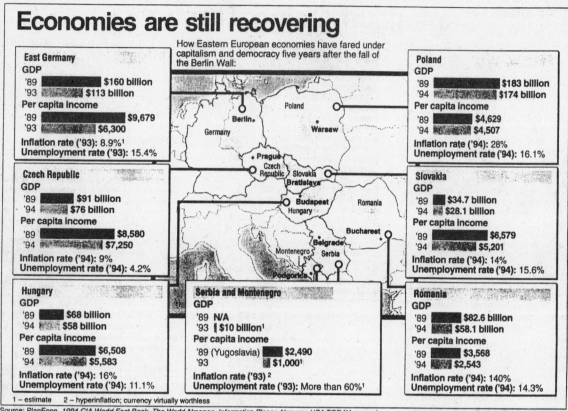

Economies are still recovering

How Eastern European economies have fared under capitalism and democracy five years after the fall of the Berlin Wall:

East Germany
GDP
'89 | $160 billion
'93 | $113 billion
Per capita income
'89 | $9,679
'93 | $6,300
Inflation rate ('93): 8.9%[1]
Unemployment rate ('93): 15.4%

Czech Republic
GDP
'89 | $91 billion
'94 | $76 billion
Per capita income
'89 | $8,580
'94 | $7,250
Inflation rate ('94): 9%
Unemployment rate ('94): 4.2%

Hungary
GDP
'89 | $68 billion
'94 | $58 billion
Per capita income
'89 | $6,508
'94 | $5,583
Inflation rate ('94): 16%
Unemployment rate ('94): 11.1%

Serbia and Montenegro
GDP
'89 N/A
'93 | $10 billion[1]
Per capita income
'89 (Yugoslavia) | $2,490
'93 | $1,000[1]
Inflation rate ('93) [2]
Unemployment rate ('93): More than 60%[1]

Poland
GDP
'89 | $183 billion
'94 | $174 billion
Per capita income
'89 | $4,629
'94 | $4,507
Inflation rate ('94): 28%
Unemployment rate ('94): 16.1%

Slovakia
GDP
'89 | $34.7 billion
'94 | $28.1 billion
Per capita income
'89 | $6,579
'94 | $5,201
Inflation rate ('94): 14%
Unemployment rate ('94): 15.6%

Romania
GDP
'89 | $82.6 billion
'94 | $58.1 billion
Per capita income
'89 | $3,568
'94 | $2,543
Inflation rate ('94): 140%
Unemployment rate ('94): 14.3%

1 — estimate   2 — hyperinflation; currency virtually worthless

Source: PlanEcon, *1994 CIA World Fact Book, The World Almanac, Information Please Almanac,* USA TODAY research

By Julie Stacey, USA TODAY

these economies and leading the drive to re-join Europe. It's not a small group — in some cases 35% to 40% of the population. These are the people making the transition a success."

ON BUSINESS CONDITIONS

Desperate for foreign investment

Bankruptcy laws and contract enforcement remain almost non-existent five years since the fall of communism. Businesses find it an ordeal to get title to the buildings and land they buy.

Taxes on individuals and businesses, which change frequently and with little notice, can be confiscatory. Romania, for instance, has a tax rate of 64% on income above $400 a month.

It can still take hours to get an international telephone line in the Czech Republic. Hungarian telephone directories are at least 20 years out of date. Mail delivery is dicey everywhere.

In most places, businesses still can't write or accept checks because banks don't offer checking or electronic banking services.

Western-style ethics have been slow to sink in. Parliamentary politicians and key bureaucrats sit on boards of the state companies they are supposed to be privatizing. In Romania, where it is common for managers to solicit bribes

before signing contracts, the leading business school has no plans to offer a course in ethics.

Eastern European politicians and businesses have had their fill of western consultants and advisers. But everywhere except Hungary, they remain desperate to attract more foreign investment. Hungary has snared $5.6 billion of the $12.6 billion in outside investment lured by the region since 1989.

In five years, the six countries have taken in just 60% of the foreign investment drawn by China last year alone.

Some western employers still complain about many eastern European workers, who they think are lazy, indifferent and unwilling to make decisions. Absenteeism and drinking on the job are not uncommon, the employers say.

"People are afraid to make decisions right up to the highest level," says John Anderson, an Ameritech executive in Hungary.

But attitudes are changing, largely because the workforce is drawing younger workers, who are more ambitious and adaptable. "Our people were uncomfortable with how important they were to us. They were used to showing up, keeping their heads down and not doing anything unless the boss told them to," says Peter Kraft, head of the American Express office in Budapest. "We demand more, and now they give it to us."

Says Gherghe Florice, furloughed from his job as a gear maker at a state-run Romanian

locomotive plant: "We are not afraid of work. I would work 10 or 12 hours a day as long as I could get paid."

Adds William Szentagotay, another American phone-company executive in Hungary: "These people are not lazy."

YOUNG VS. OLD

English speakers have an edge

An increasing number of eastern Europeans in the 40-to-55 age range, are members of what Hungarians call "the lost generation." It consists of workers too young to retire and too old, in the eyes of their bosses, to learn new ways. "They cannot change," Niemczycki says, his feelings echoing those of many other executives.

Workers who speak English, regardless of their age, usually can find work. But English speakers are rare because many of the Communist regimes discouraged students from learning English until the 1980s. In many cases, people who learned English were blacklisted and had both job promotions and travel restricted.

"We are experiencing only the dark side of capitalism," says Erno Keleti, 46, who managed Hungary's largest bookstore until it went private. He has been out of work since spring. "The younger generation gets all the opportunity."

(cont.)

WHAT'S AHEAD

Fears of social unrest

By late 1995, the Czech Republic will have moved all but a few state-controlled enterprises into the hands of management-led buyout groups, foreign investors and public shareholders.

But the Czechs are far ahead of their neighbors. In every other country, there are hundreds of large industrial companies still soaking up state subsidies. Most have bloated payrolls, outdated technology and no export markets for products they used to sell within the Soviet bloc.

When they are eventually privatized, they will dump tens of thousands more workers onto the unemployment rolls, possibly triggering social unrest.

Another worry is the growing resentment of the region's have-nots. They tend to suspect anyone prospering of having ties to mafia or old communist insiders.

"Growing disparities in income and wealth are inevitable," says Czech Prime Minister Vaclav Klaus. "We have to defend the idea that they're inevitable."

In fact, many of the most successful businesses in the region are run by former party insiders. To have excluded former party members from buying state companies "would have thrown the process into chaos," says Jiri Skalicky, Czech privatization minister. "We had two million party members. To get good work at that time meant joining the party or making some kind of compromise. The people who are able to be entrepreneurs, who have the education and means, they had to have made some compromises in the past."

NO GOING BACK

'Central Europeans' now

Despite widespread nostalgia for the security offered by the old system, few people say they're eager for a return to communism and the isolation and authoritarianism that came with it.

Eastern Europeans are looking and acting more and more like western Europeans. Increasingly, in fact, they are turning their backs on Russia and the East, insisting on being called central Europeans.

"The old system collapsed, it's history," says Aleksandr Kwasniewski, a leading Polish socialist who was sports minister in Poland's last communist government. "No serious person or party is interested in seeing it come back."

Making Inroads

Japan's Imports Rise, And U.S. Companies Are Gaining New Sales

The Strong Yen and a Surge In Competitiveness Pry Open the Market a Bit

Bargain Beer and Cheap PCs

TOKYO — It's April, and, as Japanese have done for centuries, Masahiro Nakajima is viewing cherry blossoms near the Imperial Palace. And guzzling a cold Budweiser.

An American beer? "I never noticed," says the city planner, looking at the red,

By Wall Street Journal staff reporters Michael Williams, Jennifer Cody and David P. Hamilton.

white and blue can. Bud, he says, "is very popular here."

Surprising as it might seem, Japan these days is sucking in imports, and some U.S. suppliers are among the big winners. Companies ranging from General Motors Corp. to Sun Microsystems Inc. to Tower Records Inc. are gaining market share on Japan Inc.'s home turf.

Exporting to this notoriously tough market still is fraught with difficulties, of course, and Japan's trade surplus against the U.S. remains vast. But in important areas, the U.S. is gaining momentum, selling to Japan products ranging from household goods to giant power generators. Those increased sales may portend a shifting economic relationship between the countries.

After dipping slightly in 1992 along with the Japanese economy, the unit volume of U.S. exports to Japan began rising last spring and has accelerated since then. It is running about 60% greater than in the mid-1980s, according to data from Japan's Economic Planning Agency. In February it was up 10% from a year earlier. And the trend shows no signs of abating. In dollar terms, Japan says, its U.S. imports rose 5.7% last year to $55.2 billion — second only to Canada among U.S. customers.

U.S. government pressure is helping, by getting Japan to lower barriers to such U.S. goods as beef and cellular phones and by prodding Japanese multinationals like Toyota Motor Corp. to buy American. The market-opening push has intensified with the Clinton administration; in fact, its tough line may have hastened the fall of Prime Minister Morihiro Hosokawa.

But many Japanese economists, businessmen and consumers attribute the changes mainly to economics rather than politics. They cite the increased competitiveness of U.S. industry and the help from a strong yen, which makes American products cheaper in economically sluggish and newly price-conscious Japan. "The Clinton administration's punch in the mouth to Hosokawa came too late," argues Paul Summerville, Asian research director at Lehman Brothers in Tokyo. "The markets have already taken over."

Widening Trade Surplus

To be sure, Japan's trade surplus with the U.S., measured in dollars, is still rising; it totaled $59 billion last year, by America's count. The main reason: The same strong yen that helps U.S. exports to Japan also inflates the dollar value of Japan's surplus. In addition, it discourages direct investment in Japan, which eventually could narrow the gap.

Moreover, Japan still maintains many trade barriers, such as regulations and informal cartels that frustrate foreign companies. By one estimate, removing all of the barriers could increase U.S. goods exports to Japan by $9 billion to $18 billion annually. "If the issue is whether Japan is buying more from the world and the U.S., certainly the answer is yes," says a U.S. embassy official in Tokyo. "There has been modest progress in making markets more open. But there's still a long way to go."

Even so, many observers contend that the U.S. may have a sizable trade deficit with Japan for the indefinite future because of the two nations' differing savings rates and industrial structures. The imbalance, in fact, may largely reflect U.S. dependence on Japanese capital to finance its investments and government deficits.

Tantalizing Prospect

However, the increase in U.S. exports, even at a time when Japan's economy is weak, offers the tantalizing prospect of denting the deficit. Japan's Nomura Research Institute expects the bilateral merchandise-trade gap to contract 5% in the Japanese fiscal year ending next March.

Sensing opportunity, U.S. companies large and small are attacking the Japanese market with new gusto. "We don't see any barriers to allowing us to sell," says Vincent Naimoli, chairman of Harvard Industries Inc., a Farmington Hills, Mich., company that exports sophisticated magnesium engine parts to Toyota. He expects "significant growth" for his business in Japan in coming years.

Two-thirds of the bilateral gap is in autos and auto parts. Last year, the U.S. Big Three sold just 19,335 vehicles in Japan, while Japanese car and light-truck exports to the U.S. totaled 1.72 million. Total imports of autos made in the U.S. rose 38% last year but still amounted to a relatively modest $1.1 billion.

Chrysler Corp. has begun racking up triple-digit sales increases for its lower-priced Jeep Cherokee, albeit from a tiny base; it sold 4,000 in Japan last year. It expects its sales of Cherokees and other Jeeps to about double this year to 10,000.

Such sales are pacing an increase in market share here for cars made in the U.S. by both Japanese and American manufacturers. In addition, GM has begun exporting Delco radios to the land of the transistor; the radios are installed on some Toyotas aimed at the U.S. market.

In sophisticated items such as airliners, which Japan doesn't make, and chemicals, where the U.S. is much more competitive, the U.S. has long run large surpluses. However, in areas such as heavy power equipment and semiconductors, evidence that the U.S. is beginning to close the notorious "manufacturing gap" is increasing. And in services such as travel and patent royalties, which don't show up in merchandise-trade numbers, Japan reports a $19 billion bilateral deficit.

The staunchest allies of American exporters are the pressures reshaping Japan's domestic economy. Slow growth and high costs are pushing consumers and companies to hunt for cheaper products and are opening up new distribution routes for imports. The strong yen, too, has made many U.S. goods an irresistible bargain. Economists say U.S. gains would continue, though more slowly, even if the yen weakened 20%.

But American businesses are also employing tactics learned from Japan's success in the U.S. American personal-computer makers, for example, have flooded the market with cut-rate PCs, demonstrating that foreigners can make inroads against entrenched competitors even in markets considered strategic by the Japanese — and without help from Uncle Sam.

Warnings in the Press

Now, the Japanese press is warning of an *American* import invasion. In last week's Nikkei Business magazine, a bird's-eye photo of Tokyo is doctored to show a green "Iron Triangle" around the Imperial Palace. The corners are three areas studded with offices of U.S. multinationals: "Little Detroit," "Silicon Town" and "International Finance Center."

American software powerhouses such as Microsoft Corp., Lotus Development

(cont.)

Corp. and Borland International Inc. have seized more than 50% of Japan's PC-software market. Without a trace of irony, some Japanese companies now howl about unfair competition. "Major U.S. software makers give more importance to gaining market share than profits," complains Takashi Inagaki, a spokesman for Justsystem Corp., Japan's largest PC-software supplier.

The pressure is increasing even in such Japanese bastions as auto parts. In a squeaky-clean garage outside Tokyo, Philip Austin, GM Japan's auto-parts vice president, shows off Toyota vehicles that his mechanics have equipped with GM parts: a car with GM seat covers, a sports truck retrofitted with GM wire.

These "demo cars," headed for Toyota headquarters, are the Trojan horses in Mr. Austin's campaign to breach Japan's tight-knit supplier networks. GM recently joined a Toyota supplier association and named a full-time Toyota "customer manager" whose job includes playing golf with Toyota engineers.

A Serious Effort

GM's tactics suggest that many U.S. companies are becoming serious about selling in Japan — and partly rebut Japanese criticism that the Americans don't try hard enough. Last year, GM exported $250 million of such parts as shock absorbers and radiators to Japan, up 25% from 1992. By 1998, GM hopes to sell $2 billion of parts to Japanese assemblers world-wide, including $450 million in Japan. It has been a long slog, though; Mr. Austin set up GM's parts operation here 11 years ago. U.S. parts still have just an estimated 1% share.

Helping him is Tadayoshi Iimura, who spearheaded the Delco sale to Toyota. A former Toyota engineer, Mr. Iimura knew the Japanese auto maker is obsessed with its standing in the J.D. Power & Associates quality ratings. He also knew that GM's Delco radios outscored Toyota's in those surveys — and used that to win orders. "There is and there will be a shift of procurement to GM parts," says Koichiro Noguchi, Toyota's general manager for international purchasing.

Certain U.S. makers of consumer products hear cash registers ringing, too. Detroit-based Stroh Brewery Co. says it shipped one million cases of beer to Japan in the year ended March 31, up from 350,000 cases a year earlier and virtually none three years ago. It expects its Japan sales to rise 50% to 100% this fiscal year.

Some in the beer industry say foreign brewers could eventually grab a 10% share of Japan's beer market, up from less than 2% today. David Jensen, a Smith Barney Shearson analyst, estimates that U.S. brewers ship beer to Japan priced as low as

19 cents per 12-ounce can vs. the 71 cents charged by Japanese makers. He believes that the Americans could undercut the Japanese even if the dollar strengthened to 200 yen from about 103 yen today.

Price Is the Lure

Some Japanese are buying American because it's cheap, not chic. In his tiny Tokyo liquor shop, Norio Suzuki sells such Stroh brands as Schlitz and Old Milwaukee for $9.32 a six-pack — 28% less than domestic beer. He gets his cut-price suds from Shigematsu & Co., an Osaka importer that opened Japan for Stroh in a guerrilla marketing campaign. In turn, the importer's managing director, Keisaburo Shigematsu, chops out layers of middlemen by faxing fliers directly to retailers and by selling in lots of 50 cases, turning down costly single-case orders.

Some consumers are cutting out the go-betweens altogether. In her cramped Tokyo apartment, Noriko Takahashi pores over a catalog from Oregon-based Hanna Andersson Corp. while her two-year-old daughter naps in the next room.

"This page has been very popular with my friends," she says, pointing to a photo of blond babies nattily decked out in purple and gold outfits. "You can't find these styles and colors in Japan."

Gun Denhart, Hanna Andersson's chief executive, says her company shipped more than $1 million of clothing to Japan last year and expects to double that this year. "One customer wrote to tell me, 'They say Japanese companies are invading the U.S. market, but I say Hanna is invading my wardrobe,'" she says with a laugh.

Those closets are getting crowded: Patagonia, Eddie Bauer and Lands' End are beefing up operations here. L.L. Bean had $27 million in Japanese mail-order sales in 1992 and plans to open a third store here this fall. "All of our [U.S.] competitors are right on our tails," says Richard Leslie, Bean's international director. Overall U.S. exports of clothing and accessories to Japan, the Ministry of Finance says, rose 52% last year to $860 million.

Canny American retailers such as Tower Records, of Sacramento, Calif., are selling the Japanese not only U.S. goods but also a whole new shopping culture. The closely held company's three-story store in Tokyo's trendy Shibuya district is blowing away the notion that success here requires copying Japanese habits and tastes.

Tower's American-made compact disks are more popular than many Japanese-imprints of the same albums. The imports are 20% cheaper, a bargain that more than makes up for the absence of Japanese-language cover notes and packaging. Tower displays albums face-out, in contrast to smaller stores that cram in disks like books on a shelf. Enthusiastic staff help by answering questions.

Such details please Rie Ishida, an 18-year-old who buys up to four CDs a month at Tower. "The feeling is good here," she shouts over a throbbing dance tune.

Keith Cahoon, Tower's Far East managing director, says his main rivals are two British outfits, Virgin Megastores and HMV. Tower's Japan stores posted sales of $122.5 million last year, up 15% from 1992.

Other U.S. companies have parlayed their technological strength into big sales. In the early 1980s, for instance, General Electric Co. finally won an order for advanced generators from Tokyo Electric Power Co., one of the world's largest utilities. Now GE is the largest supplier of such generators in Japan — beating out companies such as Toshiba Corp. and Hitachi Ltd. Tepco is its biggest customer.

"Japanese companies just can't make those generators," says Akira Arai, a Tepco executive general manager. GE has a very Japanese-style competitive advantage, leveraging skills honed in its jet-engine operations and applying them to power turbines — much like a Japanese keiretsu industrial group.

The going wasn't always smooth. Once, Mr. Arai recalls, a GE generator broke down, and a standoff developed when GE engineers wanted to take only the defective part back to the factory for repair instead of removing the entire machine for tests, as is customary here. But after days of talks, GE agreed to take back the entire generator. "We now understand one another," Mr. Arai says.

Importing Ideas

As significant as imports of products are imports of American ideas. Japan's major consumer-electronics and semiconductor makers have staked their best hopes for future hit products on U.S. designs and technology. So pervasive is Japanese dependence on U.S. ideas—ranging from microprocessor designs to Apple Computer Inc.'s Newton pocket computer — that some Japanese executives are warning that their companies risk becoming "subcontractors" to U.S. rivals.

In the past, widespread licensing of U.S. technology has tended to build up Japanese competitors — and eliminate the U.S. technological lead. These days, however, most U.S. companies are keeping a much tighter grip on their ideas — making it harder for the Japanese to catch up by copying. U.S.-based biotech companies, for example, have retained rights to the bestselling biotech drugs in Japan.

Others, such as Sun Microsystems, have licensed their technology widely—and still reap huge rewards. Sun brought its computer workstations in the mid-1980s to Japan and signed up Fujitsu Ltd. as a key partner. Fujitsu not only made chips for the computers but also slapped its brand on Sun machines and distributed them as its own — a tactic used by American companies in the 1970s during the Japanese electronics onslaught.

Yet Sun has emerged triumphant and is unworried by Fujitsu's recent introduction of its own Sun clones. In 1993, Sun captured a 27% share of the roughly $5 billion workstation market in Japan, up from 24% the year before, according to International Data Corp. Fujitsu's share, meanwhile, slipped to 14% from 15%.

What probably ensures that the U.S. export growth will continue is that plenty of Japanese are getting rich by riding it. Furniture merchant Katsuhisa Otsuka is one of them.

At a recent induction ceremony for new employees of Otsuka Kagu Ltd., he welcomed three ruddy-faced Americans, representatives of the furniture makers that he chose to help him supply Japan's largest furniture store. A U.S. diplomat praised Mr. Otsuka for importing chairs and tables from North Carolina. "Please import more," he said.

Mr. Otsuka aims to please. "Japanese consumers want foreign products," he says. "This is a company of the future."

Uruguay talks settle key issues

By Bill Montague
USA TODAY

GATT AGREEMENT OPENS DOOR TO TRADE

A global trade deal may be just hours away, but it will be years before the USA reaps the full benefits.

Negotiators from 117 countries huddled in Geneva Tuesday night, putting finishing touches on a deal expanding the General Agreement on Tariffs and Trade, a 45-year-old treaty that sets rules for world trade.

An agreement would wrap up seven years of tortuous talks, dubbed the Uruguay Round for the Latin American country where the negotiations started in 1986. The deal would take effect July 1, 1995.

Early Tuesday, U.S. and European officials cleared the way for a GATT deal when they agreed to set aside unresolved disputes involving several issues, including Europe's barriers to U.S. movie and television exports. That should allow negotiators from the 117 countries to agree on a draft of a deal by tonight's midnight deadline.

Negotiators still are haggling over a host of issues, so details may not be clear for weeks or even months. But world leaders appear to have met some of the goals they set for the round. "We're now on the verge of a historical victory to open foreign markets," President Clinton said Tuesday.

What's at stake? Economists say a GATT deal could add billions to the U.S. economy by phasing out tariffs and quotas here and abroad. Cheaper imports would help keep inflation low in this country, while a surge in exports would create millions of jobs.

But don't hold your breath. The benefits of the Uruguay Round, while substantial, won't be noticeable for years — even decades. In the short term, an agreement would be a big psychological boost to investor confidence. And most experts agree that a breakdown of the GATT talks would have shaken global financial markets. But the world's big industrial nations — including the USA — still face a host of serious problems: excessive debt, sluggish consumer demand, declining investment. GATT won't make them go away. "General Motors isn't going to build a single extra car next year because of GATT," says Brian Fabbri, U.S. economist for Britain's Midland Bank. "GATT isn't going to end the recessions in Japan or Europe. In the short term, it doesn't mean too much."

Longer term, there's little question the USA would benefit. For the first time, the Uruguay Round extends GATT to cover agriculture, where the USA is one of the world's most competitive producers. It also breaks ground by extending free-trade rules to cover some services, such as construction and tourism. Services now account for 19% of all trade, a share that has grown steadily the past two decades. And while the USA runs a big deficit in merchandise trade, it has an enormous surplus in services — an estimated $59 billion this year. That total is bound to grow if the Uruguay Round succeeds.

Another plus: Negotiators are close to a deal on tighter protections for intellectual property, such as copyrights and patents. That should cut the bootleg production of U.S. drugs, computer software and other licensed products in the Third World. IBM estimates it currently loses more than $1 billion a year in revenue due to foreign software pirating.

Studies by DRI/McGraw-Hill, an economic consulting firm, suggest that the new GATT agreements could add up to $350 billion to U.S. gross domestic product in 2005, 10 years after the deal takes effect. It also would create 2 million jobs during that period. But in a $6 trillion economy, those gains may be hard to see. "From one day to the next you aren't going to notice the impact," says Robert Hormats, vice chairman of Goldman Sachs International.

Still, the Uruguay Round should have a major impact on some U.S. industries and companies:

▶ **Aircraft.** The agreement includes stricter limits on government subsidies for all manufactured products, including aircraft. In addition, the GATT deal would incorporate a 1992 pact between the USA and the European Community that specifically limits EC research and development subsidies to Airbus Industrie, the world's second-largest commercial-aircraft maker. "This is a big breakthrough for us," says Larry Clarkson, Boeing's vice president for international development.

▶ **Heavy equipment.** The treaty should play well in Peoria, Ill. — home of Caterpillar, the giant equipment maker. The Uruguay Round's tariff cuts could generate $125 million in revenue a year for the company, says spokesman Timothy Elder. Last year, foreign sales accounted for about one-third of Caterpillar's $10 billion in revenue.

▶ **Textiles and apparel.** U.S. companies would have to survive without strict quotas that now limit clothing imports from cheaper Third World producers. Those quotas would be phased out over 10 years — not the 15 years U.S. companies had sought. "We're giving away the store and getting nothing in return," says Bill Farley, chairman of Fruit of the Loom. He says the 2 million jobs in the U.S. textile industry could be at risk if the Uruguay Round is approved.

▶ **Agriculture.** For the first time, GATT rules would be extended to agriculture. That would cut foreign government subsidies, tariffs and quotas that put U.S. farmers at a disadvantage. "We'll have to decrease our export subsidies, too," says Dean Kleckner of the American Farm Bureau Association. "But we're low-cost producers so it won't hurt us." Japan and South Korea would drop their bans on rice imports. One flaw: Europe would get extra time to phase out subsidies. That doesn't please U.S. farm leaders. "We are disappointed our minimal objectives were not met in some areas," Kleckner says.

▶ **Computers.** U.S. officials pushed hard to eliminate tariffs on a range of high-tech goods, including semiconductors, computer parts and telecommunications equipment. But the EC would only agree to lower some tariffs. "We are disappointed in the tariff reductions on semiconductors," says John Hatch of the American Electronics Association.

▶ **Financial Services.** Negotiators so far have failed to agree on terms that would allow banks, brokerages and insurance companies to compete freely abroad — a key U.S. goal. Top Treasury Department officials reportedly were continuing talks on the issue in Geneva Tuesday night.

But while the corporations and trade associations scrutinize the fine print, GATT supporters say the main benefits from a GATT deal will accrue to consumers. Although U.S. tariffs already are quite low — they average 4% — cutting them further would allow retailers to cut prices of many items, from luggage to fine china. "It would be a big victory for the consumer" says Laura Melillo, a spokeswoman for R.H. Macy.

(cont.)

Consumers for World Trade, a free-trade lobby in Washington, says lifting quotas on textiles and apparel would save the average U.S. family of four $550 a year by forcing U.S. firms to compete with cheaper foreign goods. Overall, U.S. consumers could gain $19 billion a year from lifting all U.S. trade barriers, according to an International Trade Administration study.

The GATT deal would hardly go that far. And even the savings from lifting U.S. textile quotas, for example, wouldn't be fully realized for a decade. "The effect on consumers wouldn't be dramatic," says Doreen Brown, president of Consumers for World Trade. "But at least it's going in the right direction."

Dirty Driving

Clean-Air Deadlines Pull 'Clunker' Vehicles Into Inspection Lines

Foes Decry New Mandates As Targeting Cars Owned By Collectors and Poor

Some States Crush for Cash

By Oscar Suris

Staff Reporter of The Wall Street Journal

Sitting outside of Bernard Murphy's West Easton, Pa., home are several hazards to the environment: two Nova SS coupes from the 1960s, two Pontiac Le-Manses from the 1970s and a rusted '69 Chevy pickup.

When they are out of tune, each is capable of spewing out more than 440 pounds of smog-causing hydrocarbons a year. That is 80 times the pollution allowed by law for most new vehicles and the equivalent of enough unburned gasoline to run a Geo Metro for 10,000 miles. Even when they are in tune, such cars are five to 15 times filthier than new cars.

Tuning isn't an issue for a car enthusiast like Mr. Murphy, who takes pride in restoring and maintaining classic automobiles. Nevertheless, his collection and others like it are at the center of the next campaign for clean air. Having already forced Detroit to address cleaning up the exhausts of new cars and trucks, federal and state politicians and regulators are turning their focus to the nation's 45 million "clunkers" — cars and trucks dating from before 1982 that produce emissions too dirty for skies protected under the Clean Air Act.

Clunker Cleanup

These vehicles make up 25% of those on the road today. But regulators, scientists and industry executives say they account for more than half the vehicle smog generated in the U.S. each year. Federal clean-air authorities want these clunkers cleaned up. They plan to start the process in January by requiring states to begin rolling out waves of federally approved "enhanced inspection and maintenance" programs wherever smog persists.

The inspections won't affect just the clunker owners, but owners of all 60 million vehicles driven in the 83 U.S. metropolitan areas where air has been deemed too dirty under 1990 amendments to the Clean Air Act. Every vehicle in these "nonattainment" areas will have to line up for a 15-minute, $20 to $40 inspection every other year. Owners whose vehicles flunk will be liable for repair expenses up to $450. After they have paid that amount, motorists needing additional repairs may receive a waiver until their next inspection.

In addition, in nearly a dozen states, governments either have considered, or already have paved the way for, voluntary programs that would pay drivers to have their polluting vehicles crushed at a scrap yard.

Pending Deadlines

Behind the push are November deadlines coming due under the federal Clean Air Act. November is when dozens of states must file plans for reducing ozone, which is increased by sun-baked auto fumes and produces smog. States that don't comply will face the withholding of hundreds of millions of dollars in federal highway funds. But rather than resort to no-drive days, mandatory car pools and limits on vehicle idling, most states are inclined to

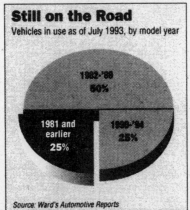

Still on the Road
Vehicles in use as of July 1993, by model year

1982-'89
50%

1981 and earlier
25%

1990-'94
25%

Source: Ward's Automotive Reports

try to get clunkers off the road by putting pressure on the drivers.

For decades, the responsibility of making cars run clean fell mostly on the shoulders and laptops of automotive engineers in Detroit. After more than two decades of being portrayed as the bad guys on clean air, auto makers have learned to play hardball, lobbying and suing over regulations that state how they must build cars and trucks. Indeed, it is partly to avoid a long, costly court fight that the Environmental Protection Agency is trying to broker a compromise — largely on Detroit's terms — in a feud over whether the Northeast will be allowed to require the sale of electric cars and to adopt California rules for auto emissions.

Ironically, with citizens being required to share the emission burden, pressure is likely to revert to Detroit in a different form: A car's emissions characteristics will join styling, cup holders and air bags on the list of features that car buyers seek.

I would junk a clunker, says Jim Salvaggio, an air-quality regulator in Pennsylvania. "There's no point putting it through an inspection."

That is just what regulators expect, once people learn the penalty for driving dirty. California, home to the nation's worst air problems, may be where clean cars acquire cachet first. A proposed Senate bill there would assign a pollution rating to every new and used vehicle up for sale. Displayed like a sticker price, the vehicle's "smog index" would also determine "pollution allowances" for 2.5 million vehicles in Southern California. The dirtier the vehicle, the fewer miles it can be driven before it is called once again for inspection. Likewise, motorists who drive the most will use up their allowances the quickest. Says Alan Uke, a San Diego entrepreneur who conceived the bill and found a senator to sponsor it: "They can lower their pollution by either driving less, by modifying their car or by buying a [cleaner] car."

Cost of Cleaner Cars

Technically, auto makers and regulators are approaching the limits as to how much cleaner vehicles can be made to run. Since the first federal emissions standards went into effect in 1968, emissions from cars have been cut by more than 90% to just one pound of smog-causing hydrocarbons for every 1,000 miles in 1993. Under California's stiff clean-air rules enacted in 1990 — the Low-Emission Vehicle program — that is to be cut another 90% to one pound for every 10,000 miles by 1997. That is less than the amount of hydrocarbons many oak trees exhale in a year.

The cost of that much more pollution reduction can add up. Estimates made available by General Motors Corp., Ford Motor Co. and Chrysler Corp. have put the cost of meeting California's Low-Emission Vehicle program — which is being considered by a dozen states in the Northeast and, in effect, includes a sales mandate for electric vehicles — at $9,800 to more than $102,100 for each ton of pollution prevented; the cost would come as auto makers raised the level of technology to meet the program's standards. Those figures compare with the estimated $10,000 to $50,000 a ton it would cost if regulations were passed to further clean stationary sources, such as smokestacks.

Moreover, critics of California's program say it is so costly to auto makers that

(cont.)

they will probably raise new-car prices, providing little incentive for consumers to dump their clunkers for cleaner cars. Some argue that a vehicle-inspection program with teeth could cost a state government just $500 to $1,700 a ton — and nudge clunker owners into newer models to avoid penalties and repair bills.

States Seek Solutions

In other states facing Clean Air Act deadlines, regulators are buying high-tech treadmills big enough to test '79 Buicks. They are trying out sensitive infrared devices that can analyze fumes from passing vehicles. And they are even thinking about putting limits on which days people can drive, the ways people can commute and how often they can start up their gasoline-powered lawn mowers.

Old cars still look like the most viable regulatory target, even though foes say stringent regulation penalizes people who would love to drive a new, environmentally friendly car but can't afford to. At an inner-city used-car lot operated by a Detroit charity, David Smith looks for a bargain among the wrecked and the dented. The 23-year-old father needs something inexpensive to drive to his job as a part-time security guard—and to school—but even the rusting hulks offered for less than $1,000 seem overpriced to him. "They're robbing people here," he says.

People like Mr. Smith depend on clunkers, says Rick Frazier, operator of the charity lot, Mother Waddles, which is named for a nun and relies on donated cars. He produces a stack of letters, most scribbled by hand, from Detroit citizens pleading for one of the beat-up cars Mr. Frazier gives away weekly. Restricted by a sparse bus system that operates infrequently between the city and suburbs, most of the writers say they can't make job interviews or doctor appointments.

Still, protest over the coming assault on clunkers has been limited, perhaps because its dimensions haven't sunk in yet. Where opposition has surfaced, it has been intense.

All it took was the passing of the federal government's toughened vehicle-inspection program in Pennsylvania to inspire Mr. Murphy, never before an activist, to pack a cooler of soda pop in his Chevy truck and drive 70 miles to Harrisburg. There, standing on the capitol steps, he led a raucous rally of some 2,000 fans of old and classic vehicles. "Something has to be done about the attack on old cars," says Mr. Murphy, a 30-year-old factory mechanic. "This is basically going to force you to buy a new car every five years."

In New Jersey, Assemblywoman Maureen Ogden last year introduced a bill under which owners could voluntarily sell their old, polluting vehicles to businesses that would have them crushed in exchange for state cleanup credits. But instead of receiving praise for her environmental efforts, she was accused by classic-car collectors of attacking their hobbies and livelihoods. "I thought, 'Oh my goodness, it's like the NRA all over again,'" she recalls, referring to the intense lobbying for which the National Rifle Association is known. Today, she says she is in the process of rewriting her bill, inserting provisions to apply to all vehicles.

Still, it is tough to make the general public passionate about clean driving. Last winter, Sun Co. of Philadelphia started using a remote-sensing device to spot pollution from passing vehicles in its metropolitan area. By beaming a ray of light across a city road and stationing a video camera a few yards away, Sun was able to spot more than 3,400 vehicles out of 75,000 screened that were spewing fumes beyond federal limits. Sun offered to pay for a tuneup for such cars and give $100 to anyone who accepted. But the participation rate was less then 20%. "People's eyes just glazed over," a Sun spokesman says.

Bounty on Clunkers

Voluntary scrappage programs look more promising. In Chicago two years ago, anyone offering an old car for destruction was offered $950. "Neat program.

Excellent purpose," said one of the 207 owners who participated. The sponsors (which included GM, Mobil Corp. and the Environmental Defense Fund) estimate that the program eliminated 43.6 tons of hydrocarbon pollution over a two-year period. Those who cashed out of their clunkers bought vehicles that were on average eight years newer.

In California, Ford and Unocal Corp., of Los Angeles, teamed up in 1990 to scrap more than 8,000 pre-1971 automobiles, as state officials handled thousands of phone inquiries from owners who had heard about the program. Unocal says the program removed 13 million pounds of pollutants a year — the equivalent of taking 150,000 new cars off the road.

Of course, there is something in these programs for the sponsoring oil companies and car makers. They get government-awarded credits that let them delay cleaning up their smokestacks. The Clean Air Act provides for such credits and even allows for them to be swapped and sold like baseball cards.

To some clunker owners, this sounds like a cynical trade favoring big, rich corporations that have something to gain for their environmentally conscious action. Moreover, some drivers point out that clunker-crushing destroys a major source of spare and used parts, making repairs tougher to perform.

Clearly, though, there are those who want to crack down on the worst polluters, whether through scrapping them or fixing them. "It is going to take 15 minutes every two years to get a vehicle inspected." says Keith McCall, a state representative in Pennsylvania. (That's a very small sacrifice to pay as an individual in this country to get clean air."

Fortress Academia Sells Security

By Ellen Graham
Staff Reporter of The Wall Street Journal

Selling a college today takes more than top professors, a powerhouse football team and lush financial-aid packages.

Try 1,500-pound-per-square-inch electromagnetic locks on residence-hall entrances, a point of pride at Seton Hall University. Or walkie-talkie-toting student patrols like those spotlighted in the University of Pennsylvania's brochures. Or a comprehensive rape-counseling program, such as that established at Boston University with last year's senior-class gift.

With college applicants jittery about rising campus violence, security poses a touchy marketing problem for academia. Urban schools, in particular, are forced to promote their myriad crime-prevention measures—but without implying that their campuses are actually dangerous. And now that colleges must by law disclose crime statistics, administrators are being drawn into a new numbers game to rival their perennial jousting over SAT scores and tuition costs.

The Campus Security Act of 1990 requires colleges to annually tally the murders, rapes, aggravated assaults and other serious crimes on their campuses, and to make the numbers available to current and prospective students. The law — pushed through Congress by the parents of a Lehigh University freshman who was murdered in her dorm by a fellow student in 1986 — has led to inevitable comparisons and rankings, a source of consternation among college administrators.

Biggest Fear

"A college's biggest fear is being labeled the capital of mayhem," says Dorothy Siegel, director of the National Campus Violence Prevention Center at Towson State University in Maryland.

At a meeting a few weeks ago, one Midwestern college administrator confided to a colleague that his school's rape statistics had shot up 200% in the past year — from one incident to three. "I can already see the headlines," he fretted.

In a compilation published in the Chronicle of Higher Education last January, 2,400 colleges reported 7,500 violent crimes for the first year of data collection, including 30 murders. Still, by far the most prevalent crime on campus is petty theft— a category omitted by the federal statute.

Negative data haven't decimated enrollments, as initially feared. Applications rose at the University of Florida in Gainesville after the 1990 serial murders there of five students, one of whom was enrolled at another nearby school.

Nor did the University of California at Berkeley see a drop in applications after the 1992 murder of a female sophomore in a busy campus office building. But W. Russell Ellis, Berkeley's vice chancellor for undergraduate affairs, says schools have no way of tracking the number of students who may be deterred from applying — or enrolling — because of security concerns. "Common sense tells me [the crime statistics] are having some impact on urban schools," he adds.

'Safest Campus in America'

USA Today published its own safety ranking of nearly 500 schools in 1990, and those with high marks—like Philadelphia's University of Pennsylvania and Temple University — cite their ratings in promotional literature.

Adelphi University in Garden City, N.Y., seized on its USA Today ranking to proclaim itself "the safest campus in America" in ads in the New York Times, Harper's and other publications. Privately, an administrator at another university calls the boast "dumb," because any school's numbers can swing wildly from year to year.

Schools are on the honor system when it comes to publishing crime statistics; the Department of Education doesn't audit the figures. While college officials and outside security consultants believe intentional underreporting is rare, most complain that the raw numbers are misleading.

New York University, in the heart of Manhattan's Greenwich Village, reported three burglaries in 1991, while Kansas State University, a school of about the same size in Manhattan, Kan., (pop. 35,000), reported 241. Pat Bosco, dean of student affairs at Kansas State, says over half those crimes involved theft of laminated parking permits hung on car mirrors. "The rationale for the law was exceptionally good," he says. "But the consumer is left with cold statistics that are inconsistant and very difficult to explain."

The rules for tabulating data are vague, and subject to wide interpretation. For one thing, the law applies to crimes occurring on campus property, but not the surrounding neighborhood. Because the Gainesville murders occurred off campus, for example, they weren't reflected in the university's crime report. Yet Johns Hopkins University had to report 13 weapons arrests — all of them involving nonstudents apprehended in and around the university medical center some miles from the main undergraduate campus in Baltimore.

The law stipulates that only crimes reported to campus security or local police need be listed in a school's crime report. Thus, offenses such as underage drinking that are often handled as disciplinary rather than police matters are underreported, particularly at private schools. (At many state universities, where campus cops often are state employees, offenses are more likely to result in arrests.)

"There's underreporting across the system," says Maurice O'Connell, vice provost for student life at American University in Washington, D.C. "We want students to have a realistic picture of the campus environment, but the current structure doesn't make for valid comparisons."

By far the thorniest debate centers on the reporting of rapes and sexual assaults. College counselors told of such crimes currently aren't obligated to report them to authorities — ostensibly to encourage victims to come forward and to protect their privacy. The government is now considering expanding this confidentiality shield to deans and residence-hall directors.

But Connie and Howard Clery, whose daughter Jeanne was the victim of the Lehigh murder, view this as a loophole that would lead to more underreporting. Already, the Clerys assert, too many schools are "cooking their crime statistics."

If nothing else, the law has forced schools to acknowledge campus crime. College presidents now huddle with Federal Bureau of Investigation agents at crime conferences, and residence halls are being fortified in a way once reserved for nuclear-research laboratories.

The surveillance cameras and "electronic enunciator" alarms figure prominently on campus tours. At LaSalle University in Philadelphia, applicants are guided through dorm security turnstiles down hallways where doors are fitted with combination locks and peepholes. "Certainly we play it up," says Brother Gerald Fitzgerald, director of admissions. "It seems to relieve the fears of parents."

Bill Whitman, a campus security consultant in Thorndale, Pa., says he gets about 20 calls a week from parents asking him to steer them to a safe campus. His advice: Schools with the highest numbers are often the most vigilant in tackling crime.

As part of its out-of-court settlement of a lawsuit filed by the Clery family, Lehigh spent over $1 million installing an electronic ID card-swipe system at all residence-hall entrances. Like many other

(cont.)

schools, Lehigh has also wired dorms with a "perimeter access system" that trips an alarm if exterior doors are propped open. Jeanne Clery's murderer, who is now on death row, entered her dorm via a propped door—the scourge of school police everywhere.

Security concerns have led, on a few campuses, to the resurrection of controls on student life not seen since *in loco parentis* rules were abandoned 20 years ago. Boston University and the University of South Carolina, for example, have reimposed some restrictions on overnight visitation privileges in dormitories.

Mindful that some 80% of all campus crime is student-perpetrated, St. Augustine's College in Raleigh, N.C., has taken yet another tack. Along with SAT scores and transcripts, it asks applicants for a statement from their hometown police attesting to whether they have criminal records. School officials stress, however, that students with police records won't necessarily be denied admission.

Banks Profit by Sweet-Talking Overdue Payers

By G. BRUCE KNECHT

Staff Reporter of THE WALL STREET JOURNAL

When Chase Manhattan Bank can't reach one of its delinquent credit-card customers by phone, it doesn't send a threatening letter. It sends a videotape.

And coming from a bank that isn't being paid its due, the tape has a surprisingly amiable tone. Far from demanding money or making threats, it oozes with understanding. "Even though you're in collection, you're still our customer," says the commentator. "You're still No. 1 with us."

The tape ends by imploring viewers to telephone a Chase representative. But even this is delivered with velvet softness: "We understand completely why you may not feel comfortable calling us to discuss your account, but we believe that together we can work it out."

Chase and other unsecured lenders are going soft. "It's not that the banks want to be nice guys," says Donald B. Kramer, the senior partner of Kramer & Frank, a St. Louis law firm that specializes in collections. "They are concerned about what happens if they aren't nice guys: If you press people too hard, it's very easy for them to jump into bankruptcy."

The head of Chase's credit-card business, John A. Ward III, is convinced that the new approach has improved the bank's collection rate. The stakes are high: Of Chase's $9.7 billion in credit-card loans, Mr. Ward says 5.6%, or $543 million, is more than 60 days past due.

The new approach took root after the recession led to a sharp increase in the number of consumers who could not pay their debts. "We began to recognize that we're pretty far down the priority list," says Edward R. Scully, the vice chairman of First USA Bank, a Wilmington, Del., subsidiary of Dallas-based First USA Inc. "People are going to pay the rent and put food on the table before they pay credit-card companies. Our leverage is not that great."

Card companies, which are the biggest providers of unsecured loans to individuals, also found that customers who cannot pay a credit-card bill generally have a number of unpaid creditors — and debtors tend to pay those they like the most.

"People would rather do business with a company that is nice to them than a company that harasses them," says Ruth Susswein, the executive director of Bank Card Holders of America, a McLean, Va., consumer-advocacy group.

It was different in the old days. Since delinquent card holders were generally viewed as unreformable deadbeats, the presumption was that the lender-creditor relationship was over. Most card issuers used threats to bully borrowers into paying at least some of what they owed. Kenneth R. Crone, Visa U.S.A.'s vice president for consumer risk, says, "We just tried to get as much out of them as we could, and then we closed their account."

The new approach is based on a radically different assumption: that most delinquent card holders are good customers who have fallen on temporary bad times. Issuers assume—indeed hope—that nonpaying card members eventually will return to good standing.

What's more, many card executives believe that recruiting new card members has become so difficult that they are better off rehabilitating existing customers than recruiting new ones. "We're in a highly competitive business," Mr. Scully says, "so we want to hang on to as many of our customers as we can."

In implementing the new strategy, card executives say the crucial ingredients are maintaining as much contact as possible and treating nonpaying customers with the same respect as other card holders. "If you lose contact with a customer, your ability to turn things around diminishes very rapidly," says Bruce C. Hammonds, the chief operating officer of MBNA America Bank, a subsidiary of MBNA Corp. of Newark, Del.

"We used to say pay now or you're out of here; we're going to refer you to a lawyer," says Suzanne Tratner, a collector who works in a Chase collections center. "Now we try to help customers. And it's true: If you take a different approach with customers, they take a different approach with you."

Chase's collectors do their best to be as friendly and upbeat as they can, particularly with card users who have no previous payment problems. "When I make the first call," says another collector, "I say, 'You've never been in collections. Has anything in your life changed? Is there anything we can do to help?'"

It is when customers refuse to talk that the videotape comes into play. The tape acknowledges Chase's desire to develop an ongoing dialogue and its commitment to treating nonpaying customers with respect. "You know when a person is first approved for a credit card it seems like everyone cares," the commentator says. "But as soon as a customer has a problem it suddenly seems like no one cares. At Chase we care about all our customers."

The bank sent about 10,000 videotapes to customers last October, and since they produced a 28% increase in customer contacts, the bank plans to send another batch of tapes in July. The tape, which cost $37,000 to produce, costs $3.50 a copy to duplicate and mail.

The hope is that customers will phone the collection department, describe their problems and agree to a revised schedule for repaying their debt. The renegotiated repayment plans include reductions in the required monthly payments and the forgiveness of fees and at least a portion of interest charges.

At Chase, the average balance of troubled accounts is about $2,500. Since the minimum payment on most cards is 2% of the outstanding balance, the average account would require a minimum monthly payment of $50. A typical repayment program would result in a $25 monthly payment.

"We don't like to advertise it, but we will reduce fees and interest," says Joseph J. Giuseffi, Chase's nationwide collections chief. "We find that if you forgive fees and some interest, people are more likely to complete the repayment programs." And according to Visa's Mr. Crone, "The people who successfully complete a repayment program rarely go into bankruptcy."

Card issuers are also more willing to accept repayment plans negotiated by the National Foundation for Consumer Credit, a nonprofit organization that negotiates on behalf of borrowers. Chase, which several years ago rejected more than 30% of the plans proposed by the organization because they were thought to be overly favorable to borrowers, now accepts almost all of them.

As collection techniques have changed, card companies say they have to find a new breed of collector. "In the old days, a good collector was persistent, demanding and sometimes abusive," says Mr. Scully of First USA. "Today, the best collectors have the attributes of a salesman."

Down-to-Earth Ads Are Aimed at Those Thinking of Heaven

* * *

Ursuline Order of Nuns, Seeing Their Numbers Dwindle, Launch Recruitment Drive

By Valerie Reitman
Staff Reporter of The Wall Street Journal

YOUNGSTOWN, Ohio — It isn't a normal advertising assignment.

Instead of promoting a lower price or better taste, the folks at a Cincinnati advertising agency are pitching something of a more celestial order: the nunhood.

Their client is the four-century-old Ursuline order, and the mission is to help the Roman Catholic sisters boost their ranks, which have plummeted in North America to fewer than 3,000 nuns scattered among 20 convents.

And it must be done subtly. After all, a hard-sell campaign probably won't make someone sign up for a lifetime commitment to poverty, chastity and obedience.

"We had to pull back, because we felt that when dealing with the soul and God, a snappy headline wouldn't be the answer to anybody's questions," says Sive/Young & Rubicam copywriter Melanie Marnich. "It's not like selling a cheeseburger."

Forget the Ruler

And so, Madison Avenue — or in this case, East Seventh Street in Cincinnati—created an image campaign to put to rest the stereotypes of the convent: the black habit, the big white collar, the hand gripped around a ruler.

Like other orders, the Ursulines had advertised in Catholic magazines, but with little success. And when they looked at their thinning and aging ranks — half as many nuns as 30 years ago — they knew something more than prayer was needed. In recent years, the nuns in Youngstown would get just a handful of inquiries annually, and sign up just one or two novices.

It is a crisis for convents everywhere, which are fast dwindling in size and in some cases disappearing. Over the past 25 years, the total number of nuns in the U.S. has fallen more than 50%, to 94,000 from 178,000.

The Ursulines decided their image needed an overhaul. They stumbled on the Cincinnati agency through a friend whose husband dealt with the firm. "They gave us an uncluttered message for a real cluttered marketplace," says Sister Jacquelyn Herpy, the nun here who is overseeing the nationwide campaign. The ad agency, which says it spent about $70,000 worth of its time, agreed to do the campaign pro bono.

A Nun for the '90s

The result is a series of print ads, a radio spot and even a direct-mail brochure that try to depict what being a nun in the 1990s is all about. The ads, which will begin running this fall, are being distributed to Ursuline convents, each of which will do a local media campaign.

One radio spot features a nun (actually an actress) talking about her busy schedule taking classes for her master's degree, doing community-service work and meeting friends: "I guess people are surprised when they find out I'm a (pause) nun."

The print ads show real Ursulines as many of them are: contemporary women in street clothes doing social projects. There is Sister Mary Scheetz, armed with hammer and nails, who renovated and now runs two houses in Youngstown for homeless families. Another ad shows Sister Pam Mueller, a speech pathologist, with a developmentally impaired boy. "Because in order to keep pace with a changing world," says the Ursuline's new slogan, 'we have to change with it. And that's what being an Ursuline is all about."

But aren't nuns supposed to be "called" to their vocation by a higher power than advertising? Indeed they are, says Sister Jacquelyn. But the image campaign "helps those who are called feel more comfortable when they hear the calling," she says.

Promoting Their Lives

"I think it's wonderful. We have to make people aware that our lives are so normal," says Sister Virginia McDermott, 78 years old.

Sister Virginia has seen a lot of changes in her 60 years in the order. Most of her colleagues have shed their habits, and many have careers beyond the teaching and hospital work that was once their mainstay. They are lawyers, social workers and community organizers.

The few new enrollees tend to be in their 20s or 30s—far older than the once-standard age of 18. In fact, the Youngstown community's newest recruit is a 50-year-old divorcee with two children and a grandchild who converted to Catholicism seven years ago. (The church annulled her marriage.)

The older sisters live in a "mother house," a sprawling complex on pastoral grounds. Their rooms have television sets and bathrooms. Upstairs is an infirmary to provide nursing care for the members as old as 98. The sisters take meals in the dining hall, have an optional daily Mass and often swim in an Olympic-size pool. "Though we live in what used to be called an institution, it's very homey, very chummy," says Sister Virginia.

The younger sisters, such as Sister Jacquelyn, who is 45, tend to live in group houses or their own apartments in the city. Sister Jacquelyn, for instance, now shares a house with three other nuns.

Hunting for Bargains, Too

The order pays for their housing, education, cars, food and travel. It also provides $75 a month for incidentals like clothing. But how does someone as stylish as Sister Jacquelyn — clad on a recent day in black culottes, pearl earrings and a gold bracelet—survive? She is a bargain-hunter, finding buys like a $300 pair of designer shoes for $3.99 in Cleveland.

That stylishness surprised the ad agency's officials. "They go to the movies, they wash cars, they wear street clothes, they do most of the things we do," says account representative Karen Bell. "But nobody knows that."

By promoting their everyday lives, the Ursuline sisters hope to counter the peer pressure that keeps some potential recruits from signing on. Some who express a calling find themselves abandoned by friends and relatives. A 37-year-old Ohio hospital technician, who didn't want to be identified, says a few of her friends stopped speaking to her when she confided that she is contemplating becoming a nun. She says one friend told her: "I couldn't go out to a bar with you or on vacation with you because I wouldn't know how to act."

Another problem the sisters are addressing is the fear of a lifetime commitment. While Sister Jacquelyn describes her life as "so full of opportunities," she also acknowledges that she is among just four members of her original class of 22 still in the order.

Now, the order is offering short-term residences of a few years to women who aren't sure they want to be nuns.

One thing the campaign doesn't show is that nuns don't always take themselves seriously. When they saw "Sister Act," the Whoopi Goldberg movie about a singer hiding out in a convent, many howled. "I was in the movie theater laughing my fool head off," says Sister Germaine Staron, 66. "If you hadn't been in the convent, you wouldn't realize how funny it was."

Indiglo Watch Lights Up Better Times For Timex

40% of sales, Indiglo moves Timex from functional to fashionable. By Elaine Underwood

Through 45 years, the Timex brand is best-known for trumpeting the lifespans of its watches with the long-running "It takes a licking and keeps on ticking" campaign. Now the Middlebury, Conn., firm can take credit for extending its customers' lives.

Consider the call forwarded to the Timex marketing department a few days ago. A Florida woman reported that her boyfriend and two fishing buddies got through a night spent clinging to their boat, capsized in Jupiter Inlet, by focusing on the reassuring blue beam of a Timex Indiglo wristwatch.

"It's not that they signaled a rescue plane with it," said Timex director of advertising Susie Watson of Indiglo's battery-lit blue face. "But they said the Indiglo was really comforting."

Watches as beacons? Good-luck charms? A talisman? It's reactions like these that make Timex's quiet corporate headquarters more akin to a crisis center. The $38 Indiglo has stood battle through L.A. earthquakes, the World Trade Center bombing and all manner of floods, storms and power outages.

One quake-struck Los Angeles couple mailed in a *Hard Copy*-style video recreation of how the Indiglo lit their way to safety after the temblor.

"Oh my God, there's glass everywhere. Put your shoes on," they said, aiming their Indiglos like flashlights on the floor. "Thanks for saving our lives, Timex." While watching the tape in Timex's boardroom, the irony overcame president Michael Jacobi, who burst out laughing. "No. Thank *you*. Thank *you*," he insisted.

Indiglo has been pumping its share of life into Timex Corp., too. Jacobi credits Indiglo with boosting Timex's 1993 sales by 30%, to $500 million. Indiglo models

accounted for 40% of all Timex units sold in 1993. This year, Indiglo will represent as much as 50% of unit sales, leading Jacobi to believe that watches with night lights will soon be as standard a feature on wristwatches as water-resistancy.

Developed with Motorola Inc. over a 15-year period, Indiglo is an electroluminscent light that is powered by the watch's 1.5- to 3-volt battery.

"The trick was to be able to drive that light bright enough with very little power," said Jacobi. And there lies the limitation. Indiglo's candlepower is restricted to small surfaces. If the dial or lit area was much larger, the integrated circuits could not power enough uniform light. "We might use it with a calculator, a mobile phone," said Jacobi. "Motorola uses it on pagers."

The technology is also making ho-hum Timex kind of hip. Just a couple years ago, Timex was elbowing Armitron for shelf space on neighborhood pharmacy counters. Now, this mass-market staple is right in the thick of the trend-driven $600 million department-store fashion watch category.

Indiglo's success has helped push Timex into retailers like Macy's and Filene's, stores that normally won't stock brands sold at mass merchandisers.

According to company research, Timex has a 27% market share among watches costing up to $100. Competitors Casio, Seiko, Lorus and Swatch all clock in with single-digit shares.

As the company did in 1993, Timex is throwing its entire 1994 ad budget of approximately $12 million behind Indiglo. The brand was introduced with an ad featuring an amorous bug buzzing around a lit watch. Timex agency Fallon McElligott, Minneapolis,

followed last Christmas with a spot of a priest avowing that Indiglo was indeed the brightest watch around.

> Developed with Motorola Corp. over a 15-year period, Indiglo is now so popular, some believe it will become as much of a standard wristwatch feature as water-resistancy. Timex is throwing its entire $12 million 1994 ad budget behind Indiglo. It's gotten the company sold into trendy retailers which formerly wouldn't stock the venerable watch brand.

Watson is also lining up some fall promotions that she hopes will tie Indiglo in with the trendy. In the fall, Timex will sponsor a major concert tour, perhaps the Rolling Stones.

"We are negotiating with a major tour organizer," said Watson, who declined to name the band. "At the venue that is going to be televised, we want to give away cardboard watches with working Indiglo dials." Part of the deal will be to have the TV cameras pan the audience when they turn on their watches.

In the Aug. 26 issue of *Entertainment Weekly*, Watson will solicit tales of Indiglo heroics with the Timex Bright Idea Contest. The L.A. earthquake couple should consider themselves entered, said Watson.

With a hit on his hands, Jacobi is quickly rolling out Indiglo timepieces in overseas markets and leveraging the technology to Timex's other watch

(cont.)

brands, such as its licensed Guess, Nautica and Disney Cinema Classics lines. He's also using Indiglo to storm into new markets and bolster soft ones such as Japan.

All this attention hasn't gone unnoticed by competitors, who are rolling out copycat watches. In May, Seiko Corp.'s Lorus division will jump in with new LumiBrite glow-in-the-dark watches.

"The reason department stores are looking at Timex more favorably is due to the overwhelming success of Indiglo," said Tony Cannilla, manager of advertising at Lorus Watches. "We want in on it, too."

Not everyone is 100% sold on Indiglo, even marketers at Callanen Corp., the Timex subsidiary that markets Guess and Monet watches. Only 10% of all Guess watches sold in 1993 featured Indiglo.

"It will never be 50% of our business, it'll grow to 20%," predicted Callanen's sales vp Bud Polley. "It is a novel thing right now. It's neat to be in a movie theater and light it up. I don't think it will be for the masses."

Bulova Corp. is only pursuing nightlight technology in the table-clock division.

"Will it become the standard for a watch as water resistancy is?" asked Bulova marketing vp Philip Shaw. "I don't think so. People buy our watches for style."

Current hot fashion brand Fossil takes the same tact.

"It's not a Fossil thing," insisted Fossil marketing vp Peter Benanti. "We are not tricks. We are styling."

Lorus' LumiBrite watch dials are coated with a similar non-radioactive compound that absorbs light during the day and re-emits it for up to five hours in the dark.

"The real benefit is our watches glow bright without having to push a button," said Cannilla, who will spend around $3 million pushing LumiBrite this year.

Perhaps the most telling sign of fashion accceptibility for the Timex brand is the opening of its first in-store boutique at Macy's Garden City, N.Y., branch, an honor typically reserved for trendy brands like Swatch and Fossil. Macy's is ceding Swatch's old space to Timex and if the move works, Eric Dauwalter, watch buyer for the chain's 59-store East Coast division, will consider opening more.

"The customer reaction over Indiglo this past Christmas was tremendous," said Dauwalter. "Consumers came in asking for it by name."

Macy's carries Timex's department-store exclusive Essentials line, basic Timex, Nautica and Guess licenses. This fall, Timex will throw another watch brand into the market—licensed Benetton watches. The Benetton line is designed to capture a younger fashion consumer than the Guess line attracts.

Unusual treatments such as colored metal bands will distinguish the line stylistically.

Indiglo dials are on tap, too. As for the ads, Watson makes it clear that Olivier Toscani, the photographer/creative director behind Benetton's controversial clothing campaign, has promised her "nice product shots."

Watson's concerns could be over. Toscani abruptly quit over creative differences with Aldo Palmeri, Benetton's powerful managing director last week. It's uncertain whether this flap will blow over or stick.

Timex picked up the Benetton watch license early this year when Bulova let its contract run out.

"Obviously, Timex is on an expansion program and the easiest way to do that is with licensed properties," said Bulova's Shaw. "I personally question their choice."

In the U.S., Benetton's sales and cachet has plunged since a high in the mid 1980s. However, Benetton should give Timex entry to watch counters in upscale European and Asian department stores.

"If we had to pick a brand to license just for the U.S., it wouldn't be Benetton," admitted Watson.

Beyond luminescence, the next revolution for the watch industry will be two-way voice communication timepieces, something Dick Tracy fans have been dreaming about for decades. AT&T is already running print ads telling consumers the age of telephone watches is nigh. The telecommunications company is also telling consumers it'll be first on the market with them. Jacobi is another believer.

"Within this decade, voice communication [in a wristwatch] is possible," he said. "The only problem is battery power."

Prototype talk/watches are so large, they can hardly be worn on the wrist. But Indiglo test models were also ungainfully big. Should Timex launch a talk/watch, consumers will undoubtedly shower the company with more tales of averted catastrophe.

When actor Paul Newman wanted to develop watches for race-car drivers and runners, he invited Timex over to his Westport, Conn., house.

"All he had on was a terrycloth bathrobe and a tie," recalled Jacobi. "He was a really funny guy."

While Newman's watch plans fizzled, Jacobi gained an Indiglo convert. "I saw a picture of him recently and he was wearing the Ironman he got from us," said Jacobi.

Maybe Newman will be in the unaccustomed position of writing a fan letter of his own someday. ∎

Finding Target Market Opportunities

U.S. mission goes beyond video games

by Kevin Maney
USA TODAY

NEW YORK--Sonic the hedgehog may become the next Mickey Mouse.

Sonic is the lead character for Sega Enterprises, a company evolving into a Walt Disney Co. for the information highway age. Sega is looking to move beyond video games the way Disney moved beyond Mickey Mouse cartoon shorts in the 1930s.

"We have a mission statement," says Thomas Kalinske, CEO of Sega of America, the powerful U.S. subsidiary of Tokyo-based Sega Enterprises. "We want to lead in interactive entertainment whether in the home or out of the home." The statement purposely omits the words "video games." To reach its broader vision, Sega has, for instance, opened a film studio and launched plans to build 50 theme parks in the USA. Last week, Sega and two partners, TeleCommunications Inc. and Time Warner, launched The Sega Channel. Analysts call it the first mass-market, two-way TV service. And most say it's a sure winner. Stan Thomas, Sega Channel's president, expects to have as many as 1 million subscribers by the end of 1995 and turn a profit in 1996. Customers in a few areas can begin using the channel today. It will be available in 14 cities by the end of this month.

"All the feedback I've heard has been extremely positive," says John Taylor, analyst at L.H. Alton. Rob Agee, editor of *Interactive Television Report* agrees. "The test results look very good."

Video games rule on The Sega Channel, but the channel creates an intriguing early version of the information highway envisioned by technology experts. Sega has 18 million game machines in U.S. homes--18% of households. Each is a digital, computerized device attached to a TV. Connect the machines through cable lines and--bingo!--Sega could deliver much more than games. "The reality is that through the game machine and The Sega Channel, we are supplying data," Thomas says. "Right now, the data is games. But it's not inconceivable that we could supply other kinds of data"--perhaps news reports or school-related information.

Thomas breezily moves back to the topic of games. He wouldn't want Sega's fun image to get sullied by too many references to data--at least not yet. This month, Sega has to concentrate on its core market. The company is shoveling $45 million into a holiday-season marketing blitz to battle rival Nintendo. Sega and Nintendo just about split the $6 billion-a-year video-game market, leaving crumbs for challengers. The video-game business, including arcade games, accounts for almost all Sega's revenue.

This year marks a transition for Sega and the rest of the video-game industry. Demand has peaked for so-called 16-bit games, the current technology. Next year, Sega and Nintendo--and an imposing new entrant, Sony--will come out with more powerful 32-bit games. New hardware, new software and new marketing campaigns could mean the market will shift in ways no one can foresee. As industries such as entertainment, computers and communications converge on the information highway, consumers will get video games delivered by many sources. More homes have personal computers with CD-ROM drives, which can run eye-catching games. Cable and phone companies plan to attach computer-like boxes to TVs to handle interactive services, including games delivered by cable or phone wires. To get ready, cable giant TCI paid $80 million for 10% of Acclaim Entertainment, a game creator, in October.

Sega sees the threats and is trying to get ahead of them. Its strategy starts at New York-based Sega Channel. The channel doesn't require a futuristic super-network. Most up-to-date cable systems can carry it. All a subscriber has to have is a Sega machine, any model, and a connection kit from the cable operator. The kit includes an adapter that plugs into the Sega machine and wires that connect the adapter to cable lines.

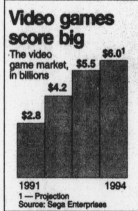

Video games score big

The video game market, in billions

$2.8 | $4.2 | $5.5 | $6.0[1]

1991   1994

1 — Projection
Source: Sega Enterprises

By Web Bryant, USA TODAY

The service likely will cost about $12 a month, though the price is left to individual cable operators. Subscribers can choose from 50 games each month, playing any or all as much as they wish. How it works:

▶ Once hooked up, turn on the TV — it doesn't matter what channel it's tuned to — and turn on the Sega machine. The Sega Channel comes on automatically.

▶ On the screen is a menu listing categories of games, including Sports Arena and Classics. Most games are ones that have been out for a while, not the current hottest sellers. Sega doesn't want the channel to bite into retail sales.

▶ Click a button on the machine to choose a category, then choose from a list of games. The game is downloaded, via your cable line, directly into your Sega machine, just as though you loaded a cartridge into the machine. Once the game is loaded, start playing.

For now, a Sega Channel subscriber can't play against a subscriber in a different house or city, but that's coming. Sega is working with Cupertino, Calif.-based Catapult to develop the capability.

Subscribers in test markets were enthusiastic. They felt the channel was a bargain, especially since buying a Sega game in a store can cost $50 or more; renting one game costs $2 to $3 for a couple of days. "Outrageous! Right on time! Saves my parents lots of money!" 7-year-old Jamie Beasley of Buffalo, wrote to The Sega Channel.

Thomas believes the channel can echo the success of Home Box Office, the premium movie service owned by Time Warner. Thomas worked at HBO for 11 years. "HBO took a medium that existed — movies — and brought it into the home in a more convenient, efficient and exciting way," he says. "We wanted to do the same with video games."

As the channel gets up and running, it will give Sega early insights into how it can take advantage of the information highway. "We'll have hands-on experience operating what everyone else is dreaming about," he says.

(cont.)

After The Sega Channel, the next step is theme parks--more specifically, virtual reality parks. Sega has built one, called Joypolis, in Yokohama, Japan. It has about 90,000 square feet, about the size of five-and-a-half football fields--a sliver compared with Disney World, but big enough to include restaurants and shops among the virtual reality rides.

Typical is a ride called Scramble Training. Sixteen people sit in a pod that can simulate motion. They don goggles and headsets. The ride immerses them in a space battle. Each shoots at bad guys. Highest scorer gets to land the spacecraft.

Visitors to Joypolis spend $40 to $50 each. Net profit margins are reportedly around 30%. Kalinske will try to transport that success to this country. He plans to build 50 U.S. parks by 2000. As the parks are built, Sega may hook them via phone lines, so a visitor in Cleveland could play a virtual reality game against someone at a Dallas park.

In the meantime, Sega this month opens a digital studio in San Francisco, not far from its U.S. headquarters in Redwood City, Calif. The studio will enable Sega to film scenes to create more realistic games or, perhaps, interactive movies. It will, says Kalinske, let the company experiment with new forms of entertainment.

The chief concern about Sega is this: "They've got a lot of balls in the air," says analyst Taylor. The company has to handle the ongoing competition, plus its new ventures. "It will be a challenging period. It's where good management rises to the top."

Sega's management seems up to it, analysts say. Kalinske, a former Mattel executive, joined Sega of America in 1990 when it was a non-factor in the U.S. market. He blasted the company, founded in Japan by U.S.-born David Rosen in 1954, past Nintendo and has made Sega of America as powerful as its parent. Sega's U.S. unit creates 85% of all software played on Sega machines worldwide.

Sega is a powerful brand name. It is one of the world's best interactive entertainment developers; almost all Nintendo games are created by outside developers. Add the cable channel, the theme parks and more, and there's a chance Sega is moving into Disney's world.

Back To School With Binney & Smith's Crayola

By Judith D. Schwartz

It's back-to-school time, and for millions of households with school-age children, that means time to stock up on crayons and other school supplies. Binney & Smith's Crayola crayons have been around since 1903. But the brand has not lost its luster, thanks to a consumer-marketing focus that has led it to branch out into new product areas while continually refreshening its basic products. The current hot growth area: toy and activity products for specific age groups. Annual sales today run in excess of $300 million, a six-fold increase from 1975. As Crayola prepares to celebrate its 90th birthday--for which colorful characters and guests will converge at Hollywood's Universal Studios in November--Binney & Smith is exploring new ways of leveraging the brand. Mike Russamano, director of toys and activities, talked about the company's product and promotional plans.

Catching the Population Wave

The Crayola brand is all about kids. Demographically, we've got a nice confluence of circumstances right now. With the echo baby boom, our target population is expanding. We can also play on nostalgia. Today's parents and grandparents grew up with Crayola. It's a name they know and feel good about.

Since inventing the crayon, Crayola has been a vital brand. But when the brand itself does the bulk of the work the temptation is to just slide and let things alone. We hit a bit of a growth lull between about 1982 to 1984, and saw that we had lost sight of our main strength: keeping in tune with what will spark the child's imagination. At that point we redirected our energies to take more of a consumer marketing approach.

> "We do quantitative and qualitative research, but to us the most important ways to determine market need are interactive and stem from our continual involvement with the crayon user. We spend a lot of time with kids."

We've also gotten more aggressive with new products. New products give kids more reason to color. If we focus on usage per child--and the average child in the U.S. will wear down 730 crayons by the age of 10--we're only going to increase it if we can offer something new. Kids are always looking for coloring subjects and ideas. In the last four or five years, we've introduced a number of new items, offering new product and package sizes and broadening the possibilities of what can be done with crayons and markers.

Name That Crayon

We do quantitative and qualitative research, but to us the most important ways to determine market need are interactive and stem from our continual involvement with the crayon user. We spend a lot of time with kids. Our roots are as an educational company and we have many programs in the community and the schools. It's not unusual for our marketers to go into a school and play with kids. Each year, we have 30,000 visitors to our two main plants, the majority of whom are children. Their comments and suggestions often trigger ideas for us.

We definitely listen to our customers, even when their preferences take us by surprise. In 1990, we "retired" eight crayon colors and introduced eight bright new colors that kids liked better, such as "Jungle Green" and "Wild Strawberry." The announcement brought such an outcry from adults that to appease the crayon loyalists (like the Raw Umber and Maize Preservation Society--RUMPS), we reissued the "old" colors in a special box. Aside from being wonderful p.r., it sold well--as did the 64-box with the sunny new colors. We saw a 200% spike in crayon sales after this.

(cont.)

Recognizing our customers' investment in our colors, we have our crayon-naming contest. We've just introduced the Big Box—with 96 crayons the biggest selection ever, including 16 as-yet un-named colors. We're inviting customers to help name the crayons. So far, we've received more than 2 million suggestions from crayon fans of all ages, everything from "Down Umber" to "Cost of Living Rose" and "James Brown." The winners will be flown out to Universal Studios for the birthday celebration.

Coloring in Playtime

We're fortunate in that we're such a strong force in our category, coloring and drawing products and arts activities. But, ultimately, we're competing for kids' leisure time. The time children spend coloring and drawing has been stable for the last nine or so years, but in the era of computer games and video around-the-clock we have to keep our brand compelling.

Our aim is to drive the business by continuing to innovate and staying focused on what kids want. New technologies have been important, particularly in the marker business. Two years ago, we came out with Changeables, special wands that with a single stroke change the color of marker drawings. This year we introduced Overwriters, which allow children to color *over* color, creating interesting effects. We found that one frustration many children have about coloring is that they need to leave room for elements in a drawing such as the sun or clouds. Overwriters give them the freedom to add pictures as they like.

The key is coming up with projects that provide opportunities to color and create. That's where the toys and activities come in. Kids love to color. We know that. By loosening up and following our sense of fun, we can promote kids' artistic imaginations and expand our growth. Already we've seen our toy-and-activity volume triple in less than 10 years to comprise 18% of our business. Consumers are finding out we make a lot more than just crayons and markers.

Jazzing Up The Market

While the typical crayon user is in the 4-to-8-year-old range, activity kits allow us to target other age segments. For example, we saw tremendous potential in the market of girls 8 to 12.

To hit this product void we've just introduced a line of six do-it-yourself boutique-style jewelry kits called "Jazzy Jewelry." We're presenting it as its own brand with the Crayola trademark in small type on the package graphics. At this age, kids want to feel grown-up, and the new branding creates a comfortable distance from childhood toys. The labeling says to a child, "This is cool stuff,"

"The average child in the U.S. will wear down 730 crayons by the age of 10. We're only going to increase it if we can offer them something new."—Russamano

but tells the parent, "This will be good."

The various kits include Glitter Gems, Hip Hoops and Funky Friendship Beads, and several use our unique technologies. Jewelry is a booming field in the kids' business right now as girls are becoming sophisticated at a younger age. With these kits they make their own, which is fun—like coloring—and helps them feel good about their creativity and skills. It's also a line that works: There are a lot of toys out there that don't fulfill advertising promises. With the Crayola name on the package, it's important to deliver.

When A Box Is Not Just A Box

At the other end of the age spectrum, we've introduced a series of kits based on themes from *Barney & Friends*, the hit children's TV show. Barney the dinosaur *owns* the under-4 crowd right now. He's big in pretend play. It was a good fit for us, so we acquired a license to the name. We have four kits shipping now, all based on themes from the show.

We're also making more creative use of our packaging by adding play value. Our 72-crayon case was extremely popular, and we now have a 96-crayon case which is like a briefcase. We've just introduced a Crayola school bus, which is "powered" by a crayon sharpener and has crayons riding in the seats. We tested this last year and got excellent response.

Inviting Kids In

Our advertising, created and executed by Averett, Free & Ginsberg, continues the theme "Crayola Rocks." The commercials are filled with upbeat music and vibrant colors, presenting Crayon in a fun, hip, "today" atmosphere. Our back-to-school flights emphasize crayons and markers for the 3-to-8 set, and for fourth quarter we'll include the activity kits.

About four years ago, we shifted our age target and started speaking directly to kids. Our research shows that young children request Crayola products and parents do the buying. This changes significantly at the age of 8. Our marketing now takes into consideration kids' growing purchasing influence and buying power. Crayola products are mostly high-impulse buys, so point-of-purchase displays play a big role in our strategy. Since parents have positive feelings about our products anyway, regardless of who initiates the purchase, they're going to be happy about it. Crayons and markers are affordable, portable and good entertainment value for the price.

We're looking forward to our anniversary celebration and continuing to introduce new products and ideas. Another ongoing goal for us is promoting consumer education and the importance of arts in the schools. More than 13 million children have participated in our Dream Makers program in elementary schools.

Our commitment is to add color to the lives of kids and adults and support artistic development. We've been touching people's lives with art for generations. Grant Wood, the midcentury painter famed for his work *American Gothic*, attributes his decision to become an artist to winning a Crayola coloring event. We want to be there with innovative products from the time a child can hold his or her first crayon, and to grow with people's skills, whether their work will hang on the refrigerator or in a museum. ∎

Bikers Give Ski Resorts Summertime Lift

By Marj Charlier

Staff Reporter of **THE WALL STREET JOURNAL**

WINTER PARK, Colo.--It may be a hot summer afternoon, but it's a perfect day to ride a ski lift up a mountain, head for the nearest trail and race downhill.

On a bicycle.

These days, it doesn't take snow to keep Winter Park Ski Resort busy. Instead of hauling skiers and snowboarders, the ski lifts this time of year carry mountain bikers and their bikes.

"We had all the amenities here," Julie Klein, a Winter Park spokeswoman, says of the resort's lifts, hotel rooms, restaurants and bars. "We might as well use them in the summer."

Until recently, most ski resorts turned into ghost towns in the summer. Now, mountain biking is giving more of these resorts year-round life.

Mountain bikes--solidly built bicycles with fat tires, flat handlebars and more than 20 gears--have invaded at least a quarter of U.S. ski resorts. Ski resorts' mountain-biking revenue is increasing as much as 60% a year. As a result, resorts have been able to hire more year-round employees, keep their restaurants and hotels open and get some extra income from their millions of dollars of fixed investments--all with little expense.

Some resorts have targeted the fast-growing sport's hard-core experts--dirt-eating, boulder-jumping, macho riders--by offering tortuous, steep and narrow "singletrack" trails. Other ski areas are trying to attract families and the not-so-fearless with gentle mountain roads and jeep paths.

In the process, some longtime skiers get to see what the slopes look like without snow while checking out one of the country's fastest-growing sports. "We never came up here in the summer before," says Dick Williams, an Evergreen, Colo., insurance-company owner and avid skier. "Now we will," he says, showing off his new mountain bike on a trail near the town of Winter Park.

For bikers accustomed to pedaling uphill on dirt and gravel roads and run-of-the-mill trails through woods, ski resorts offer the advantage of a lift up the mountain. But with rocks, tree stumps and sharp turns, mountain biking can be scary. Crashes aren't uncommon. In fact, ski resorts like bikers because, unlike skiers, they brag about falling down and don't complain when their bikes get damaged.

Mammoth Mountain in Southern California has 50 miles of bike trails. Before Mammoth began offering mountain biking in 1990, it did little in the summer but run its gondola for sightseers. Now the resort has attracted enough summer business to justify building a climbing wall and a rope obstacle course to keep visitors busy, and the resort is planning more summer activities. Mammoth's bike trails also have attracted Northern Californians. "We're seeing a phenomenal number of people coming down," says summer marketing manager Jennifer Renner.

Of course, "phenomenal" is a relative term: Mountain biking is nowhere near as big as skiing. Mammoth, which attracts about a million skiers a year, is expecting only about 20,000 bike riders this year. And Winter Park, which has more than a million skiers last season, attracted only 12,400 bikers last year.

Moreover, hard-core mountain bikers--who are mostly in their 20s--don't have big budgets and don't need them. An all-day lift ticket for one person with bike at Winter Park runs $15 in the summer, compared with $38 in the winter. At Killington Ski Resort in Vermont, which offers tennis and golf as well as mountain biking, bike riders spend very little compared with skiers, golfers and tennis players. "They may rent a bike and buy lunch, but chances are they leave after that," says a spokesman for the resort. Killington's biking revenue rose 60% last year over the year before but still accounted for only 20% to 25% of the resort's total summer business.

But the added business from mountain *(continues...)*

(cont.)

biking comes at negligible cost. The same trails used by skiers often can accommodate bicycles without any construction. The SilverCreek ski resort, Winter Park's neighbor about 90 miles west of Denver, spent less than $1,000 on maps and signs that turned the terrain into a mountain-bike area. Deer Valley, in Utah, estimates it has spent only about $5,000 to $10,000 on its bike program. Winter Park, which took the extra steps of cutting new trails and retrofitting its ski lifts, still spent only about $100,000 to accommodate the new sport.

Some big resorts like Vail and Beaver Creek in Colorado have found a national audience for their programs by staging mountain-bike races that attract TV coverage — and that also help their year-round business. Indeed, promoting skiing may be the biggest benefit some resorts get from mountain biking. The second most often cited reason for choosing a ski resort (after recommendation from a friend) is a prior summer experience in the area, says Allan Whitescarver, SilverCreek's marketing director. His resort makes no money from its low-key biking program, but he hopes Denver residents who discover the resort's easy biking trails may come back to try the unintimidating ski slopes.

Mr. Whitescarver promotes Silver-Creek as a gentler alternative to Winter Park's more challenging trails. Other resorts, too, have found that many customers want easier terrain after finding their mildest trails — laid out by mountain-bike experts — were too tough for beginners. "We weren't seeing a lot of injuries" among beginners, says Skip King, a spokesman for Sunday River, a resort in Maine. "But they weren't having a lot of fun." The resort reconfigured its trails this year, adding some less demanding terrain.

Perhaps nowhere has mountain biking had a bigger impact than at Winter Park. Before mountain biking, the towns of Winter Park and nearby Fraser dried up in the summer. The Fraser River valley's year-round population of about 1,000 couldn't support the area's shops, restaurants and hotels on its own. But in the past five years, Winter Park has become a mountain-bike mecca, with 45 miles of tough trails on the mountain connected to 600 miles of easier trails and logging roads in the valley. A dozen bike shops — some of them ski shops that transform themselves for the summer—offer rentals and repairs.

Winter Park's total summer-program employment has increased to 40 people from 26. The resort keeps 12 of its ski patrollers on staff year round, up from four, making it easier to retain good people from season to season, says Jack Mason, Winter Park's summer-program director. (Mr. Mason heads the ski patrol in the winter.)

Summer sales-tax revenue in the towns of Winter Park and Fraser has risen 80% since lift-served mountain biking began four years ago, and reservations at local hotels are up 54%. Summer visitors are staying longer, and mountain biking has helped boost use of the resort's alpine slide and miniature golf course. "Now we have a critical mass of activities," Mr. Mason says. "There's enough things to do for people to stick around more than a couple of hours."

Photography Companies Focus on Niches

By Joan E. Rigdon
Staff Reporter of The Wall Street Journal

Photo companies want to cash in on your family.

With film sales down for the second consecutive year, filmmakers are working harder to exploit promising niche markets: moms, kids and older folks.

Next week, the tiny Konica USA Inc. unit of Konica Corp., Tokyo, is to begin shipping 400-speed "baby film," which is designed "to bring out the very delicate skin tones of young children's faces," product literature asserts. To push the film, Konica is holding a sweepstakes with a $25,000 scholarship as grand prize.

In May, Eastman Kodak Co., the No. 1 U.S. filmmaker, plans to start shipping children's photo hobby kits to Kmart Corp., Wal-Mart Stores Inc. and other mass merchandisers. To reach older people, it's training its own retirees to teach photography to members of their retirement homes and churches. And later this year, Polaroid Corp. plans to promote some products through the American Association of Retired Persons.

Soap Operas

New ad strategies are in the works, too. After decades of advertising on general-interest family shows, film companies are branching out to soap operas and cable TV. Both Konica and Kodak will advertise on daytime soaps this summer to reach mothers, while Kodak will also push film to teens on "Beverly Hills 90210" and MTV. In print, Kodak is considering shifting some print-ad dollars to such magazines as Seniors, Working Mother and Your Prom.

The renewed focus on niche markets is a matter of survival. Last year, U.S. consumers bought 718 million rolls of film, down 4% from 748 million a year earlier and down 5.4% from 759 million in 1990. "We need more growth," says Bob LaPerle, Kodak's general manager, consumer products and programs.

"Locating the customer is getting more difficult," says Barry Harrand, marketing-research director at Photo Marketing Association, a trade group. "It's more important to differentiate products and services."

Industry watchers had attributed dwindling demand for film to the weak economy and growing popularity of camcorders. But Kodak research attributes the slump to shifting demographics. As younger and older people have gained buying power, companies' marketing strategies haven't kept pace. "You can't just think of the consumer as an imaginary 18-to-45-year-old person," says Mr. LaPerle.

Of course, film companies have marketed to family segments before. Most companies have an entry-level camera aimed at children. Kodak and archrival Fuji Photo Film USA, a unit of Fuji Photo Film Co., Tokyo, have given away free film in promotions with schools; four years ago, Polaroid launched its instant "Cool Cam" camera to a lukewarm children's market.

Foolproof Cameras

And nearly all camera makers have tried to appeal to children and older people with foolproof cameras that focus and advance film automatically. Fuji cameras also are self-loading, so users don't have to thread film onto sprockets.

That's a great boon for older people. "I've gone through the Nikon stage where you focus. Now I want to have everything automatic," says Carol Johnston, a 50-year-old activities coordinator at the Senior Center of West Seattle.

Foolproof features have made cardboard cameras the fastest-growing segment of the photo market. With the film already inside, they don't have to be loaded or unloaded; once the roll is shot, picture takers simply give the entire camera to a photo lab that develops the pictures and recycles parts of the camera.

The real growth market is the elderly. Although most are on fixed incomes, they generally have more time to visit grandchildren or indulge in such hobbies as bird-watching; both are major picture-taking opportunities.

Polaroid figures that there are three types of elderly person: active, hobbyists and inactive. "We call them the go-gos, the low-gos and the no-gos. And we're going after the go-gos" says Mario Castaneda, marketing manager, new-business development.

Marketing to older people is sometimes as easy as changing a product package or making a knob bigger. Kodak and Fuji have put larger print on their film boxes, and Polaroid is eliminating some fine print to make room for larger film-speed numbers. Last month, Kodak introduced a new version of its panoramic cardboard camera, with a magnifying lens over the exposure-number indicator.

Polaroid became interested in the elderly market in 1991, when its studies showed that older people use its instant-photo products more than any other age group. Since then, the company has been advertising in Modern Maturity; this April, it will also advertise in New Choices, a Reader's Digest magazine for wealthy older people.

Fuji, which has positioned itself as the film company for young, hip customers, says it also tries to appeal to the elderly, generally with cameras that load film without any threading and have clearly marked controls. But now that the population is aging, "we're going to have to be looking more at the senior market," a spokesman says.

Of course, there are pitfalls to niche marketing. Several film executives snickered and rolled their eyes, for instance, when they heard about Konica's baby-film product, which sells at a 58-cent premium to Konica's 200-speed film. Konica counters that the baby film has sold successfully at premium prices for three years in Japan and for 18 months in Canada.

Children are an especially tough market. Polaroid's Cool Cam instant cameras, targeted at 9-to-14-year-olds, were popular with college students, who liked the bright colors, but a turnoff to younger children, who didn't like the name. "They thought it was a little hokey," concedes Mr. Castaneda. "You try to speak to kids in their own language. They're pretty smart. They catch on."

Kodak has high hopes for its Photo FX hobby kits for children, based on feedback from focus groups. But it's less sure about a new product, Story Albums, which children illustrate with pictues of their friends and families. Kodak says the $10 albums have sold well in test markets in Boston and Chicago, but it's too early to tell whether the product will be launched nationwide.

Reprinted from the March 12, 1993 issue, by permission of *The Wall Street Journal* ©1993 Dow Jones & Company, Inc. All Rights Reserved Worldwide.

Waterbed Makers Target Younger, Groovier Snoozers

By Gregory A. Patterson
Staff Reporter of The Wall Street Journal

Remember waterbeds? In the 1970s, they were the counterculture's pleasure zones, dressed up with black lights and peacock feathers.

That allure has ebbed in recent years. Today's younger generation tends to view waterbeds as impractical—too bulky, too expensive and, ultimately, too retro. "I just think of disco music when I think of a waterbed," says Kim Christy, 26 years old, a Chicago speech pathologist. Waterbed mattress sales fell to 2.5 million last year, down 34% from a peak of 3.8 million in 1988. By contrast, traditional mattress sales topped 16.8 million last year.

No wonder the waterbed industry is trying to put some bounce back in its business by touting technological and design advances in the new beds. One innovation is the "softsided" waterbed, which fits into standard-size bed frames. Fiber that rims the mattress sides makes the waterbed easier to remove—a real problem with early waterbeds, which were simple vinyl pouches filled with water.

A more recent design change is the placement of a layer of fiber just below the surface of the water, which helps give more firm support to a sleeper's back. In addition, many water mattresses now contain two separate chambers so that the temperature of each can vary.

With these products, the industry is courting babyboomers, its most loyal audience. It's also wooing the over-60 generation by touting the health benefits of waterbeds in treating arthritis and even bed sores.

But the industry is now taking special aim at the under-30 crowd. The Waterbed Council, the industry's trade association, proclaims in a print campaign that boldly borrows from Oldsmobile: "It's not your parents' waterbed."

"We've done a terrible job of appealing to Generation X," says Michael Geraghty, 45, president of Strata Flotation, based in Torrence, Calif. "The industry was started by guys who were all 20 to 25 years old. Their target demographic group was themselves," he says.

Mr. Geraghty believes the industry could capture half the bedding market (it has a 15% share now) if consumers only knew how much better waterbeds are today. But to get that message across, industry officials admit they must destroy the waterbed's hippie-culture image and also deal with those recurring waterbed horror tales of flooded apartments and seasick users.

They hope humor, as well as truth, in advertising will work with the younger set. Strata Flotation, together with Waterbed Emporium, a West Coast retailer, runs a television commercial, for instance, that shows two people sleeping in a waterbed seemingly undisturbed amid the rumbling of an earthquake. The announcer says: "A Strata mattress is so downright comfortable you can sleep through almost anything. (Pause.) Maybe that's why they are so popular in California."

In Baltimore, Steven Ginsburg, president and owner of Waterbed Galleries, advertises on hard-rock radio stations to attract younger buyers, and he offers financing incentives such as no money down and no interest payments for a year. He's even stopped calling his product a waterbed. "It's a flotation mattress," he declares. In Phoenix, Sun Valley Waterbed goes after the MTV generation by advertising—where else?—on MTV. "If we lose Generation X," says Richard House, Sun Valley's president, "it will be a pretty tough loss to recover from."

Simmons Co., an Atlanta-based manufacturer, expects to demonstrate its products by holding waterbed races on campuses throughout the southeast and midwest this fall. The company will hand out accompanying T-shirts that read: "I only sleep with the best."

The Waterbed Council, based in Marlton, N.J., hopes a half-hour infomercial it has produced will persuade consumers of the technological and design advances in today's waterbeds. The infomercial airs in the middle of the night where it has a good chance of catching its target audience: People in need of a better night's sleep.

To dispel consumers' worries about undulating waves, the infomercial claims that new, tougher vinyl cases for waterbed mattresses all but eliminate waves. Then, copying a Lexus car commercial, the infomercial shows a man walking across the foot of a waterbed mattress without spilling a half-filled glass of wine at the head. "Once you've been in a waterbed, you know you'll never get seasick," the woman announcer says.

At Peppers Waterbeds in Elmhurst, Ill., manager Michael Lannan prominently displays a wall chart that shows how waterbeds distribute the pressure of the body's weight more evenly than innerspring mattresses, thus promoting sounder sleep. His sales pitch includes a claim that waterbed sleepers toss and turn two-thirds less than people who sleep on innerspring mattresses.

"You spent the first nine months of your life in water, and you should have never left it," he says, contending that the quality of one's work depends largely on getting

(cont.)

a good night's sleep.

Perhaps the biggest concession to Generation X that Mr. Lannan's store has made is selling futons, the mattress of choice for today's hipsters. Futons are cotton-filled mattresses that look like over-sized bedrolls. They are popular among young people because the mattresses can convert easily from a bed to a couch.

While noting that futon sales are strong, Mr. Lannan maintains that his primary objective for offering futons is to attract prospective waterbed customers. "We convert them over to flotation sleep," he says.

Targeting the New Professional Woman

♀ × $ = ?

Execs at Jockey--an archetypal man products company--copped to the women's market and doubled sales. Gerry Meyers offers a roadmap in "Targeting the New Professional Woman."

W omen run to extremes," a French philosopher observed. "They are either better or worse than men." Understanding the fairer sex is an older pursuit than questioning the meaning of life. Amid society and culture's redefintion of women's roles, marketers are struggling to come up with new ways to reach the "new woman." Is she a professional, or a mother/homemaker? And what marketing strategy does she respond to most favorably?

In her soon-to-be published book, "Targeting The New Professional Woman," ($32.50 from Probus Publishing, Chicago) Gerry Meyers argues that the 57 million working women in America women are different enough from both men and their predecessors that they must be approached with an entirely new set of values, sensibilities and sensitivities. Meyers is president of the Dallas-based Meyers Group, a marketing firm that helps manufacturers who have been accustomed to selling products to male customers begin to establish footholds in women's markets. As Howard Colley, former president of Jockey International said, "Approximately half of the people in the world are women . . . As a man's underwear company, this simple recognition allowed Jockey to double in volume."

There are numerous segments within the woman's market. In many cases, she is the purchasing agent for the family. In this role, she buys for herself and for others. Today, many single women are primary buyers. They are the ultimate consumer who will use the product or service. In the business world, the corporate buyer is also a purchasing agent. She buys for her company rather than for her own personal use.

In the last 20 years, the number of single adults has nearly doubled. Today there are more than 73 million singles, the majority of which are women. Young women put off marriage for careers; middle-aged women get divorced, never marry, or become widows.

In 1985, 36% of the women in the United States were single with no children, 9% were single heads-of-households with dependent children, 28% were married, but had no dependent children at home, and 27% were married with children. Interestingly, 72% of women believe they can have a complete and happy life if they remain single; 23% disagree. However, 57% of women think men must be married to be happy. The vast majority, 94%, saw a combina-

(cont.)

tion of marriage with a career and/or children as the ideal lifestyle.

Within the singles group are many subsegments. There are teenage girls, young women in their twenties, baby boomers, single professionals who have never married and probably never will, divorced women of various ages, single parents, and widows.

Young single women are a marketer's dream. They have discretionary income and few responsibilities other than themselves. They are often considered more selfish because their spending emphasis is self-centered.

"Single women have more time. They browse in stores more. It is an entertainment and social experience, where they feel comfortable and powerful," said Janice Leeming, editor-in-chief of the newsletter "Marketing to Women." Generation X women seem to worry less about the recession, are less concerned about planning for the future financially and love to travel. "Travel is very important to younger singles," stated Leeming. "They like to travel abroad, are more adventurous, and enjoy everything from the beach to mountain climbing. Around 51% of the time, women in their twenties prefer to vacation in new places, compared to the overall average of 43%."

As single women begin to age, their priorities change. Baby boomers begin to plan for the future, and are more concerned about money when the economy is in a recession. As they mature, retirement planning, IRAs, and mutual funds take on more significance to them.

The singles market is an untapped segment for life and disability insurance. Selling insurance to single women is an excellent way to build a new dimension into a company's or agent's customer base. Generally, these women are underinsured and have a more positive view of insurance than men. Frequently, the market is overlooked because there isn't a male head of household buying insurance to protect his family. Insurance agents need to rethink their marketing strategies and target this undiscovered group.

When young women marry, their priorities change. Their lifestyle becomes more traditional. Their new emphasis is on family and children they plan to have. Saving for a house becomes important. When they become parents, they have more demands on their money, and their purchasing patterns shift dramatically.

When a married woman with children becomes a single parent, another major shift takes place. She is totally unlike the carefree single woman with no children. Young, single, working women who enjoy the freedom of their own income and the material things they can buy with it are diametrically different from struggling-to-get-by young, single mothers.

Single mothers are among the poorest demographic group in America and it is a growing segment. Today, 75% of the nations's poor are woman and children. White women and children represent 51% of those living in poverty. Blacks, Hispanics, ethnic minorities, and white males make up 49%. These women count every penny, comparison shop and use a lot of coupons.

Married women redeem and collect

Young single women are a marketer's dream. . . . discretionary income and few responsibilities except themselves.

coupons even more than single women, although both groups are heavy users. This group often works on a very tight budget, because women as a whole earn less and frequently pay more for basically the same product or service than a man does. These women are usually the caretakers of small children.

"As family and traditional values continue to play a predominant role in our society, even women without children will spend more on children," claimed

Leeming. "They will buy for siblings, for friends' children, and for extended family members."

While married women, especially young wives, have returned to the basics and enjoy cooking from scratch, single women eat more frozen dinners than their married counterparts and eat in restaurants more often.

Food companies are recognizing the phenomenon of the single-person household and are repackaging their products in individual servings. Frozen gourmet dinners, microwave breakfasts, smaller cans of soups and juices and one-serving coffee packets have all appeared on store shelves. Salad bars have become a staple at grocery stores, so singles can purchase variety without waste. Single women between 18 and 24 make fewer food shopping trips than married women or women with children. While other categories of people eat at restaurants six times a month, single women dine out nearly nine times monthly.

Married women make more major food shopping trips than single women. But the biggest difference in shopping habits between the two groups is the amount of money spent weekly by married and single women for food. Around 44% of married women spend $100 or more per week on groceries, while only 16% of single women spend at that level. Conversely, only 15% of married women spend less than $50 per week, while nearly half of all single women do. While 75% of single women say they cook very often, 94% of married women cook most of the family meals.

Singles of both genders have entered the real estate market. According to home builders, 25% of first-time home buyers are single and 54% of condominium purchasers are single. Like those in other industries, home builders have found out that women who live alone want security, services, and social opportunities. Many companies that design and manage health clubs choose multi-residential buildings for their facilities that have a high percentage of singles.

In the automotive industry, 61% of

new car buyers under 25 are female, according to the Motor Vehicle Manufacturers Association. Women between the ages of 25 and 34 will be the buyers of 1.6 million imported cars and 1.9 million domestic cars, according to a report by *Cosmopolitan* magazine entitled, "The Changing Course of American Women."

Women between 35 and 44 will purchase 1.5 million new import cars and 2.2 million domestic cars. These two age categories represent 46% of all female new car buyers.

The majority of female first-time car buyers are single.

"The image of the car is more important to young, single women than the female population as a whole. Like their stylish clothes, they see cars as a reflection of themselves—who they are," said Leeming. Single women, or women with no children, are more likely to buy a sportier car, while married women with children tend to buy more practical vehicles including minivans and sports utility vehicles.

Lifestyle changes created by working women have affected most industries. While greeting cards may not be as visible a sign of changing times as automobiles, card companies, nevertheless, have also undergone transitions in the marketing of their products.

With sales flat, greeting card companies began to look for new markets. Hallmark, Gibson and American Greeting began creating cards appropriate for announcing divorce, as well as marriage. Many have added cards about dieting, dating, congratulations to fellow employees and other contemporary topics to their lines.

With women buying 90% of all greeting cards, it isn't surprising that astute marketers would concentrate on that market. Some have hired women writers and psychologists to create sayings and designs that speak to women.

Card companies aren't the only businesses focusing on the more than 20 million Americans who live alone—triple the number living alone in 1960. Between 1970 and 1986, the number of singles living

alone between the ages of 25 and 34 increased 346%. Singles between 35 and 44 rose 258%.

As single-person households increase three times faster than other households, they become a ripe target for many companies. The diversity of the live-alone single is astounding; it includes young women just out of school, baby boomers and divorced, widowed and never-

As single women begin to age, their priorities change. Baby boomers begin to be concerned about money during a recession.

married women. More than 60% of those living alone are women.

Since loneliness is a byproduct of living alone, many companies have developed strategies tapping into this emotion. As the singles-bar scene faded, video dating services like Great Expectations have sprung up and have prospered. Located in nearly 50 different cities, Great Expectations has signed up thousands of singles searching for that perfect mate, or at least a fun companion. Dating services are a big business in the 1990s. Technology has picked up where humans have failed. Computers access thousands and thousands of files in their quests to match compatible partners. Trade-show organizers have also cashed in on this trend with singles fairs that travel to various cities annually.

Despite women's growing interest, sports is still more a man's world than a woman's. The Winter Olympic Games is the only major sports event watched by more women than men. In participatory sports, men play baseball twice as often as women play softball. They like hunting, basketball, football, racquetball, and

scuba diving more. Women are far more involved in aerobics. These figures are important to sports marketers of equipment and apparel, sports and fitness centers, and other sports-related items.

Equally important to a manufacturer's marketing strategy is the development of programs to deal with a declining sales. The beer industry's sudden interest in the women's market has everything to do with good business. As distributors and marketers watched consumption fall from 194.9 million barrels in 1990 to 190.7 million barrels in 1991, they had nowhere to turn but to women to boost sagging sales. With the overall decline in consumption over the last 10 years and the introduction of low-alcohol and low-calorie brands, women have caught beer marketers' attention.

While brewers are still trying to sort out if women are their market, or if they can be, the statistics still indicate that men decided nearly twice as often as women what brand of beer to buy. Men also influence the choice of the brand of liquor more than women. Of course, changing their advertising and targeting premium and light beers to women could change those demographics, as breweries are discovering.

Women will never be major consumers of beer if commercials continue to be patronizing and designed to appeal only to male drinkers. According to Steve LeResche, director of public communications at Anheuser-Busch Co., things are changing. Brewers have an interest in marketing to women because of their greater buying power. But it hasn't been a smooth transition as beer marketers try to gain an edge on this untapped market.

Beer marketing efforts aimed at women have caused concerns by health organizations, just as the increase in cigarette usage by women did. Because beer drinkers are traditionally a younger market, critics complain that they are targeting women of childbearing age. Marketers need to understand there is a middle ground. Ads that the growing number of women beer drinkers don't find offensive can be targeted to their primary audience--men.

Identifying growth segments is a critical aspect of a marketer's job. Many companies have identified women as a growth market and have made inroads into securing their business. Others have only paid lip service to the concept that women are a distinct market that must be addressed by every industry hoping to maintain market position in this decade. Procter & Gamble has always considered women its major market for household products. As I watched two of their laundry detergents' advertising and promotional strategies shift, I thought P&G was attuned to the changing demographics of the marketplace. Not so.

I questioned Lynn Hailey, Procter & Gamble spokesperson, about All-Temperature Cheer. I noticed their ads always included males; a mother teaching a son going off to school, a boyfriend-girlfriend, or two people of the opposite sex in a laundromat. Obviously, P&G had concluded that as more women went to work, married later, and got divorced, men would be doing more laundry. In other words, just as women were buying more cars and gold jewelry, men were buying traditional "women's" products as well. But according to Hailey, that wasn't the intent. Too bad. Men are an untapped market that could be expanded into a profitable market segment.

Next I asked about Tide. With its bright orange and yellow colors splashed across NASCAR race cars and crew uniforms, Tide was targeting the 43 million women who attend NASCAR events, as well as the millions more who view the sport. There is nothing wrong with this new venue, and many other products aimed at women are seeking this outlet. However, I believe deliberately targeting the male attendees that use Tide would be an excellent idea. What other avenues could be used to capture the single male customer's business? Just as GM has learned it must market to women, so should P&G and other companies that have primarily targeted women develop campaign strategies aimed at capturing the emerging male market.

As more women are looking for convenient, quick meals and other time-saving products designed with the busy, professional women in mind, manufacturers should take advantage of the secondary male market that would provide a whole new segment.

Staying in tune with your customers, modernizing your product to reflect the lifestyle changes that are happening with your primary customer, and looking for new, income-generating secondary markets are vital to the growth and prosperity of many companies in this competitive marketplace. Change is not gender biased. Both men's and women's lifestyles are in transition. Astute marketers are reacting quickly to the changing demographics and buying patterns of today's men, as well as today's women.

Marketers need to learn the lifestyle of the new mother is different when she gives birth to her first child when she is 31, not 21.

When trying to market to a new segment, marketers must meet the challenge by examining the target market, evaluating its potential, developing a fresh perspective, and exploring the attitudes and needs of the new segment.

As has already been established, men and women react to information differently. When segmenting the market, marketers need to remember that there are numerous differences depending on the age, income, occupation, lifestyle, personality style, and a whole range of other factors. Women still have certain innate characteristics, and these should be considered when creating effective marketing programs.

Campaigns are a mass-media effort and, while individual characteristics should be addressed, general traits must not be forgotten either.

As marketers use demographic information, patterns and trends become obvious. In 1990, the population of the United States was slightly more than 250 million. It is projected that by 2000, it will be 268 million, and by 2050, it will be 309 million. As baby boomers continue to mature, they will skew the age demographics upward. For instance, in 1970 there were only 17.7 million women between 30 and 44. In 1988 there were 26.3 million women in that age category.

In addition, women are marrying later, and having their children at a later age. The number of childless women between the ages of 25 and 29 rose from 31% in 1976 to 41% in 1988. Today, one out of every four babies is born to a woman over 30.

As marketers develop new programs, promotions, and product strategies, they need to be cognizant of how the lifestyle of the new mother is different when she gives birth to her first child when she is 31, not 21.

What kinds of products and services do these women want? What is the most effective way to target them with their now even busier lifestyle?

Old questions and outdated premises just won't work anymore.

Marketers need a fresh approach and a comprehensive look at the woman's market. The demographics of age, sex, income, and occupation are certainly aspects to consider in formulating marketing strategies for the late 1990s and the next century. But marketers need to include the human element as well. ∎

Reprinted from the January 31,1994 issue of *Brandweek*, © 1994 ASM Communications, Inc. Used with permission from *Brandweek*.

Vacationing Families Head Downtown to Welcoming Arms of Business Hotels

By James S. Hirsch
Staff Reporter of The Wall Street Journal

CHICAGO--In the atrium lounge of the Chicago Hilton and Towers, couples linger over late-night drinks as Travis Jeffords racks up a game of pool. A barmaid scurries toward him and hands over his special order: Four cherries on a toothpick.

Spoils abound for Travis, who is a nine-year-old from Austin, Texas, and is visiting Chicago over a weekend with his family. "When you're here," Travis says, waving his sticky fingers at Hilton's marble and bronze appointments, "you just feel like a king."

Treating customers like royalty has always been the goal of huge convention hotels like this one. What is different is that families, not just executives, are now receiving the red-carpet treatment. The result is that summer travelers are flocking not only to tree-lined resorts and beach properties--where children have always been welcome--but also to traditional business hotels in big cities and suburbs.

Not everyone is pleased when strollers fill the lobby. Business travelers who are stuck working over the weekend cringe when children race the elevators or hop aboard bell carts. And hotel employees have to hustle to accommodate special needs of families. But weekend vacations reflect changing patterns in leisure travel. Discount air fares that require Saturday-night stays have made weekend travel more affordable; and many two-career couples, prevented from taking long trips because of their jobs, prefer brief escapes. Full-service hotels--with pay-per-view movies, fitness centers and diverse dining options--also appeal to a baby-boom generation accustomed to one-stop shopping.

"Weekend getaways are part of marriage maintenance," says Cindy Van Der Boom of Dayton, Ohio, as she leans back in a hot tub in the Chicago Hilton fitness center.

For their part, hotel chains like Hilton, Hyatt, Marriott and Westin have had to rethink their pitch to customers. Over the years, these lodging companies have tried to associate themselves with power lunches, not potty seats. **Hilton Hotels Corp.** used to call itself "America's business address." High-ranking executives, with their sophisticated styles and expense accounts, brought cash and cachet. Families brought tight budgets, asked a thousand questions and were ignored by marketers.

Not surprisingly, business hotels were typically ghost towns on weekends. But by the 1990s, they were often abandoned during the week as well, thanks to the recession and tougher competition. So in recent years, full-service properties have all but begged kids to fill their empty rooms.

Most hotels have always discounted weekend rates and allowed children to stay in their parents' room for free. The battle for families is mostly fought with amenities and services, including special children's menus, cribs, bed rails, video games, even apparel. **Four Seasons Hotels** Inc. offers flameproof bathrobes for kids.

Creating the right family environment is one goal. During weekends at the Costa Mesa Marriott Suites in Orange County, Calif., employees dress down and toasters are put on the breakfast buffet. Just like home, but for $79 a night.

Festive marketing helps. The Hyatt Regency Reston in Reston, Va., uses its 21 executive suites for weekend slumber parties. The kids, no more than 10, throw down their sleeping bags in the living room, and the grownups stay out of harm's way in the adjoining bedroom. Special training is also part of the mix. At the Westin Canal Place in downtown New Orleans, bellmen are instructed to keep children preoccupied while parents check in, and the restaurant's maitre d' tries to seat families away from the briefcase and portable-phone crowd.

But trying to isolate young mischiefs in a hotel is futile, and some grizzled guests resent the weekend invasion. At the pool in the Chicago Hilton, collisions occur between adults swimming laps and children playing water games.

Have hotels' courtship of families worked? A good example is the Chicago Hilton, a 1,153-room urban colossus. "When I started here six years ago, [families] were an afterthought," says Michael Webb, the hotel's director of housekeeping services. "If they came, they came."

But since initiating its "Vacation Station" program three years ago, which includes gifts and games for kids, the Chicago Hilton has tripled its number of cribs in its inventory to 150, put gummy bears in minibars and installed a pay-for-view movie system that allows parents to deactivate adult films.

The upshot: Saturday nights are usually sold out and Friday nights average 80% occupancy levels, while weekday levels hover in the low 60s.

Not that everyone is thrilled by the hotel experience. Waiting for the delivery of a Domino's pizza outside the hotel, Josh Solyer, 13, of Columbia, Ill., is asked about the excitement of staying in what was once the largest property in the world. "I've been here six or seven times," he shrugs. "I know the hotel by now."

SNACK TIME? GIVE ME MY CEREAL BOWL!

Looking to expand brands and sales, ready-to-eat cerealmakers are positioning product as other-than-breakfast time snack food

By Betsy Spethmann

A funny thing happened to General Mills on the way to a new product for consumers who are too busy to sit down for breakfast before they leave for work.

The cerealmaker found that people would be happy to eat cereal "all day long," General Mills marketer Barry Davis recalls. "We saw that potential and said, 'Gee, this is bigger than the 'breakfast-on-the-run' market.'"

Thus was born "Fingos," General Mills' new "eat-from-the-box" finger-food cereal for other-than-breakfast-time snacking. General Mills is not alone.

Makers of ready-to-eat cereals looking for opportunities for growth increasingly are positioning new products and line extensions in a decidedly snack-oriented way.

Kellogg's Rice Krispies Treats—the marshmallow-cereal recipe Moms have been serving up for years—has been so successful since the cereal's January introduction, Kellogg has run ads apologizing for product shortages. It racked up sales of $5.3 million in just 12 weeks, with its only marketing support being two free-standing inserts.

Ralston's bagged Chex Snack Mix is one of that company's fastest-growing products, racking up sales of $46 million last year, according to Information Resources Inc.

Cereal-market watchers say it was only natural for cereals to start bumping up against snacks. The economic incentive is substantial. Americans spent $7.3 billion on ready-to-eat cereals last year, and are expected to spend $8 billion by the time this year is out. But that's only about one-third of what they spend on snacks. Americans buy $26.6 billion in snacks annually.

Getting consumers to eat cereals for midmorning snacks, after-school treats or in front of TV at night may not be as much of a stretch as it first appears. About 7% of ready-to-eat breakfast cereal already is being consumed at times other than breakfast. In addition, eating trends are putting marketers into a position to expand that.

Cereals are "basically grains," said Bill Spencer, a consultant with Ryan Management Group in Westport, Conn. Grains are the base of the U.S. Department of Agriculture's new "food pyramid." As more consumers "become educated on that, we'll see more and more extended uses of cereal."

General Mills is hoping 80% of Fingos' consumption is at times other than breakfast.

Dollar sales for ready-to-eat cereals are up 4.8% for the year ended Feb. 20, according to A.C. Nielsen.

Kellogg, the category leader, held 36.1% of the market with sales of $2.6 billion, up 3.7% from the prior year. General Mills, the No. 2 manufacturer, had 29.2% of the category, with sales up 4.8% to $2.1 billion.

General Mills chose to introduce a new brand name with Fingos rather than use an existing brand because it wants to create a new category, said Davis, marketing manager for the product. "We're very focused on getting people to think about cereal differently," he said. "The whole finesse to our marketing is convincing people to eat cereal all day long."

Big G welcomes competition; competition would help expand the category.

But category-building presents some formidable marketing challenges. General Mills will spend $34 million on heavy in-store and event sampling and TV advertising as the product rolls out nationally this year. It'll be one of General Mills' biggest sampling efforts ever, Davis said. DDB Needham, Chicago, handles the account.

Part of Fingos' distinction is made by its packaging, a tall, thin box that shows fingers feeding a wide-open mouth. Large retail accounts are putting up to nine facings in the middle of the cereal aisle. That immediately communicates a distinction, Davis said.

Davis credits Needham's creative team with Fingos' tightly integrated marketing.

"We took the concept to them and worked with them on its positioning," marketer Davis said. "Everything (in the marketing mix) easily grows out of our positioning as a cereal you eat with your fingers.

"Most people know cereal is a reasonable balance between being healthy and good-tasting," Davis went on. "It's not extremely healthy or decadent. It's popular because it's nice, it tastes good, and you don't have to feel guilty for eating it."

(cont.)

While Fingos may establish a "decent niche as a specialty item," Spencer believes "there's just not going to be a mainstream snack in the cereal aisle. Shoppers aren't into impulse snack buying in that location."

That's fine with General Mills.

"We don't want to be the noun 'snack.' We want to be cereal," Big G's Davis said.

Though Fingos' success remains to be

> ## "Cereal marketers are looking for crossover opportunities. They've seen it happen with cookies, crackers and snacks."—Bill Spencer

seen, Rice Krispies Treats cereal has set the cereal aisle on fire.

"They bingoed with this one," said Nancy Rodriguez, president of Food Marketing Support Services in Oak Park, Ill., and, equally important, a mother with kids hooked on the cereal. "I'd say this is a bullseye product for Kellogg."

When production is back up for Rice Krispies Treats cereal, the company will consider national advertising, likely TV. The plans for Rice Krispies Treats won't affect marketing for Rice Krispies, a Kellogg spokeswoman said. It will still be positioned as an all-family cereal as well as an ingredient in homemade Rice Krispies snacks.

That advertising, handled by Leo Burnett USA, targets consumers who like to cook; consumers more interested in convenience are the aim of Rice Krispies Treats cereal.

Rodriguez thinks Kellogg doesn't have to worry about cannibalizing regular Rice Krispies. The new cereal "still uses Rice Krispies, so what difference does it make? Those sales are going to Kellogg, period," she said. In fact, Kellogg could double usage because Rice Krispies Treats cereal is a great afterschool snack, she said.

General Mills' Cheerios brand has long been the reigning brand for preschool snacks. Yellow-box Cheerios has been marketed as a toddler finger food for about 12 years, via print ads from Saatchi & Saatchi Advertising, N.Y. Big G counts on parents of toddlers for a substantial percentage of the brand's sales, a spokeswoman said.

General Mills also has pitched Cheerios as a snack ingredient, especially during the oat bran craze of the mid-80s. A recipe for Hot Buttered O's—Cheerios sauteed in garlic butter—was popular then, the spokeswoman said.

Ralston Purina's newest Chex cereal carries its own snack: mini graham crackers. Graham Chex and Crispy Mini-Grahams cereal was introduced nationally in February, backed by TV that broke late in March, couponing and in-pack sampling. A blend of rice and graham cereal biscuits with tiny graham crackers, Graham Chex and Crispy Mini-Grahams is positioned as a family cereal.

Being a snack ingredient is key to Ralston's Chex cereal, with an estimated third of Chex cereal sold as an ingredient for Chex Party Mix.

Ralston's shift of Chex Snack Mix to a bag from box and its introduction last June of a small bag has helped sales, by shifting to a snack from a cereal mentality, a source said. Snack Mix hasn't cannibalized Chex cereal sales because each targets different consumers and is merchandised differently, the source said.

For several years, Nabisco, Keebler and Frito-Lay, among others, have been blurring the line between crackers and salty snacks with products like Zingers, Wheatables and Doritos snack crackers.

"Cereals are becoming more like snacks, snacks more like crackers, crackers like cookies—it's one big circle," Spencer said. "Cereal marketers are looking for crossover opportunities because they've seen it happen with cookies, crackers and snacks."

And with reason.

"Cereals and snacks aren't all that different," Spencer said. "They start with a grain-based dough, and either bake it for cereal or usually fry it for snacks. Most cereal is sweetened and most snacks are salty, but they're not different from an equity perspective." ∎

Reprinted from the May 3, 1993, issue of *Brandweek*, © 1993 ASM Communications, Inc. Used with permission from *Brandweek*.

Evaluating Opportunities in the Changing Marketing Environment

Local Trauma

Ambulance Companies Fight Municipalities For Emergency Market

Firefighters Coming to Aid Of Victims Must Compete With Private Paramedics

Drawing a 'Map of Conquest'

By Robert Tomsho
Staff Reporter of The Wall Street Journal

SACRAMENTO, Calif. — With sirens screaming, Sacramento Fire Department paramedics sped to a midnight shooting at the Round Table Bar.

After police checked for the gunmen, the emergency squad rushed in — only to find that the competition had beaten them, entering through another door. Already treating the wounded man was a crew from American Medical Response Inc., a for-profit Boston-based ambulance company that moved into this market in February.

An angry Sacramento Fire Department chief ordered the AMR crew to turn over the bleeding victim. But the crew members refused, saying they had arrived first.

From Oregon to New York, the market for emergency medical services—EMS—is engulfed in bitter fighting. On one side are a small but aggressive group of ambulance entrepreneurs who smell profit amid health-care's extensive changes. On the other are fire departments whose very existence could be at stake. The outcome will determine who responds to medical emergencies, how long they take and what they are equipped to do once there. "You could call it the ambulance war, because that's what it is," says George Burke, spokesman for the International Association of Fire Fighters, a labor union.

A Growing Need

At stake is the $5 billion market for transporting patients to the hospital. Private ambulance companies and most fire departments typically bill patients or their insurers. Depending upon how much of the cost is subsidized by local government, trips can cost anywhere from $100 to $1,000. Local governments typically decide which ambulance services can operate within their boundaries and, in many cases, help pay for transporting indigent patients.

This market is growing by an estimated 8% a year and is expected to expand even more as health-care change intensifies. With hospitals discharging patients earlier, more of them need ambulances to go home or return for treatment. Also, as hospitals drop unprofitable specialties, more patients are being taxied from one facility to another for different services. Finally, the uninsured increasingly are being treated at home by paramedics—prompting most authors of government reform proposals to call for increased reimbursement for ambulance services.

Little wonder that for-profit chains are popping up. Besides AMR, Laidlaw Inc., the Canadian waste-management and transportation concern, has expanded aggressively through its MedTrans unit based in San Diego. So has CareLine Inc. of Irvine, Calif.

Gobbling Up Little Guys

In two years, such chains have snared an estimated 15% of the U.S. ambulance market, gobbling up scores of the mom-and-pop operators that once dominated the industry. "It has changed the composition of the ambulance service in major parts of this country," says James Page, a consultant and publisher of the Journal of Emergency Medical Services. "It's almost like a map of conquest."

But local firefighters seek to conquer that same territory. While many large cities fund and operate separate EMS departments, elsewhere fire departments have long responded to 911 calls, usually only to extricate crash victims, stop bleeding and otherwise stabilize patients. After those services, for which fire departments typically aren't reimbursed, patients are whisked to the hospital by ambulance firms that do get reimbursed.

Now, firefighters want to provide—and be paid for—the ambulance service, in part because their success at fighting fires has left them seeking a new purpose.

Victims of Success?

Thanks to sprinkler systems, tougher building codes and fire-prevention campaigns, reported fires in the U.S. fell 23% between 1982 and 1992, according to the National Fire Protection Association. Last year, fires accounted for 13% of the 15.3 million calls to which U.S. fire departments responded, while 57% involved requests for medical aid. Budgetarily speaking, "the fire service has shored up its whole operation with EMS," says Doug Brown, an executive with the International Association of Fire Chiefs. "You couldn't justify your budget without that."

The worst fear of firefighters is that EMS firms will attempt to take over firefighting, too. In recent years, firefighter unions have fended off urban expansion moves by Rural Metro Corp., a Scottsdale, Ariz., concern that is already providing firefighting services to many Arizona and Tennessee communities that have outgrown their volunteer departments.

Meanwhile, in Louisiana, a for-profit EMS firm, Acadian Ambulance Service Inc., based in Lafayette, has started a 311 line. Although the line is supposed to be for nonemergency calls only, fire departments and government emergency-services agencies have protested that citizens will confuse it with the state's 911 number. "In a crisis situation, we don't want people to have to stop and think," says Martha Carter, 911 administrator for Shreveport's Caddo Parish.

Acadian co-owner Richard Zuschlag counters that he "would never do anything to harm 911," adding that callers who mistakenly call his 311 line with a life-and-death emergency are immediately patched through to the 911 operator.

Thus far, neither side has an undisputed financial edge. Fire departments note that they have much of the personnel and equipment in place to offer EMS. But even departments used to responding to all 911 calls would need to get some added equipment and people to start transporting patients to hospitals — and for-profit firms say taxpayers don't seem eager to finance that. "Look at the last Election Day," says W. Earl Riggs, chairman of AMR's Western operations. "People are not in the mood to spend a hell of a lot more money than they are already spending."

A look at AMR shows how aggressive these new firms are. The two-year-old public company has acquired more than 30 smaller ambulance companies. It has more than 1,000 ambulances, with operations in 16 states. For the nine months ended Sept. 30, net income rose 49%, to $10.9 million, from the year before. Revenue nearly doubled, to $291.5 million.

Advantage of Size

"We are able to use technology that the little guy couldn't use," says James McGrath, an AMR director and co-founder, noting that the company dispatches and tracks ambulances by satellite. The result, the company contends, is that its service is more professional and less expensive, considering that local governments pay for the equipment used by fire departments.

Yet when it comes to patient care, for-profit firms face greater skepticism than fire departments. Consider its operations in the Sacramento market.

For years, the city had a thinly regulated web of ambulance fiefs. Ownership changed frequently, quality varied widely and ambulances routinely arrived late. Most were staffed by "emergency medical technicians," who, unlike paramedics, aren't licensed to administer drugs or complex life-saving procedures. Some arrived without gurneys. In a notable 1990 incident, a 15-year-old crash victim died after her ambulance ran out of gas five blocks from a hospital.

So Sacramento invited its fire department to begin offering the service. "We didn't just wake up one morning and say that we ought to take over the ambulance business," says Jack Crist, a Sacramento deputy city manager. "The private ambulance companies did this to themselves."

Fighting City Hall

In February, however, AMR established its Sacramento beachhead by acquiring a large regional ambulance company that had already scooped up most of the little ones. AMR promised first-rate service and paramedic care — and fierce competition to local firefighters.

The skirmishes have been ceaseless. In January, the City Council divided up the city geographically, giving roughly one-third to fire-department EMS crews, with the rest being covered by AMR units. AMR and other private providers began lobbying for a state law to make it harder for cities to get into the ambulance business.

On the street, the fire department has accused AMR of trying to undermine its operation by snatching patients from wealthy neighborhoods and shunning low-income areas. AMR calls that accusation "totally false," adding that it provides service without regard to location or a patient's ability to pay. Nonetheless, early on, the fire department put extra ambulances in the central business district, claiming that AMR was picking off calls from state office buildings, where workers were likely to be insured.

AMR says its ambulances responded at such buildings only when fire-department vehicles were busy or when its ambulances were passing through a fire-department zone on their way back from a hospital. They claim that dispatchers, who are local government employees, have shunned AMR ambulances even when they are closest to a call.

On the Go

Unlike the fire department, whose crews remain at fire stations until called, AMR squads are constantly on the go. Stationed at convenience stores, street corners and hospitals, they relocate regularly as one unit is called to an emergency and others shift to cover the area.

Critics say the system leads to paramedic burnout. "We hear complaints from paramedics that they are moving 30 times over a 12-hour shift," says Mr. Page, the consultant, "and that they can't find a clean place to go to the bathroom, or wash up after a bloody mess."

AMR executives deny that and say the system allows them to cover a city more efficiently and shift resources away from downtown offices to bedroom communities when the workday is finished. They argue that they have improved pay and benefits for private paramedics, provided them with good sanitary facilities and monitored their hours and stress levels carefully. "The industry has come a long way," says Mr. Riggs, the AMR executive. "We have top-notch people."

But in local emergency rooms and on the street, the tension is evident. "The stress is phenomenal," says AMR paramedic Heidi Corrado, as she and partner Adam Blitz race through rush-hour traffic to reach a man who has overdosed on a potentially lethal antidepressant. They arrive at a run-down, darkened house just seconds behind a Sacramento ladder truck sent from a fire station. Inside, a husky, tattooed man sits at a kitchen table groggily mumbling about a half-consumed bottle of pills buried in his tattered backpack.

No Love Lost

Although they arrived first, the four firefighters watch silently as Mr. Blitz questions the man, fishes out his pills and takes him outside to the waiting AMR ambulance. During the entire encounter, the firefighters and private paramedics barely speak.

Later, Mr. Blitz grumbles that, in the old days, firefighters used to help out the private paramedics by taking vital signs, fetching blankets and carrying gurneys. Now, he says, "it's getting to the point where they are not doing anything."

Such battles could be decided on political rather than economic grounds. This summer, the fire department proposed taking over all emergency ambulance service. In the City Council debates that followed, each side accused the other of raiding jobs, juggling data and putting public safety at risk. While members of the firefighters' union threatened to campaign against opposing council members, the union representing AMR paramedics took out a newspaper ad claiming the fire department's plan amounted to a "takeover of private industry."

In November, the City Council voted to turn over the entire operation to the fire department as of March 1. The move will effectively restrict AMR to nonemergency calls in the city. The company says it will be forced to lay off about 140 of its 275 local employees and sell some of its vehicles.

The fire department's plan calls for hiring 65 more people and putting 12 ambulances on the street, eight of them around the clock. The department contends that, if it can collect on just 48% of its billings, the system will be self-sustaining. "If it doesn't work that way," says Fire Chief Gary Costamagna, "I know that this City Council will move to privatize it quickly."

That is what AMR is banking on. Instead of moving on, the company will continue covering a few outlying communities and handling nonemergency business while maneuvering to take back the Sacramento market.

The company already has filed suit in federal court here claiming that the local-government dispatch center is violating federal antitrust law by denying it equal access to 911 calls.

AMR executives also have begun courting some of the area's managed-care networks, says Earl Riggs, AMR's top executive in Northern California. With or without the city contract, being a network's exclusive EMS provider would mean controlling a big chunk of the paying patients.

"And then," he adds, "let the fire departments have the indigent patients."

Revolution in store for record shops

Technology for making CDs in-store likely to jazz up sales; home delivery may be next

By Kevin Maney
USA TODAY

FORT LAUDERDALE, Fla. — Imagine walking into a record store and finding everything you want, even that rare old Harry Nilsson album you've been searching for.

You never have to rely on a clerk wearing black nail polish (male or female). Your selections are printed on the spot in minutes.

And you always leave satisfied.

Now, imagine never having to set foot in a record store and instead buying any album, any time, over cable TV or phone lines by using a remote control while sitting on your couch. The album gets recorded on your home digital audio tape machine.

No, those aren't just descriptions of music lovers' heaven. A revolution is coming to the business of selling recorded music, touched off last week by an announcement by Blockbuster Entertainment and IBM that they're building high-tech kiosks for record stores that can pull an album out of a central computer and print it on a compact disc. The same system, combined with fiber-optic telephone or cable TV lines, interactive television and digital tape machines could someday pipe albums into homes.

"The technology is here," says David Lundeen, who heads the venture for Blockbuster, based here. "We have a working prototype."

At least one small high-tech company is secretively working on home-delivery technology, says Gary Arlen, a Bethesda, Md., telecommunications consultant. Other big companies, including Tele-Communications Inc. and Time Warner, are interested in the concept of selling music by wire. "Home delivery of hits could get intriguing," Arlen says.

Blockbuster has been working on its system with IBM since last year. The system eventually could work for on-site duplication of videotapes and video games, too. Blockbuster owns 238 Sound Warehouse and Music Plus record stores and more than 3,000 video-rental outlets. All those places also sell video games.

The technology originally was called Soundsational, but the name has been changed to New-Leaf Entertainment to show that it will apply to more than audio products. Besides, Lundeen says, Blockbuster Chairman Wayne Huizenga kept mispronouncing it Soundsensational.

If the NewLeaf system works and is adopted by record retailers and record labels, record stores may look more like video-game arcades by the late-1990s, says Thomas Gage, vice president of telecommunications for Gemini Consulting. "There would be no need for racks and racks of inventory," he says. Instead, stores would be lined with up to 80 kiosks, each armed with a video touch screen and headphones.

As Lundeen tells it, a customer would go into a kiosk and touch buttons on the screen to go through menus. The menus could list recordings by artist, album title, song title, whatever. Theoretically, you could find the title of any album ever made, from Nilsson's out-of-print *Son of Schmilsson* to Eric Clapton's popular *Unplugged*.

You'd swipe your Blockbuster card through the NewLeaf kiosk's card reader, and it would know who you are and what you've bought at Blockbuster-owned stores in the past. "It could know that you like Eric Clapton and Jeff Beck and suggest that you might like Robert Cray," Lundeen says. If you wished, the kiosk could then play a couple of Cray songs for you on the headphones or show Cray's latest video on the screen.

When you decided what you wanted to buy, you would hit a button.

The kiosk would be linked — probably by fiber-optic lines or satellite — to central Blockbuster computers that stored a digital version of all the recordings the company was authorized to sell. The computer would send a digital copy of the album back to the kiosk and send payment to the record company that produced the album.

Back in the record store, the kiosk that is hooked to a high-speed CD duplicating machine would copy the music onto a CD for you. A high-quality, color laser printer would put out the album cover and lyric sheet. Lundeen says the packaging would look almost as nice as current

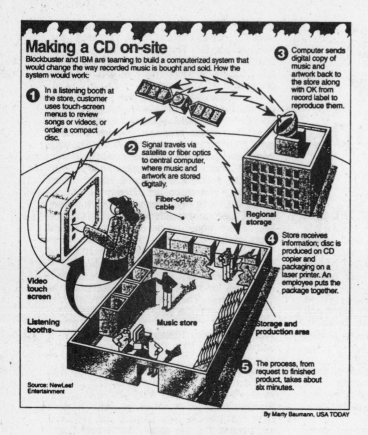

Making a CD on-site

Blockbuster and IBM are teaming to build a computerized system that would change the way recorded music is bought and sold. How the system would work:

1 In a listening booth at the store, customer uses touch-screen menus to review songs or videos, or order a compact disc.

2 Signal travels via satellite or fiber optics to central computer, where music and artwork are stored digitally.

3 Computer sends digital copy of music and artwork back to the store along with OK from record label to reproduce them.

4 Store receives information; disc is produced on CD copier and packaging on a laser printer. An employee puts the package together.

5 The process, from request to finished product, takes about six minutes.

Fiber-optic cable

Regional storage

Video touch screen

Listening booths

Music store

Storage and production area

Source: NewLeaf Entertainment

By Marty Baumann, USA TODAY

packages. More complicated books that sometimes come with CDs might be tough to re-create, but they could be mailed to buyers.

And that's it. The whole process, from ordering the album to having it in your hands, is supposed to take six minutes.

It's also supposed to light up record retailing, which had $9 billion in revenue in 1992. Blockbuster bought the Sound Warehouse and Music Plus chains last year, and executives sound a little appalled at what Lundeen calls the gross inefficiencies of music retailing.

Record stores haven't changed much since the 1950s. They buy and store lots of copies of popular albums and few or no copies of older or more obscure recordings. That may shield the stores from getting stuck with inventory that's not selling, but it often means stores miss sales. Blockbuster figures that 60% of people who walk into a record store know what they want. Of those, 43% leave empty-handed.

Blockbuster hopes NewLeaf can change that — the first kiosks likely will sit alongside traditional bins of CDs and deliver only albums a customer can't find in the store.

The technology isn't expected to be that expensive. Lundeen says a complete system for a typical record store in a mall would cost $75,000 to $200,000 — about what the total inventory for the store costs. One other note: Transportation adds up to $3 to the cost of a CD. Stores could either pocket what they'd save by printing their own CDs or slash prices.

Record labels will have to get on board if NewLeaf is to succeed, and that could be a problem. Major record labels Sony and Warner reacted angrily, saying they hadn't been contacted by Blockbuster or IBM and wouldn't cooperate. But they and other record labels may come around. "It seems kind of crazy to have any position at this early stage," says Don Rose, president of independent record label Rykodisc.

Telecommunications experts say NewLeaf is only a beginning. The step after that is selling music directly into homes. In that case, your TV set — hooked to phone lines or a cable TV box — would act much like the NewLeaf kiosks, offering menus and choices of music that you could select using a remote control. The TV would also be wired to your cassette deck or digital audio tape machine. Choose a record, punch in a credit-card number to pay for it and sit back while your home stereo records the music. The packaging would arrive in the mail.

In fact, NewLeaf may grow into technology that could serve homes, Lundeen says. NewLeaf is "a step between now and then," he says.

Other pieces of home delivery systems are moving into place. Music already is becoming a part of cable TV.

A company called Digital Cable Radio, for instance, is available to about 5 million cable customers. Customers get up to 56 channels of CD-quality music piped into their homes. A special tuner plugs into the cable box and into a stereo system.

Major investors in DCR — including Time Warner, Sony Software, Cox Cable and General Instrument — are betting that the company can grow into something more than just a fancy radio. It could be a way to market recordings. In fact, DCR already has a tie-in with Tower Records: Call a phone number, order a CD and Tower delivers it to your home — the old-fashioned way, by car.

Consultant Arien warns against too-high expectations for music by wire. Even if the technology works wonderfully, it may take time for consumers to get the hang of it.

But to anyone who has tramped in and out of a half-dozen record stores looking for the Del-Lords' first album, the technology can't come soon enough.

It's a Mail Thing: Electronic Messaging Gets a Rating—Ex

* * *

Some Computer Chiefs Dump It as the Masses Invade The 'I-Way'; Bozos Beware

By G. PASCAL ZACHARY
Staff Reporter of THE WALL STREET JOURNAL

Adrian Rietveld spends considerable time helping to plug his software company's electronic-mail programs, which have sold more than a million copies. So, how best to reach *him*? "Just phone me," insists the chief executive of WordPerfect Corp. "I get too many e-mails."

John Sculley, Apple Computer Inc.'s ex-chairman, tells his pals to fax — not e-mail—important messages.

Denise Caruso, an oft-quoted computer pundit, recently removed her e-mail address from her business card. "I don't want people to get that close," she says.

One computer executive even shuts down his company's e-mail system for half the work day—he finds it unproductive.

Mail Chauvinists

The information highway may bring a new era of democracy and openness, as its boosters suggest, but you wouldn't know it from the e-mail lifestyles of the "I-way's" rich and famous. E-mail was supposed to be the great social leveler — Bill Clinton himself has an e-mail address accessible, in theory, to all.

But top executives and other Very Important People are finding that an unguarded e-mail address is like a published phone number: It encourages irksome contact from the electronic masses. Last year, for example, critics blitzed William Gates, chairman of Microsoft Corp., with protest e-mail after the company fired an employee who used his Microsoft e-mail address to launch broadsides against Ukrainian Communists. More recently, when the New Yorker published Mr. Gates's e-mail address in a profile, more than 5,000 messages poured in. This is about as profound as they got: "I fervently believe that the key to immortality is living a life worth remembering."

Indeed, one of the problems is that e-mail doesn't always live up to its early promise as a tool providing instant communication of vital or worthy information. Instead, in many cases, it has become a phenomenal way to communicate trivia,

says Mitch Kertzman, chairman of Powersoft Corp. Among hundreds of messages Mr. Kertzman got last week: a note to all employees from a worker seeking to sell a dog. If not for the advice of lawyers and psychologists, a number of the software company's e-mail abusers "would've been caned a long time ago," he says.

Junk in the Net

An effusive e-mailer has tremendous power and reach. One message can be multiplied into thousands using simple commands. And now, everyone down to the local hardware store has e-mail; in fact, the Electronic Messaging Association estimates that the number of people sending e-mail will grow 50% this year to as many as 60 million.

"E-mail is part of the whole movement to 24-hour accessibility," says John Staudenmaier, a historian of technology at the University of Detroit. "It's disgusting, way too much. It leads to an overload that will spawn a backlash."

Lashing back at immoderate e-mailers, Andrew Grove, Intel Corp.'s chief executive officer, pointedly tells subordinates to stop copying him on inane material. WordPerfect's Mr. Rietveld, who gets up to 150 e-mail messages a day, has ordered employees not to broadcast nonessential memos like notices of softball practices.

But desperate times sometimes call for desperate measures. Charles Wang, chairman of software giant Computer Associates International Inc., no longer sends or reads e-mail—though his company sells an e-mail software package. Mr. Wang also shuts down the company's e-mail system for five hours a day so employees can get some work done. "As a leader in a company, you have to go to an extreme to demonstrate a point," he says. With subordinates copying their bosses on practically every memo they write, "It's become a cover-your-ass tool," Mr. Wang adds.

Free at Last

Other e-mail slaves are liberating themselves as well. "I totally wasted a third of my life this way," says Gary Chapman, a vocal advocate of federal funding to bring the information highway, including e-mail, to the homes of poor Americans. But not long ago, Mr. Chapman suddenly found himself without an e-mail address — and freed from the grim task of reviewing upward of 80 electronic messages a day. "When I went cold turkey on e-mail, I could think of what I was going to do at the office and then do it — without having my agenda diverted," he says.

Fools Rush In . . .

Productivity aside, many CEOs secretly fear unbridled e-mail is just too

democratic, says Langdon Winner, a political scientist and social critic at Rensselaer Polytechnic Institute in Troy, N.Y. "E-mail is a powerful tool to promote communication and flatten hierarchies," Mr. Winner says. "But what nobody wants to admit is that people in an organization have different amounts of power and status. And that those who are better off want to restore a degree of isolation."

Fortunately, there is the bozo filter.

Microsoft's Mr. Gates, an unabashed e-mailer, uses special software — a "bozo filter" in cyber-slang—that culls mail from strangers and sends it into an electronic archive, where the mail sits unless he searches for it. The filter is programmed so that only mail from Microsoft employees, or from Mr. Gates's high-profile friends like Tom Brokaw, gets through. (It apparently works: He hasn't responded to a year's worth of e-mail messages from this reporter.)

But it didn't filter out Connie Chung. Mr. Gates agreed to an interview on her "Eye-to-Eye" show partly because he was impressed that she e-mailed her interview request. Mr. Gates walked out of the recent interview Tonya Harding-style, though, when Ms. Chung pressed him with irritating questions. She also kept pronouncing MS-DOS, a core Microsoft product, as "dos," the Spanish word for two. This might have all been avoided had Mr. Gates learned from the network that an aide to Ms. Chung, and not Ms. Chung herself, sent the e-mail message.

Weakly Reader

For those executives who can't quite seem to pull the plug on e-mail, there is an alternative. At AST Research Inc., Chairman Safi Qureshey has an aide reply to many messages, leaving some employees wondering whether a missive is really from the big cheese. Mr. Qureshey reluctantly concedes that savvy staffers have figured out how to tell the difference. (Clue: The aide writes with proper capitalization, while Mr. Qureshey writes in either all capitals or all lowercase.)

Of course, there are those who can't get enough e-mail. One such addict is Scott McNealy, chairman of Sun Microsystems Inc., whose 13,000 employees e-mail an astonishing 1.5 million messages a day. As if the 200 electronic messages that land in Mr. McNealy's e-mailbox on a busy day aren't enough, Mr. McNealy even sends himself e-mail. A recent missive: "Scott, your fiancee's birthday is next Friday. Don't forget, dummy."

Flexing Muscles

Clinton's Regulators Zero In on Companies With Renewed Fervor

Conservatives and Businesses Fume Over the Impact Of Government Activists

Banks, OSHA, Food Fights

By LAURIE McGINLEY
Staff Reporter of THE WALL STREET JOURNAL

WASHINGTON — Earlier this year, Joseph Dear sent the construction industry a message: Get the lead out—or else.

In February, Mr. Dear, the head of the Occupational Safety and Health Administration, proposed a $1.3 million fine for Manganas Painting Co. in Canonsburg, Pa., for allegedly exposing workers to lead hazards during a bridge-painting job. In June, he slapped Pittsburgh's E. Smalis Painting Co. with a $5 million fine for similar violations, the highest penalty ever levied against a single construction company. Both firms deny the allegations and are contesting the fines. "OSHA just wants to hurt people and collect money," says Andrew Manganas, who manages his father's firm. "They should get a real job."

Mr. Dear isn't apologizing. With OSHA inspection forces understaffed and worker-injury and illness rates rising, he figures he has to hit the worst offenders hard to set an example for everyone else. "We're pointed in the right direction," he says.

"I tell our companies, 'Watch out for OSHA,' " says Peter Eide of the U.S. Chamber of Commerce. "They have the power to make life miserable, and they are."

OSHA's Mr. Dear is just one of a number of Clinton administration regulators who, after 12 years of relatively laid-back Republican rule, are making life miserable for companies that violate their standards of corporate behavior. Many were slow to get going in the early months of the Clinton presidency because of appointment and staffing delays. But now these regulators are stepping up enforcement and other activities with a fervor unseen in years, particularly on consumer and investor protection, worker safety, equal access to credit and civil rights—and they are starting to have an impact

On Monday, for example, Transportation Secretary Federico Pena overruled the views of some of his technical experts to find that General Motors Corp. pickup trucks with side-mounted gasoline tanks were defective — even though the vehicles passed the government's own safety standards. Other regulators are investigating the way drug companies sell their products, sniffing about the quality of indoor air and revamping school menus.

Moreover, with President Clinton facing two years of potential gridlock with a Congress that is expected to include more Republicans, the regulators may represent his best hope of achieving economic and social goals. Administration activists over the next two years are likely "to push the envelope further and further," predicts Ben Vandegrift, a Washington lawyer.

'Out of Control'

Some of the efforts undoubtedly will hurt the corporate bottom line, and many businessmen and conservatives are fuming. "Clinton talks the talk of the new Democrat and the reformist, but he doesn't walk the walk," says Edward Hudgins, director of regulatory studies for the Cato Institute, a public-policy think tank in Washington. "What you have is a government out of control." Susan Eckerly of the Heritage Foundation in Washington says some of the initiatives, such as one under development at OSHA for repetitive-stress injuries, could have "tremendous ramifications for the economy."

But many of Mr. Clinton's appointees also seem eager to minimize the costs of regulation and to continue deregulation in some areas.

Comptroller of the Currency Eugene Ludwig, for instance, is pushing hard to force companies to pursue fair-lending practices, but he also is streamlining examination procedures for smaller banks and trying to trim red tape. "He is the quintessential Clinton regulator," says Karen Shaw, president of ISD/Shaw Inc., a bank-consulting firm in Washington. "He's someone with a social conscience and a market orientation."

Regulatory Arsenal

In some cases, the new Democratic regulators don't represent a sharp break from the Bush administration. In fact, during Mr. Bush's tenure, Congress passed several sweeping new laws, such as the 1990 Clean Air Act and the Americans With Disabilities Act, that expanded regulators' authority over business far more than anything in the Clinton years.

But many Bush political appointees, while issuing new rules, were reluctant to make full use of their regulatory arsenal and often faced roadblocks from the White House when they did. Now the situation has turned around, and many regulators

are using their existing tools to the maximum.

Menu labeling is one example. After passage of the 1990 food-labeling law, the Food and Drug Administration began working on rules governing when entrees could be described as "light" or "low fat," for example. But Bush appointees in the Office of Management and Budget said the law didn't apply to restaurant menus and blocked the effort—a policy reversed by the Clinton administration. Now the FDA is working on the rules.

A more dramatic example occurred in August, when Chevy Chase Federal Savings Bank agreed to open offices in the poorer, predominantly black neighborhoods of Washington to settle Justice Department charges of lending discrimination. The bank denied the allegations. Under the hand of Chairwoman Ann Brown, a former consumer activist, the previously moribund Consumer Product Safety Commission has begun tackling an eclectic mix of safety issues, including high-lead Chinese crayons, fireworks and five-gallon buckets (thought to be a drowning hazard for toddlers).

Here are three Clinton activists that bear watching:

Joseph Dear

Confirmed less than a year ago, the 43-year-old Mr. Dear got off to a slow start but now is moving forward with one of the most ambitious regulatory agendas in OSHA's history.

Businesses already are choking on his indoor-air-quality proposal, which would require them to attack so-called sick-building syndrome by taking aggressive action against indoor contaminants. OSHA puts the cost of compliance at $8 billion a year, although it claims the resulting productivity gains would total almost $15 billion a year. So far, the proposal has drawn a record 100,000 comments, many lambasting a provision to ban smoking in most workplaces, except in separately ventilated areas. A dozen letters were so hostile they were turned over to law-enforcement authorities.

Employers also are fretting about Mr. Dear's next big project: rules that would require them to find and fix the causes of repetitive-stress injuries, an often-debilitating malady. The National Association of Manufacturers is putting together a 100-member Coalition on Ergonomics to work on the issue — a sure sign of a fight waiting to happen. The OSHA chief also plans steps aimed at countering workplace violence as well as the tuberculosis threat faced by health workers. He also is pushing new standards long stuck in the pipeline, such as one dating back to 1971 on asbestos.

A onetime labor activist and former head of Washington state's Department of

Labor and Industries, Mr. Dear says he knows industry is apprehensive, and promises a "high degree of consultation" in "trying to find common ground."

That approach rankles organized labor, which believes talkfests with business and "reinventing OSHA"—another Dear priority — won't do much for worker safety. "The concern I have," says Margaret Seminario, the AFL-CIO's health and safety director, "is that with the administration, and Joe in particular, the strength is in managing, but the job isn't managing. It's providing leadership, using the bully pulpit. There's a sense of urgency missing from this administration."

Mr. Dear says he hopes to blunt such criticism by intensifying enforcement. He has raised the minimum fine for serious, willful health and safety violations fivefold to $25,000. And with only 2,100 state and federal inspectors available to police six million workplaces, he must target the "bad actors." Still, no matter what his course, he says, "I'm going to get criticized by both sides, probably with some justification."

Eugene Ludwig

When he was appointed comptroller, most bankers didn't know who he was. Now they do. To them, Mr. Ludwig is "the Antichrist of community lending," says Ms. Shaw, the analyst.

For almost two years, the 48-year-old Mr. Ludwig, who regulates more than 3,300 national banks, has pressed banks to end discriminatory loan practices and to step up lending and other services in areas long shunned, from the Bedford-Stuyvesant section of Brooklyn, N.Y., to the Navajo Nation in the Southwest. His activism is in stark contrast to his Republican predecessors, who paid "almost no attention" to social issues, says William Isaac, who was chairman of the Federal Deposit Insurance Corp. under President Reagan and an FDIC board member under President Carter. "People say, 'The GOP didn't care,' but mostly it was that the banking system fell apart. The regulators were struggling to keep the business from blowing up."

Now that bank profits are up, the Clinton administration sees the industry as a way to pump capital into neglected communities. Along with the other banking regulators, Mr. Ludwig is overhauling the rules that require banks to invest in low-income neighborhoods. He is the only bank regulator to use "testers" — people who secretly apply for loans to see if mortgage lenders treat people differently based on race.

Moreover, he has referred 10 potential lending-discrimination cases to the Justice Department and the Department of Housing and Urban Development for possible prosecution; only one referral from the Comptroller's office ever had taken place

previously. "He is head and shoulders above anybody who has been in that job," says Allen Fishbein, general counsel for the nonprofit Center for Community Change.

"We've tried very hard to get this right and not go on a witch hunt," Mr. Ludwig says.

Bankers nevertheless complain they are being used to push the administration's social goals because there isn't enough federal money for urban problems. "You shouldn't use private business for public purposes," says Kenneth Guenther, executive vice president of the Independent Bankers Association of America in Washington. "If you want a program, the taxpayers should pay for it." But he admits banks are changing their ways as a direct result of the administration's policies. Many now use testers of their own to see if they are following fair-lending laws and conduct outreach programs for local residents.

Mr. Ludwig is a longtime friend of President Clinton's (the two met on the boat to England where they studied at Oxford University, and they attended Yale Law School together). Like many Clinton regulators, he didn't spend his career at consumer groups, but at a blue-chip law firm; he was a partner at the Washington firm of Covington & Burling, which represents NationsBank, one of the country's largest banking companies. While pushing hard on fair lending, he also wants greater opportunities for banks. He strongly supports letting them sell insurance and securities to compete with other financial institutions.

Still, he has gotten roughed up by all sides in trying to revise the rules aimed at increasing lending to poorer neighborhoods. The first proposal, issued in December, drew flak from bankers, who said it was too heavy-handed, and from community activists, who said it was too timid. One community group dubbed Mr. Ludwig "the Cowardly Comptroller." A more recent proposal softened, but didn't end, the criticism. "It's a hugely contentious area," Mr. Ludwig says.

Ellen Haas

Ellen Haas has spent most of her adult life starting food fights.

To protest high food prices in the early 1970s, she picketed supermarkets in suburban Maryland and, along with Ms. Brown, now the head of the Consumer Product Safety Commission, threw bones down the steps of the U.S. Capitol.

"We said, 'Congress, you won't give us bones,' or something stupid like that," she recalls. As head of Public Voice for Food and Health Policy in Washington, which she founded in 1982, she successfully won changes in meat grading to emphasize leaner meats and ruffled feathers over her

outspoken demands for improved poultry and seafood inspection methods.

Now she is working to overhaul the $4.7 billion federal school-lunch program—which provides subsidized meals to 25 million children at 92,000 schools — to reduce fat, sodium and cholesterol. This time, though, she is the powerful insider, the assistant agriculture secretary for food and consumer services, with control over more than a dozen national feeding programs, including food stamps, and 60% of the department's budget.

Rolled out on June 8 with immense fanfare, Ms. Haas's proposal would require that school lunches meet the U.S. dietary guidelines by reducing total calories derived from fat to 30% from the current average of 38%, and by lowering calories from saturated fat to 10%. Her goals drew extensive praise, but her methods elicited a lot of grumbling.

Under her plan for "Nutrient Standard Menu Planning," schools would follow a complex, computerized process to count nutrients such as niacin, calcium and fat.

The National Milk Producers Federation called her plan a "costly, impractical government-controlled program" that would cost dairy farmers $200 million a year in reduced government purchases of some high-fat commodities such as cheese and butter. The American Frozen Food Institute initially was miffed that the name of the program was "Fresh Start." (It was later changed to "Healthy Kids.") Consumer groups, including Public Voice and the Center for Science in the Public Interest in Washington, while applauding the effort, urged that the rules be extended to cover fast foods, including hamburgers and pizza, which are served in a la carte lines and aren't currently regulated by the government.

But the toughest criticism was served up by the American School Food Service Association in Alexandria, Va., which represents 66,000 food-service workers. The group, arguing that Ms. Haas's plan was too cumbersome, complained vociferously to Congress. Shortly before lawmakers left for the year, they ordered Ms. Haas to develop an additional option for meeting the dietary guidelines that the group says would be easier to implement. While the food workers consider it a major victory, Ms. Haas calls it a "technical correction" that won't impede her goal of ensuring that school meals comply with the dietary guidelines. Whatever the final details of regulations, which are due out next year, Ms. Haas's high-profile campaign to overhaul school menus has set off a scramble among the industry to develop and market lower-fat cheeses and meats for sale to schools and to the Agriculture Department, which purchases about $700 million a

(cont.)

year in commodities for the program.

The 55-year-old Ms. Haas, known for her savviness with the media and industry, recently staged a coup by persuading Walt Disney Co. to produce commercials featuring two animated bug-eating characters from "The Lion King" to teach children about nutrition. But in the past, her dealings with business have caused waves; while she was head of Public Voice, she accepted funding from some big food producers, which some fellow activists criticized as a conflict of interest.

Ms. Haas says learning to work with business has been part of a natural process of moving from confrontation to consensus. "As I grew up and moved up," she says, "I realized I had to make changes within the system."

22

Movable Feasts: More People Dine and Drive

By Kathleen Deveny

Staff Reporter of The Wall Street Journal

Forget about fat or cholesterol. The greatest hazard at mealtime these days may be oncoming traffic.

Pressed for time or simply craving privacy, more people are eating meals in their cars--often while driving. This year, one of every 10 meals purchased in a restaurant will be consumed in a car, according to Harry Balzer, a vice president of NPD Group, a Chicago company that tracks people's eating habits. That's up about 24% from 1985, Mr. Balzer says.

Gary Stibel, a principal with New England Consulting Group in Westport, Conn., thinks the figure is even higher" When snacks from convenience stores are included, he says, the incidence of eating and driving may be as high as one in six meals. "Consumers are very proud when they use time more efficiently," he says.

Longer commutes, coupled with the growing availability of fast-food drive-throughs, have spawned a new breed of motorist, who hoist a hot dog or hamburger in one hand and drive with the other.

Bill Edwards, 36 years old, is one of them. As president of a small Chicago company that sells chemical storage systems, he drives 40,000 miles a year to visit prospective customers. On a straightaway, Mr. Edwards says, he can eat, talk on the phone, and take notes while driving. "I don't want to lose time, and the food usually isn't worth stopping for," he says. "But my ties are always a disaster."

Some food marketers have started pitching products to consumers like Mr. Edwards. A commercial for **Kellogg** Co.'s Nutri-Grain cereal bars, for example, features the members of a car pool becoming irritable when they realize they don't have time to stop for breakfast. The last man on the route saves the morning with a box of breakfast bars. Burger King Corp., a unit of **Grand Metropolitan** PLC, is testing a new pocket-like sandwich wrapper that is easier to pick up and put down--a benefit in stop-and-go traffic.

In addition to quick fuel, a burger behind the wheel can provide respite from responsibilities, says Steve Barnett, an anthropologist and principal with Global Business Network, which tracks consumer behavior. Mr. Barnett, a former director of product planning for Nissan North America, says some people today get upset if their commute is too short because it's the only time they have to themselves. "Work is hectic, home is hectic, but the car is always quiet," he says.

Some Behavioral experts say the urge to eat in the car may run even deeper. People need to balance sensory stimulation, says Michael T. Marsden, a dean at Northern Michigan University who has done extensive research on car culture in America. When driving a car, Mr. Marsden says, we become visually overstimulated. To create a sense of equilibrium, we stimulate our other senses by listening to the radio and munching on something. That's why people like to eat popcorn while they're watching a movie, he says.

That makes sense to Mike Ventola, 27, a graduate student at Rutgers University in New Jersey. His one-hour commute from Brooklyn, N.Y., often stretches to two if traffic is congested But saving time isn't his main motivation for snacking behind the wheel. "I try to choose food that takes a long time to eat because it calms me down," he says.

To broaden its appeal among drivers, **Southland** Corp., operator of 7-Eleven convenience stores and perhaps the nation's largest vendor of car cuisine, is toying with more healthful snacks, including a grilled breast of chicken sandwich shaped like a hot dog and a car-friendly crudite tray, now being tested in Texas, which features bit-sized pieces of cauliflower and broccoli and a spill-proof reservoir for salad dressing. The company is also trying to push fresh fruit and has found that its carry-out clientele favors easy-to-eat varieties, such as applies or melon chunks, over more cumbersome oranges.

Southland isn't abandoning its junk-food heritage. The company also sells a hot-dog-like breakfast sausage and dreams of creating such desserts as cheesecake on a stick. The company acknowledges that, for many customers, the car is a haven from good nutrition.

"The car is my hideaway," confesses Karen Raskopf, merchandising communications manager for Southland. "I can get myself one cookie, get in the car and eat it, and I don't have to answer for it."

Eating behind the wheel can be a perilous habit. The National Highway Traffic Safety Administration doesn't calculate the number of accidents that involve meals, but estimates that inattentive behavior, which includes eating as well as chatting on the phone, played a role in 7% of fatal car crashes in 1992, the most recent year for which statistics are available.

Not all marketers, consequentially, are willing to pitch their products as car fare. Although drive-through customers now account for about 55% of sales in restaurants, where the service is available, **McDonald's** Corp. ostensibly discourages eating and driving. "We don't encourage people to eat while they are driving for safety reasons," says a spokesman for the burger chain. There are exceptions, however. "French fries are eminently eatable in the car," the spokesman adds, "because they only require two fingers."

The makers of automobiles have been loath to encourage behind-the-wheel eating. Since the late 1980s, however, they have lavished attention on the built-in cup-holder, creating ever sturdier models. **Chrysler** Corp.

(cont.)

now offers square drink holders for kids' juice boxes in some of its minivans and jumbo-sized versions to accommodate 7-Eleven's "Big Gulp" cups. But Chrysler says it has no plans at this point to develop a tray-- or any other device--that might make eating and driving easier and neater.

"We kind of discourage eating in the car," says Jim Ebejer, chief of interior design for all vehicles at Chrysler.

The auto makers have technical problems to overcome before they can design an eating tray. The dashboard area of most cars is already crowded, and there isn't much room in the door, either. The only logical solution would be a tray that would fold out of the console between the two front seats, say Mr. Barnett, the consultant who once worked for Nissan. Moreover, safety rules prescribe that all objects that extend into the main compartment of a vehicle must be what Mr. Ebejer call "friendly on impact."

Kathy Reinhart, who lives in Cincinnati, wishes the car companies would relent. She says her 14-year-old son Nick eats one or two fast-food meals a week in the car, as she drives him home from basketball practice. "For every dropped french fry or spilled Coke, I wonder, why couldn't there be a tray that comes out of the glove compartment?" she says. "You know, maybe something on hinges." Some industry experts think the car companies will eventually come around to equipping cars for mealtime. Eating in the car is a reality that manufacturers won't ignore forever, says Christopher Cedergren, a consultant with AutoPacific Group Inc. "Ten years ago, drink holders were unheard of, but now everybody has them," Mr. Cedergren says. "The next step will be making some place to put food."

23

Kellogg reports brisk cereal sales in India

By Mir Maqbool Alam Khan

BOMBAY—Kellogg Co. says its newly introduced corn, wheat and basmati flakes breakfast cereals are selling faster than hotcakes in this urban area. And the U.S. cereal giant expects annual nationwide sales to hit $26 million in three years, in a country where the market is just $2 million now.

Kellogg's marketing concentrates on convincing Indians to take time for breakfast and consume a lighter, more nutritious morning meal.

Although advertising didn't kick off until a week after the products hit the shelves Sept. 17, such ready enthusiasm caused Kellogg to up its original sales projections.

The long-term prospects have convinced Kellogg to invest $30 million in the business. Kellogg's All Bran, Bran Flakes and Raisin Bran will be introduced as well, with all cereals available nationwide by next year.

The marketer faces a more daunting challenge in changing breakfast habits in non-Westernized small cities and rural areas. According to a market penetration study by the Indian Market Research Bureau, while countrywide penetration of cookies is currently at 88% and potato chips 64%, corn flakes and hot cereal were a minuscule 3%. An earlier study said 22% of Indians now skip breakfast.

To convince consumers to switch to a lighter, more nutritious diet, Kellogg is introducing rice flakes using basmati, a premium aromatic rice.

The whole line is being backed with a $450,000 multimedia campaign through December, with three 30-second TV spots featuring a family around the breakfast table. The commercials use a common Kellogg theme for the Asia/Pacific, addressing overeating as well as the ill effects of a bread and butter diet and skipping breakfast.

The campaign "does leave behind a suggestion that current fried breakfasts are not the best things you could provide your family to begin the day," said Anil Bhatia, senior VP-general manager at Hindustan Thompson Associates.

Kellogg also plans to sponsor a TV special featuring a panel of nutritionists, dietitians and physicians on the government-run Doordarshan Network.

The company is already sponsoring "Kellogg's Breakfast Show," a morning talk show that runs daily on radio. The first guest celebrity in early October was Sushmita Sen, Miss Universe 1994.

Kellogg is also sponsoring two message boards on the main Bombay commuter thoroughfare featuring healthful advice from medical experts.

Informative and copy-heavy ads are being placed in English and local-language newspapers, and women's and health magazines.

"To me, the Indian market is similar to the Mexican market because the Mexicans also used to consume a hot, savory breakfast," said Damindra Dias, Kellogg India's managing director. "We are saying, 'Take the right food. Don't fill yourself with fat the first thing in the morning.' "

It took Kellogg an arduous 20 years to crack the Mexican market, and more than six years to convince the French to pass up croissants and the Japanese to lay down their chopsticks in favor of cereal in milk.

Problems arise "where there are very entrenched ethnic [breakfast] habits," Ms. Dias said.

Kellogg claims its patience and the general influence of Western media will win over the 75 million urban upper middle-class Indians who are initially being targeted.

Kellogg's Corn Flakes and Wheat Flakes are priced at exactly double that of other brands in the market. The most popular brand is Mohan Meakin's New Life Corn Flakes.

The brand has been selling for decades in larger cities such as Bombay, but its sales are tiny compared with players in more developed cereal markets. ☐

Getting Information for
Marketing Decisions

Old Market Research Tricks
No Match for New Technology

By Bart Ziegler

Staff Reporter of The Wall Street Journal

Munching popcorn and sipping red wine, executives from Hewlett-Packard Co. peer through a one-way mirror at a dozen New Yorkers, searching for insights into consumer opinions on interactive television and software.

This well-educated, high-income "focus group" should be a natural constituency for such equipment, but before research leader Brooke Warrick begins, he asks how many of the people present are familiar with interactive TV. Only a few hands go up: It seems even these dream consumers aren't sure what the interactive age is all about.

That's the problem with doing market research for the information highway: It's like asking 19th century Americans their opinions on airline travel. The result has been contradictory and questionable findings.

Mr. Warrick has found that consumers want new services zapped to their TV sets rather than a personal computer; after all, consumers tell him, a PC is a *work* device. But other research shows that more than 50% of consumers want to use a home PC for entertainment, says Inteco Corp., Norwalk, Conn. And while most surveys show movies on demand will be the "killer application" that drives the highway, Lou Harris & Associates finds such frivolous fare is the *least* popular feature; people really want "information," Harris says.

"There is an enormous amount of flying in the dark," notes Thomas Gage, a vice president at Gemini Consulting, Morristown, N.J., who advises communications companies. Cable and phone companies have used survey results to justify spending billions of dollars to build interactive networks. But "standard market research techniques—focus groups, questionnaires, telephone research—are extremely weak ways of predicting how people might behave with a product they barely understand," Mr. Gage says. And most companies have been in too much of a hurry to use newer, more sophisticated techniques.

Companies recognize the problem, but they say they have little choice. "We layer a responsible conservatism" on the results, says Scott Ferris, who oversees research efforts for U S West Inc.'s interactive TV unit.

Consumers are notorious for defying the rosy predictions of surveys when it comes to new technology products, says research expert Glen Urban, dean of the Sloan School of Management at the Massachusetts Institute of Technology. A key problem is that consumers in focus groups and surveys often vastly overstate the likelihood that they will buy a new product, he says.

Computer makers, for example, had high hopes last year for handheld "personal digital assistants." But despite enthusiastic early research reports, the gadgets sold poorly. Early studies on cellular phone service also predicted huge demand, Mr. Urban says, but "it took 10 to 15 years to get to the levels they were talking about."

This research dilemma has prompted some companies to start building systems even before deciding which services to offer. They say the only way to really find out what services customers will pay for is to test a system in their living rooms. "There really is no substitute for getting real consumer feedback based on actually utilizing these services," says Tom Feige, who oversees Time Warner Inc.'s Orlando, Fla., test of 4,000 homes, set to start late this year. He calls the system "the world's most advanced telecommunications research laboratory."

But even this approach may produce misleading results, says Roberta Chicos of Mercer Management Consulting Inc., Lexington, Mass. Customers could be turned off by the design or by the limits of the current technology, rather than by the interactive services themselves. There may appear to be little demand for home shopping, for example, but the fault may lie in a klunky on-screen "navigation" system, she says.

If the tests sour users because of faulty or immature technology, the entire market could be set back, says Nicholas Donatiello Jr., president of the San Francisco research firm Odyssey L.P. "It's far more important to be right, not first," he adds.

And since interactive tests involve at most a few thousand households, which haven't been randomly selected, results can't be used to predict national demand, experts say. "These aren't market tests," a researcher says. "A lot of these tests are for Wall Street—to show [these companies] are out front and to drive up their stock price." Time Warner's Mr. Feige responds that the Orlando test will be big and will involve a cross section of consumers.

Some experts, including MIT's Mr. Urban, believe the only reliable way to find out whether consumers will buy a nonexistent product is to create a realistic, computer-based simulation. He worked on a team that conducted such "information acceleration" research for a proposed electric car for General Motors Corp. The research included videotaped interviews with supposed experts on the car, as well as dummy ads, fake magazine articles,

(cont.)

price lists and a simulated tour of the car on a computer screen, followed by a test drive of a prototype.

Cable and phone companies are doing some simulations. U S West plans to use interactive kiosks to mimic proposed services for consumer tests, but that research won't yield results until the middle of next year — well after the company's test in Omaha begins. **Bell Atlantic** Corp. took some consumers into a mocked-up living room, where they tried a prototype interactive TV device. But none of this is as elaborate as the "information acceleration" technique.

Gemini Consulting's Mr. Gage suggests combining research into how "early adopters" use existing interactive services, such as America Online, with in-depth studies of unmet consumer needs. That would involve spending time in people's homes to see what services might be useful, he says.

Few, if any, companies have used so elaborate an approach. For now they rely more on early interactive tests that are like an arrow shot into the air, says Joe Kellagher, research director for Bell Atlantic's video division. "You don't know where the target is — it may be directly behind you," he says, then adds hopefully: "Eventually you get on the target and work toward the bull's-eye."

A POTENT NEW TOOL FOR SELLING:
DATABASE MARKETING

It may not be celebrated as a national holiday, but it's a pretty big deal around here. Happy birthday from the Claridge Casino Hotel, Atlantic City.

What time is it now in Israel? What is Mama cooking today? We at AT&T know exactly how you feel and are aware of your need to call and speak with those close to you whenever you wish.

Dear Nabisco All-Star Legends Collector: As a participant in last year's offer, you are being given a sneak preview of our 1994 All-Star Legends cards. Be the first on your block to order these special limited-edition cards....

Does it seem as if a lot of companies are taking quite a friendly interest in your life these days? Helping you mark your birthday? Soothing your homesickness? Giving you an early peek at something new? If this kind of stuff is turning up in your mailbox more often, you're not alone. You're on the receiving end of a sophisticated, high-tech twist to the ancient art of persuasion. It goes by different names—database marketing, relationship marketing, one-to-one marketing. But it all adds up to the same thing: Companies are collecting mountains of information about you, crunching it to predict how likely you are to buy a product, and using that knowledge to craft a marketing message precisely calibrated to get you to do so.

It amounts to one of the biggest changes in marketing since "new and improved." First came the mass market, that vast, undifferentiated body of consumers who received identical, mass-produced products and messages—any color of car they wanted, so long as it was black. Then came market segmentation, which divided still-anonymous consumers into smaller groups with common demographic or psychographic characteristics. Now, new generations of faster, more powerful computers are enabling marketers to zero in on ever-smaller niches of the population, ultimately aiming for the smallest consumer segment of all: the individual.

A growing number of marketers are investing millions of dollars to build databases that enable them to figure out who their customers are and what it takes to secure their loyalty. Direct marketers have long been in the van-guard of database users: Catalogs, record clubs, and credit-card companies have always needed their customers' names and addresses to do business with them. But database marketing is now moving into the marketing mainstream, as everyone from packaged-goods companies to auto makers comes to believe that in the fragmented, fiercely competitive marketplace of the 1990s, nothing is more powerful than knowledge about customers' individual practices and preferences.

HOG-TIED. In 1992, for example, General Motors Corp. joined with MasterCard to offer the GM Card. As a result, GM now has a database of 12 million GM card-holders, and it surveys them to learn what they're driving, when they next plan to buy a car or truck, and what kind of vehicle they would like. Then, if a cardholder expresses an interest in, say, sport-utility vehicles, the card unit mails out information on its truck line and passes the cardholder's name along to the appropriate division.

Blockbuster Entertainment Corp. is using its database of 36 million house-

---

HOW IT WORKS

1. THE PRODUCT

2. INTO THE DATABASE MAW
You may think you're just sending in a coupon, filling out a warranty card, or entering a sweepstakes. But to a marketer, you're also volunteering information about yourself--data that gets fed into a computer, where it's combined with more information from public records.

3. DIGESTING THE DATA
Using sophisticated statistical techniques, the computer merges different sets of data into a coherent, consolidated database. Then, with powerful software, brand managers can "drill down" into the data to any level of detail they require.

4. AN IDEAL CONSUMER
The computer identifies a model consumer of a chosen product based on the common characteristics of high-volume users. Next, clusters of consumers who share those characteristics--interests, incomes, brand loyalties, for instance--can be identified as targets for marketing efforts.

5. USING THE KNOWLEDGE
The data can be used in many ways: to determine the values of coupons and who should get them; to develop new products and ensure that the appropriate consumers know about them; to tailor ad messages and aim them at the right audience.

6. SHARING DATA WITH RETAILERS
Cash-register scanners provide reams of information about exactly what shoppers are buying at specific stores. Merged with the manufacturer's data, this intelligence helps to plan local promotional mailings, fine-tune shelf displays, and design store layouts.

7. REFINING THE DATABASE
The database is continually updated with information collected from product-oriented clubs, responses to coupons, calls to 800 numbers, and sweepstakes entries, as well as with new lists from outside sources.

holds and 2 million daily transactions to help its video-rental customers select movies and steer them to other Blockbuster subsidiaries. In Richmond, Va., the company is testing a computerized system that recommends 10 movie titles based on a customer's prior rentals. The suggestions are printed on a card that also offers targeted promotions. Customers who have rented children's films, for example, might get a discount at Discovery Zone, Blockbuster's play-center subsidiary.

Kraft General Foods Inc. has amassed a list of more than 30 million users of its products who have provided their names when sending in coupons or responding to some other KGF promotion. Based on the interests they've expressed in surveys, it regularly sends them tips on such things as nutrition and exercise—as well as recipes and coupons for specific brands. The company figures that the more information consumers have about a product, the likelier they'll be to use more of it (sample tip: Use Miracle Whip instead of butter for grilling sandwiches). KGF constantly refines its database by sending surveys to the names on its list.

Like KGF, Harley-Davidson Inc. wants to urge customers to keep using its products. That's why it mails the 256,000 members of its Harley Owners Group (HOG) a bimonthly magazine packed with listings of regional, national, and international events to encourage owners to get out on the road and use their bikes. House of Seagram uses its 10 million-name database for loyalty-building programs for existing products. It might send premiums tied to proofs of purchase—a pair of snifters, say, to someone who bought its Martell cognac. Seagram uses surveys to identify likely buyers of new products, as well as drinkers of rival brands it can send offers to. RJR Nabisco Holdings Corp. is building a database that identifies, among other things, households that have responded to past promotions.

Over on the tobacco side of RJR Nabisco's business, database marketing has long been practiced in earnest. For cigarette makers, it's a virtue born of necessity. Facing increasing restrictions on advertising, Philip Morris Cos. and RJR have assembled huge databases of smokers they can reach directly. For example, by requiring consumers who respond to offers of free shirts, sleeping bags, or other merchandise to fill out detailed questionnaires. Philip Morris has built a list of some 26 million smokers' names and addresses. The companies use their lists both to market to

smokers with coupons and promotions and to enlist grassroots support for their lobbying efforts.

Consumers appear to be responding to the precision marketing. But of course, this private intelligence-gathering gives some people the creeps. At best, critics say, targeted marketing efforts are intrusive and annoying. At worst, the collection, manipulation, and combination of lists of personal information amount to an ominous invasion of privacy. Such concerns aren't fazing the marketing types, though. According to Donnelley Marketing Inc.'s annual survey of promotional practices, 56% of manufacturers and retailers are currently building a database, an additional 10% plan to do so, and 85% believe they'll need database marketing to be competitive past the year 2000. "It is one of the most important marketing developments of the 1990s," says marketing guru Stan Rapp, chairman of consultants Cross Rapp Associates.

Why all the activity? In part, it's in the name of the relentless drive to make marketing more efficient. Seagram knows that most U.S. adults aren't likely prospects for its distilled spirits: Two-thirds of them haven't had a single drink of liquor in the past 30 days. As a result, notes Richard P. Shaw, vice-president for marketing communications at Seagram, mass-market advertising has "a great deal of what we would call nonproductive reach." Of course, many conventional promotions, and much typical junk mail, are similarly wasted because they're aimed at too broad an audience. "We're trying to kill off junk mail--junk mail defined as 'anything I didn't ask for and wouldn't be interested in,'" says Barrington I. Hill, London-based senior vice-president for product development at American Express Travel Related Services Co., which has been using its detailed database to send carefully aimed promotions to cardholders.

SIMULACRUM. Marketers increasingly are recognizing that past customer behavior, as recorded in actual business transactions, is by far the best indicator of future buying patterns. "It's not true that demographics is destiny," says Matt Kuckuk, senior principal at American Management Systems Inc.'s Financial Industry Group. Merely knowing Mr. Jones's Zip Code or income generally yields less insight--and opportunity--than knowing, say, that he has just applied for his first joint

checking account. That probably signals a marriage, which means future openings to sell a mortgage, life insurance, long-term investments, perhaps even a college loan.

It's a kind of cybernetic intimacy: In ever-expanding processing power, marketers see an opportunity to close the gap that has widened between companies and their customers with the rise of mass markets, mass media, and mass merchants. Database marketing, they believe, can create a silicon simulacrum of the old-fashioned relationship people used to have with the corner grocer, butcher, or baker. "A database is sort of a collective memory," says Richard G. Barlow, president of Frequency Marketing Inc., a Cincinnati-based consulting firm. "It deals with you in the same personalized way as a mom-and-pop grocery store, where they knew customers by name and stocked what they wanted."

Consider the dilemma of a busy casino. In the old days, the pit boss kept notebooks on frequent players. Periodically, he would pick a name from the notebook, call the high roller up, and offer a free room for the weekend. Today, with thousands of visitors trooping through on any given day, "it's virtually impossible to get to know people on a first-name basis," says Robert M. Renneisen Jr., CEO of Claridge Hotel & Casino Corp.

Now, the casino's computer keeps tabs on visitors who use its frequent-gamblers' card and sends out offers every day. Claridge's Comp-Card Gold, which offers discounts and tips on upcoming events, has 350,000 active members. They get offers ranging from $10 in coins for slot machines to monogrammed bathrobes and door-to-door limo service. "It's made us more efficient," says Renneisen. "We can target our dollars directly to customers who justify the costs."

"GREATER VALUE." In addition, by weaving relationships with its customers, a company can make it inconvenient for consumers to switch to a competitor. Don Peppers, co-author of *The One to One Future,* one of the bibles of the new marketing, cites MCI Communications Corp.'s Friends & Family long-distance discount plan. To get the discount, the customer has to form a network of friends and family members--"a substantial investment in time and energy on the consumer's part," he notes. Changing long-distance carriers means having to "reinvent my

(cont.)

relationship," Peppers says.

All these efforts to forge ties to consumers are based on the same fundamental idea: There's no more important asset than a happy customer. Happy customers remain customers, and it's much cheaper to keep existing customers than to find new ones. Michael D. Keefe, director of Harley-Davidson's HOG, is reluctant even to call the process marketing. "It's more like customer bonding," he says. "If people use the motorcycle, they'll stay involved. If there's nowhere to ride, no place to go, the motorcycle stays in the garage, the battery goes dead, and a year from now, they just sell it."

Some database marketers say their promotional offers garner response rates in double digits, considerably higher than the typical 2% to 4% for junk mail. For example, the targeted promotions that Hilton Hotels Corp. offers senior citizens in its Senior Honors frequent-traveler program, which features discounts and travel tips, have persuaded close to half of the club's members to take previously unplanned trips that included stays at Hilton hotels. And KGF says its offers those listed on its database get significantly higher response rates than standard mass-market coupons. The database, says John T. Kuendig, vice-president for market development, is a list of steady consumers who "have a greater value to the brand."

NO CHOICE. Database marketing has its skeptics, of course. An earlier flush of enthusiasm prompted by the spread of checkout scanners in the 1980s ended in widespread disappointment: Many companies were too overwhelmed by the sheer quantity of data to do anything useful with the information. And some critics say these efforts to reach out and touch individual consumers haven't demonstrated their usefulness in many product categories. Programs that identify frequent customers and reward them may make sense for airlines, but consumers have rejected the "frequent-eater" programs offered by some fast-food chains as being not worth the bother.

Still, many companies believe they have no choice but to brave the data-base-marketing frontier. For one thing, most manufacturers are waging an information war with the retailers that stock their products. Large supermarket chains and giant mass merchandisers, such as Wal-Mart Stores Inc., have grown increasingly sophisticated in their use of checkout-scanner data to keep track of sales. They now base many of their choices about what to stock, what to promote, and what to charge on that information. To shape those decisions to their advantage, manufacturers need persuasive information of their own. "To the extent we have built up relationships with our consumers and know which ones will respond, we can work with retailers to help them build their businesses," says KGF's Kuendig.

BUSYBODY QUESTIONS. Databases start with information from the consumer. In transactional businesses, such as charge cards, banking, or catalogs, that's easy: The marketer simply collects information on the sale. For other marketers, the challenge is to get consumers to volunteer the data about themselves. Many packaged-goods marketers collect information that consumers divulge when they call 800 numbers or mail in coupons. In its surveys, Seagram tracks consumers' names and addresses, the brands and types of alcohol they drink, their sex, birthdate, income, and how many bottles they purchase in an average month. And GM went into the credit-card business not just to build loyalty and offer cardholders rebates on cars but also because it saw the billing process as a way to harvest reams of data about consumers. "This is a gold mine," says H. D. "Hank" Weed, general marketing manager for the GM Card.

Having assembled a list of consumers, the marketer then mixes in information from other sources. Research houses such as Donnelley, Metromail, and R. L. Polk glean vast amounts of data from public records—drivers' licenses, auto registrations, and mortgage-tax rolls. Even income, the most sensitive subject, can be estimated based on mortgages and automobile registrations. Such information isn't cheap, though. This year, for instance, Ohio sold its drivers'-license and car-registration lists to TRW Inc. for $375,000.

Wittingly or unwittingly, consumers often offer plenty of data about themselves. Think of all those busybody questions on a warranty card: What's your age, income, occupation, education, and marital status? How many children? Do you hunt, fish, or play tennis? If you think none of that has much to do with the guarantee on that radio you just bought, you're right. But National Demographics & Lifestyles Inc., based in Denver, collects those warranty cards and the precious information they reveal, then resells it to database marketers.

Increasingly, the computer itself is sifting through such data for patterns that will predict behavior. Using neural-network software, computers can plow through masses of data and determine how specified variables may depend on one another (page 62). For example, what combination of income level, investment activity, and credit-card spending is most likely to be seen among people who are in the market for mortgages? Once the network has come up with a highly specific profile of some class of customer, it's easier to find new customers matching that profile and aim at them with customized direct-marketing schemes.

Most marketers consider the greatest benefit of the databases simply to be identifying who their current customers are and how much business the company is doing with them. First Commerce Corp., a $6.4 billion New Orleans bank holding company with five banks, has been using this technology to retain current customers and build its business. Its customers, like those at every bank, tend to bank with several institutions. But by analyzing the data available on its current checking customers, First Commerce can try to win more of them as credit-card customers, too. The work is done with a combination of PCs and a mainframe storing hundreds of thousands of records. On a fast PC, a neural-network run can take from 30 to 60 minutes to complete.

Where there are millions of records to sift through, so-called massively parallel database computers, at typical prices of $1 million or more, may be required. These machines gang together scores or even hundreds of the fastest microprocessors around, giving them the oomph to respond in minutes to complex database queries. Marketers call these complex searches "drilling down." With such speed at hand, companies can search their databases more frequently and feel freer to experiment with new strategies. "Before parallel computing, you just didn't have the juice required," says Doug Cheney, director of program development at AT&T Global Information Solutions, the former NCR Corp. and a maker of parallel database computers.

WEATHER REPORTS. Massively parallel processors from Thinking Machines Inc. are a key technology for American Express Co. Before the systems were in place, the amount of information the company could keep on each cardmember was limited to basic stuff, such as the cardmember's name and address, how long he or she had been a cardholder, and how much the cardmember had spent in the past year.

With massively parallel processing, AmEx could vastly expand the profile of every customer. "We basically store every transaction," says product-development executive Hill.

Now, 70 workstations at the American Express Decision Sciences center in Phoenix race through mountains of data on millions of AmEx cardmembers--the stores they shop in, the places they travel to, the restaurants they've eaten in,. and even the economic conditions and weather in the areas where they live.

Every month for a little more than a year, AmEx has been using that information to send out precisely aimed offers. They go out in millions of customized monthly bills that the company says amount to individualized newsletters sent to a growing number of customers around the world. On one British cardmember's recent statement, a British Airways flight triggered an offer, printed adjacent to the transaction, of special deals on weekend getaways to New York and continental Europe. A purchase at Harrod's triggered a notice of a special sale at the store for AmEx cardholders. Since its introduction in Ireland in March, 1993, this "relationship billing" has been rolled out through Europe, Canada, and Mexico. AmEx has seen an increase of 15% to 20% in year-over-year cardmember spending in Europe and gives the new billing format much of

the credit. Next year, AmEx plans to introduce relationship billing in its biggest market, the U.S.

Heavy computing firepower isn't always necessary, though. For some efforts, all it may take is a few thousand dollars' worth of hardware and software. Using a Macintosh personal computer, Yuri Radzievsky has built a database of Russian, Polish, and Israeli immigrants to the U.S. By combing lists of subscriptions to foreign-language newspapers and buyers of tickets to events such as tours by Russian entertainers, his YAR Communications has assembled lists of 50,000 Russians, 75,000 Poles, and 30,000 Israelis in the U.S. Such information is of real value to client AT&T—telephone service, after all, is one of the first things new arrivals want when they set up their households.

Using the lists, AT&T has mailed Hebrew- and Russian-language offers of discounts on calls home. "Every marketer's dream is to be able to target those little slices," says Sandra K. Shellenberger, district manager of diversified marketers and multicultural marketing communications for AT&T. Response rates for such database-directed offers sometimes run as high as 20% to 30%, she says, compared with the low single digits for broader, more conventional direct mail.

Where will it all end? Few predict that database marketing will supplant mass marketing. Still, many targeted direct-mail campaigns are as glossy as any big-budget ad campaign. The mail-

ings Seagram sends out feature lush photos and long, story-spinning blocks of copy discussing such matters as the proper way to drink single-malt scotch. Seagram also plans to rely heavily on database marketing to penetrate emerging markets, such as India and Thailand, where the proportion of affluent drinkers is so small that the use of mass media would be especially wasteful.

There's no doubt technology is shaking up traditional marketing methods. Marketers, after all, have been accustomed to thinking in broad swaths, such as adults 18 to 34 or women 25 to 49. Now, a typical AmEx segment might be business travelers who have bought jewelry abroad in the past month. Some of the offers the company has sent out in bills have gone to as few as 20 people. Says Hill: "This is a strange experience for the marketing people."

Can a faceless, distant marketer re-create the personal relationships consumers used to have with the people they did business with? More and more companies are betting that the answer is yes as they reach out to envelop customers in an automated embrace.

By Jonathan Berry, with John Verity, in New York, Kathleen Kerwin in Detroit, Gail DeGeorge in Miami, and bureau reports

26.

Focus Groups Meeting In Cyberspace

MORE MARKET researchers are getting wired on computer networks and finding that focus groups in cyberspace are faster and cheaper than the old-fashioned kind.

The latest and potentially biggest venture involves BKG America, a New York research firm specializing in children, teens and Generation X. It has an exclusive agreement with America Online to conduct electronic research with five- to 29-year-olds. BKG will collect data via broad surveys and in-depth electronic chat sessions and sell the findings to corporate and ad agency clients. The service, American Dialogue, begins this month, with BKG electronically probing 600 households with five- to 12-year-olds.

Marian Salzman, BKG America president, says marketers want real-time feedback, particularly from the 20- to 29-year-olds who make up Generation X.

Other companies are doing consumer research on line. Viacom's Nickelodeon network established its own private forum of eight-to-12-year-olds last year on the CompuServe network, a unit of H & R Block. Prodigy Services, a joint venture of International Business Machines and Sears, Roebuck, markets a focus-group package to companies and counts the three major television networks among its users.

BKG plans to wire up 5,000 to 10,000 children and young adults by offering them free America Online software. Electronic participants also get $35 to $50 per session — the amount paid to members of traditional focus groups.

Electronic research is cheaper than gathering data face to face, Ms. Salzman says. A typical in-person focus group costs $4,000, she estimates. Electronically, it could be done for $1,500. And although electronic research doesn't yet allow visual observation, Ms. Salzman says that isn't a problem. "The degree of intimacy in this medium makes up for what you're losing," she says.

Consumer experts are intrigued by the idea but caution that it won't replace traditional focus groups yet. Barbara Feigin, executive vice president at Grey Advertising, notes online users are "a tiny sliver of the population." Users—mostly upscale, highly educated men—are a fine subject for research about high-tech products, she says, but not mass-market items. "They aren't the true target," she says. "They're not the ones who are going to buy it."

27

THEY KNOW WHERE YOU LIVE--AND HOW YOU BUY

If you consume, you can't hide from Zip Code seer Claritas

You're 35 years old. The price tag on your suits shows that you're a success. You drive a Volvo. You know your way around the olive-oil section of the store, buy fresh-ground coffee, and go on scuba-diving trips. You're living out your own, individual version of the good life in the suburbs. You're unique--not some demographic cliche.

Wrong. You're a prime example of "Kids & Cul-de-Sacs," one of 22 new consumer groups in PRIZM, Claritas Inc.'s demographic taxonomy of American by postal Zip Code. For the past 20 years, PRIZM (Potential Rating Index by Zip Market) has been among marketers' favorite tools for finding consumers. Restaurant chains, banks, and stores use the Alexandria (Va.) company's PRIZM to pinpoint the best locations for new outlets. Direct marketers tap it to target mailings. Ad agencies comb PRIZM for insights on consumers. Often, they find surprises: "Executive Suites" has a lot of Spam fans; the blue-collar households of "Rural Industria" are a good market for pagers; and "Golden Ponds" seniors love theme parks.

SCANNER WARS. The new upgrade, which brings the total number of consumer segments in PRIZM to 62, is the latest sign of how the nation's increasing ethnic and economic complexity is changing consumer marketing. Old PRIZM standbys, such as "Furs & Station Wagons" and "Shotguns & Pickups"--PRIZM is as well-known for its fanciful names as its insights--are being joined by new clusters. "American Dreams" reflects new waves of immigrants. "Kids & Cul-de-Sacs" points to the new migration to the suburbs. "Young Literati" taps Generation X. There's even a place for aging hippies--"New Ecotopia." Behind the cutesy names are important trends, Claritas executives say. "The goal," notes David Miller, 43, the quiet, lanky statistician behind PRIZM, "is getting the right message

to the right person."

The new upgrade, which will debut in February, is also the latest volley in marketing's information wars. The number of companies keeping data bases of individual consumers has exploded. Supermarket checkout scanners, meanwhile, are enabling legions of marketers to track how their products really fare on the ground. Some say that leaves PRIZM--which lumps people into

groups--at a disadvantage. "The future lies with technologies that count real people and actual purchases," says Laurel Cutler, worldwide director of marketing planning for ad agency Foote, Cone & Belding Communications Inc.

Demand for information has been particularly feverish in this sluggish economic recovery. In many categories, marketers can increase sales only by capturing market share. Good research is a competitive advantage, says Cutler. Claritas,

which had 1993 sales of $35 million and is a division of the Dutch company, VNU, can't afford to fall behind.

PRIZM is founded on the notion that "birds of a feather flock together." The idea is that people who live in the same neighborhood tend to buy the same types of things. Jonathan Robbin, who designed the original PRIZM data base, broke U.S. Census Bureau data into Zip

Codes and analyzed each for social rank, mobility, ethnicity, family life cycle, and housing. The Census data are supplemented with market-research surveys and other statistics from suppliers such as A.C. Nielsen Co. and information from 1,600 municipal and regional agencies. The current version of PRIZM segments America not only by Zip codes by block tracts and Zip-plus-four as well. The most expensive model, including mapping software, costs more than $100,000 a year to license.

FACTOIDS OF THE NEW AMERICA
Three of PRIZM's new demographic clusters, with selected traits and median household income

AMERICAN DREAMS
The emerging, upscale, ethnic, big-city mosaic; one in five is foreign born.
LIFESTYLE: Import cars, *Elle*, Mueslix, tennis weekends, designer jeans.
INCOME: $46,100.

RURAL INDUSTRIA
Young families in heartland offices and factories.
LIFESTYLE: Trucks, *True Story*, Shake'n Bake, fishing trips, tropical fish.
INCOME: $22,900.

CASHMERE & COUNTRY CLUBS
Aging baby boomers living the good life in the suburbs.
LIFESTYLE: Mercedes, *Golf Digest*, salt substitutes, European getaways, high-end TVs.
INCOME: $68,600.

(cont.)

But reports go for as little as $99.
VIBE APPEAL. Marketers in a broad range of industries are ponying up. Premier Bank in Baton Rouge, La., merges PRIZM with its internal data base to find neighborhoods with lots of households that match the traits of its best customers. Ad agency Ammirati & Puris Inc. combined PRIZM with other research to create MasterCard's "Smart Money" ads.

Time Inc. Ventures used it to get its new urban-culture magazine *VIBE* over a hump. Advertisers were convinced *VIBE* was just for inner-city kids. PRIZM showed it also appealed to white-collar "Young Influentials" and middle-aged "Money & Brains." The result: ad buys from vodka and consumer-electronics marketers.

Ultimately, that's where the consumer-research wars will be won: sales. In these tough times, figures Claritas, what marketer wouldn't be piqued by the notion that those blase "Young Literati" buy lots of Cheerios?

By Christina Del Valle in Alexandria, Va., with Jon Berry in New York

28

Data Raids

Rivals Duel Bitterly For Job of Supplying Market Information

IRI Steals Back an Executive Nielsen Previously Stole; Both Sides Steal Clients

Scanning the Retail World

By GABRIELLA STERN and RICHARD GIBSON
Staff Reporters of THE WALL STREET JOURNAL.

When his phone rang at 4:30 a.m. a week ago Friday, Dun & Bradstreet Corp. President Robert Weissman thought it was a drunk calling a wrong number.

No such luck. It was Serge Okun, the president of D&B's A.C. Nielsen unit, on the line from Bangkok with some urgent news. George R. Garrick, hired just four months earlier to rejuvenate Nielsen's U.S. market-research business, had suddenly quit. Worse, he was returning to his former employer and Nielsen's archfoe, Information Resources Inc.

Mr. Okun immediately canceled a big budget meeting in the Thai capital and flew home to help with damage control. And within hours, Mr. Weissman himself was on the phone reassuring major clients like Kraft General Foods and Coca-Cola that they needn't be concerned — even though D&B had issued a news release saying it was "shocked" by Mr. Garrick's move.

The aggressiveness of this reaction was typical of the Nielsen-IRI rivalry, one of the more intense in American business. Both companies delight in bad-mouthing each other to prospective clients, and celebrate even when a small customer switches sides. They also regularly raid personnel in what one industry operative calls "cut-the-head-off" sorties.

Mystery Packets

For example, after Mr. Garrick's first defection — when he went from IRI to Nielsen in June — Nielsen clients and executives began receiving packages containing memos Mr. Garrick had written at IRI criticizing Nielsen. IRI's chairman and chief executive, Gian Fulgoni, says the memos were intended for internal use, adding that he doesn't know how they came to be mailed.

At IRI's annual companywide celebration last summer, a staffer mocked Nielsen as a stodgy place by dressing up like an old geezer. Says IRI President Magid Abraham: "We are mortal enemies."

It's easy to see why. At stake are lucrative contracts with the world's largest makers of consumer products. All are hungry for the data IRI and Nielsen collect round the clock from client supermarkets, drugstores and mass merchandisers. More numbers are created every time a box of cereal or bar of soap passes over a checkout scanner. IRI estimates it gathers 100 million new records each week.

The wealth of data ultimately affects what shoppers can buy. Retailers use the information to stock shelves and adjust prices, and manufacturers use it to decide how many of which kinds of products to make, and how to market them. (The Wall Street Journal uses some, too, getting data from IRI to compile its twice-weekly "MarketScan" feature on consumer-product trends. The Journal also uses Nielsen as a source for marketing data.)

Appetite for Data

Multinational behemoths like Procter & Gamble and Unilever have a growing appetite for shopper data as they seek to wring costs from manufacturing, distribution and marketing operations. The Kraft General Foods unit of Philip Morris, for example, spent an estimated $24 million last year on data from Nielsen. Battling for this business, Nielsen and IRI seek to underprice each other, while each claiming its interpretation of the data is superior.

"We want to be No. 1 and we're religious fanatics about it," says IRI Chairman Fulgoni. Observes Mr. Weissman of D&B: "We have in IRI what I characterize as an extremely angry competitor."

The hostility dates back to 1987, when D&B sought to acquire IRI for $455 million in stock, only to be thwarted by the Federal Trade Commission on antitrust grounds. During the four months the FTC studied the takeover, IRI's business was stalled and it lost millions in revenue. Mr. Fulgoni became enraged when he learned that Nielsen was noting IRI's losses in presentations to clients. "They used the stuff they found during due diligence to develop their business plans, and used the fact that we'd lost money during this period," Mr. Fulgoni says. "That just drove us bananas." Mr. Weissman says D&B didn't do anything unseemly.

Purloined Accounts

IRI's executives redoubled their efforts to cut into Nielsen's business. Over the next few years, they stole many of Nielsen's domestic consumer-products clients. Using a technological advantage in scanner software plus lots of promotion, IRI won major corporate clients: PepsiCo, Campbell Soup, R.J. Reynolds Tobacco, H.J. Heinz, Tambrands and Bristol-Myers Squibb.

IRI's 1992 revenue of $276.4 million, though up 24% from 1991, remains far behind Nielsen's $1.3 billion world-wide. The gap in the U.S. is narrower than that suggests, however, because only about $515 million of Nielsen's 1992 revenue was domestic, and of that about a third came from Nielsen Media Research, the TV-rating service. According to industry estimates, IRI's U.S. revenue was $241.6 million. Overseas, Nielsen is far ahead of IRI.

The research business remains lucrative for both companies, yielding profit margins in the teens, but IRI has had steeper profit growth. Last year it earned $19.2 million, up 25% from 1991. D&B doesn't break out Nielsen's earnings.

Some industry analysts fault Nielsen for being slower than IRI to recognize that data alone are just a commodity — that the key to winning contracts is analysis of the data. Nielsen's service has also occasionally drawn fire. An executive whose health-care products company switched to IRI in 1991 says: "We were seeing consistent problems with Nielsen—missing data, misstated data, deleting data without notifying us."

A Nielsen spokeswoman says data quality was an issue for a time after the company introduced a sophisticated software package that analyzed data differently. "There were misunderstandings as to accuracy," she says.

It took several jolting contract losses to spur Nielsen to action. Early last year, the company wrested the Kraft account from IRI — it already had General Foods — reportedly by offering a 30% price discount.

IRI retaliated, picking off P&G's giant account from Nielsen. But P&G, playing the rivals against each other, ended up paying at least 50% less than it had under its Nielsen contract, people close to the situation say.

IRI went on to score several more coups, adding such accounts as Kellogg, Borden and Burroughs-Wellcome. Despite their willingness to deal, the data companies keep profit margins up by adding more services and expanding their clientele, as checkout scanners spread even to rural convenience stores and gas stations.

When Nielsen's president, John Costello, quit last winter, D&B saw the chance for a shake-up, and enticed Mr. Garrick away from IRI's London headquarters to do the job. The 41-year-old Mr. Garrick reportedly told friends he felt unappreciated by his IRI superiors back in Chicago,

(cont.)

and he and his wife were eager to return to the U.S. At Nielsen there was jubilation.

But IRI's Mr. Fulgoni was furious. He had personally recruited the bright engineer-cum-M.B.A. from Purdue University. Now he fired off a fax to Mr. Garrick with a Mark Twain quotation: "If you pick up a starving dog and make him prosperous, he will not bite you. This is the principal difference between a dog and a man."

George R. Garrick

Mr. Garrick, though shaken by IRI's anger, sought to turn it to his advantage. After learning that his memos critical of Nielsen were being leaked, he invited Nielsen employees to read his assessments. "I don't regret anything I said here," some recall him saying.

Such candor won him favor at Nielsen, where he saw himself as an agent of change. Indeed, one reason D&B hired him, Mr. Weissman says, was that Nielsen was seen as "a little uptight." Mr. Garrick joined as president and chief operating officer of Nielsen Marketing Research North America and then became CEO.

One thing he did in his short time there was to foster a more relaxed climate. He replaced initials on nameplates with first names, installed a casual dress code and located his office so it was open to staffers. He also poked fun at the organization, once saying that somewhere in the corporate archives was a book spelling out "43 ways to say 'up' and 43 ways to say 'down,'" according to a Nielsen manager.

But he also urged sales employees to listen carefully during staff meetings, warning that they would be given a test afterward. He cut layers of management and recruited some outsiders, including former IRI colleagues.

Mr. Garrick spent much of his time calling on clients. He often took along two IRI recruits, causing some resentment back at Nielsen's Northbrook, Ill., headquarters. Some employees also felt he was indiscreet to call Nielsen "dysfunctional" in an August newspaper interview.

But clients were bowled over. "Most exciting to us was that he felt [Nielsen's] focus should be on helping clients get more value out of the information we were purchasing," says a senior marketing executive at a Midwestern food company. She recalls Mr. Garrick displaying a chart where one line represented information available and another showed its average use. "There was clearly a gap and he positioned Nielsen as trying to address it," the executive says.

A deft salesman, Mr. Garrick won the entire Colgate-Palmolive account for Nielsen, which previously had been divided with IRI.

But not everything went smoothly. According to Mr. Garrick, a problem arose over how much money D&B would give Nielsen. Mr. Weissman says he told Mr. Garrick that, like a field general, Mr. Garrick was asking for a lot of guns and bullets in order to win the war. But "we need to talk," Mr. Weissman added, "because there are too many guns and bullets on your list." However, he says, Mr. Garrick quit before they had a chance to talk seriously.

In an interview last week, Mr. Garrick said he decided to leave Nielsen and return to IRI because "the realities of what I was expected to do were a lot different from the expectations I'd been given when I was recruited." But Mr. Weissman says that Mr. Garrick had no reason to be dissatisfied since the 1994 budget process wasn't even over when he left.

When word got back to IRI that Mr. Garrick was unhappy, it seized the chance to weaken Nielsen. Two weeks ago, IRI's Mr. Abraham met Mr. Garrick for dinner. After telling him he was "a person our people hate to hate," Mr. Abraham says he "popped the question about what it would take" to win him back. Two nights later they met at Mr. Fulgoni's Chicago townhouse and had what Mr. Garrick calls a "bury-the-hatchet dinner."

Neither he nor IRI officials will say what the company offered to entice him back, although people close to the situation say his base pay is about equal to the approximately $450,000 he earned at Nielsen. The carrot at IRI apparently was a hefty package of long-term stock options. Mr. Garrick, who had felt he was moving up the IRI ladder too slowly before, also has a new position: president and CEO of IRI North America.

On Friday, D&B named Mr. Garrick's Nielsen successor, David J.S. Flaschen, 37, a software executive in the company's London office, who it said would lead "an aggressive new strategy" for Nielsen.

As for Mr. Garrick, D&B says it is reviewing its options. "We're frankly troubled — as are some of our customers — by some of the things that IRI has done over the past week, and we're actively exploring their implications," Mr. Weissman says. He is sorry Mr. Garrick left, but "life will go on." Still, it promises to be more austere. Nielsen, which has cut world-wide staff by several thousand already, plans further reductions.

Since the announcement that Mr. Garrick would return to IRI, that company's shares have risen 6.2%, closing Friday at $38.75 in over-the-counter trading. D&B's shares have edged up a bit, closing Friday at $66.875 on the New York Stock Exchange.

With Mr. Garrick back, IRI vows "to increase the pressure on our cross-town rivals even more," a memo to employees from Messrs. Fulgoni and Abraham says. "George's departure from IRI was similar to a temporary and painful breakup in a relationship. Both parties don't realize what they have until they are apart."

29

DATA GAP

When it comes to understanding black consumers, most companies are surprisingly ingorant.

By Carolyn Phillips

What marketers don't know about black consumers could fill volumes. and finally, it's beginning to.

Inside giant consumer-products companies, at market-research firms, on university campuses and in black-oriented media, the effort to gather information on African-American consumers is taking off. Spurred by a growing recognition of the importance of this $270 billion-a-year market, as well as by recent missteps on the part of those who failed to read it correctly, researchers are looking far beyond the sometimes meager in-house reports that for decades were virtually the only intelligence there was on the subject. The result is that gaps in U.S. marketing data are being filled with the kind of hard evidence it takes to sway advertisers, product developers and bankers.

"Companies are beginning to recognize that America is turning brown," says Lafayette Jones, the president of Segmented Marketing Systems Inc. in Winston-Salem, N.C. He sees the 1990 U.S. census as "a wake-up call to corporate America," showing as it did that nonwhite portions of the population are the fastest growing. However, he adds, when most executives ponder this enormous market, "the first thing they understand is that they don't know anything about it."

Clouded Vision

Last summer, for example, **American Sports Data** Inc., a research concern in Hartsdale, N.Y., reported that its studies "indicate that racial stereotypes may be clouding key marketing targets from the view of sporting-goods companies." The work demonstrated that blacks are participating in such activities as tennis and running to "a far greater extent than is suggested by the conventional wisdom."

Harvey Lauer, the president of American Sports Data, also points out that the industry's notion that blacks account for a hugely disproportionate share of the athletic-footwear market is a myth. "In 1991," he notes, "blacks purchased 12.2% of the 342 million pairs of athletic shoes in the U.S., compared with their 12.1% representation in the population."

Research by the **Wellington Group**, an Oaklyn, N.J., market-research firm, showed **Procter & Gamble** Co. that while its Crest brand toothpaste may be No. 1 overall, it loses out among black consumers to **Colgate-Palmolive** Co.'s Colgate brand. Working with an adver-tising agency hired by **Chrysler** Corp., Wellington also learned that white consumers were typically sold on performance and quality when shopping for a car, while black buyers were more committed to style and American-made models.

In some cases, the distinctions are more subtle. "It's not simply that we use different products," observes Eugene Morris, the president of the Chicago-based ad agency E. Morris Ltd. "Sometimes we use the same product in a different way." Mr. Morris cites a survey that **Nestle** SA's Carnation division conducted to find out about buyers of its Instant Breakfast. The result, he says, revealed that "in certain areas [there is] a high incidence of black usage, even though African-Americans are not particularly diet conscious and don't embrace those products to the same degree as the general population." It turned out that the product is being used, not as a breakfast substitute, but as a breakfast supplement.

Following the Leaders

As such information becomes available, more companies are jumping on the bandwagon. "Tight economic times have forced them to say, 'Hey, what about this black market thing?'" says Ken Smikle, who publishes a monthly trade newsletter in Chicago called Target Market News. "Look at the leading companies in any category and ask, 'Are they involved in aggressively marketing to African-American consumers?'" he instructs, then does the drill himself. "Fast food? McDonald's. Yes. Soft drinks? Coca-Cola. Yes."

In fact, **Coca-Cola** Co. is somewhat unusual in that it has been researching black consumer tastes for more than 30 years. And it has taken the findings to heart: After a study by Mr. Morris's agency discovered that African-American typically prefer larger servings of soft drinks, Coke began using 16-ounce containers instead of the 12-ounce size in ads directed toward blacks.

"We were vitally interested [in the black consumer market] at Coca-Cola," says Charles Morrison, a former Coke executive whose year-old management consulting firm in Atlanta specializes in ethnic marketing.

Some companies, though, have been much less careful in their attention. Apart from the obvious incentives of competition and the market's size, the need for more and better insight into minority consumers has become apparent after several recent corporate embarrassments.

"A lot of [companies] hit some land mines," says Jerome Williams, an assistant professor of marketing at Pennsylvania State University. He recalls the negative publicity and the outrage in the black community over attempts by **G. Heileman Brewing** Co. and **RJR Nabisco** Inc. to launch PowerMaster malt liquor and Uptown cigarettes, respectively. Ultimately, he says, "these firms realized you just can't rush into these things" without doing the right kind of homework and then learning how to apply the findings in the appropriate way.

Heileman officials decline to comment on the attempts to market PowerMaster. RJR, which acknowledges targeting black consumers, never launched Uptown. Maura Payne, a company spokeswoman, says the failure "wasn't a question of not having adequate research or not interpreting it properly...Our problem came from the antismoking community."

Lost in Translation

For the most part, however, "people doing the research don't always know what they're doing," says Mr. Morris, the advertising executive. Often it's language that gets in the way. One large advertising agency was relying on research it thought showed that a lot of black people read TV Guide, Mr. Morris recalls, when in fact black respondents were saying that they looked at television listings of all sorts. "And it's not just terminology," he explains. "If you don't understand the body language and all those things, it's easy to miss something."

Even in mainstream advertising, companies have found that there is much to ascertain about what doesn't work for black consumers. Mr. Williams of Penn State refers, for instance, to an ad from the Benetton clothing chain that showed a black hand and a white hand handcuffed together. The image was intended to convey the idea of racial harmony, but the reactions from blacks who

Spending Patterns

Overall, the average black household spends $19,130.44 each year on consumer goods, 35% less than the $29,546.92 spent by the average nonblack household. But black consumers spend more than white consumers on a variety of products. Here are some.

	AVERAGE ANNUAL PER-HOUSEHOLD SPENDING		PERCENT DIFFERENCE
	BLACK	NONBLACK	
Television sets (rental)	$ 2.91	$ .91	219.8%
Boys' nightwear	5.76	1.81	218.2
Boys' pants	44.56	15.12	194.7
Appliances (rental)	5.17	1.87	176.5
Materials for plastering, panels, roofing, etc.	1.16	0.49	136.7
Boys' underwear	5.92	2.57	130.4
Boys' hosiery	7.30	3.19	128.8
Coin-operated apparel laundry and dry cleaning	64.50	30.63	109.6
Boys' footwear	43.33	21.09	105.5
Refrigerator, freezers (rental)	15.78	7.98	97.7
Infant accessories	8.71	4.48	94.4
Washing machines (rental)	11.45	6.00	90.8
Pork, excluding ham bacon and pork chops	53.80	29.28	83.7
Boys' suits, sports coats, vests	5.18	2.85	81.8
Coin-operated laundry and dry cleaning (nonclothing)	8.25	4.60	79.4
VCR, radio and sound equipment (rental)	2.27	1.29	76.0
Repair or maintenance services	12.81	7.59	68.8
Taxi fares, not on trips	9.69	6.10	58.9
Sugar	28.02	18.25	53.5
Radios	10.97	7.23	51.7
Sausage	26.15	17.71	47.7
Rice	17.88	12.27	45.7
Noncarbonated fruit-flavored drinks	32.21	22.26	44.7
Bacon	28.99	20.20	43.5
Pork chops	39.62	27.99	41.6
Fresh and frozen fish	52.71	38.91	35.5
Calculators (household)	2.89	2.15	34.4
Chuck roast	15.27	11.72	30.3
Termite/pest control products	.35	.27	29.6
Boys' sweaters	5.77	4.50	28.2
Baby food	26.59	21.17	25.6
Boys' shorts, short sets	6.87	5.50	24.9
Flour	7.78	6.31	23.3
Women's hosiery	31.71	25.99	22.0
Frankfurters	23.84	19.83	20.2
Boys' accessories	5.54	4.61	20.2

Sources: American Demographics magazine; Bureau of Labor Statistics, Consumer Expenditure Survey, 1990

saw it were very negative. "They saw a white police officer locking up a black criminal," says Mr. Williams. "They saw chains, shackles, bondage."

Although work done by smaller firms has often been tagged as "asterisk research"--meaning that the sample sizes and methodology are considered inadequate for producing accurate, representative results--the big companies that dominate market research have been slow to tackle the subject. This is partly because they tend to wait for their clients to request specific types of research.

It's an issue of supply and demand," explains Anna Fountas, president of the syndicated research division of giant **Simmons Market Research Bureau** Inc. in New York. Ms. Fountas says that while Simmons has in certain cases done customized research on black consumers, her own division, which produces reports for broad distribution, has never done a study in which the sample population has been entirely black.

A second major factor in the big firms' tardiness is that studying the black consumer market requires a new approach, with different sample structures and different questions. And marketing executives, argues Mr. Morrison, the consultant, "are creatures of habit."

A Skewed Picture

Traditional research firms have been hampered by "methodology and research-gathering techniques that haven't recognized diversity," says Debra Johnson-Hall, president of **Johnson & Associates Marketing** Inc. in Chicago. For one thing, she notes, such firms have relied too heavily on phone sampling and mail surveys--tactics that usually fail to yield a representative cross-section of blacks.

Al Wellington, the head of the Wellington Group, agrees: "Random-digit dialing techniques simply don't work. Blacks are not randomly distributed. We're clustered." Random dialing, he explains, typically yields a sample that's only 6% to 8% black--roughly half the level of black representation in the general population. And the

blacks who do wind up being contacted, he adds, tend to have values more in line with those of suburban residents.

Another problem with phone polling is more intractable. Particularly in urban areas, researchers calling to gather survey data commonly run into the same obstacle encountered by census takers: suspicion about those seeking personal information.

Thus, "you have people who go house to house," Mr. Morris says. But this isn't always a workable option in such areas as the inner city: "My office is about a mile from the Cabrini-Green housing projects. There's no way you can tell me that the average demographer is going house to house in Cabrini-Green. Nobody is talking to those people."

A number of researchers advocate so-called intercept strategies for reaching black consumers. These techniques involve questioning subjects at schools, churches, recreation centers or even on the street.

In 1990, **Deloitte & Touche**, one of the nation's largest accounting firms, teamed up with **Impact Resources** Inc., a Columbus, Ohio, market-research company, to do just that. Researchers set up tables in malls and retail centers, and talked to tens of thousands of consumers, making sure to tap racial minorities in proportion to the general population. When it comes to interpreting the data from such efforts, Christine Donovan, a research associate at Deloitte in New York, says she works closely with marketing specialists from the black women's magazine Essence, a black travel group and others.

The work has drawn notice in the business world. Stuart Crane, an Impact Resources vice president, says that while customers for the company's general-market studies are usually media concerns using the data to sell ads, requests for the black-consumer study "come more from consumer-products manufacturers and retailers."

As Mr. Smikle, the newsletter publisher, points out, "If there's no research, even an African-American marketing executive is ill equipped to make the argument as to how and why a company ought to market to black consumers."

Buyer Behavior

30

Population growing at a furious rate

By Margaret L. Usdansky
USA TODAY

In the next minute, 268 babies will be born.

Ninety-eight people will die.

The math is simple, but staggering. The world's population is growing by 170 people a minute, so fast that the number of people on the already crowded planet could more than double from 5.6 billion today to as many as 12.5 billion by 2050.

These mindboggling numbers are at the heart of a problem so pervasive that--even though most in the USA do not directly see it-- it affects everything from the quality of the air we breathe and the water we drink to worldwide resources and stability.

"We are now adding the equivalent of one China's worth of people every 10 years, one Mexico's worth of people every single year," says Vice President Gore. "Societies cannot maintain stability with that kind of ... growth."

In September, Gore leads the USA's delegation to the most important worldwide population conference in a decade, where more than 170 countries will try to agree on a plan to slow population growth.

And while the threat of world population growth has faded from the nation's consciousness along with such phrases as "population explosion," experts agree September's International Conference on Population and Development in Cairo, Egypt, comes at a critical moment.

At issue: whether the number of people on the planet by 2050 will come closer to the United Nation's high estimate of 12.5 billion or its low estimate of 7.8 billion.

Many experts say it's impossible to overstate the implications.

"If we do not stabilize population with justice, humanity and mercy ... it will be done for us by nature, and it will be done brutally," says Nobel Prize winner Henry Kendall of the

Crowding of the planet

Growing 2.8 people per second

The world population grows by almost 90 million a year:

Year	89,458,000
Month	7,454,834
Week	1,720,346
Day	245,050
Hour	10,212
Minute	170
Second	2.8

Source: USA TODAY research

Largest countries

Population in millions, 1994

China	1,192.0
India	911.6
USA	260.8
Indonesia	199.7
Brazil	155.3

By Marty Baumann, USA TODAY

Union of Concerned Scientists.

Already, conference delegates have drafted a 113-page plan that sets ambitious goals, from universal access to family planning to equal education of girls, lower infant mortality and higher status for women.

Of course there's no assurance that countries signing any plan will follow it. And the Catholic Church is waging a major challenge to the plan because it endorses contraception and includes abortion as a part of reproductive health care.

Moreover, the complexity of any worldwide proposal is enormous, and must thread its way through countless cultural taboos, social norms and religious practices.

But at base, what the conference comes down to is helping people like Amina Mohammad Irshad of Bombay, India.

For 10 years, Irshad and her husband have lived on a piece of pavement 4 feet by 6 feet. Burlap bags tied to a lamppost provide their only shelter, and they pay one rupee, about 3 cents, for each use of a toilet. A milky stream of garbage runs by the curb where Irshad cooks.

Four children have been born to them since they tried to improve their lives by moving here from Calcutta, where, Irshad says, "There

was nothing to eat and living conditions were terrible."

That is how one woman sees it.

This is how National Academy of Sciences president Bruce Alberts sees it: "Science and technology can do a lot of things, but what they cannot do is make finite resources support an infinite population."

The problem is not that population programs haven't worked. They have achieved a remarkable amount in the short period since the USA and the United Nations began funding them in the late 1960s:

▶ The average number of children born to a woman in the developing world has fallen from 6 to 4.

▶ The number of married women using contraception has risen from under 10% to almost half.

▶ Annual population growth has dropped from 2.1% to 1.6%.

But birth rates haven't fallen fast enough to keep pace with even more dramatic declines in infant and child mortality, which, though good news, mean more babies survive to have children of their own.

And although the rate of population growth has declined, the world gains almost 90 million newcomers each year, more than 85 million of them in developing countries.

Progress toward reducing the average number of children born to

(cont.)

women varies dramatically region to region, country to country:

▶ Some of the most dramatic success stories have occurred in Asia. Between 1960 and 1994, Thailand reduced its birth rate from an average of 6.4 children per woman to 2.2., while birth rates in Sri Lanka dropped from 5.3 to 2.5.

Other countries such as India, where birth rates fell from 5.9 to 3.6, have made progress — but not nearly enough to stabilize growth.

▶ Birth rates also plunged in Latin America, where the average Mexican woman now has 3.2 children, down from 6.7.

▶ Progress has been slowest in Subsaharan Africa, where, despite very recent fertility declines in Kenya, Botswana and Zimbabwe, the average woman still has 6.4 children. In Mali, it's 7.3.

▶ In the developed world, population growth has slowed to a near halt.

Spain has the lowest fertility, with an average of 1.2 children per woman. In Japan it's 1.5, in Germany, 1.3.

In the USA, the average woman has 2.1 children.

A number of signs point to growing consensus about the need and means for reducing worldwide population growth, and many experts think the upcoming conference has a real chance to make a difference.

Not only do most countries with rapid population growth want to reduce it, but the USA — which downplayed the issue during the Reagan-Bush years — is taking on a leadership role.

And there is growing support for some kind of family planning, even in nations traditionally opposed to such programs, including Muslim countries like Iran and Catholic countries like Peru.

Even with agreement, reducing population growth is complicated.

Still, many experts and ordinary citizens alike think it's a goal of growing importance, and not just for Third World countries. These days, many problems, such as diminishing resources, have global implications.

"Those who are rich, it is time for you to share your riches," says Bisi Ogunleye, president of a Nigerian woman's association, who will attend the conference. "If you don't, the poor will share their poverty."

Contributing: Ellen Hale, Gannett News Service, reporting from India

31

Marketers Pay Attention! Ethnics Comprise 25% of the U.S.

Minorities are majorities in one of every six U.S. cities. By Michael J. McDermott

Like other kinds of niche efforts, ethnic marketing has long been the domain of a handful of minority-owned companies. But increasingly, companies such as Soft Sheen Products and Goya Foods are going head-to-head with the likes of Procter & Gamble and Sara Lee.

The reason is a simple one: demographics. Lafayette Jones, executive vp of Segmented Marketing Services Inc. (SMSI), a Winston-Salem, N.C.-based marketing firm that specializes in ethnic marketing, calls data from the most recent U.S. Census report a "wake-up call for marketers."

Already, people of African, Asian, Hispanic and Native American ancestry account for 25% of the U.S. population. In a little more than five years, they will comprise a third of all consumers in this country. By 2010, non-whites are projected to make up the majority of the populations of California and Texas.

In some of the nation's largest markets—New York, Washington, Atlanta—more than half the residents are non-whites, and in some cases up to 70% of those populations are minorities.

That trend has been accelerated by the arrival of almost 10 million immigrants during the 1980s, mostly from Asia and Latin America. Minorities now make up the majority of the residents in about half of the 90 California cities with populations of 50,000 or more. "Minority majorities" are the norm in one of every six U.S. cities.

It should come as no surprise, then, that at least half of all Fortune 500 companies have launched some ethnic marketing initiatives, according to Gary Berman, president of Market Segment Research, a Coral Gables, Fla.-based firm specializing in ethnic market research. Berman projects that ethnic marketing

expenditures will double to more than $1 billion by the end of this decade. Still, Berman is surprised that more mainstream marketers haven't targeted what appears to be a mushrooming market.

Part of the problem in entering the field has been that non-ethnic marketers simply did not know how to attack the developing market.

"Ethnic consumers are not simply white consumers with different-colored skin," said Geri Duncan Jones, executive director of the American Health and Beauty Aids Institute, a Chicago-based trade association of ethnic beauty care products companies.

In the same vein, Jones faults many mainstream marketers for confusing message exposure with message receptivity.

"Black consumers, like other segments of the population, respond best to tailored, personalized invitations to purchase," he said. "But those invitations simply don't get delivered to most black consumers via the general media."

There are signs that mainstream marketers are beginning to get the message. Within the past year, leading retailers including J.C. Penney, Montgomery Ward and Sears, Roebuck and Co. have announced plans to sell merchandise specifically targeted to black and Hispanic consumers.

Direct marketing giant Spiegel Inc. has launched "E Style," a series of women's apparel catalogs targeted to readers of Johnson Publishing Co.'s Ebony magazine.

Arcadia, Calif.-based supermarketer Vons Cos. has created a new store format targeted to the Hispanic market. Its Tianguis prototype has been hailed as the standard bearer for marketing to the Latino population of southern California.

The store emphasizes the fresh pro-

duce, poultry and other ingredients that are important to its Hispanic customers' meal preparation habits, and its merchandise mix acknowledges the different preferences among Mexicans, Filipinos, Central Americans and other distinct ethnic groups within the overall Hispanic market. The store layout seeks to recreate the atmosphere of a Latin American open-air market.

In other cases, mainstream marketers are learning the lessons of ethnic marketing the hard way, as minority entrepreneurs have sprung up to exploit market niches.

For example, Mattel Inc. has long offered black Barbie dolls that are identical to the original Barbies, with the exception of their skin color. Consumer dissatisfaction with that half-hearted measure prompted Olmec Corp., a New York-based black-owned company, to introduce Imani, a Barbie-type doll with authentic African-American features.

Such ethnic marketing gaffes are likely to become a rarity as mainstream companies begin to hone their ethnic marketing skills. Realizing the complexity of targeting minority consumers, marketers are running more ethnic focus groups, hiring minority-owned firms as consultants and experimenting with specialized marketing programs as a prelude to full-blown launches.

One such effort was recently conducted by Hillshire Farms & Kahn's, a Cincinnati-based smoked sausage and lunch meat subsidiary of Sara Lee Corp.

"Disfrute el sabor de lo mejor," which translates to, "Enjoy the taste of the best," was the tag line of a Spanish language campaign for Hillshire Farms last year that included 15 different radio spots, recipe tear pads, a recipe booklet and two free standing insert coupon drops. The radio spots featured Chef Pepin, a popular figure on Univision, a Spanish-language television network.

"This effort made sense for us for a number of reasons," said Marianne O'Dwyer, smoked sausage product manager at Hillshire Farms & Kahn's. "Hispanics are much bigger consumers of smoked sausage than the general population. As a group, they are also less concerned about fat and cholesterol."

The widespread use of scanning technology by all types of retail outlets is making it easier for them to successfully target ethnic consumers.

The proliferation of cable channels is also opening up opportunities for marketers to communicate targeted messages to specific ethnic audiences.

Big-name brands like McDonald's, Sears, Procter & Gamble, Nike and MasterCard were the force behind a 14% increase in ad spending at Hispanic media in 1993. Similar increases are projected for 1994, although the growth in Hispanic media is now fueled by smaller companies in areas such as financial services and regional retailing.

"The ethnic market is becoming a target for all sorts of companies," said Market Segment Research's Berman. "Banks, credit card companies, insurance companies, they're all finding they have strong market opportunities here, as long as they approach the market in the right way."

Marketers who would hitch their wagons to the ethnic juggernaut must be circumspect with the messages they issue.

Jones, Berman and other ethnic marketing specialists are in consensus: ethnic markets are not homogeneous.

"An inner-city black youth is not going to respond to the same marketing messages as a middle-aged black professional living in the suburbs," said Neil Harris, director of international marketing at Johnson Products Co., a black-owned health and beauty aids firm. "They may not even be interested in the same products."

Diversity can be even more pronounced among other ethnic groups. The U.S. Census Bureau tracks 16 different nationalities under the umbrella heading of "Asian" in its surveys. The Hispanic market in this country consists of people from at least 25 countries.

Another key for marketers is to avoid advertising campaigns that condescend or patronize, said SMSI's Jones.

G. Heileman Brewing Co. offended the black community with a controversial marketing campaign for its PowerMaster malt liquor, a potent brew that relied on stereotypical imagery to target inner-city black youths. Special interest group backlash forced Heileman to pull the brand. Heileman later quietly introduced a product to the market identical to PowerMaster under the Colt 45 Premium Malt Liquor name, which the brewer calls a line extension.

"Marketers must recognize the differences among ethnic groups, and they must create marketing programs that appeal to the individual wants and needs of

Marketers who would hitch their wagons to the ethnic juggernaut must be wary. Ethnic markets are not homogeneous. The Census Bureau tracks 16 nationalities under the heading of "Asian."

those disparate groups," said Jones. "But all the while they must maintain respect and understanding for those differences. That, in a nutshell, is what effective ethnic marketing is all about." ∎

Michael J. McDermott is a freelance writer based in Carmel, N.Y. who frequently writes about marketing issues.

High-Tech Marketers Try to Attract Women Without Causing Offense

BY KYLE POPE
Staff Reporter of THE WALL STREET JOURNAL

In an effort to broaden the appeal of personal computers, **Tandy** Corp. in 1990 introduced what was then a radical plan: marketing its machines to women.

Its new computers, advertised as the simplest ever, came with software for making Christmas lists, recipe programs and a feature that could be used to take inventory of silverware and china. But many women were offended by the ditzy homemaker stereotype, and the campaign fizzled.

Technology companies haven't given up hope of attracting more women customers; if anything, the desire is even stronger today. With the home PC market booming and women controlling more household budgets, high-tech companies realize they have to look beyond their hard-core, male base. "Women have obviously popped up on the radar screen," says Mal Ransom, vice president of **Packard-Bell Electronics** Inc., a Westlake Village, Calif., PC maker.

The catch, as Packard-Bell and others have found, is developing campaigns that don't alienate more customers than they attract.

Though most of the efforts are still in the planning stages, even the prospect of a computer campaign tailored for women makes some women angry. "My natural cynicism is: Why are they trying to con me?" says Catrina McAuliffe, a senior vice president at an advertising agency in San Francisco. "Why should I buy anything that men won't?"

For many years, computer marketing has reflected the fact that men are the predominant users of personal computers. Experts guess that 85% of the most experienced PC users are male, and Micrografx Inc., a Richardson, Texas, software company, estimates that men buy 70% of the computer software purchased.

But that's slowly changing because more professional women are using computers, and single-parent households led by women are increasing. Link Resources Corp., a New York consulting concern, found in a recent survey that 26% of the households with computers count women as their primary users. That comes out to about 8.3 million households, up sharply from the 4.4 million reported in 1989.

Moreover, the next generation of women is even more computer literate. Many women now in their 40s weren't raised with computers, notes Cheryl Currid, a Houston technology consultant, but their daughters are already comfortable with the machines. When it came time for gift lists last Christmas, for instance, Ms. Currid says her 11-year-old daughter sent her wish list via e-mail.

So far, **Compaq Computer** Corp. has led the latest marketing push. The Houston PC giant has taken a direct approach with TV commercials aimed squarely at work-at-home moms. One spot shows a woman putting her child to bed, then heading to her Compaq PC for some late-night work.

Digital Equipment Corp. has been more subtle, replacing its sports-oriented print advertising with messages deemed more gender neutral.

Predictably, even the most timid early moves have attracted grumbling. Some women say they're offended that computer ads in fashion and home-and-garden magazines focus on how easy the systems are to use. Others say the focus on children's software—considered by marketers to be a surefire way to women's pocketbooks—ignores the army of female managers who long ago mastered the most complex spreadsheets and engineering software.

"I wouldn't know how to put a recipe in a computer, but I can sure balance my finances," Ms. Currid says.

Women PC users, as well as corporate marketing experts, say there are ways technology companies can target women without offending. Carol Thompson, until recently the owner of a ComputerLand franchise in Austin, Texas, notes that training classes and service programs were popular among women customers, as were female salespeople.

Tandy, the electronics retailer based in Fort Worth, Texas, plans to start an electronics-repair program and gift-delivery service to boost the image of its flagship Radio Shack chain. The hope is that women, who are still responsible for most household gift-giving, will find the service a time-saver.

At Digital, which is considering a PC line for the home market, engineers are studying such details as the weight of their machines and how difficult it will be for women to pull them out of the box.

Meanwhile, computer publishing giants like Ziff-Davis Publishing Co. and CMP Publications Inc. are targeting women in new family-oriented publications called Family PC and Home PC, set to make their debut later this year. The magazines will include reviews of educational and entertainment software, as well as articles on ways people can use their computers.

Packard-Bell has resisted pitching to women a multimedia software package called Navigator that uses rooms of a house as icons to help guide users through the machine. Says Mr. Ransom: "A 486SX 25 will do the same for you whether you're a man, woman or child."

That said, Mr. Ransom notes that Packard-Bell will begin advertising its wares in Working Woman magazine later this year. He says the company's pitch will be essentially the same as in its other advertising, which focuses on the user-friendliness of the company's machines and Packard-Bell's wide distribution network.

Michael W. Baldwin, who runs the Compaq account for ad agency Ammirati & Puris in New York, argues that the issue for marketers is experience rather than gender. The industry's challenge, he says, is to attract the uninitiated. That focus will force computer companies to broaden their appeal, which will, by default, engage women who aren't as familiar with the machines.

"It's like an outsider comes into a meeting that is very inbred and asks a simple question and everybody stops in their tracks," says Mr. Baldwin. Trying to appeal to new customers "is going to make sure that the manufacturers don't get away with using shorthand."

Perhaps the message for marketers attempting to reach women, then, is not to try so hard. "My view," says Ms. McAuliffe, the advertising executive, "is that it's best just to treat them as intelligent human beings."

CLASS
IN AMERICA

Old socioeconomic rankings have given way to the increasing segmentation of the U.S. population, and more Americans are unsure where they stand.

by Kenneth Labich

LIKE IT OR NOT, all of us are largely defined, at least in the eyes of others, according to an elaborate set of criteria—how much we earn, what we do for a living, who our parents are, where and how long we attended school, how we speak, what we wear, where we live, and how we react to the issues of the day. It all adds up to our socioeconomic class, our ranking in U.S. society. In a process as natural as sunrise, a few folks are consigned to the ranks of the chiefs, the rest of us to more middling places among the workers and drones.

Many Americans are more than a little confused about just where they stand in the great hierarchy these days. In part, they are resonating with the broad egalitarian strain that runs through the center of the nation's history and culture. To acknowledge any interest in class status or to spend much time thinking about socioeconomic ranking is to behave in some way vaguely un-American. More important, Americans are responding to changes in the U.S. economic and cultural fabric—and in the workplace—that have blurred old-time class distinctions and, in many cases, redefined bedrock status issues.

The outline of America's class structure may have seemed simpler just a decade or so ago, when Rutgers University professor Paul Fussell published a widely read primer on the subject. Fussell identified nine distinct socioeconomic classes, ranging from an elite class, virtually invisible behind the tall walls of their mansions, to a wretched underclass, equally invisible in their hovels. In between, in Fussell's universe, were an effete upper class he found "impervious to ideas," an upper-middle class that had earned its status and looked with some disdain on those living off inherited money, a vast and essentially insecure middle class ever concerned about social indiscretions, and several levels of blue-collar "proles" whose tastes were unrefined and predict-

able. Wrote Fussell: "There isn't anyone in any of these theaters who isn't scared to death that he's going to stumble, waffle his lines, or otherwise bomb."

That same level of anxiety may still be present, but many of the rules that once defined Americans' class status have been thrown into marked confusion in recent years. One of the most dramatic changes has been the apparent fragmentation of U.S. society into scores of distinct subcultures, each with unique tastes and yearnings of the sort that once distinguished broad social classes.

Even a few years ago demographers could mark out a large chunk of the populace—say, married couples 30 to 54 years of age making over $40,000—and safely predict many of the group's responses to questions ranging from presidential choice to preferred brand of mustard. Now marketers and others interested in reaching a specific group must focus much further down. Claritas Inc., a market research firm in Alexandria, Virginia, has identified 62 distinct classes, each with its own set of beliefs and aspirations.

At the top are three classes of the so-called Suburban Elite, super-rich families with substantial assets and a taste for expensive cars and other lush consumer goodies. At the bottom are poor isolated country families, a group Claritas labels Hard Scrabble, and single-parent families in the inner city. The company terms this group Public Assistance.

In between are dozens of classes of varying affluence and differing behavior—the upwardly mobile Young Influentials, ex-urban executive families labeled God's Country, retirement-town senior citizens known as Golden Ponders, African American service-worker families called Downtown Dixie–Style. You may be a Young Suburbanite who drives a hatchback, listens to all-news radio, and carries department-

store credit cards. You make the same kind of money as a person of the Blue-Chip Blue class, but you probably drink imported rather than domestic beer and are far less likely to be interested in powerboat racing. Says Michael Mancini, product marketing manager at Claritas: "What we are really doing is taking a lot of demographic information and making it more real, bringing it to life."

This trend toward fragmentation into smaller social classes or subgroups is, if anything, accelerating. Watts Wacker, resident futurist at the consulting firm Yankelovich Partners, points to the intricate personal networks forming daily through on-line computer services. Says Wacker: "People who believed they were the only one in the world who thought a certain way are finding like-minded allies all the time. They are forming fraternities of strangers."

Recent economic trends have added to the disintegration of old class lines. According to a 1991 study by the National Opinion Research Center, nearly one-half of all Americans consider themselves to be middle class. But many thousands of the jobs that provided for a comfortable middle-class lifestyle have simply vanished. Between 1980 and 1986, according to the Bureau of Labor Statistics, some 780,000 foremen, supervisors, and section chiefs lost their jobs due to layoffs and plant closings. In the years since, many thousands of division heads, assistant directors, assistant managers, and vice presidents have suffered the same fate.

Even if these folks were able to find new jobs, they often had to take severe pay cuts. Nearly five million of the 13.6 million new full-time jobs added between 1979 and 1989 paid less than $13,000 a year after adjusting for inflation. In 1979, the Census Bureau calculated that 18.9% of full-time workers had low-wage jobs; by 1992, that figure had jumped to 25.7%.

REPORTER ASSOCIATE *Ann Sample*

THE NUMBER of younger families able to own their own homes, the classic badge of middle-class status, sums up the tale: Though low interest rates have pumped up the market of late, the long-term trend in incomes has made it more difficult for newcomers to get into that market. Over 60% of people ages 30 to 34 owned their own homes in 1973; that percentage had dwindled to 51.5% by 1990.

What has evolved, in the estimation of Boston University sociologist Alan Wolfe, is two distinct sets of subgroups within the vast middle class, each defined by different opportunities, expectations, and outlooks. The first, more established middle class moved up during the 1950s and 1960s—or moved out to the suburbs—when the continuation of growth was assumed and opportunity abundant. Many people in these strata have survived the recent economic dislocations and remain reasonably confident that they will muddle through somehow. Many are also politically and culturally liberal, and fairly casual about religion.

Not so more recent arrivals to the middle class, many of them African American, Asian American, and white ethnics in the ranks of civil servants or blue-collar workers whose jobs have been threatened. These folks are often rigidly conservative, standing fast by traditional middle-class pieties. They are also reeling from the economic dislocations taking place. Wolfe says that millions of these relative newcomers to the middle class are now clinging fiercely to their hard-won gains. "A kind of desperation has started up," says Wolfe. "People are out there fighting like mad to hold on to whatever status they have achieved." One result of these new divisions: heightened antipathy between groups.

While class structure in the U.S. has been fragmenting, barriers between the scores of new subclasses have been hardening. Vast changes in the workplace have been partly responsible. Labor Secretary Robert Reich has pointed out that one group of workers, making up about 20% of the U.S. labor force, has been able to keep up with new technology and remain globally competitive. This group, which Reich calls "symbolic analysts," includes such professionals as engineers, investment bankers, accountants, lawyers, systems analysts, and consultants of all types.

But the other 80% has not fared nearly as well in Reich's view. These folks--assembly-line workers, data processors, most retail salespeople, cashiers, and a whole range of blue-collar service workers--are falling further behind the curve, both economically and in their grasp of changing realities. And more and

more, these two groups share less and less. Says Reich: "No longer are Americans rising and falling together, as if in one large national boat. We are, increasingly, in different, smaller boats."

This increasing separation between groups is most glaringly evident when it comes to housing. Birds of a feather are flocking ever closer together, finding residences in close proximity to others of their economic and cultural ilk. Market researchers can now pinpoint the class status and buying patterns of just about everyone in the U.S. on a neighborhood-by-neighborhood basis. Says Josh Ostroff, a principal at a Massachusetts research firm called Virtual Media Resources: "Once I know where you live, I don't need to know a whole lot more about you."

Claritas Inc. has broken down the entire U.S. into geodemographic clusters, some as small as 300 households. If you are at the highest level of the Suburban Elite class, you live in Blueblood Estates territory like Scarsdale, outside New York; Winnetka, outside Chicago; or Atherton, south of San Francisco. You probably own a new convertible, read one or more of the business magazines, and maintain a full-service brokerage account. If you are an Urban Gold Coaster, you are likely to live on the Upper East Side in Manhattan, along Lake Michigan in Chicago, or in the Pacific Heights section of San Francisco. Your tastes probably run toward sailing and informational TV, and you most likely have at least $10,000 invested in the stock market.

As one might expect, rapidly expanding direct-mail companies are among the most

aggressive clients for this sort of research. Such enterprises sent out 13.5 billion catalogues last year, accounting for more than $50 billion in sales, and much of their success is due to knowing which addresses are populated by Lands' End types and which by L.L. Beanies. If you drive a new Volvo you will probably be on the list for catalogues full of preppy clothing from J. Crew or the Smith & Hawken gardening catalogue, with its $50 trowels. If you subscribe to *Guns & Ammo* and drive a Dodge, you are more likely to be on the list for Sears or Publishers' Clearing House.

Advertising agencies make liberal use of such status information as well, as they tailor the hundreds of messages we are bombarded with each day to increasingly specific audiences. The appeal to our class aspirations can be subtle or blatant, as in those Ralph Lauren ads in which all the models appear to be fourth-generation Princetonians. But the key to nearly all such advertising is to touch off a personal response, to signal the consumer that this product or service is appropriate for his or her taste and social status. Says Malcolm MacDougall, chief creative officer at Ally & Gargano in Manhattan: "The trick is getting people to think 'This beer is me' or 'This magazine is me.'"

With the U.S. class structure now so fragmented, advertisers are forced to hone in ever more closely on specific targets. "You've got to use a rifle instead of a shotgun," says MacDougall. Advertisers must also take into account the fact that tastes of

CLASS DISTINCTIONS: You are what you choose		LOWER MIDDLE	MIDDLE	UPPER MIDDLE
Car	1980s	Hyundai	Chevrolet Celebrity	Mercedes
	1990s	Geo	Chrysler minivan	Range Rover
Business shoe (men)	1980s	Sneakers	Wingtips	Cap toes
	1990s	Boots	Rockports	Loafers
Business shoe (women)	1980s	Spike-heel pumps	Mid-heel pump	High-heel pumps
	1990s	High-heel pumps	Dressy flats	One-inch pumps
Alcoholic beverage	1980s	Domestic beer	White wine spritzer	Dom Perignon
	1990s	Domestic lite beer	California Chardonnay	Cristal
Leisure pursuit	1980s	Watching sports	Going to movies	Golf
	1990s	Playing sports	Renting movies	Playing with computers
Hero	1980s	Roseanne Barr	Ronald Reagan	Michael Milken
	1990s	Kathie Lee Gifford	Janet Reno	Rush Limbaugh

FORTUNE CHART

(cont.)

classes and subgroups are shifting more rapidly now than decades ago. At MacDougall's agency, for example, copywriters working on the Saks Fifth Avenue account have begun emphasizing that gold jewelry is a solid investment. In the 1980s, when opulence was more in favor, they would have appealed more overtly to gold as a pure status symbol.

The complexities of such status symbols have helped muddy the waters for many Americans trying to find their place in the new hierarchy. At the same time, most of us would like to avoid being seen as striving too hard to appropriate the right symbols. We make cartoons of those hapless middle-class strivers, grasping at the next rung, who name their children Chauncey or Dierdre, keep temperamental pets with long pedigrees, and take up ruinously expensive sports like sailing.

AND JUST WATCH OUT for the next shift in tastes: If the Eighties were about greed and ostentation for the uppers, the Nineties are about value and self-fulfillment. The experts observe that affluent tastes now run more toward the utilitarian: A Range Rover or Ford Explorer, rather than a Mercedes, is the vehicle of choice, and a bank credit card with frequent-flier miles attached seems to make more sense than American Express Platinum with a high annual fee. Dressing down seems more practical as well—loafers instead of lace-ups for men, one-inch pumps rather than high heels for women. Those $115 Hermès ties may come off as a little foppish these days, and top executives even at GM have taken to wearing open collars to work on Friday.

Clothing, of course, has always been a peculiarly resonant class symbol, and wearing what is appropriate for one's status at work and play remains a major concern for many Americans. Writes Alison Lurie, in her book *The Language of Clothes*: "The man who goes to buy a winter coat may simultaneously want it to shelter him from bad weather, look expensive and formidable, announce that he is sophisticated and rugged, attract a certain sort of sexual partner, and magically invest him with the qualities of Robert Redford."

On the job, your wardrobe goes to the heart of class status. Many a regiment in the vast army of blue-collar workers, everyone from postal employees to the kids behind the counter at McDonald's, are issued uniforms that let the world know they are in a subservient service role. Most of the rest of us have more latitude about our business wardrobe but are limited by our sense of status and appropriateness. Should you try to dress as well as your boss or try to fit in with the crowd? Fussell is particularly amused by men who spend enormous sums on their clothes but cannot master the casual elegance of the upper classes. Says he: "The principle of not-too-neat is crucial in men's clothing."

THE CONFUSION many Americans feel trying to gauge their position in the hierarchy of classes is compounded by dramatic changes transforming the workplace, the arena where most of us still earn our status points. Take the upwardly mobile manager. Not very long ago the path to class glory was clear. You landed in a management-training program at some large company, kept your nose clean and your eyes open, acquired a mentor or two. If you were smart and lucky, you eventually found yourself battling it out with a few others for one of the top positions. If not, you hung around loyally as a general manager or vice president until the right moment and then were assured all the money you would ever need for a comfortable retirement. There was absolutely no confusion about your class status; you were an Executive, with all the perks and status appurtenant thereto.

Just about no piece of that old template remains intact these days. The best way to enter the managerial cadre may still be to join a so-called academy company, a McKinsey, General Electric, Citicorp, or PepsiCo, where you can learn the key levers, the core strengths and weaknesses, of any business. But according to top executive recruiters, many big, prestigious companies—and smaller employers for that matter—are hiring fewer liberal-arts grads and MBAs who require a lot of training. Instead, they favor engineers and techies who can actually add value the first day on the job.

This trend toward the specialist is evident further down the ladder, as well. The Bureau of Labor Statistics estimates that technical jobs—encompassing everything from software programming to air-conditioning repair—will increase 37% by 2005, vs. 20% for all other jobs. Much of the growth in the ranks of technicians will come at the expense of old-style manufacturing operatives.

Some observers of the corporate scene say that once on the job, would-be managerial types find that sharp elbows have become a good deal more valuable than politeness. With fewer management jobs available and far more bottom-line pressure everywhere, the high-status prizes now go only to those willing to be hyperaggressive about doing what's necessary to achieve results. Says Robert Salwen, a principal at the management consultant firm William M. Mercer: "There's a lot less sentimentality in the workplace today. It's all about who can deliver the goods quickest—you eat what you kill."

Confusingly, other experts argue that such drive isn't enough; that, indeed, it may be an impediment to progress through the managerial ranks. Because so much of business has been decentralized, this argument goes, companies now depend on a small corporate staff of flexible, smart, analytically trained people. These folks must be comfortable with leading-edge technologies, should think globally, and ideally should be adept at dealmaking with strategic partners. They also have to be squeaky clean. "Increasingly, top executives must embody the company's ethics," says Dayton Ogden, chief executive of the executive-search firm SpencerStuart. And they have to display a key new talent: handling an increasingly diverse work force. With people ever more vigilantly maintaining their separateness, their ethnic and cultural identity, on the job, the new manager must find ways to integrate their efforts.

IS IT POSSIBLE to get beyond fretting over one's status? Paul Fussell, in his treatise on class in America, winds up with a chapter about what he calls an X Class—folks who have expanded beyond the boundaries of class consciousness and live their lives caring not a fig what others think. These X Classers behave in what most would consider an unconventional manner, and all of us probably know someone who tries to break the mold at least some of the time. Futurist Wacker of Yankelovitch Partners, who lives and works in the affluent suburb of Westport, Connecticut, wears shorts to church on Sunday and resolutely refuses to use a computer.

The trouble is, if enough people start behaving like that, some marketing whiz will no doubt classify them: the Iconoclasts, or some such. In truth, there is scant escape from the class consciousness that surrounds us, and most of us will probably continue to respond to a range of status pressures and signals, even as these pressures and signals become harder to parse. **F**

Reprinted from the February 7, 1994 issue of *Fortune*, Copyright,© 1994 Time Inc. All rights reserved.

HBA Companies are Making Hay with a Little Horse Sense

Yes, it's horse-care products for two-legged creatures. By Pam Weisz

Can Mane 'N Tail compete on a drugstore shampoo shelf with Head & Shoulders? Straight Arrow, a Lehigh Valley, Pa.-based maker of animal-care products, including Mane 'N Tail, a shampoo for horses, thinks so.

The company is among a small, but growing group of animal-care product companies, which, after learning their products were being used by horse owners, discovered they could also target the two-legged market.

After building up a following among the equine set, companies like Straight Arrow and Minneapolis-based Palm Beach Beauty have repackaged their horse shampoos and placed them in salons and drugstores to compete with hair-care giants like Procter & Gamble and Nexxus.

The appeal of the products is simple, said Gene Carter, executive vice president of marketing and sales for Straight Arrow, which had sales of $30 million last year.

"Here's a $100,000 animal that looks beautiful. People want the same thing for their hair," he said.

A multimillion dollar print and TV campaign breaks in mid-summer to support the company's two new brands, Equenne, sold in salons, and Conceived by Nature, which is in mass-market. Both products have the same ingredients as the company's original horse shampoo, Mane 'N Tail, which is still sold in feed stores and tack shops.

Straight Arrow began to explore the idea of marketing to humans three years ago, after research done by Carter and company president Roger Dunavant revealed that as many as 10 bottles of Mane 'N Tail out of a case of 12 were being used on people.

The company went about making some changes, and it stated on the label that the product was safe for humans and it emphasized a protein-rich formula.

The hard work has its rewards. As word spread, the company saw sales grow from $500,000 five years ago to $30 million last year. Carter expects sales to jump to $60 million this year, as a result of advertising and promotions, which will include product displays at horse shows and giveaways of Mustang convertibles.

The ad campaign plays up the horse connection.

"The concept of the ad is the horse is glad the humans finally got their own product," Carter said.

The Equenne and Conceived by Nature lines, which include styling aids in addition to the original shampoo, had a precedent in another Straight Arrow product, a muscle relaxing liniment called Mineral Ice. Bristol-Myers Squibb has been selling Mineral Ice to humans since 1990, with sales last year of $17.6 million.

Straight Arrow's healthy increase in sales led marketers at Palm Beach Beauty to launch their Lucky Kentucky line of upscale hair care products this year.

Like Straight Arrow, Palm Beach Beauty continues to sell products for horses. But if sales continue to grow, both companies could find themselves contemplating the decision made by New York-based Barrielle, maker of Barielle Nail Strengthener Cream. The product was originally called Hoof Care and was developed to prevent splitting and cracking in hooves. Seventeen years ago the product moved into department stores, and soon after the horse version was taken off the market. The product is now in about 2,000 retail locations--none of which cater to the equestrian set.

Barrielle still uses a horse in its print ads. One advertisement features a photo of a woman and a horse, and a product shot, with the words, "Why neither of these ladies has splits, chips or cracks in her nails."

Carter swears Straight Arrow will not abandon its four-legged customers.

"We remind people to use it on their animals, too," he said.

War Stories From the Sandbox: What Kids Say

'Everyone in school has one, Mom!' By Dr. Selina S. Guber and Jon Berry

"You've *gahht* to see this jacket I saw," implores Christie. "It's soooo nice! I want it soooo bad! Can I get it? Ah, come on, Mom! I'll pay for it, I swear! If you buy it for me, I'll pay you back!"

Around her, in the focus-group facility, a group of 12- to 14-year old girls are convulsed in laughter at the scene they've seen so many times themselves. "My mom," said Linda, 12, "like, she'll say no a few times. Then she'll say maybe, probably to have me stop bugging her. Then I'll bug her again anyway."

"And if she still says no?" the moderator asks.

"Then I say *everyone* in school has one. 'It's really nice, Mom. You don't understand.'"

"And if she still says no?"

"Then I go ask my dad," Linda shrugs. "I'll tell him I *swear* I'll pay it back."

"And does he give in?"

"Yeah, usually. Moms are tough. They don't care. Dads are easy. They say, 'You're still my little girl.'"

"So you get the money?"

"Yeah, usually," chimes in Karen, 13, a veteran of the shopping wars of attrition. "Most of the time."

"And do you pay it back?"

"Sometimes," said Linda. "They eventually forget."

"They want you to stop bugging them," said Christie. "It's like, 'Stop bothering me. Take the money and *go!*'"

"How do you girls get so good at this?"

"Practice!"

*   *   *

Parents may cut back on eating out. They may put off buying a new refrigerator for another year, or start putting private-label canned corn in the grocery cart. But no one brags about cutting back on their kids. Parents always want to do well by their kids. Having

been raised in the affluence of the '60s and '70s, in perhaps the apex of American consumer culture, parents are particularly sensitive to providing for their children's needs today. That's normally thought of as the impetus behind the meteoric growth of Nintendo and Sega, and periodic frenzies over short-supply toys like Cabbage Patch Dolls. It's also been responsible for the growth of parent-approved, educational toys like Lego building blocks and *Carmen Sandiego* computer games, and the tripling of sales of children's books.

And, as the echo baby boom that began in the 1980s toddles into the school-age years, it's generating interest in college funds. It won't be that long, after all, until the bulge that's swelling elementary schools now will go off to college. The college-age population is at its absolute dearth now. The years 1973-76 were the low point of births, averaging 3.15 million per year. From there, it was all up; 4.18 million kids were born in 1990. And, while the aging of the Baby Boom will affect births--the leading edge of the boomers will be 54 in the year 2000--the Census Bureau expects births to stay above 3.9 million through the end of the decade.

> *The U.S.' population of kids has been growing since the '70s, and will remain at high levels through the '90s.*

Marketers' storehouses of information about kids have grown as kids' marketers have taken an increasingly disciplined approach to the market. But some of the best teachers have been experience. Herewith, then, some "war stories from the sandbox."

*   *   *

It's true that kids know more about drugs, crime, pollution and other social problems than past generations. But family values run deep. Asked what is the most important thing in their lives, the overwhelming majority of kids say "family." Money and careers are also-rans.

In focus groups with Children's Market Research, kids have shown an unflagging interest even in family sitcoms. *Cosby*, *Growing Pains*, *Charles in Charge* and other such shows have found new audiences in reruns, in new generations of kids who were too young to see the shows the first time around.

Many parents, glad to spend time with their kids, let the younger generation set the viewing agenda. One dad of a 4-year-old, 6-year-old and 13-year-old said he never watches *60 Minutes*, his favorite show, because he'd rather watch what the kids are watching.

Kids, in turn, are pitching in more, to take some of the burden off their two-career parents. "I set the table," said a 7-year-old girl. "After dinner, my brother and I wash the dishes." "All my children do chores," one mother told Children's Market Research during a series of focus groups in Denver, St. Louis and Metro Park, N.J. "I wouldn't be able to work if they didn't."

* * *

The best experts on kids are kids themselves. But talking to them, in a research setting, isn't easy. It's easy for a child to feel intimidated in a focus group or interview room. Kids should be grouped with kids of similar ages. There may not be much difference between a 35-year-old man and a 40-year-old man. But kids go through enormous developmental changes in a five-year span.

Most focus groups rooms have a big conference table. But, for kids, that can be an encumbrance. Pushing the table to the side and putting the chairs in a circle makes the setting friendlier, and opens up space for role-playing, games and other activities. Younger children, like 5 year olds, might like to play duck-duck goose to loosen up. It's important to be clear about the purpose of the session: "This is how we get our information to make products," the moderator might say. "There are no right or wrong answers. We want to know what you think."

Picture-drawing and secret ballots can draw out some kids who feel awkward about articulating their feelings. Children have drawn rainbows around products,

or shown happy families sitting around a table eating a product—sure signs of endorsement. On the other hand, Children's Market Research once saw a child draw a picture of a product being dumped into a trash can.

* * * *

You also can learn about interactions between parent and child by observing it in

action. A researcher, for example, set up in a breakfast cereal aisle to watch purchase decisions, then interview the parents and kids. When the cart wheeled by, some kids would break away from their parents and make a beeline for their favorite brand. Most parents gave in right away. Only one stood her ground, and made the child return the sugar-coated

TUBE CULTURE
Top TV viewing times of children 6 to 14
(by percent)

	Total	Boys	Girls
After school (Mon.-Fri., 5 p.m.-8 p.m.)	29.2	29.6	28.8
Kids primetime (Mon.-Sat., 8 p.m.-10 p.m. and Sun., 7 p.m.-10 p.m.)	28.0	28.7	27.2
Sat. morning (8 a.m.-1 p.m.)	24.1	25.7	22.5
After school (Mon.-Fri., 3 p.m.-5 p.m.)	21.1	20.5	21.6
Sat. evening (5 p.m-8 p.m.)	14.9	17.5	12.1
Sun. evening (5 p.m.-7 p.m.)	12.1	14.7	9.4
Sat. daytime (1 p.m.-5 p.m.)	10.1	12.2	7.9
Sun. daytime (1 p.m.-5 p.m.)	9.6	12.3	6.8
Sun. morning (8 a.m.-1 p.m.)	9.3	10.1	8.5
Early morning (Mon.-Fri., 6 a.m.-9 a.m.)	9.1	10.7	8.6

Source: CMR Kidtrends Report, based on data from The Simmons Kids Study (1991)

IT'S THE FOOD
Reasons why child's favorite restaurant is his/her favorite
(kids 6-14, by percent)

	Total	Boys	Girls
Best foods	55.0	54.4	55.6
Best toys/prizes	23.7	23.8	23.6
Best meal packs	19.7	19.8	19.7
Have the most fun	16.0	14.3	17.9
Best playgrounds	14.8	14.6	15.0
Child's friends go	12.2	11.6	12.8
Best birthday parties	6.2	6.3	6.0
Other reason	15.9	17.2	14.5

Source: CMR Kidtrends Report, based on data from The Simmons Kids Study (1991)

GAME GEAR
Percent use, ownership of various electronic equipment by boys, girls
(by percent)

	Total	Boys	Girls
Camera	49.4	46.3	52.7
Clock radio	46.6	46.4	46.7
Pocket or hand-held calculator	45.6	47.3	43.8
Portable stereo radio (boom box)	43.8	42.5	45.1
Portable/walk-about stereo with headphones (Walkman)	41.2	41.6	40.7
Compact or console stereo (all-in-one)	22.9	21.2	24.6
Stereo receiver/tuner/amplifier (all-in-one)	19.2	21.1	17.2
Separate stereo components	15.8	16.3	15.3
Camcorder	12.5	11.6	13.4
Compact disc player	12.3	11.8	12.8
None of these	5.9	5.7	6.1

Source: CMR Kidtrends Report, based on data from The Simmons Kids Study (1991)

(cont.)

cereal for a raisin bran. Several, though, went into bargaining sessions: The kid could have the sweet cereal "if you'll get this healthier one and eat it some mornings too." Or, "OK, but we're going to buy raisins for you to eat in your lunch this week instead of cookies."

* * *

It's important to make it easy for a child to talk in research. Some researchers use computer software to engage kids in interviews; others ask kids to choose from a range of happy faces to angry faces. But there are limits. A 10-year-old boy's mother once came into an interview room and seated herself behind the child. She proceeded to answer the questions for the child—the research equivalent of back-seat driving.

* * *

Having a good idea is not enough. You have to follow through with common-sense decisions. Once, a company called Children's Market Research to research a children's cologne the company planned to produce. The research turned up three findings. Kids were receptive to the idea. But the kids—the boys in particular—were uncomfortable with the strategy to make unisex colognes. Yet the biggest problem was price. At almost $10 a bottle, the product was beyond the reach of weekly allowances. Grandparents might pick up a bottle; parents would have preferred $5. The product didn't last.

* * *

Some products straddle markets, to try to meet both children's desires and parents' concerns. As healthy eating has become more of an issue for grown-ups, opportunities have grown for products that straddle adults' wishes with kids' tastes.

Dannon's Sprinkl'ins is one example. Dannon was convinced yogurt was not at its market potential in the U.S. The company went out and talked to kids. It found kids thought yogurt wasn't nearly as much fun as "green slime pudding and other snacks kids have to choose from," as Dannon vice president-marketing Bob Wallach put it. Moreover, Dannon found kids have surprising autonomy over what they eat: one in three make their own breakfast, and one in five make their own lunch.

THE BIG STORES
Stores visited by child in the last four weeks, in order (by percent)

	Total	Boys	Girls
K mart	47.8	46.4	49.2
J.C. Penney	31.3	26.3	36.6
Wal-Mart	28.4	28.2	28.6
Sears	26.2	25.3	27.2
Toys R Us	22.4	23.0	21.8
Target Stores	14.9	13.4	16.5
Payless	14.5	12.3	16.7
Kay Bee Toys	14.2	15.1	13.3
Woolworth/Woolco	11.4	11.9	10.9
Montgomery Ward	11.3	11.5	11.1
Mervyn's	9.3	7.3	11.4
Ames	8.6	9.7	7.4
Kids R Us	8.6	8.2	9.1

Source: CMR Kidtrends Report, based on data from The Simmons Kids Study (1991)

Dannon tested 48 concepts, then whittled the list to four. The most intriguing was a yogurt cup that would come with a packet of multicolored sweet sprinkles that would be sprinkled into the yogurt, and mixed by the child. Dannon went back and tested names: Sprinkl'ins won. Early results have been encouraging.

* * *

Old toys never die; they just wait for kids to grow up, become parents, and buy them for their kids. Or so it seems. Hasbro has reissued "classic" models of its G.I. Joe. Creepie Crawlers and Erector sets have been restaged. Children's board games have seen a resurgence. Some observers have noted that Hula-Hoop sales go up every few years, as a new crop of parents comes along. Hula-Hoops were perhaps the quintessential '50s toy phenomenon—some 25 million were sold the first year on the market. Parents had so much fun swiveling their hips to keep the hoop in the air, they apparently figured their kids would, too. Call it "the Hula Hoop factor."

* * *

How do kids get what they want? "I just keep talking about it and say that all my friends have it until my parents buy it," one girl said in a focus group.

"I tell them, 'I'll never ask for anything again," another girl said.

"I just keep asking them for it," a third girl said.

Marketers can't tell kids to nag. It's not allowed. But—once a product gets the inside track in the peer group—word-of-mouth probably does more than market-

ing could. Research has shown kids weigh in on a broad range of family purchases. "My brother and I wanted to go to Florida," an 11-year-old girl said. "We asked my dad. We just kept on asking. My mom wanted to go, too. We went."

* * *

What trends will drive the children's market in the years to come? The environment is very important to kids: Thanks to

"OK, we'll get the sweet cereal. But we're going to buy raisins for you to eat in your lunch this week instead of cookies."

programs in schools, they often are more educated about environmental issues than their parents. "We have a big blue bin in our garage," said Judy, an 11-year-old from Allentown, Pa., who takes the lead on her family's recycling. "My mom tries to help. But I guess it's hard to teach an old dog new tricks."

Health and fitness, and eating well—concerns in the adult world as well—seem likely to trickle down to children

(cont.)

also. Athletes are to kids today what rock stars were in the 1960s and what cowboys were in an earlier age. Michael Jordan, Shaquille O'Neal and Bo Jackson have become role models for playing on team sports, staying in shape and watching what you eat.

Education is increasingly on families' minds as well. With schools under financial pressures, many parents are stepping in to backstop the system by enriching their kids' activities at home with educational software, books, and educational toys and games. ∎

From Marketing To And Through Kids, McGraw-Hill. Guber is president of Children's Market Research, N.Y. Berry is a BRANDWEEK editor.

Reprinted from the July 5, 1993 issue of *Brandweek,* © 1993 ASM Communications, Inc. Used with permission from *Brandweek.*

36

Booked Up

Big Accounting Firms, Striving to Cut Costs, Irritate Small Clients

Many Companies Say Service Has Slipped Badly, Hurt In Part by Staff Turnover

'I Got Tired of Being Ignored'

By LEE BERTON
Staff Reporter of THE WALL STREET JOURNAL

Mark Feinstein says he hired Arthur Young & Co. six years ago because he heard that the big accounting firm gave small businesses "dynamite service."

But soon thereafter, he contends, the service fizzled. Arthur Young merged with Ernst & Whinney to form Ernst & Young, and, to cut costs, the huge new firm began slashing staff.

"In the first two years, I'd get a call back the same day when I had questions," Mr. Feinstein says. "After the merger, it took up to a week to get a response. Ernst & Young kept switching staff, who dragged their heels."

Six months ago, Mr. Feinstein's Lincoln, R.I., video-rental company, Northeast Management Inc., switched from Ernst & Young, the nation's second-biggest accounting firm, to Kahn, Litwin & Co., a Providence, R.I., firm with one office and a staff of only 17. "I got tired of being ignored," Mr. Feinstein says.

Many Similar Complaints

An Ernst & Young partner declines to comment specifically on Mr. Feinstein's complaints. A spokesman for Ernst & Young says it continues to give good service to small companies. But similar complaints across the country go far toward explaining why many big companies in field after field are losing clients to smaller competitors.

Personal attention can be crucial in the service sector, which has grown to 54% of gross domestic product from 47% a decade ago. When staff cutbacks take hold and tougher competition puts pressure on prices and fees, big companies tend to focus their resources on big clients. As a result, small clients feel like second-class citizens while still paying high prices.

Some big companies, such as International Business Machines Corp. and Xerox Corp., find serving many small customers too uneconomic. Five years ago, IBM sold all its midrange computers directly to small business, but today independent distributors sell about half of these machines in the U.S. Xerox also says it increasingly sells to small businesses through distributors and retailers.

"It's impossible to serve every single customer as we did in previous years," says Peter Thonis, an IBM spokesman. With IBM's work force down to 255,000 from 406,000 in 1986, "we're now more willing" to sell through intermediaries, he adds. He concedes that some small customers are "probably upset."

Shifting Business

In big-time accounting, where mergers and slow revenue growth have intensified cost-cutting, many small clients are so irritated they are leaving, shifting to regional and local firms. In the past two years, the Big Six accounting firms lost 239 public audit clients to local firms, while gaining only 159 such clients, according to a study by Strafford Publications Inc., which publishes the Public Accounting Report newsletter. In the early 1980s, when the accounting business was booming, the Big Six won many more clients away from local firms than they lost, accountants say.

"Today, the pressure on Big Six partners to bring in big bucks is enormous," says Mark Carr, editor of the newsletter. "Partners can't be as responsive to small business, which pays small fees, as they once were." Annual audit fees typically range from $5,000 to $50,000 for small companies, but from $1 million to $10 million—even more—for big ones.

"We have to continue to evaluate clients [to] see which ones it makes sense for us to stick with as winners," says Larry Davidson, an Ernst & Young partner. Big accounting firms also say they are weeding out small-company audits that risk costly malpractice litigation.

Slipping in the Surveys

Surveys of 400 small-business owners by Cicco & Associates, a Murraysville, Pa., consulting firm, show their disillusionment with the big firms. In last year's study, big accounting firms ranked ninth of 12 industry groups in responsiveness to small-business needs; six years ago, they ranked first. Only 33% of the owners last year considered *any* big accounting firms responsive to small-business needs, down sharply from 45% in the 1988 survey.

"Our surveys show that after mergers and staff reductions at their firms, accountants' attention was diverted to internal company politics, and small-business clients suffer because the big accounting firms dare not ignore their biggest customers paying the largest fees," says John Cicco, president of the consulting firm.

Many smaller clients feel especially shortchanged in the personnel assigned to them. Major accounting firms are shifting small clients among employees so often that the practice is known as "churn and burn," says Jay Nisberg, a Richfield, Conn., consultant to accounting firms.

Such staff changes caused the Terence Cardinal Cooke Health Care Center in New York to fire KPMG Peat Marwick, its auditor for three years, last October and hire Urbach, Kahn & Werlin, a 35-partner firm in Manhattan.

"In our first audit, we were able to keep the same staff from Peat during the entire year," says David Arditt, the center's interim chief financial officer. "But in recent years, all three audit staff members were changed every year, and Peat staff members who did the annual audit were different from those who reviewed our quarterly figures during the year."

In one instance, a junior auditor from Peat who had never worked on Medicaid forms took 10 hours to learn how to fill out an 80-page form for long-term care, Mr. Arditt says, whereas the previous staffer who had worked with the forms did the job within an hour. Taking the extra time to train auditors unfamiliar with the forms helped raise audit costs 20%, he estimates.

Marianne Treglia, chief financial officer at the center until last December, says that when Peat was first hired, "its staff would work a full day and treat us like members of the family." But last year, she says, new Peat staffers "who were very young and inexperienced" treated the center's people "like we were servants." She adds: "They'd come in late and leave early, disappear in the middle of the day and ask that medical records at the other end of the building be brought to them when they should have gone and fetched them themselves."

Patrick E. Donnellan Jr., a former Peat partner who headed the center's audit, says, "Staff backup from Peat was sufficient." He declines comment on the other complaints.

Asked whether recent staff cutbacks have hurt Peat's relationships with some clients, Jon Madonna, Peat's chairman, says that those who were let go were less productive and that those who remain work hard to give all clients top service. "We do not differentiate between small and big clients and attempt to give every company we serve top priority," he says.

Small Clients' Complaints

But some small clients think that only auditors' billing departments are giving them top priority these days. Indeed, rising fees are helping drive small clients away from Big Six firms, especially if clients feel they are getting poor service.

(cont.)

Peter Ottmar, president of Attleboro Radio Association Inc., a radio-station and real-estate company in Attleboro, Mass., dropped Deloitte & Touche's Boston office three years ago. Deloitte had increased its annual audit fee to nearly $50,000 from $38,000. The new auditor, Kahn Litwin, charges only $28,000, Mr. Ottmar says.

Another reason Attleboro Radio fired Deloitte was that it "sharply downgraded its service to us," Mr. Ottmar says. He says Deloitte's failure to give proper advice on depreciation cost investors in the company up to $50,000 in extra taxes.

"We're a Sub S corporation so that tax savings pass directly to the owners," he notes. Sub S corporations don't pay taxes and pass profits directly to owners, who are taxed like partners. "But because of poor advice from Deloitte, we weren't taking enough depreciation, which reduces our taxes, on our electrical equipment cable," he asserts. "We called them four times on this issue, and they ignored us like we were invisible. Their lack of knowledge cost us tax money."

D. Gibson Hammond Jr., the Deloitte partner who headed the audit, declines comment on Mr. Ottmar's criticisms.

In some cases, fees are prompting clients to abandon relationships with big firms that stretch back decades. After 30 years with Ernst & Young, which has 1,800 partners, Southern Michigan Bancorp Inc., of Coldwater, Mich., switched last year to Crowe Chizek & Co., which has 80 partners. The bank cut its annual audit and tax-preparation fees by 40% to $30,000, says Julie Redmond, the bank holding company's controller.

Rapid Turnover Noted

Like Attleboro Radio, the banking company says money wasn't the only issue. "A decade ago, before accounting firms began to cut staff, Ernst was very responsive, and its staff would remain on the account longer," Ms. Redmond says. "But in recent years, the Ernst & Young staff below manager would change every year. It was very frustrating to deal with lower-level staff who were replaced so often."

Ms. Redmond says such treatment "made us want to ask, 'Why are the auditors having so much turnover?' " She says that when she asked Ernst & Young about new accounting rules, it took two to three days for the firm to get the answer from its experts at the home office.

But when she asked Crowe Chizek about a new accounting rule on retirement benefits recently, the firm's top expert on the rule contacted the bank immediately, she says. "When you're closing books at the end of the month, an extra day wasted is very critical," she adds.

Robert Jansen, a partner at Ernst & Young's Kalamazoo, Mich., office, which had serviced the bank prior to its switch, says, "We valued our relationship with the bank and were disappointed that they left us." He declines further comment.

Today's complaints of neglect represent a sharp change. In the early and middle 1980s, major accounting firms eagerly sought out small clients. Arthur Young began offering start-up companies a broad array of auditing, tax and consulting services usually available only to big companies. In 1986, it began honoring a small-company "entrepreneur of the year" at a glitzy annual party.

Some major accounting firms still emphasize their efforts to serve small companies, even setting up separate departments to do so. But many in the industry say a big change in the economics of accounting makes it harder every year for major firms to offer anything like equal service to both large and small clients.

In both 1992 and 1993, the Big Six's U.S. revenue grew only 4% year-to-year, less than half the firms' growth rate in the early 1980s, says Arthur Bowman, editor of Bowman's Accounting Report, a monthly newsletter. In contrast, many small firms are posting sharp gains. "Our revenues rose 20% or more in both 1993 and 1992," says Lawrence Kahn, a partner in Kahn

Litwin, and the firm increased its audit staff to six from four.

A big factor is overhead. Small firms don't have huge national office expenses. Moreover, their partners generally earn from a third to 40% less than do Big Six partners, who average more than $250,000 annually, Mr. Bowman estimates.

The big firms are responding to slower growth and profit pressures by cutting staff. Reversing the growth of earlier years, their total audit staff dropped 17% from 1988 to 1992, the latest year for which figures are available, the Public Accounting Report says.

The firms also have cut the number of partners, the experienced people who are supposed to guide younger staffers. Peat Marwick, Ernst & Young, Deloitte & Touche and Coopers & Lybrand have reduced their partner ranks by 8% to 14%. In some cases, mergers hastened the process. Price Waterhouse has made selective personnel cuts, and the number of Arthur Andersen's certified public accountants has remained static since 1982.

Mr. Nisberg, the consultant, says big firms will stay lean, and partners will be "stretched in so many directions that they can't afford to develop rapport with clients." The partners "must be hustling for big clients with big fees all the time."

Frederick Nydegger, a former Peat Marwick partner who lost his job in a 1991 purge of partners, says: "In the good old days, you could take small-business owners to dinner and discuss their problems without worrying about chargeable hours. Now, Peat partners tell me that chargeable time with big clients is No. 1 on its hit parade." He says the change is a big reason that most of his small-business clients at Peat are no longer there.

37

HOW NOT TO BUY
300,000 PERSONAL COMPUTERS

The Air Force's procurement reforms couldn't prevent a fiasco

Computer makers were ecstatic in May, 1991, when the U.S. Air Force announced plans to buy 300,000 personal computers. Not only was Desktop IV worth up to $1 billion, but the Pentagon hoped that the deal's streamlined procurement process could serve as a model for the future.

Nearly two years and no—as in zero—computers later, PC makers and the Pentagon alike are wondering if the government can ever rationalize the Byzantine way it buys high-tech gear. The latest evidence says it will take much more than good intentions to cut through the costly, many-layered wasteland of purchasing red tape.

Consider this: On Feb. 16, the Air Force put on hold its award of Desktop IV to Zenith Data Systems Corp. and reseller Government Technology Services Inc. It was the third time in a year that sore bid-losers had successfully thrown sand in the gears. Now, the Pentagon may have to start the process over once more. "It looks like sheer idiocy," says Robert A. Dornan, senior vice-president of Federal Sources Inc., a contract consultant in McLean, Va.

ONE CHANCE. Could the debacle have been avoided? Air Force Major Charles H. Mather once had high hopes. "The way we were doing it in the past was absurd," he says. His plan for Desktop IV mandated simpler, less cluttered guidelines to produce simpler, easily evaluated bids. A shorter request for proposals would deter losers from tying up the contract with appeals pinned to obscure details. And in a break from past protocol, bidders would submit only a single, final offer—no negotiation, no revisions.

When issued, the Desktop IV proposal filled 10 pages instead of the usual 150. It specified only that PCs be able to run Microsoft Corp.'s Windows and other standard software. To make life even easier for bidders, the Air Force distributed its specs through electronic bulletin boards and gave on-line answers to computer makers' questions. In November, 1991, from a slate of 22 bidders, the Air Force awarded the deal to CompuAdd Corp. in Austin, Tex., and Sysorex Information Systems Inc. in Falls Church, Va.

The new buying system worked just fine, it turned out, but the elaborate processes surrounding it remained seriously flawed. When the government purchases anything, it is bound by thousands of rules designed to prevent corruption and favoritism. As soon as the Air Force picked the winners, losing bidders complained that procurement officers had erred by rejecting proposals on minor technical grounds. Indeed, one bid was disqualified because it failed to include the price of a single spare part, another when a section was left blank rather than marked "not applicable." The protests had the desired effect: In January, 1992, the GSA's Board of Contract Appeals canceled the award.

That April, the Air Force tried again, requesting new bids by summer. And in September, it gave the job to Zenith Data Systems, a division of France's Groupe Bull. Again, losers screamed, this time raising the politically sensitive issue of foreign ownership, among other objections. Inevitably, politicians got into the act. Representative J. J. Pickle (D-Tex.) wrote Defense Secretary Dick Cheney on behalf of his constituent, CompuAdd. Because Zenith was French-owned, he said, "we have grave concerns about the security of data stored on these computers." The GSA appeals panel held 10 days of hearings, waded through 4,000 pages of documents and, in late December, told the Air Force to give it one more shot.

BACK IN LIMBO. Still hoping to salvage a contract from the fiasco, the Air Force reviewed the bids and split the order between Zenith Data and GTSI. But Electronic Data Systems Corp. and CompuAdd objected that Zenith Data was selling foreign-made monitors and the Air Force should have considered awarding the contract to more than two companies. Now, the contract is in limbo once more. The GSA has until April to decide whether to approve the award, kill it, or get the military to pick another bidder.

Until a resolution is reached, the military is stuck buying most computers under its 1989 Desktop III specification--a disaster in its own right. The winner then, Unisys Corp., which hoped to gain a foothold in the government PC market. It bid so low that it was losing money on each unit. But now, PC prices have plunged so steeply that every time it purchases a Unisys

May, 1991
Air Force invites bids on $1 billion contract for 300,000 personal computers. It says it will streamline the procurement process and announce a winner by fall.

November, 1991
CompuAdd and Sysorex Information Systems win competition. Rivals object, government retreats and restarts contest.

September, 1992
Zenith Data Systems, owned by France's Groupe Bull, wins this round.

December, 1992
Unhappy rivals object again. Under fire for awarding deal to foreign-based supplier, the government reconsiders again. Zenith contract is voided.

February, 1993
Air Force names Zenith winner again, but this time gives contractor Government Technology Services a piece of the action. Miffed competitors quickly cry foul. Government suspends deal again.

machine, the government pays a premium--for outdated computers based on Intel 80386 processors.

Can the ordeal get much worse? Sure, if everyone keeps bickering. "The fault is with industry for spending more time and energy in trying to prevent this award than in preparing the best possible proposal in the first place," says Thomas Buchsbaum, vice-president for federal systems at Zenith Data. Unless vendors support true reform—which must include limits on endless appeals—Desktop IV will, alas, stand as a monument to everything that can go wrong.

By Mark Lewyn in Washington

On-Line Service Offers
Fast Lane to Small Businesses

IndustryNet Links Plugged-In Manufacturers to Free Data Network

By STEPHANIE N. MEHTA
Staff Reporter of THE WALL STREET JOURNAL

Last year, Gary Vangelder needed information about some hard-to-find equipment—and he needed it fast.

The quality-assurance manager for Ritchey Metals Co. faced a tight deadline on a proposal to automate the small zinc-alloy maker in Bethel Park, Pa. He used to locate special supplies by scouring catalogs and blindly calling dozens of potential suppliers.

No longer. Instead, Mr. Vangelder posted a message on a special computer network for manufacturers. He heard from several suppliers a few days later. Without the on-line service, he says, his search "would have been very difficult."

Mr. Vangelder and countless other small manufacturers are now turning to on-line computer networks to gain instant information about products, communicate with other industry players and accelerate their supply searches. IndustryNet, the network used by Mr. Vangelder, says it has grown to about 150,000 individual users at thousands of manufacturing concerns since its inception last year, for example.

Even Out the Playing Field

An industrial on-line service can help small manufacturers to keep up with bigger competitors, says Ken Stork, a manufacturing consultant in Naperville, Ill. Many big manufacturers have direct computer connections with their distributors and can get orders filled at the push of a button. Small manufacturers are less likely to have such relationships, he adds.

IndustryNet helps to even out the playing field between big and small concerns, says Donald H. Jones, president of Franklin McKee Corp., a Pittsburgh company that operates IndustryNet as part of its Automated News Network publishing unit. Any manufacturer can log on to the free network, which offers advertisements, message boards, new-product announcements and electronic mailboxes geared to an industrial audience. "We're automating the buying and selling process," Mr. Jones says.

To be sure, on-line services do pose certain limitations. Supply searches conducted electronically still reach only those suppliers and distributors plugged into the system. Right now, manufacturers can make queries and order literature about products, but they can't buy items electronically. And Ritchey's Mr. Vangelder says replies to his messages seeking supplies sometimes trickle in months after his deadline.

Some firms have found networks to be a useful secret weapon in dealing with customers and contacts who are not plugged in, however. At Livingston Products Inc., a small diversified manufacturer in Wheeling, Ill., manufacturing manager Jon Pentz uses IndustryNet to check out suppliers' selections and prices. He says he sometimes uses that information to bargain with other suppliers and distributors that don't subscribe to the network.

International Reach

While some small manufacturers use regional bulletin boards and general interest on-line services such as CompuServe, America Online and Prodigy, IndustryNet has emerged as perhaps the most popular network for the manufacturing sector, many users say.

Medium-sized manufacturers also are tapping into IndustryNet's electronic marketplace. Wheaton Industries Inc., a Millville, N.J., container maker with more than $600 million in annual sales, recently used the network to find guardrails for one of its plants, reports Leon Horin, a Wheaton Industries project director.

Part of IndustryNet's appeal is its international reach, thanks to a link with the Internet, a world-wide computer network. But IndustryNet's most attractive feature

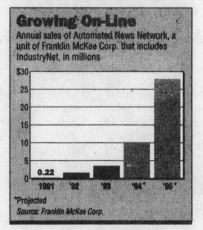

Growing On-Line
Annual sales of Automated News Network, a unit of Franklin McKee Corp. that includes IndustryNet, in millions

*Projected
Source: Franklin McKee Corp.

is that it is free, small companies say. National advertisers, such as International Business Machines Corp. and Honeywell Inc., bear the cost of running the service. Such big concerns pay between $8,000 and $40,000 a year to market their products and services, while regional advertisers pay between $1,500 and $15,000 a year to reach a more limited audience, according to IndustryNet's Mr. Jones.

Yet even IndustyNet cannot take the place of face-to-face meetings, where people can haggle about prices and strike bargains, Ritchey's Mr. Vangelder notes.

Nevertheless, Mr. Jones insists that on-line services will continue to grow in popularity as more small manufacturers use personal computers to conduct business. He expects the number of IndustryNet users to more than triple in 1995.

Meanwhile, Mr. Jones says, IndustryNet plans to upgrade its service so users can place orders on line. He eventually wants to turn IndustryNet into an industrial "shopping mall" through which manufacturers of all sizes could order everything from financial services and educational materials to ball bearings.

Of course, enthusiasm for on-line services isn't limited to small and midsized manufacturers. About one-fourth of all home-based businesses, for example, use modems, according to Find/SVP, a New York based research outfit. Major national on-line services such as CompuServe now feature special forums or so-called "user groups" for small-business owners. "Small businesses want to act bigger and appear more professional with the customer," says Mark Kutner, president of small-business services for Bell Atlantic Corp. in Philadelphia.

Mr. Pentz of Livingston Products, agrees. On IndustryNet, he says, nobody need know that he works for a six-engineer firm. When he used to contact possible distributors, "a lot of places didn't have time to mess with you because you weren't talking in tens of thousands" of dollars of orders, he says.

But when he makes a request for information or supplies through IndustryNet, Mr. Pentz says, he finds that the response is surprisingly rapid. "It allows us to be able to act like a big guy," he adds.

TO SELL IN JAPAN, JUST KEEP TRYING

To move mountains, salespeople sometimes have to climb them. Literally. In the dark, huffing with clients all the way to the summit of Mount Fuji in the ritual trek to glimpse the sunrise. TRW has done that and more in its quest to sell Japanese carmakers parts ranging from engine valves to air bags.

Has walking the extra mile paid off? You bet. In the past seven years, TRW's annual worldwide sales to Japanese auto companies have swelled more than sevenfold to $500 million, accounting for 10% of the company's total auto parts sales last year. Even though Japan's carmakers are in a slump, TRW expects sales to keep growing, reaching $1.5 billion by 1997, about equal to its business today with Detroit.

Success in Japan couldn't have come at a better time for TRW, helping the Cleveland conglomerate's rebound to profitability. The company, which also has defense and credit-rating businesses, had suffered a series of mishaps. In 1990, defective air bags led to a costly recall by Ford, GM, Honda and Mazda. The next year an explosion at one of the company's main air bag plants shut down production for a few weeks. Meanwhile, consumers were howling over errors in credit reports issued by TRW's high-tech credit-rating service. When the dust settled in 1991, the company had lost $140 million and sales had declined 3% to $7.9 billion. Since then, it has been fighting its way back, making money in the past three quarters.

TRW's auto parts business in Japan has blossomed from tiny seeds in unpromising soil. Though the company had formed a joint venture to make engine valves in 1964, the operation was hardly a high priority. By 1981, TRW had only one employee in Tokyo to handle the sale of auto parts to all of Asia. When Joe Gorman, 55, became CEO in 1985, he made selling to Japanese automakers a major goal. Says Gorman: "All you had to do was look at parking lots around America. We all knew what was happening. Given the trend lines, we might as well go out of the automotive business if we aren't providing the Japanese with some major portion of our products."

His first move was to build up the sales force. While that boosted sales a bit, it wasn't enough. So Gorman tried a more indirect approach. TRW invested heavily in joint ventures with Japanese companies supplying the U.S. plants of Toyota and Nissan. Once these carmakers began using TRW parts for their U.S. cars, it was a relatively easy step for TRW to begin supplying them back in Japan. Meanwhile, one of TRW's early partners in Japan offered to sell its share of a thriving joint venture, TRW SI of Nagoya, which made steering systems. The company had close connections with four groups of Japanese parts suppliers that work directly with Japanese automakers.

While other American suppliers may sell a handful of specialized parts in one or two categories, TRW is now providing a full line: valves, steering systems, air bags and seatbelts, and electronics. Except for air bag components and some electronics, TRW makes these products in Japan. In addition, the company is working its way into the design labs of Japanese carmakers, something few of its peers have done.

The center of TRW's success is clearly its air bag technology. The restraint devices are complex systems that draw parts from several vendors. Currently TRW supplies air bag-triggering sensors for half the cars Japanese companies sell abroad and 35% of those they sell in Japan. The sensor, which detects in a split second whether a collision is serious enough to warrant the bag's inflation, is the most complicated and costliest part of the system.

TRW has sold ten million sensors since 1988 and expects to more than double annual sales of air bag components by 1996. But industry experts point out that the market for air bags is undergoing a technological metamorphosis as automakers search for safer, cheaper ways to build the devices. And that means more competition, especially from Japanese parts makers. Honda uses TRW air bags in its large sedans but has turned to Nippon Koki, a Japanese maker, for its smaller cars.

Gorman, who also is president of the U.S.-Japan Business Council, says he's ready for the competition. He hopes to starting making air bag components in Japan later in the decade. He also plans to send additional American engineers across the Pacific to work more closely with Japanese car designers--and climb more mountains.

- Emily Thornton

Product

40

The ticket to ride: Smart cards

Travel agent, expense-report system in palm of your hand

By Julie Schmit
USA TODAY

New technology will soon make an ordinary trip extraordinary.

Within five years, most people won't call a travel agent to book a trip. You'll do it yourself on a computer. You'll answer simple questions: where to; from where; what time; what airline. Your computer — fed with the same information travel agents get — will find the lowest fare. If you need a rental car or hotel, you'll reserve it, too.

Trip planned, you'll insert your "smart card," a credit-card look-alike with a computer chip, into your computer. Your reservations will be transferred to it. At the airport, you'll swipe your card through an electronic reader to board. No need to carry a paper airline ticket or wait in line for a boarding pass. When you get to your destination, you'll go to the rental-car lot, insert your card into a machine and see the car keys pop out. When you arrive at your hotel, you'll swipe your card through another reader in the lobby to check in. When you get to your room, your card will open the door. You won't get a key.

Your smart card will be your credit card and personal record keeper, too. The cost of your flight, rental car, hotel and meals will be recorded on the card. Once back at the office, you'll insert it into your computer. It'll transfer your expenses onto a report. No receipts needed.

"This isn't Star Wars stuff anymore," says Steve Weiss, senior vice president of Marriott Hotels. "Some of it is five years away, some of it will be in limited use this year," agrees Terry Redmond of Rosenbluth Travel, one of the world's largest travel agencies.

The emerging technologies will make travel easier to plan and do. Travel agencies, telephone companies, soft-ware providers and others are laying the groundwork. Airlines, hotels and car-rental firms are taking steps of their own. When it comes together, consumers will have easy access to the same information travel agents get. By using smart cards, fliers will be able to go from parking lot to jet to hotel room without talking to anyone or waiting in lines.

"In the next year, someone will board an airline using a smart card," says Richard Mandelbaum, AT&T's chief smart-card scientist.

AT&T has been developing smart cards for 10 years, but they're just starting to come into use. Smart cards can store up to three pages of typewritten text — anything from checking and credit-card numbers to frequent-flier numbers and seat preferences. If airlines used smart cards, they wouldn't need paper tickets and fliers would be better off. Today, tickets do little but slow the travel process. Fliers can make reservations over the telephone, but they have to pick up a ticket or wait for it to be delivered. Fliers can change reservations with a phone call. But they have to wait in line at the airport to change the paper ticket, too. If you make a reservation with a smart card, you'll change it the way you made it — on your own computer. "Airline tickets are dinosaurs," says United Airlines' Greg Couper, director of services planning.

Frequent business travelers will be first to see big changes in planning and taking trips:

▶ This year, Holiday Inn will have frequent guests test "Herbie," a hand-held computer called a personal digital assistant, or PDA. Herbie will put the resources of a travel agency into a traveler's hand. Using its built-in cellular telephone, Herbie will dial into computer reservation systems. Travelers will tell Herbie when and where they want to go. Herbie will find the lowest airfares and best car-rental deals. But the only hotels Herbie will find are Holiday Inns. By giving frequent guests PDA power, Holiday Inn hopes to keep their loyalty. Because PDAs can be used while somebody is on the run, Steve Jacobs, senior vice president of Holiday Inn, expects them to become the No. 1 way frequent travelers make travel plans. "Anyone who wants to survive and prosper from 1995 on is looking at this technology," he adds.

▶ Sprint announced last week a voice-activated calling-card service. The software recognizes callers' voices so they don't have to dial 14-digit ID numbers. Marriott, for one, expects such technology to someday let frequent guests call Marriott and say nothing but, "It's me. I need a room Tuesday in Chicago." The software would recognize the voice and book a room based on the guest's past booking practices.

▶ United Airlines is testing electronic gate readers at Chicago O'Hare airport. The machines read a magnetic strip on the back of the airline ticket. The strip is coded with the flier's name, seat and flight. Fliers swipe the ticket through the reader and board. By having an electronic reader instead of a gate agent, United speeds boarding and gets fliers accustomed to automation. A smart card would be read the same way. This year, United plans to put the readers in three more airports.

▶ Improvements in electronic mail are giving business travelers more control over their travel arrangements. Today, it can take three to 10 telephone calls between a traveler and a travel agent to book a trip. With new e-mail systems, no phone calls are made. Travelers fill out electronic travel request forms on their computers. They're sent by e-mail to a computer at a travel agency. The computer finds the best travel option and sends an e-mail itinerary back to the traveler. One system, SABRExpress — owned by American Airlines parent AMR — will be tested this year by 10 to 20 companies.

The emerging interactive technologies promise to bring less-frequent travelers into the fold, too. In Birmingham, Mich., and Denton, Texas, a cable television pilot program lets 200 households buy airline tickets by TV and pay for them by punching a credit-card number into a keypad. This year, Bell Atlantic hopes to run a bigger test in 38,000 homes in Toms River, N.J. Future Vision of Philadelphia, a data-gathering company, will supply a travel database of flights, fares and video of resorts, hotels and tourist destinations. "You'll be able to walk a beach outside the hotel you want to stay at," Redmond says. To book a trip, consumers will use remotes.

No one is looking at the new technologies harder than travel agents, whose livelihood is threatened. Today, travel agents book 80% of airline tickets and get about a 10% commission on each one. For airlines, commissions are their third-biggest operating expense and one they'd love to reduce. They will as consumers book more trips themselves. To protect themselves, big travel agencies are trying to help companies manage travel better instead of just booking trips.

At Carlson Travel, 80% of new corporate contracts are based on fees, not commissions. The more Carlson saves a company, the more it makes. It uses special software to make sure travelers follow corporate travel policies. American Express even has software that makes expense reporting easier. When a traveler puts charges on an AmEx card, AmEx can transfer those charges to an electronic expense form and send that to the traveler's accounting department. Accounting gets expense reports faster and travelers don't have to take time to do the paperwork.

On the leisure side of the business, agencies hope to feed the interactive networks. Rosenbluth is working with Bell Atlantic and Future Vision in the Toms River test. Once the consumer decides on an itinerary, Rosenbluth will take the information, make the reservation, print the airline tickets and mail them. If airline tickets become obsolete, Rosenbluth would still gather the travel information.

Mom-and-pop travel agencies, which book a lot of leisure travel, won't disappear overnight, either. If optimists are right, 50% of U.S. homes will have interactive TVs within 10 years. But many consumers may still prefer the human touch to a computer.

The USA is, after all, still a nation of consumers who cannot program a VCR.

KinderCare Learning Centers

NEW LESSONS IN CUSTOMER SERVICE

IT HASN'T ALL been fun on the jungle gym for the biggest player in the game of caring for tiny tots. KinderCare's business is one of the world's toughest and most emotionally charged. A junk-bond-financed diversification binge by its former parent Enstar Group in the late 1980s eventually forced the Montgomery, Alabama, company into bankruptcy. But in April, after five months, it emerged from that time-out for bad behavior as the nation's only publicly traded company devoted solely to child care. To lure back wary investors, CEO Tull Gearreald, 48, a former Merrill Lynch investment banker, is pursuing a strategy that would serve any manager well: Listen to customers, and act on what they tell you.

To battle teacher turnover--a huge complaint among parents and the bane of an industry where low wages and long hours are the norm--Gearreald is requiring new caregivers at KinderCare's 1,160 centers in 39 states to take a 12-hour "survival training course." Teachers get paid for their time and learn the company's teaching methods, conduct guidelines, and techniques for dealing effectively with parents. "They used to learn this on the job, which can be very stressful and discouraging," says Gearreald. "We hope the training tells them, 'We think you're valuable, so we're making an investment in you.'"

In January, KinderCare opened its first center catering expressly to commuters. In a renovated supermarket in Lombard, Illinois, steps away from the busy Metra train station that runs into Chicago, it gives harried moms and dads a convenient one-shop stop at rush hour. Robert Schiel, vice president of the new KinderCare at Work division, notes, "We even have fresh coffee." The hours are a bit longer than normal too--6 A.M. to 7 P.M.--again, at the request of commuting parents. The company is talking to transportation authorities in New York, San Francisco, and Washington, D.C., about similar sites.

KinderCare is listening to kids as well. Its new Kid's Choice centers accept only children age 6 and up. Bigger kids, says Gearreald, whose own son, Bud, 4, attends a KinderCare in Montgomery, often gripe about having to "hang around babies." The appeal for kids: computers to use for homework or games, and a big-screen TV for movies. (Gearreald vows it will not be tuned to MTV all day.) The appeal for Kinder-Care: Such centers, located in shopping strips and malls, are cheaper to equip and launch—$200,000, vs. $1 million for a typical stand-alone facility—and cheaper to operate, since they require full staffing only before and after school. The first Kid's Choice center opened in mid-August in El Paso, Texas, and Gearreald plans to roll out 25 more by March.

So far this progress hasn't shown up in KinderCare's share price, which is languishing around $12 after initially shooting to $17 when the company came out of Chapter 11. Its toughest competitors are small, neighborhood child-care providers that offer considerably fewer amenities and services but usually cost less—KinderCare's typical weekly charge ranges from $80 to $120. An added burden: Interest payments on its $237 million in debt still eat up nearly a third of operating income. Says an analyst who admires the company: "It's going to take a couple of decent quarters to get KinderCare on investors' radar screens again."

Alan Dorsey, director of research for Value Investing Partners in Westport, Connecticut, thinks that will happen in the next 18 months. He estimates KinderCare will earn $27.3 million on sales of $468 million, or $1.15 a share, in the 1994 fiscal year ending in May, and $33.3 million on revenues of $507 million, or $1.40 a share, in fiscal 1995.

GEARREALD insists KinderCare can achieve this growth without chasing the unrelated businesses—retailing, banking, and insurance—that enticed his predecessor, company founder Perry Mendel. One huge potential market: building child-care centers for big employers or running their existing facilities for a fee. KinderCare is already operating centers for 35 large organizations, including Citicorp and Walt Disney, and expects to have 40 or so signed on by October.

It also plans to open its first overseas center in Britain by fall 1994 and may eventually expand into New Zealand and Australia. "We'd like to stay in countries with a common language," says Gearreald. "There are enough cultural differences we'll have to work out." Makes sense. For an outfit that prides itself on listening, merely adjusting to a new argot—nappies instead of diapers, and pushchairs instead of strollers—should be challenge enough. – **Susan Caminiti**

Chinese cereal (left) copies Kellogg's packaging, and Chinese facial tissues use well-known American name.

Chinese Flagrantly Copy Trademarks of Foreigners

By Marcus W. Brauchli
Staff Reporter of The Wall Street Journal

Visit a Chinese store these days and you'll catch glimpses of America: the bright red of a Colgate toothpaste box, canned foods in Del Monte green, the Kellogg's Corn Flakes rooster.

But the toothpaste is Cologate. The cans of "Cream Style Corn" are made by a company called Jia Long. And the rooster adorns a box of Kongalu Corn Strips. "Kongalu," says the box, is "the trustworthy sign of quality which is famous around the world."

Kongalu is indeed well-known in Battle Creek, Mich., Kellogg Co.'s headquarters, where company lawyers are considering their options. "We will take whatever action is available to us under Chinese law" to stop what Kellogg considers a flagrant violation of its well-known trademark, vows a spokesman.

Audacious copying of foreign trademarks, copyrights and patents is rampant in China, the world's fastest growing and potentially biggest consumer market. Brands are ripped off: Bausch & Lomb's Ray Ban sunglasses become Ran Bans. Products are copied: Virtually any Madonna album is available for $1 or less. And well-known names are exploited in strange new ways: One company markets Rambo facial tissues, in pink and blue.

The problem is so serious that the Clinton administration is weighing a special investigation under Section 301 of the U.S. Trade Act. Washington must decide by June 30 whether to proceed. If the U.S. Trade Representative determines that U.S. companies have been hurt, such an investigation could ultimately lead to sanctions. Already, U.S. officials put the annual damage at $800 million.

At issue is China's actual protection of so-called intellectual-property rights. Although Beijing has promised to stop infringements, a senior U.S. trade official says that China hasn't done nearly enough to head off a special 301 investigation.

"I have real confidence if the political will is there, it will be carried out," says the official. "What's lacking right now is political will."

Violations of intellectual-property rights afflict most industries and businesses doing business in China. Microsoft Corp. says Chinese software pirates cost it $30 million a year, and the amount is growing. The Motion Picture Association says virtually all the $45 million or so in videotape and laser-disk sales in China last year were fakes. Beijing Jeep Corp., a Chrysler Corp. joint venture, found more than 2,000 four-wheel-drive vehicles designed to look nearly identical to its popular Cherokee model.

Even the powerful suffer: Within weeks after the daughter of China's patriarch, Deng Xiaoping, published a biography called "My Father, Deng Xiaoping," thousands of illegal copies were flooding bookstores in major cities. This month, Deng Rong won a legal case against one publisher among the many who produced tens of thousands of illicit copies of her book.

Spurred by such embarrassments and eager to avoid a trade tussle with the U.S., Beijing has passed tough laws for dealing with counterfeiters and last year set up special intellectual-property rights tribunals.

"It's quite clear that in terms of a comprehensive legal framework, China has done an excellent job," says David Buxbaum, a leading China lawyer who is pursuing 12 intellectual-property rights cases through the new courts. But he worries that some of the judges assigned to the new courts may be unfamiliar with the concept of intellectual property. "It's only beginning to dawn on people that copyrights and trademarks are property," Mr. Buxbaum says.

While the legal concepts may be new, China is staging a huge propaganda campaign to show that it is trying to grasp them. The government says it handles more than 13,000 trademark-infringement and counterfeiting cases each year, of which about 500 involve foreign companies. The U.S. has the largest number of the 59,466 foreign trademarks registered in China.

For the most part, Chinese enforcement so far has meant police raids on street markets or stores that sell counterfeit software, compact disks or laser disks. Few factories have been shut down, to the dismay of U.S. trade officials.

It's not that the factories are secret. Indeed, U.S. trade officials recently visited the biggest of China's 26 known CD factories, Shen Fei Laser Optical Systems Co., in Shenzhen, just across the border from Hong Kong. The U.S. says it has given the names, addresses and telephone numbers of major counterfeit CD manufacturers to Chinese authorities.

"We've in a joking manner offered to provide them with satellite photography if that would be helpful," the senior U.S. official says.

CDs, laser disks and software have attracted the heaviest publicity, in part because losses have been big and those relatively glitzy industries have aggressive lobbies in Washington. Pirated music accounts for half of China's nearly $700 million a year in recording sales. And the software industry estimates that 94% of the software sold in China is fake, a loss industry puts at $595 million.

Yet consumer-products companies are being hit just as hard. Shampoos, soaps, toys, clothing and shoes are all being copied. Particularly vulnerable are those made in China: Exact copies of products made by Procter & Gamble Inc., Colgate-Palmolive Corp., Reebok and Nike are

(cont.)

common throughout southern China. "They'll actually hire workers away from the real factories," says an executive.

Most companies in China like to keep low profiles in trade disputes, so few will comment publicly about their troubles.

But as with most issues in China, the companies say privately that the intellectual property-rights infringements are compounded by China's size. Even if they succeed in wiping out a counterfeiter in one city, fakes can pop up somewhere else overnight.

Double Entendre: The Life And The Life of Pepsi Max

The name's the same, but the game is not. By Karen Benezra

In the early days of colas, one of the trickiest parts was to get a Coke to taste the same as every other Coke. Likewise for Pepsi, no matter what fountain or bottle was the source. But in today's wacky world of soft drinks—the soda jerk days a faint memory—it figures that a company is doing its best to market sodas under a single name that taste different, depending where on the planet you make your purchase.

Such is the odd life of Pepsi-Cola's fledgling Pepsi Max, a mid-calorie soft drink rolling out in Canada. A sugar-free soda—also named Pepsi Max—is pushing through European markets and is set to swing into Latin America and Asia.

Same name, same package. Different products. Pizza Hut and McDonald's tweak formulations to adapt pizzas or Big Macs to local market tastes, but Pepsi Max's split personality may turn into quite a cola conundrum.

The sugar-free Pepsi Max developed for global markets is aimed at consumers who have notoriously shunned diet drinks. With a rollout to 20 countries by year end, Pepsi Max sales are expected to reach $250 million. Still, a sugar-free Pepsi Max is not likely to hit the United States where it would compete directly with the well-established Diet Pepsi franchise. Also, one of its key ingredients, a sweetner called acesulfame-K, has not been approved by the FDA.

But Pepsi is keeping a sharp eye on its Canadian mid-calorie soft drink and may introduce *that* version to American palates. "We want to make sure there's a consumer reason for being and we won't do anything unless we're convinced that mid-calorie says something people care about," said Craig Weatherup, president of Pepsi-Cola North America, referring to Canada as a "big test market."

Both Max products were born of different challenges. Outside the U.S., where Coke outsells Pepsi more than 3 to 1, diet drinks have been a tough sell, accounting for less than 5% of beverage sales. Quaffing diet sodas, by and large, presents image problems for European men. Pepsi decided a one-calorie product with the "mouth-feel" of a regular cola, would appeal to consumers looking for strong flavor but no diet after-taste. Finally, they gave the product a strong blue and red package with bold graphics designed by Peterson Blyth Pearson and a $40 million advertising campaign. TV ads mimic a strategy used by Mountain Dew, another Pepsi entry, featuring rock climbers and sky divers. In Britain, Pepsi Max drew 1.2% of supermarket cola sales while diet Coke lost 0.4%. Pepsi Max drinkers also boosted the company's total volume, said international marketing director Mark Blecher.

In Canada, Pepsi's market research indicated that roughly a third of consumers switched back and forth between regular and diet soft drinks. Also, a surge in private label brands—whose shares leaped past both cola giants in 1993—left Pepsi in need of a quick fix to boost sales. Their answer: Pepsi Max, advertising "All the taste of Pepsi, with 1/3 less calories."

Introduced via sampling that hit 1 million consumers in nine cities, mid-cal Pepsi Max, which contains sugar, is "exceeding expectations," said Jeff Lobb, vp-marketing at Pepsi-Cola Canada. Ads from J. Walter Thompson, Toronto, pairs *Seinfeld* stars Juliet Louis-Dreyfus with Jason Alexander and *Cheers* pals George Wendt and John Retzenberger.

A mid-calorie beverage is also being developed by rival Coke, which has tinkered with the idea since 1980 using such code names as Project Midway and Project Fog (*Brandweek*, Jan. 31). And while the market appears ripe for a drink with anywhere from 40 to 100 calories, it could pose problems. "You fear that a mid-calorie product will make people abandon the full sugar or diet lines," said consultant Tom Pirko of Bevmark, N.Y.

Worse still, a diet product containing sugar could turn off customers in droves, much like New Coke was spurned by Coke traditionalists in 1985. "If you're a diet person, 50 calories is as bad as 150," said Chester Kane of consulting agency Kane Bortree & Associates, N.Y.

But with diet soft drink sales falling in the U.S. for a second year in the face of bottled waters, juices and teas, there may be little choice but to bring a mid-calorie product to the masses. And that's when Pepsi Max could be forced to leave one of its personas behind. ∎

ATTACK OF THE FIGHTING BRANDS

From diapers to beer, major labels are jousting with store brands

"Miller High Life—the champagne of bottled beers."
"It's Miller Time."

In years gone by, such Madison Avenue-spun slogans got beer drinkers to pony up premium prices for Miller High Life. Despite the havoc that micro beers, import beers, discount beers, and such have wreaked on High Life of late, Miller Brewing Co. has found there's still some sparkle in the brand. Just not as a premium-priced brew.

Miller is one of a clutch of marketers trying to breathe new life into tired old brands. They're slashing the prices of some well-known products and repositioning them as higher-grade alternatives to the store brands and other low-priced fare that appeal to budget-minded shoppers. Procter & Gamble Co. has cut prices on a fistful of old standbys by 12% to 33% over the past 14 months, shifting them to what it terms a "mid tier" in pricing. Among them: Joy dishwashing detergent, Era liquid laundry detergent, Luvs disposable diapers, and Camay beauty soap. In its own twist on the formula, Eastman Kodak Co. is fighting store brands with a new low-priced, seasonal film, Funtime.

Such "fighting brands" have often been deployed by marketers as temporary measures to keep customers during recessions. But marketers see this current wave as more than a temporary phenomenon. They view it as a response to the fragmentation of the mass marketplace by taste and, increasingly, economic insecurity. Marketers say many consumers have become switchers, trading back and forth between branded products and store brands. The trend has spurred the growth of private-label products, which have risen from 18.2% of supermarket unit sales in 1989 to 19.7% last year, according to Information Resources Inc.

BREWING SALES. For manufacturers, the midtier brands offer several benefits. They can help a marketer corral switchers without setting off price wars on premium brands. They keep factories humming. And they save old brands from the scrap heap, letting companies milk the equity of years of ads. Miller has brought back the "Miller Time" line in ads to tap nostalgia for High Life.

TO THE RESCUE
Manufacturers are using different strategies to protect their market shares.

PROCTER & GAMBLE dropped prices on some products to put pressure on store brands and rivals while protecting its higher-priced brands.

MILLER BREWING dropped prices on Miller High Life and revived the old "Miller Time" ads to go after store and discount brands.

KODAK will launch funtime, a new low-price film aimed at store brands. It will be offered only in the spring and fall.

Until recently, such price-tiering has been confined to a few categories. P&G has employed tiering in shampoos in the U.S., in diapers in Venezuela and Germany, and in laundry detergents in the developing world. Now, fighting brands are spreading and scoring victories. Despite a flat beer market, High Life's sales jumped 9%, to 4.9 million barrels, last year after Miller cut its price 20% or more in most markets. A 12-pack of High Life that cost $6.99 two years ago

in Ohio can now be had for $4.99. "The impact was fairly immediate," says Jeffrey P. Schouten, director of pricing for the Philip Morris Cos. unit. Luvs' market share in unit volume is up from 11% to 12.9% since its price was cut by 16% last May, arresting a severe slide.

HIGH-LOW. The challenge is to calibrate a fighting brand to make it good enough to draw consumers from low-priced rivals but not so good it clobbers the marketer's top brands or its profit margins. To offset the lower margins on its Funtime film, for example, Kodak is also launching a high-end film for special occasions, Kodak Royal Gold. On Luvs, P&G eliminated jumbo packages, streamlined package design, simplified printing on the diapers, and trimmed down promotions.

Even so, industry sources say Luvs initially cannibalized Pampers' sales; Pampers recovered when it introduced a new, thinner diaper in the fall. P&G's total unit share rose to 40% in December but slipped back to 39.6% in February. That's up from last April's 39.2% but not by much.

Other marketers figure that if they can't beat store brands, they might as well make them. That's what RJR Nabisco Inc. may do: It recently disclosed plans to test-market private-label cookies and crackers in some stores. Such moves underscore the power of retailers, who love the fat margins on store brands. Retailers are said to make 8% to 12% on store-brand diapers. As part of the Luvs repositioning, P&G has said, it has fattened retailers' margins to 8.6% from 3.3%. Still, some retailers, such as most divisions of Safeway Inc., no longer stock Luvs. In the end, fighting brands won't be contenders if retailers don't give them the chance to duke it out.

By Jonathan Berry in New York and Zachary Schiller in Cleveland, with Richard A. Melcher in Chicago and Mark Maremont in Boston

The Mystique of the Brand:
Jarred, Bagged, Boxed, Canned
A brand's equity protector is the package itself

By Betsy Spethman

Twelve suburban women sit around a focus group table, psyching themselves up to talk about cat food for two hours. Through the course of the evening, only two things really perk them up: The chance to describe their cats, and a vacuum-packed foil bag of cat food.

Even before they've examined the nuggets of cat food, most have said they would buy it, intrigued by the high-tech, brick-like bag they've come to expect to see in the coffee aisle, certainly, but never spotted before among the cans, boxes and bags of pet foods.

It's a point increasingly driven home to marketers of food, health and beauty product lines and over-the-counter drugs: the package is the brand. When you've done everything you can to make your product taste good, work effectively, cost less, you can still distinguish it with a package none of your competitors can copy.

As media channels proliferate, prospective customers split into harder and harder to reach audience and readership segments. Without an impressive return on investment from mass media advertising, the packaging's role in influencing a customer's moment of purchase has expanded dramatically.

"Marketers are paying more attention to package design because products are so much more at parity these days," said David Wisnom, senior consultant for Landor Associates. "When differentiation through taste, color and other product elements has reached parity, packaging makes the critical difference."

A case in point is Pepsi-Cola Co.'s reaction to Coca-Cola's vaunted plasticization of its hallowed curved bottle.

"It's not something Pepsi could do," said Rob Meyer, director of packaging innovation for Pepsi. "But we want to level that playing field. I'd like to do a new package every few years. It's tough operationally, but that's what this category needs. We can't build business on distribution and price, but packaging is a way to build excitement without changing the formula or adding products that'll cannibalize the line."

> "Packaging is a way to build excitement without changing the formula." -- *Pepsi's Meyer*

Pepsi's building a stable of designs with monikers like: "Fast Break," a 20-oz. resealable, curved bottle; "Big Slam," a one-liter bottle geared to convenience stores; "Pepsi Junior," a resealable 12-oz. plastic "can" testing in Cleveland and Birmingham; and "Block Party," a 30-can version of "The Cube." Pepsi's turned that 24-can multipack into a promotional tool, carrying coupons from marketers like Nabisco, Breyer's, Thermos and Spalding (*Brandweek*, June 13). "The Cube is some real estate we can have fun with," Meyer said.

Perrier also made its distinctive package the centerpiece of promotion, shrink-wrapping original artwork onto bottles sold through restaurants. Alport Lipson Glass, Chicago, handled that effort.

Licensees are cashing in on the recognizability of McDonald's packages, selling neckties in mock fry and burger boxes in department stores.

Beyond good looks, the best designs extend a brand by bringing some intrinsic value to the product itself, said Patrick Whitney, professor and directory of the Institute of Design at Illinois Institute of Technology. "It's a constant dance we see as marketers balance identity and utility; they want to be different and offer some benefit to the consumer," said Scott Talgo, principal of brand equity consultancy St. James Group.

Packaged goods marketers are paying special attention these days to delivery systems, Wisnom said. That's prompted in part by the success of club stores, whose giant packs are better if they're resealable. A unique delivery system, like Mentadent toothpaste's double pump, can cement a brand's image. And designs based on consumers' use of a package "make consumers feel like the manufacturer cares about them. That leaves a good taste in their mouths," said Jonathan Prinz, president of Schechter Group.

Drug companies have capitalized on that as they fight off private label. Procter & Gamble boasts an easy-to-open yet childproof cap on its Aleve analgesic.

Tylenol touts its Fast Cap, designed for older adults. "These convenience moves add value, but if a competitor can copy it, it's more of a tactical move than a strategic brand-protection," Talgo said. It ends up being a bonus for container makers, though, giving them a ready market for innovative packages that may have required expensive retooling to produce. Proprietary packaging, especially patented designs, prevents knockoffs; it's become common practice for marketers to patent a specific design and then build a moat around it by copyrighting several similar designs.

Knockoffs have become especially irksome to hba and otc drug brands. Massengill last year redesigned douche boxes with proprietary elements like a signet "M" and gold seal to prevent knockoffs. "They had been very lax about private label encroachment; one day they looked at competitors and couldn't tell them apart from Massengill. Now they've wiped the slate clean and will be very vigilant" protecting the brand, said Flavio Gomez, partner of SBG Group, which handled the redesign.

Consumers' concerns for the environment pressures marketers to avoid wasteful packaging. While that cuts down the surface area for graphics, it could be better for marketers in the long run. "That greater ecological pressure may reawaken interest in proprietary shapes," said Prinz. The most likely candidates are jarred and bottled items like condiments; glass is easy to shape, and a distinctive jar means an added value to consumers. Cartons, on the other hand, are more expensive to shape and more difficult to protect from infringement.

And some ecological advances come at a cost. When Hanes dropped the plastic egg for L'eggs hosiery in 1991 and moved to a gabled box, "There's no question they lost something," Prinz said.

"It's an interesting challenge," said Allen Adamson, executive director of Landor Associates. "That egg structure had been tied to a function; without the function, I'm not sure the shape is relevant to the future equity of the brand. And the question is, how do you capture that shape graphically?"

Graphics get tinkered with more frequently than structure because it's a cheaper and faster way to update a brand. Category leaders often use well-recognized graphics to extend their clout into new categories. Sun Diamond Growers of California is rolling out new packaging for Sun-Maid dried fruits that uses the Sun-Maid woman and bright red used by the No. 1 raisin brand. SBG Partners, San Francisco, handled the redesign. Frito-Lay borrowed the equity in the Taco Bell name and graphics with its supermarket line of Taco Bell-branded food, designed by Schechter Group.

But package design must be carefully integrated with product, distribution and service designs, Whitney said. "If you just gussy up the package to fend off private label, that's like driving by looking in the rearview mirror. You have to design systemically and add some intrinsic value, or you'll be left competing in some small consumer niches--either the very rich or the very naive consumer."

Officials say 'check it out' for better diet

Whether it's percentages or grams, 'There's something for everybody'

By Nanci Hellmich
USA TODAY

ROCKVILLE, Md. — David Kessler, commissioner of the Food and Drug Administration, is bouncing through the aisles of a Giant grocery store, approaching customers and giving them a crash course on the new food label.

Right now, he's in the salad dressing aisle where he's cornered Polly Long.

"Do you have a minute? Would you like to learn how to use the new food label? It'll just take a minute."

He starts rooting through her cart. Together they look at the Nutrition Facts panels — labels that will be required on thousands of grocery items by next Sunday. They discover the bread that Long selected has no fiber, the cheese she has picked is very high in fat, ditto the milk.

"I need to go empty my grocery cart," she laughs. "I'm feeding my kids high-fat foods."

No, you don't, he reassures. "Here's your low-fat yogurt. Total fat: 5%. Is it low? Yes, it's low."

Then he dashes off to get more milk to show her the fat difference between skim milk, 2% milk and whole milk.

Someone *stop* that man.

Kessler, who ordinarily goes to the grocery store only on "special runs," has made this trip to stir up media attention.

And who can blame him? After years of hard work by the government, industry and consumer groups, and an estimated cost of $1 billion to $1.5 billion to food companies, Kessler wants to make sure shoppers use the new labels.

Many foods already have them, but Sunday is the deadline: Almost all processed foods manufactured after that must have the new Nutrition Facts panel or risk FDA action. Some old labels will be around until product supplies are used up.

The panel lists key nutrients, including fat, saturated fat, cholesterol and sodium in grams or milligrams. It also shows how the nutrient fits into a daily diet.

The labeling is mandatory for most foods — including processed meats — but voluntary at fresh produce and seafood counters. It's also voluntary for single-ingredient meat and poultry products, regulated by the Department of Agriculture.

At a news conference today, Kessler will launch a public education campaign and unveil two new public service announcements for television.

One stars Kirby Puckett of the Minnesota Twins and Roger Clemens of the Boston Red Sox. Clemens pitches a ball to Donna Shalala, secretary of Health and Human Services. She says: "For a healthier diet, use the new food label. Check it out."

A similar message will be flashed on Major League stadium scoreboards and the electronic message boards on the Goodyear blimps and in New York City's Times Square.

And Curious George, the lively monkey character in children's books, will be the mascot for material aimed at kids.

Plenty of people applaud the new labels.

It's a "public health milestone," says Bruce Silverglade of the Center for Science in the Public Interest, a leading crusaders for label reform. CSPI would like more improvements.

Kessler admits fine-tuning is necessary, especially with serving sizes. But he thinks the new rules are an important step to help consumers figure out what they're really eating.

In addition to panel requirement, the government set up:

▶ Strict definitions for descriptive terms used on the front of products such as "fat free," "low-fat" and "reduced calorie."

▶ Limits on health claims. Only seven different ones are permitted — including that calcium reduces risk of osteoporosis and a high-fiber, low-fat diet reduces risk of some cancers.

But the Nutrition Facts panel is Kessler's crusade of the day. The latest dietary information has been condensed into a few square inches, he says. A major key to using it is understanding a new term that's used on the panel: "percent daily value."

"What daily value really means is your daily allotment" of that nutrient, Kessler says.

For instance, if the daily value for the fat in a serving of a product is 35%, then it provides 35% of your total fat for a day.

Shoppers can use the percent daily value to compare products or to figure out how the food fits into that day's diet.

"Kids get this in a second. Kids understand these numbers," says Kessler. "They understand when I say to them 20% of your fat for the day is in one of those servings."

Kessler continues his race through the store. In front of the snack shelves he points out that the serving size of potato chips is now given in number of chips, not just ounces; in the lunch meat aisle, he compares saturated fat in different packages.

He stops grocery shoppers Phyllis and Albert Schindler.

"Most people don't understand milligrams and grams. If I asked you — 8 grams of saturated fat — would you know if that was a lot or a little?"

"I wouldn't be absolutely sure," says Phyllis Schindler.

"Let me show you. Go to the percent daily value column and see what this product has in one serving. One serving of this has 38% of your daily allotment. Is that high or low?"

It's high, says Albert.

Which is easier — looking at grams or looking at percent of fat? Kessler quizzes.

Looking at the percent, Albert answers.

Yes, Kessler says. Here's a simple rule: "Less than 5% of your daily value in a product is low."

All the daily values are based on a 2,000-calorie-a-day diet, but not everyone eats that amount. "You may eat 1,900 calories, and I may eat 2,300 calories," says Kessler, "but you get a ballpark" percentage on the package.

If you're more interested in counting fat grams, that's fine. "If a person still wants to know the grams, that's still in the label," he says. "There's a lot of information. There's something on that label for everybody."

To make sure that all the information on packages is correct, the FDA is doing lab analysis on hundreds of products.

But after all this, will shoppers really use the new label?

Kessler is optimistic. In 1990, about 30% of people decided whether to buy a product based on the nutrition information panel. A new FDA survey two months ago showed 55% of customers made their decision based on the Nutrition Facts panel. And that's before the education campaign began, says Kessler.

Regina Hildwine of the National Food Processors Association takes a wait-and-see approach.

If consumers don't understand the new label over time, she says, the FDA will have to "give it some serious reconsideration. But a lot of people have and will continue to expend a lot of energy to make sure consumers 'get it.'"

And Kessler is one of them. He's racing to the ice cream aisle: "Look at the difference," he says, clutching two frozen packages. "Eight percent saturated fat on a triple brownie yogurt and 50% on premium vanilla ice cream . . ."

Anatomy of a Fad: How Clear Products Were Hot and Then Suddenly Were Not

By Kathleen Deveny
Staff Reporter of The Wall Street Journal

Clear products are going the way of oat bran, hair mousse and minifoods—marketing fads that enjoyed a few years of almost hysterical popularity and then all but disappeared.

In the past few years, marketers created transparent versions of dozens of products, from colas and dishwashing soaps to beer, deodorant and gasoline, in an effort to portray them as purer, milder and more natural. But like most marketing fads, clear was undone because of a proliferation of me-too products, and products that stretched the original concept too far. "Saturday Night Live" even spoofed the trend with a parody commercial for Crystal Gravy ("you can see your meat!").

"Clear is dead," says Lynn Dornblaser, publisher of New Product News. Adds Tom Pirko, a beverage industry consultant: "Clear was last year's color."

Data provided by Information Resources Inc.'s InfoScan service suggest the future for many clear products is murky. Sales of Clearly Canadian soft drinks fell 35.7% in supermarkets, drugstores and mass-merchandise outlets during the 13 weeks ended Jan. 2. Sales of Ivory clear dishwashing liquid dropped 27.3%, while sales of Mennen Lady Speed Stick Crystal fell 15.5%. Miller Clear, a transparent beer, is already gone.

Crystal Pepsi, the most hyped of the clear products, has sustained its growth largely because of heavy promotions; even so, it has fallen short of **PepsiCo** Inc.'s expectations. A few other clear products, such as **Bristol-Myers Squibb** Co.'s Ban Clear deodorant and **Warner-Lambert** Co.'s Caladryl Clear anti-itch medication, continue to grow.

The rise and fall of clear products illustrate how even the most sophisticated marketers get drawn into fads. In many cases, companies simply mistake fleeting fashions for lasting shifts in consumer preferences. Other marketers recognize a fad for what it is but don't want to lose customers to rivals, even temporarily. Still other companies try to exploit fads by quickly launching products that don't require large investments.

Indeed, there are risks to ignoring fads—as companies that ignored salsa and gourmet coffees discovered. Both **Procter & Gamble** Co. and **Colgate-Palmolive** Co. initially scoffed at **Church & Dwight** Co.'s Arm & Hammer Dental Care baking soda toothpaste. But consumers apparently

AT THE CHECKOUT					
Future of Transparent Products: Unclear Based on sales of selected clear products in supermarkets, drugstores and mass-merchandise outlets during the 13 weeks ended Jan.2					
BRAND	MANUFACTURER	SALES ($ millions)	% CHANGE FROM YEAR EARLIER	UNIT SALES (millions)	% CHANGE FROM YEAR EARLIER
Ivory clear dishwashing soap	Procter & Gamble	20.2	−27.3	12.3	−24.4
Clearly Canadian soft drink	Clearly Canadian Beverage	19.0	−35.7	10.2	−35.6
Crystal Pepsi soft drink	PepsiCo	11.8	169.2	7.8	261.6
Ban Clear deodorant	Bristol-Myers Squibb	5.7	36.3	2.4	30.0
Palmolive Sensitive Skin dishwashing soap	Colgate-Palmolive	5.1	−12.6	3.5	12.0
Mennen Crystal Clean deodorant	Colgate-Palmolive	2.9	−15.5	1.6	−7.4
Rembrandt Mouth Refreshing Rinse*	Den-Mat	1.2	—	0.3	—

*New brand

Source: Information Resources Inc.

liked the slightly salty taste and gritty texture of the Arm & Hammer product. Baking soda toothpastes now have annual sales of nearly $300 million, and both big marketers have belatedly created baking soda toothpastes.

One problem with fad marketing is that consumers' attention spans are so unpredictable. Traditional methods of market research, including focus groups, can't accurately estimate how long consumers will stick with a new product. Give a new product to a group of consumers, ask them what they think, and a faddish item will always appear to be a winner, says Gary Stibel, a principal with New England Consulting Group in Westport, Conn. "Hand anybody a Hula-Hoop, and they'll have fun with it—at first."

In the early days, clear products seemed more promising than many marketing fads. Using the absence of color to conjure up purity, lightness and wholesomeness dovetailed with several broad shifts in consumer behavior. Aging baby boomers were moving from conspicuous consumption to abstinence, from alcohol to sparkling water. Meanwhile, environmentally conscious consumers began gravitat-

ing toward products that contained fewer harsh or unnecessary ingredients.

When Clearly Canadian Beverage Corp., based in Vancouver, British Columbia, began testing a new soft drink in 1988, younger consumers liked the concept of a clear soft drink: "Clear was equated with natural," says Glen Foreman, chief operating officer of Clearly Canadian. "It reinforced the idea that you get what you see."

In the next few years, consumer products companies latched onto the clear concept. Colgate-Palmolive spent a decade and $6 million developing a sensitive skin version of its well-known green dishwashing liquid, Palmolive. After testing light blue and yellow versions, the company found that consumers overwhelmingly preferred a clear formula. By then, a Colgate spokesman says, the company was tracking the success of Ban Clear deodorant on the West Coast and rushed out a clear deodorant of its own, Lady Speed Stick Crystal Clean.

By 1992, the trend had become a fad. Colgate brought out a clear version of its Softsoap hand soap. A few months later, Procter & Gamble launched a clear version

(cont.)

of its well-known Ivory dishwashing liquid. Then Coors Brewing Co. began testing a clear malt beverage called Zima. Consumers started filling up their cars with Amoco Crystal Clear Ultimate gasoline. And Den-Mat Corp. launched its clear Rembrandt Mouth Refreshing Rinse.

Marketing experts say media attention to the clear phenomenon put more pressure on marketers to act. "I sat in meetings with people who said 'Let's do clear because clear is hot,'" says Doug Hall, president of Richard Saunders International, a Cincinnati firm that evaluates new products.

The beginning of the end of clear, some marketing experts said, was marked by the arrival of such products as clear beer and clear gasoline. "The appearance of clear products that didn't fit the positioning debased the original concept of clear," says John Quelch, a marketing professor at Harvard Business School. "These are parasite products."

At the same time, consumers began to balk at paying higher prices for products that actually claimed to have fewer ingredients. And price competition between nearly indistinguishable rivals quickly be-

gan to cut into sales of some products.

That clear products are already passe comes as no surprise to Dani Houchin, 25 years old. Ms. Houchin, who works as a training consultant in Manhattan, used to drink clear soft drinks, but has switched back to seltzer. "When I first started drinking them, I thought they were interesting," she says. "But once it became a fad I thought, 'This isn't cool anymore.'"

48

Their appeal could run for the long haul

By James R. Healey   USA TODAY

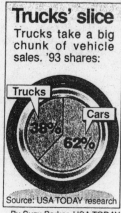

Trucks' slice

Trucks take a big chunk of vehicle sales. '93 shares:

Trucks **38%**

Cars **62%**

Source: USA TODAY research

By Suzy Parker, USA TODAY

DETROIT — Trucks, trucks, trucks.

Flashy pickups, hot-rod minivans and heavy-duty sport-utilities are roaring from all the nooks at the North American International Auto Show here. Trucks account for 14 of the 32 models making worldwide debuts at the Detroit show, the year's biggest auto exhibition.

They range from mild — Honda's conservative Odyssey minivan — to wild — Chrysler's bitty Plymouth Back Pack, a pocket-size pickup for the surf and mountain bike set. The $23,000 Odyssey is on sale this month. Back Pack, a concept truck designed to test public reaction, may not go on sale for years, if ever.

The popularity of trucks — pickups, vans and sport utilities — has been growing fast. Trucks accounted for about 38% of vehicle sales in the USA in 1993, a figure that probably rose to 40% last year, according to J.D. Power and Associates. That would be much higher than 27% a decade ago. The fresh blast of attention they're getting at this year's Detroit show signals carmakers suspect the boom could last forever. Fancy trucks do as much nowadays as sports cars once did to jazz up a company's image and draw potential customers.

Automakers are banking on a lasting truck boom. Ford Motor remodeled a factory so it can build up to 450,000 of its redesigned Explorer sport utilities a year, up from a maximum of about 310,000. General Motors cranked up a crash program to launch full-size, four-door sport utilities this spring after just 26 months of development.

Cadillac, Mercury, Lexus, even Jaguar all are considering adding trucks. Toyota and Nissan will redesign their small pickups and compact sport utilities soon. Nissan is clamoring for more minivans from its joint venture with Ford. Mercedes-Benz is building a factory in Alabama to make sport utilities in 1997.

Does all that mean there is no end in sight? Or is it like the stock market: Once everybody joins the party, it's over? "There are two schools. One is there's no limit. The other is that people will wake up and decide that they really do like cars, that a truck is not going to be their vehicle of choice for the rest of their lives," says Gordon Wangers of Automotive Marketing Consultants. "I haven't decided where I come down."

Ray Windecker, head of the research firm American Autodatum, has decided: "Contrary to popular opinion, truck fads don't last any longer than car fads."

But the industry's bets are on a long, healthy life for pickups, vans and sport-utilities. There's plenty of evidence at the show at Cobo Hall downtown here. It opens to the pub-

(cont.)

lic Saturday. From the show floor, a glimpse of:

▶ **Trucks of today.** GM's Chevrolet Tahoe and GMC Yukon four-door, full-size sport utilities — which went into production last month — go on sale in March. Their strong point: They are the only full-size four-doors. They fill the gap between the Ford Explorer, biggest of the com-

Top 10 vehicles

Four of the 10 best-selling vehicles in the USA are trucks. The top sellers, through November:

Rank	Vehicle
1.	Ford F-series pickup
2.	Chevrolet C-K pickup
3.	Ford Taurus
4.	Honda Accord
5.	Ford Ranger
6.	Ford Escort
7.	Toyota Camry
8.	Saturn (all models)
9.	Ford Explorer
10.	Dodge Caravan

Source: J.D. Power and Associates

pact sport utilities, and GM's giant Suburban, which can seat nine. All the full-size sport utilities so far have been two-door models. Expect a price range of $28,000 to $32,000 for the GM models. Ford plans a contender to come in about a year.

The management team that took over GM nearly three years ago figured a big four-door was a no-brainer. "This was one of the first programs they approved," says Ed Schoener, a manager of the four-door Tahoe development. "This was a targeted, quick-to-market vehicle." GM simplified the manufacturing and kept costly factory retooling to a minimum. Yukon and Tahoe four-doors are identical, inside and out, to GM's full-size pickups and the Suburban from the front bumper back to just behind the front door. But the frame underneath is a new design, stiffened and fitted with an updated front suspension to make the Yukon-

/Tahoe ride, steer and handle with car-like smoothness.

Chrysler's 1996 minivans go on sale in April starting at about $19,000. To fend off the herd of competitors since it pioneered small vans in 1984, Chrysler's first overhaul of the minivan features plenty of friendly features, including an optional sliding door on the driver's side.

Honda's Odyssey minivan is aimed at buyers who value smoothness and refinement more than space. It is sized to compete with the smallest minivans, such as the Mercury Villager and twin, the Nissan Quest. Odyssey is based on the Accord sedan, so it drives more like a car than a truck. Honda argues that Odyssey is a car. Honda designed it to meet all U.S. car — not truck — safety, pollution and fuel-economy standards, hoping to draw buyers seeking a refined minivan.

▶ **Trucks of tomorrow.** Ford's Triton show truck is a disguised version of its next-generation F-series full-size pickup. Production of the '96 F-series begins late this year. The production model is expected to lose the bulging hood scoop and aggressive grille for more conservative front-end styling. But Ford says Triton is the harbinger of its redone F trucks, the country's best-selling vehicles. The '96 F trucks will be the first to use modern, overhead-camshaft V-8 engines instead of the antiquated, inefficient pushrod-style engines that have powered pickups for decades. Most cars switched to overhead camshaft engines years ago to improve fuel efficiency and performance.

Ford also is showing a hot-rod minivan called SHO-Star — short for Super High Output Windstar. It's a radical idea. Minivan makers haven't produced sports models, thinking that few van buyers want sporty looks and high performance. SHO-Star boasts a 3-liter V-6 that Ford says pumps out at least 220 horsepower. It has a five-speed manual gearbox, rare in a minivan. It

rides on a taut suspension built more for hauling through tight corners than for hauling Little Leaguers. Ford insists it's only a concept vehicle for the car-show circuit. In the next breath, executives say most special goodies on SHO-Star already are in production, or are slightly modified versions of regular production items. That's what car bosses usually say when they have decided to produce the vehicle, but want feedback from auto-show crowds first.

▶ **Trucks of the next century.** Those could mainly be lightweight, low-power minitrucks, if fuel-economy regulations for trucks continue to tighten as auto executives fear. Chrysler's Plymouth Back Pack is one way to package pickup truck usefulness with sports-car spiffiness. Back Pack — or something like it — probably wouldn't hit the market for several years. It's aimed at young buyers who can't afford two cars, so want one to do everything. Back Pack seats two — three if passengers are skinny — in the front cab.

Kristin Bowen, Plymouth market researcher, says that twentysomething truck buyers demand room for hauling and have an affinity for bicycles. So Back Pack is rigged to easily handle a pair of bikes. And, she says, their trucks have to be fun and simple, "because they have enough hassles in their lives." So Back Pack has plenty of crannies for storage, one even marked "stuff." The driver's seat swivels so the driver, when stopped, can face a foldout computer table built into the passenger's seat. The numbers and other markings on the dashboard are cartoonish. Horn buttons, for instance, are illustrated with big-mouth trumpets.

But will there still be a healthy truck market by the time Back Pack and its ilk arrive? Says Jim Perkins, Chevy general manager: "How high is up? How far can this (truck) market go? We don't know."

Contributing: James Cox

Gillette Succeeds As Others Fail By Reinventing Itself

By Peter J. Flatow

What did Microsoft, Intel and Ford do that General Motors and IBM didn't? What did Gillette find out in the nick of time? Regardless of size or category dominance, if you don't reinvent your franchise, someone else will.

Reinventing your franchise requires foresight. It requires the courage to challenge conventional wisdom. It means having the confidence to think outside the comfort zone. It taps all of the company's resources to leverage its assets and skills. It has the power to increase sales and profits.

Consider Gillette. Razors and blades account for a third of Gillette's sales and two-thirds of its operating income. But there was a period when the advantages of this lucrative business were almost lost. After dominating the category for years, Gillette found itself fending off corporate raiders because it lost sight of what drives the business engine. How Gillette turned its fortunes around is the story of a successful reinvention.

In the mid-1970s, BIC introduced the disposable razor in Europe. Wary about moving into disposables, and realizing they would cannibalize sales of its far more lucrative shaving systems, Gillette nonetheless introduced Good News! as the first disposable razor in the U.S.

Though Gillette continued to develop superior shaving systems—improving upon the twin-bladed Trac II with the

Peter J. Flatow is president of CoKnowledge, a Westport, Conn., consultancy specializing in franchise reinvention.

pivot-headed Atra in 1977—it quickly incorporated improvements into disposable models. Competitors followed. Consumers, seeing little reason to pay a 44% premium for system razors, flocked to disposables. Gillette's once 72% share of the wet-shave market declined to 56%. And its problems continued.

Disposables were growing by 17% a year, while system sales were declining by 1%. By 1985, Gillette put more than 60% of its consumer ad spending behind disposables. As a result, disposables captured 60% of category units and 53% of dollars at drastically lower price points and profit margins. In 1987, Gillette spent only one-fourth of the $61 million it spent in 1975 on media advertising.

In Europe, management felt Gillette was giving up on the two principles that had made the company successful: technological leadership; smart marketing. They challenged the belief that the market was inevitably to be dominated by disposables. All marketing support was thrown behind shaving systems, with the result that shaving systems' market share increased by more than 10%, leading a resurgence in sales and profits.

As often happens, an oustide factor became the catalyst for reinvention. In 1986, chairman Colman Mockler Jr., in the heat of a proxy battle, promised stockholders that Gillette management would increse their value more than the raiders could. It was time to roll the dice.

For years, design engineers had tinkered with a system that set thin blades on springs so the razor followed the contours of the face. It would eventually be called the Sensor. Development costs exceeded $200 million before the first unit was sold at retail. But the simultaneous launch of Sensor in the U.S. and Europe in 1990, supported by a $100 million marketing budget, was hugely successful. By 1992, sales of Sensor and Lady Sensor exceeded $500 million.

Gillette successfully reinvented its franchise by doing what it did best, *better*. Sensor returned Gillette to providing the consumer with a superior shave, and away from competing on price.

Reinvention of existing products or services is much more likely to succeed than new product development, new business development or acquisition for two major reasons:

1) The costs and risks of reinventing the franchise are substantially lower because the tools, systems, talents and skills are already in place.

2) The rewards can be considerably higher, since a company is starting with what it knows and the learning curve is flatter.

Microsoft knows. Intel knows. Ford knows. To generate real growth in the 1990s, managers of even successful brands cannot just respond to change. They must anticipate change. They must be a catalyst for change. They must continually reinvent their franchise. ∎

Reprinted from the May 3, 1993 issue of *Brandweek*, © 1993 ASM Communications, Inc. Used with permission from *Brandweek*.

Detergent Wars Bubble Over in Europe

Unilever, P&G Campaigns Become Dirty Business

By Cacilie Rohwedder
Staff Reporter of The Wall Street Journal

LONDON—It was a well-deserved vacation. Tony Lee, a British chemist for **Unilever Group**, had spent months working on a detergent formula that he and his company were certain would take the world by storm. For soap scientists, it was likened "to the Holy Grail."

But while Dr. Lee was skiing in California last March, an unusual visitor turned up at Unilever's headquarters in London—Edwin Artzt, chairman of **Procter & Gamble** Co., rival of the Anglo-Dutch consumer-goods concern. Mr. Artzt carried a fearsome message to Unilever executives: He said P&G had scientific evidence that Dr. Lee's miracle soap damaged clothes. And if Unilever didn't cancel the product's scheduled launch in 11 days, P&G would tell the world.

Upon his return, Dr. Lee began a weekend of frenzied testing at Unilever's Liverpool laboratory. But he couldn't find anything wrong with his detergent. Unilever's conclusion: the issue was more public relations than fabric damage.

Dirty Business

Thus began Europe's soap war, an unrelenting battle between two of the world's largest consumer-goods companies to smear each other's products and grab a bigger share of the $10 billion European soap market. In the process, both proved beyond all doubt that selling soap has become a dirty business.

In June, Unilever finally admitted to a flaw in its new soap — marketed in Europe under the names Persil Power, Omo Power and Skip Power — and came out with a toned-down version. In the meantime, P&G—and later, German soap-maker **Henkel KGaA**—turned the affair into a public-relations disaster for Unilever.

Such animosity is new for an industry that until recently kept its dirty laundry to itself. Back in 1987, when Unilever found that a new P&G detergent caused allergies, it quietly shared the news with its rival. Though P&G rejected the charge, it did stop the product's European test launch soon after. Two years later, P&G tests showed that Unilever's then-new Breeze brand harmed clothes, and it asked for data proving the detergent really did "care for clothes," as Unilever's advertising claimed. The issue disappeared without the world knowing.

What has changed is that world-wide recession, stagnation in Western markets and spiraling marketing costs have turned a friendly business into cutthroat competition. "In the eyes of many corporate leaders, normal marketing strategies don't suffice anymore," said Joachim Klewes, a management consultant in Duesseldorf. "As a result, they increasingly exploit weaknesses of a competitor rather than stress their own strengths."

For Unilever, Persil Power was the "biggest, widest, fastest roll-out ever," executives said. The company spent $175 million developing the product and another $292 million on marketing in 1994 alone. The firm was particularly hard-pressed to get its product onto store shelves knowing that P&G would introduce its own new washing powder, Ariel Futur, just a few months later.

The escalating soap spat has taken a toll on Unilever's market share, although it hasn't so far seriously damaged the company's bottom line. Data supplied to P&G by market-research firm Nielsen reveals that in Britain alone, Unilever's share of the detergent market dropped to 28.2% in October from 32.6% at its April launch. Persil Power has fared even worse, losing almost half its initial 4.4% market share in Britain, according to Nielsen. By contrast, P&G's U.K. share rose to 52.4% by the third week of October, up from 50.6% April 30.

Posting third-quarter earnings Nov. 11, Unilever said detergent profits had declined in Europe, but didn't specify by how much. European sales of concentrated washing powder account for less than 2% of Unilever's $42 billion in world-wide sales. Pretax profit rose 11% to £724 million ($1.1 billion), while revenue increased 9%.

Privately, Unilever executives claim that P&G created this controversy to clean out store shelves for its September launch of Ariel Futur. P&G denies this. Industry insiders suspect P&G's offensive may have been used to keep Persil Power out of the U.S. market.

Clothing Damage Charges

At the heart of the dispute is a manganese complex molecule that Unilever says enhances Persil Power's performance—and that its rivals say damages fabric. P&G officials adopted their strident tone with Unilever, they said, because they feared that the manganese complex molecule would stick to clothes, even if a different detergent were used later. And with one-third of consumers switching detergent brands every four months, P&G said it worried that damage caused by Persil Power could be blamed on some of its brands.

The conflict came to light April 27, when a Dutch newspaper reported that P&G was testing Persil Power. Unilever retaliated, calling P&G's allegations about the detergent "complete nonsense" and filing an injunction to prevent P&G from further "denigrating" Unilever products containing manganese.

But Unilever withdrew the court action June 3, conceding that its washing powder harms garments "under extreme laboratory conditions." The company also announced it would change Persil Power's formula and launch a new product containing less of the contested manganese substance. It was the same day that P&G's outside tests came back. The results tore Persil Power to pieces.

The conflict escalated quickly when P&G hand-delivered the test results and its photographs of damaged boxer shorts to Britain's largest newspapers. The tabloid the Sun was only too happy to display the torn and faded underwear on its business page June 7.

Unilever contests the lab results.

Behind closed doors, Unilever also lashes out at Henkel, Europe's third-largest detergent maker. Henkel initially stayed out of the debate, but eventually sided with P&G. In a single press release, Henkel cited in-house tests confirming that Persil Power can ruin clothes.

Henkel said it entered the P&G-Unilever dispute to prevent Persil Power from being confused with its own Persil brand, which the company sells across Europe except in Britain and France.

P&G argues it didn't show bad manners either, insisting that it went public only when Unilever persistently refused to pull its product from shelves. Both P&G and Henkel say they have known about both the advantages and problems of manganese for a long time and were surprised about Unilever's launch of the substance as a "revolution" in laundry detergent.

Shoppers Advisory

Soon after Unilever withdrew its court action, P&G's side of the story got some support. In early June, Consumentenbond, the Dutch consumer organization, advised shoppers against using Persil Power, citing its own tests which found a greater-than-usual wear-and-tear effect. Even tests of the revised formula rated the formula as "poor" for washing at 40 degrees Celsius (104 degrees Fahrenheit) and "very poor" at 60 degrees Celsius.

Unilever responds that Consumentenbond's conclusions were "partial and biased." To P&G's outrage, Unilever said it sees no problem with the revamped product, launched in late June and which contains 80% less manganese than the original. P&G said the problem is the same even with the watered-down version and Unilever should withdraw it as well.

(cont.)

Unilever spent the summer polishing Persil Power's tarnished image. The company offered price cuts and published newspaper ads with a toll-free telephone number for advice and full reimbursement for damaged clothes.

Since then, hostile silence has largely reigned. But embittered Unilever executives say the battle isn't over, and pledge to "remove the question mark this has put on some of our brands." Experts speculate Unilever is awaiting the performance of Ariel Futur.

51

FLOPS

TOO MANY NEW PRODUCTS FAIL.

HERE'S WHY--AND HOW TO DO BETTER

Egg rolls for dinner: What a great idea! That was the thinking behind the decision to launch a line of La Choy frozen egg rolls in 1988. Not measly little appetizer egg rolls, mind you: What managers for the Hunt-Wesson Inc. brand envisioned were big, meaty egg rolls that a consumer would happily eat as a main course. The egg roll offensive would complement another new idea, the Fresh and Lite line of low-fat frozen Chinese entrees. After all, La Choy was a well-known brand name, thanks to its canned goods; ethnic cuisine was soaring in popularity; so were frozen meals. What could go wrong?

Plenty, as La Choy discovered when it rolled out its egg rolls into the East and Midwest. For starters, they couldn't be microwaved, because the shells got soggy. And it took a very long 30 minutes to heat these giant entrees in an oven. The other Fresh and Lite products didn't set the world on fire, either. For one thing, there was the name. "It sounded more like a feminine-hygiene product," says Linda Krakowsky, an ad executive who worked on the campaign. "And it was hard to say it was fresh anyway, because it was frozen." Two years later, La Choy executives pulled the plug on both the monster egg rolls and the Fresh and Lite line: Today they say they never had the market clout to make these products succeed.

In the long and inglorious history of new-product flops, La Choy is not alone. Put in the context of such historic screwups as Ford Motor Co.'s Edsel (estimated losses: $250 million), RCA's VideoDisc player ($500 million), and Time Inc.'s *TV-Cable Week* ($47 million), a few soggy egg rolls don't seem all that catastrophic. Producing flops is part of doing business in every industry,

from consumer products, where relentless competition for store shelf space drives many new products to quick extinction, to electronics, where rapid technological change dooms many newcomers even after a promising start. Remember the Osborne portable computer?

IS FAILURE ESSENTIAL? And the flops and near-dlops just keep coming. Among recent events: Dell Computer Corp. admits it messed up its notebook launch. Toyota Motor Corp. records disappointing initial sales for its much-heralded T100 pickup truck. Coca-Cola Co. struggles to succeed with what looked like a nifty idea--a tiny soda fountain it had designed for office use.

Overall, the new-product battleground is a scene of awful carnage. Chicago consultants Kuczmarski & Associates just studied the success rates for 11,000 new products launched by 77 manufacturing, service, and consumer-products companies. They found that only a little more than half--56%--of all products that actually get launched are still on the market five years later.

Other studies peg the long-term success rate of new products closer to 65%. But everyone agrees that most ideas never even make it into test markets. Companies had to cook up 13 new-product ideas before they came up with a winner, according to

> Turning more new products into hits looks like the final frontier. Companies could, says Wharton's Wind, "Double the bottom line."

Kuczmarski. "Clearly, all is not well," say Robert G. Cooper, a professor of marketing at McMaster University in Hamilton, Ont. A specialist in new-product development, he cites a Booz Allen & Hamilton Inc study that some 46% of all new-product development costs go to failures. That's an improvement from the 1960s. Still, he adds: "If half of a factory's output ended up as defects, you'd shut the place down."

Clearly, too, such inefficiency makes a tempting target for today's lean and hungry corporations searching for ways to cut costs and increase productivity. For U.S. companies that spent the 1980s improving efficiency and boosting quality, and that now face vicious competitive battles in slow-growth markets, raising the success rate of new products increasingly looks like one of the final frontiers. "Industry has been enormously successful at wringing operational defects out of the system," says William BonDurant, a top marketing executive at Hewlett-Packard Co. "But then you look at failure rates for new products, and they haven't changed much in 25 years. There has to be a way to drive that rate down." Adds Yoram Wind, a professor of marketing at the Wharton School: "If companies can improve their effectiveness at launching new products, they could double their bottom line. It's one of the few areas left with the greatest potential for improvement."

To be sure, there's a school of thought, ardently advocated by some executives who devote their lives to devising new products, that insists a certain rate of failure is essential. Says Brian Swette, general manager for new business at Pepsi-Cola Co.: "If you're batting a thousand with all your new products, you're doing something wrong." A perfect new-

(cont.)

product record, he argues, means a company isn't taking necessary risks to develop new markets. Then, too, failure often lays the groundwork for a future success. The classic example: The not-very-sticky glue that technicians at 3M Co. turned into Post-It notes.

Yet that philosophical view isn't keeping companies from taking a much sterner attitude toward new-product development in a broad array of industries. The No. 1 priority at the Marketing Science Institute, a research group backed by such heavies as Procter & Gamble Co. and Apple Computer Inc., is the improvement of new-product development. Companies as different as Hewlett-Packard, Motorola, Colgate-Palmolive, and Chrysler have been tackling new-product issues, too. They want to figure out how invention, in-house teamwork, and customer involvement will compress development time, unleash a flood of successful new products--and keep flops at bay.

PRODUCT CHAMPIONS. It's a riddle that requires a company to understand not just its markets and customers, but itself. Sure, says Abbie Griffin, professor of marketing and production management at the University of Chicago, product development means figuring out what customers want and developing an offering to meet that need. But, she adds, it also means considering what a company is best at, how it goes about the business of devising and marketing new products, and the path those products must follow as they move through the company's infrastructure.

And the more executives, academics, and consultants delve into what it takes to make a success, the more hurdles they discover a new product must overcome. When executives at Hewlett-Packard's Medical Products Group studied 10 of their new-product failures along with 10 of their successes, they were surprised to identify a total of 14 essential tasks that determined which products worked and which didn't. The steps covered a wide range of corporate skills. Among them: figuring out which new products play to a com-

pany's core strengths, understanding how a new product should be sold, and getting an early fix on a project's costs. "We found if you missed on just 2 of the 14 factors, you failed with your product," says Mark Halloran, chief of research and development. Other studies have pinpointed the same need to master a wide range of disciplines in order to achieve success.

So what are the steps to new-product nirvana?

For starters, a new product must satisfy a customer's needs, not a manager's. Every new product needs a champion, of course--someone who believes in an idea and is willing to take risks to see that idea grow. But advocacy can easily turn into self-deception, dedication into wishful thinking. That's a painful lesson Steve Jobs learned. The visionary founder of Apple Computer tried to repeat his success at NeXT Inc., the start-up company that developed the sleek, black NeXT desktop computer. After burning through $200 million of investment funds, NeXT stopped shipping the $10,000 computer in February of this year. It's now concentrating on its far more promising software.

What Happened? As Richard A. Page, NeXT co-founder and former hardware vice-president, put it a few months ago, when he quit: "The customers know what they want." And what they don't. For starters, they did not want Jobs's optical drive instead of the usual floppy drive. The new feature made it tough to switch work from a PC to NeXT. Even after a floppy drive was added, the machine itself remained slow, and there wasn't much software available to run on it.

True, the machine had nifty features, such as hi-fi sound. But even though Jobs tried to attract various kinds of customers, NeXT never overcame its essential, customer-hostile flaws. Students found it too expensive, even after discounts. Engineers preferred desktop workstations from Sun Microsystems Inc. Although he has dropped it, Jobs insists that the NeXT computer was the right product: It was just too late to compete with the more powerful

machines already out there. Yet if he had listened to customers and gone with more standard technology earlier on, analysts say, he might have had a chance.

BLIND TO THE SIGNS. Jobs was right about one thing: It's important to get to market swiftly. But it's even more important to get quality and pricing right the first time--even if that means delay. That's the painful lesson Cadillac learned with its Allante. When General Motors Corp. launched the model with great expectations in 1987, Cadillac managers had hoped the $54,700 coupe would bestow an aura of sexy Euro-styling on the division's whole line and expand its customer base to the younger buyers being lured away by BMW and Mercedes-Benz. It didn't exactly work out that way: The Allante went out of production July 16, the victim of a too hasty launch and a failure to offer the right mix of price, quality, and features to finicky consumers.

For starters, the car, with its 170-horsepower engine, was underpowered compared with foreign rivals. The body, handcrafted at the Pininfarina workshop in Turin, Italy, was attractive, but not especially distinctive or well made. The roof leaked, and squeaks and wind noise marred the luxury-car hush.

These were all clear signs that the car's handlers should have waited and ironed out the bugs. But signs work only when they're heeded. One executive that worked on the Allante later on says that Cadillac couldn't bring itself to delay the launch. "They had made a big hoopla about the introduction of this car, and when the car wasn't ready, they didn't want to make the hard choice and hold back," he says. The result was a car too small and expensive for core Cadillac buyers, but not really good enough to lure import buyers. No wonder Cadillac sold fewer than half the expected 4,000 Allantes in the 1987 model year. And it never sold even half its goal of 7,000 cars in subsequent years.

By the time GM decided to pull the plug, Allante (now priced at $61,675) had finally become the ultra-smooth, high-performance luxury coupe it was originally intended to be. Cadillac had added the 295-horsepower multi-valve V-8 Northstar engine and an electronically controlled transmission. But buyers were thoroughly confused. It was five years too late.

Taking a different view, Cadillac's general manager, John O. Grettenberger, says: "The car was a victim of economics, not a failure." He says a financially strapped GM finally had to focus on its core models. Allante's initial problems, he says, were not a result of haste. They were normal for a new venture in a market that Cadillac was just entering. And although he "would have liked to see it sell in greater numbers," Grettenberger says the Allante taught Cadillac valuable lessons in marketing and technology that have made the Seville Touring Sedan a success.

Of course, if Allante had gone through a more successful launch, it might have had a longer life. But even getting the new product right from the start is no guarantee of success: It must still be sold in the right way, through the right channels. A study by Cooper of McMaster shows that new-product managers double their chances of success when they successfully match a new product with the right sales force and distribution system.

"EMOTIONAL SELL." Huffy Corp., for example, the successful $700 million bike maker, did careful research before it launched a new bicycle it dubbed the Cross Sport, a combination of the sturdy mountain bike popular with teenagers and the thin-framed, nimbler racing bike. Huffy conducted two separate series of market focus groups in shopping malls across the country, where randomly selected children and adults viewed the bikes and ranked them. The bikes met with shoppers' approval. So far, so good. In the summer of 1991, Cross Sports were shipped out to mass retailers, such as the Kmart and Toys 'R' Us, chains, where Huffy already did most of its business.

That was the mistake.

As Richard L. Molen, Huffy president and chief executive, explains the company's slipup, the researchers missed one key piece of information. These special, hybrid bikes, aimed at adults and, at $159, priced 15% higher than other Huffy bikes, needed individual sales attention by the sort of knowledgeable salespeople who work only in bike specialty shops. Instead, Huffy's Cross Sports were supposed to be sold by the harried general salespeople at mass retailers such as Kmart. Result: "It was a $5 million mistake," says Molen. By 1992, the company had slashed Cross Sport production 75%, and recorded an earnings drop of 30%.

A corollary of "Know thy sales channel" is another rule: Don't sell a product just because you need something new to pump through the sales channel you have already mastered. In 1989, BIC Corp. introduced a small $5 glass flask of perfume, to be sold in the supermarkets and drugstore chains where BIC had so much distribution clout. After much hoopla, BIC sold $5.6 million worth of Parfum BIC in the U.S. before withdrawing it from stores in the first half of 1990. The cost: about $11 million.

The problem: Perfume is hardly as disposable and utilitarian as a bag of razors. Says Mark A. Laracy, president of Parfums de Coeur Ltd., in Darien, Conn., which does about $70 million a year by mass marketing knockoffs of pricey scents: "Fragrance is an emotional sell to women. But the BIC package wasn't feminine. It looked like a cigarette lighter."

TOO-SUBTLE QUAFF. Even if the product is fine and its distribution channel is right, though, it may still come to grief if consumers don't understand its benefits. Three years ago, for example, brewers fell in love with dry beer, quaffs that were supposed to have a cleaner finish. Many thought dry beer could be the boost their industry needed. Anheuser-Busch Cos., Coors Co., and a clutch of smaller foreign brewers shipped 4.6 million barrels of dry beer in 1990.

But by 1992, shipments had fallen to 3.7 million barrels--a minuscule drop of the industry's 197 million-barrel total--and brewers will be lucky to do even that much this year. Pretty sorry returns on the $40 million-plus spent in advertising for the category. Coors Vice-Chairman Peter H. Coors figures dry beer appeals to only 2% of all beer drinkers. "At the time, it seemed like an intelligent decision," he says. "Knowing what we do now, we probably wouldn't have gone with it."

What Coors knows now is that consumers, who usually only spend a few seconds in a store or bar choosing a beer--or any product--are not going to take the time needed to understand a too-subtle product like dry beer. As marketing consultant Jack Trout puts it, "Nobody can figure out what the hell dry beer is. The opposite of wet beer? It's never been explained." And it probably never can be.

Numerous as the pitfalls are, it's possible for companies to avoid them. But improving the odds in new-product development often takes some fundamental rethinking of the way a company approaches its markets and manages its own operations. Chrysler in the 1980s, for example, was a textbook case of how not to devise new products. Ignoring the need for continuing innovation, the carmarker relied throughout the decade on the K-car platform it introduced in 1981. Such models as a too-narrow New Yorker sedan were launched and flopped. In addition, Chairman Lee A. Iacocca used his influence the wrong way, walking into Chrysler's styling studios and ordering up more chrome or opera windows with a wave of the hand.

As sales flagged in 1989, Chrysler President Robert A. Lutz finally convinced top executives that the company had to change its ways. So Lutz and Francois J. Castaing, Chrysler's engineering chief, threw out their old, compartmentalized approach to new-product development, in which a project would pass from research to engineering to manufacturing, and finally on to marketing. Instead borrowing from Japanese practices, cross-functional teams of engineers, market researchers, marketers, stylists, and manufacturing engineers began working together to design and build new models. The team approach has chopped by 40% the time it takes to develop a new car or truck. One important result: the hot LH line of sedans.

SIX STAGES. Other companies are also using team approaches to hone their new-product processes. Colgate-Palmolive Co. had a string of new-product flops in the 1980s, most notably Fab 1 Shot. The product, a slug of detergent, softener and an antistatic ingredient in a soluble bag, was supposed to save consumers time and hassle, but instead it irritated users, who couldn't adjust the mix to suit their own needs. Since 1989, Colgate has overhauled its new-product process to concentrate cross-functional teams on far fewer product ideas and speed up global rollouts of the most promising products.

Now, only about 20% of ideas make it to prototype, down from around 50%. And each idea must meet specific criteria at six different stages that lead from development to achieving a commercially-viable product. While Colgate hasn't yet won a reputation as a new-products runaway winner, its latest introductions, such as Precision toothbrush and Standup toothpaste, have been successes.

Other companies have learned to get back to their core strengths. Campbell Soup Co. dismayed consumers and stockholders alike in the 1980s by pouring out almost 160 new products a year, with a success rate of at most 20%. "We didn't stay close to home," says former North and South American Div. President Herb Baum. The failures included such notable bobbles as Campbell's Fresh Chef line of fresh salads and soups, which had a shelf life of a week. The company was constantly misjudging which dishes would sell and which wouldn't. "We never knew what to make," says Baum. The result was spoiled food and irritated supermarket owners.

Now Campbell has cut back new products 20% to around 120 a year. And those are mostly in areas it knows best, such as canned soups, sauces, and baked goods. When the company ventures into new areas, it is with something such as Pepperidge Farm canned gravy, which uses technologies Campbell understands and brand names that it has already established.

INSPIRING CASES. The likes of Chrysler, Colgate, and Campbell have plenty of incentive to improve the odds for their new offerings: There appears to be a strong correlation between new-product success and a company's health. According to Thomas P. Hustad, editor of the *Journal of Product Innovation Management*, the companies that lead their industries in profitability and sales growth get 49% of their revenues from products developed in the past five years. The least successful get only 11% of sales from new products.

There are also plenty of specific cases to inspire and terrify. Gillette Co.'s stock has soared since it introduced its new Sensor razor. IBM's has floundered since it amply demonstrated its ineptitude at creating new product lines that pay. But IBM has also shown how it is possible to change: Its small ThinkPad computer is a big new-product success.

Whether it's frozen egg rolls or micro-chips, the message is clear: A company cannot avoid every flop. But if it learns from its mistakes, it can surely flop a lot less often. And understanding failure is clearly a key to success in this ferociously competitive decade.

By Christopher Power in New York, with Kathleen Kerwin in Detroit, Ronald Grover in Los Angeles, Keith Alexander in Pittsburgh, Robert D. Hof in San Francisco, and bureau reports

Place

52

QVC draws wares from everywhere

'Quest for America's Best' gives entrepreneurs a shot at the big time

By Katy Kelly
USA TODAY

We're gonna change our style of livin'
And if that ain't enough
Then we'll change the way we strut our stuff.
— There'll Be Some Changes Made

SAN ANTONIO — "Aunt" Betty Townsend and her lady friends have been singing all the way from Burleson. Their van is loaded with crock pots, tenderloins and the spice mixes that have made Aunt Betty, 57, the patron saint of the Burleson Volunteer Fire Department. The five-hour drive is an investment in the change they hope to make.

Real change, not chump change. A change that would propel Aunt Betty and her Shut Up and Eat It seasoning to national fame. A change that would let her friend Toni Kemetz bag her job at the Dairy Queen and work full-time in Aunt Betty's kitchens. A change that might just make Aunt Betty really, really rich.

Townsend is one of 228 Texans who got themselves and the best they have to offer to the Alamodome to impress the buyers for the world's largest shopping network, QVC.

This is the beginning of QVC's Quest For America's Best, a $20 million, state-by-state search for unsung inventions made by real people and regional businesses who want a shot at the big time. It's a chance to sell their product to the network's 50 million free-spending households.

To be considered, the invention must be made in the USA, already be in production, retail for more than $15, be UPS shippable, and the vendor must provide QVC with at least $10,000 worth of the product in time for it to hit the airwaves (Jan. 2, 1995 in Texas) live from QVC's mobile studio. In each state QVC will pick 20 products and five alternates.

Why do it? Because several successful minutes of QVC airtime can be better than a winning lotto ticket. "It's not going to make a dog into a good product but if it's a good product they'll make it a great (one)," says Jack Camhi, president of Houston-based jewelry business I.G. Gold.

Camhi should know. Post QVC, "We went from single digit millions

(cont.)

to multimillions." His $240 gold-lamé necklaces sold "$700,000 in less than an hour," he says. His Eterna Gold ring "sold out in two minutes."

Waiting isn't easy on any of the potential tycoons. They check out the competition: Shrimp and salsa, Southwestern button covers, jewelry and spot removers, a pantyhose preserver, golf clubs and fishing poles, decorator toilet seats and portable stairs for short-legged dogs. And more. Much more.

Pharmacist/lawyer Sam McCloud, 45, is the brains behind Luv'n Feet. For him, marriage is the mother of invention. "My wife was having a problem with her heels. She said, 'I wish there was something to take away rough skin.'"

He mixed his first tries in the kitchen and eventually hired professionals to fine-tune the product. "Five or six years" and $20,000 later his wife had soft feet, he had Luv'n Feet, and "I'm working two to three jobs" to pay for it.

Being an entrepreneur "is stressful and it's stupid. The reason I do it is I can't help myself," he laughs.

Cosmotologist Billie Davis, 35, and her boyfriend, emu and ostrich rancher Joseph Sekula, 36, are just as driven. He went to an emu auction and came home with a byproduct, emu oil. The couple used it to develop skin-care products. "We believe emu oil is going to play a big part in the future."

Cassie Hall, 49, is in the egg business. Collectible sugar eggs, heavily decorated with elaborate frosting, with tiny, costumed, 3-D animal figures visible through peepholes. She's been making them for 23 years and can turn out 250-300 a month. They come with a signed certificate and retail between $150-$200.

Hairstylists Pat Bell and Linda Lacy came up with their product when they got tired of seeing expensive curling irons get gunked up with baked-on oils and hair sprays. "People were throwing away perfectly good irons," says Bell. After much experimentation, "We got with a chemist... had it made and bottled."

The result, Sparkling Irons, works well on steam irons, too, but the road to clean has extracted a toll. The making and promoting of the product has meant spending "savings, bill money, expense money," says Bell.

On a center table in the basement of the Alamodome, the Zaps-It guys push a paper cup toward the nose of a visitor, who belatedly learns it's contents: chemically simulated urine. Not the real stuff but uncomfortably close. They need it to prove the point. A quick squirt of the enzyme-filled Zaps-It changes it into water and carbon dioxide, which doesn't smell a bit bad. They figure they've got a winner. "Wherever you have people, you have odors," says Care Labs president Paul Kehrer.

Nearby is John Trube, 29, who came up with the Cadillac Boot Jack after "I hurt my back really bad water skiing and I couldn't wear my cowboy boots anymore because I couldn't (bend down to) get them off." He bills his wooden boot jack as as "The best way in America to take off your boots."

"I'm not trying to sell it or anything," he deadpans. But if the demand is there, he — and the 10 carpenters who assist him — can turn out about 500 a week.

Waiting for the outcome "makes you nervous," says Rosemary Hayes.

Hayes was trying to make the birdseed nylon net puffs often handed out at weddings when she came up with the Rice Bagger. "I just took some balsa wood and I just started messing with it," she says.

Her husband modified the original and Hayes took it to a tool-and-die man. For $23,000, he made a mold which pops out perfect Lucite forms. The ribbon clips to the top. The net slips through a hole in the middle. A scooper measures out the rice. Tie it and voila, a perfect mini bag of rice.

Her total investment, including boxes, ads and patent attorney: $52,000. She borrowed against her savings including $25,600 she won in Vegas and $4,500 she earned in residuals when she made a commercial for X-14 bathroom cleaner. So far, she's sold about 2,000 Rice Baggers, which retail for $14.95.

Ralph Garrett, 32, and his wife, Kim, of Sand Flat, Texas, own Shoestring Creations, a four-person company that makes painted chests and tables out of wood strips. "We were bothered by the waste of wood in furniture building," she says explaining the genesis of their idea.

What will they do if they're among the chosen people? "Buy everybody we know a table saw and put them to work," jokes Ralph.

The QVC judges work the rooms, seeing dozens of people and products every few hours, finishing in time for the next wave to set up.

Picking winners "is not a formula," explains Bill Lane, QVC director of new merchandise development, as he samples the results of a make-your-own fajita kit. "The key is to bring customers (regional) products they would not ordinarily have had."

Twenty-four hours later he has picked his players. The Cadillac Boot Jack, the Fiesta Fajita Kit, Fabuloso Frozen Margarita mix, Shoestring Creations' painted chest and the Fantasy sugar eggs are among the winners. Zaps-It is an alternate. Aunt Betty didn't make it. But there's a chance her wares might pop up during a regular show, says Lane. She's the lady in red. You can't miss her.

53

CONTACT-LENS SELLERS
JUST DON'T SEE EYE-TO-EYE

Upstart mail-order outfits vs. optometrists and manufacturers

When Richard King lost a contact lens recently, he called Lens Express, a Deerfield Beach, Fla., mail-order company. But since his prescription was more than two years old, Lens Express declined to sell him a lens without a new exam. And the eight optometrists King contacted near his West Texas home refused to release his prescription so that he could order directly.

Lens Express finally found King an optometrist--167 miles away--who gave him an exam and called in the prescription. King's saving by going mail order: perhaps $300 over two years, he says. But he's steamed at what he sees as a maze of greed and conflict of interest. "Optometrists do have a responsibility to follow up on first-time contact lenses," he complains. "But the replacement source is none of their business."

HIGH MARKUPS. King's story is the product of a fray involving contact-lens manufacturers, eye-care professionals, and, ultimately, the estimated 25 million wearers of contact lenses in the U.S. At issue: Can lens makers and doctors legally restrict how their eye-care products are sold? The Florida Attorney General is investigating possible civil antitrust violations, particularly by manufacturers that won't sell to mail-order companies and some retailers. The Federal Trade Commission is conducting its own inquiry.

It's a chaotic battle, and the absence of well-defined federal regulations isn't helping. The Food & Drug Administration regulates the manufacture of contact lenses and labels them a "medical device," to be dispensed by professionals or by prescription, but leaves states to see to the details. The FTC, for its part, requires that eyeglass prescriptions be released to consumers, but it says nothing about contact lenses. Meanwhile, only 13 states require that ophthalmologists and optometrists release contact-lens prescriptions to consumers.

The government probes promise to heighten the turmoil that is already engulfing the lens industry. Manufacturing costs have plummeted, and the introduction of disposable products has weakened consumer loyalty to their doctors as sources of supply. Lenses are viewed increasingly by purchasers as a commodity, and they no longer command the fat margins that they once did.

> Lens Express claims eye doctors commonly refuse to send a patient's prescription.

So it's no surprise that mail-order outfits and other outlets--among them discount retailer Wal-Mart Stores and such warehouse chains as Costco and Price Club--have begun competing with the independent optometrists and opticians who once monopolized distribution. "We shot ourselves in our own foot," says Ronald P. Snyder, a Fort Lauderdale optometrist. "When contact lenses came out, we marked them up such that we allowed someone else to get in." Now, mail order alone accounts for about 5% of the $1.8 billion annual retail contact-lens market, and other retailers' share is growing.

Lens Express, the largest American lens mail-order operation, says that its sales have doubled every year since 1986, to $40 million this year. That growth, however, hasn't gone unnoticed. The Texas Attorney General is suing Lens Express for deceptive trade practices, an action that the company contends was instigated by the Texas Board of Optometry, which denies it. And President Brian O'Neill says that optometrists and opticians have led attempts in several states to enact legislation that would allow lens manufacturers to sell only to eye-care

professionals, shutting out companies like his.

THE BLACKLIST. One such attempt last year, in Florida, caught the attention of the Florida Consumer Action Network, which lodged a complaint with the state Attorney General. The result: a wide-ranging investigation that has sought documentation and testimony from across the industry. The Florida investigators are looking into manufacturers' refusal to sell lenses, directly or through distributors, to mail-order houses and discounters that don't have eye-care professionals on-site.

Manufacturers don't deny that they seek to limit distribution. Indeed, the three largest contact-lens manufacturers--Bausch & Lomb, CIBA-Vision Optics, a unit of CIBA-Geigy, and Vistakon, a Johnson & Johnson subsidiary--all say that they won't sell to mail-order outfits because those companies don't have on-site professionals to "fit" lenses on patients. The same policy applies to some retailers. "This is a health issue, period," says Harold O. Johnson, president of Bausch & Lomb's contact-lens division. "This is a medical device that is in direct contact with the cornea and is controlled by the FDA and by prescription."

Indeed, B&L requires distributors to sign contract agreements to sell only to professionals. And CIBA won't sell to Sam's Clubs. Vistakon keeps a blacklist of mail-order houses, optometrists, and outfits it suspects are supplying mail-order companies.

SHUT OUT? Mail-order companies contend that these policies are driven by economics, not concern for patients, since replacement lenses rarely are fitted by professionals. Optometrists can write prescriptions with annual expiration dates, if they wish, in order to make sure that patients return for eye exams.

For their part, eye-care profession-

(cont.)

als say they worry that consumers will get prescriptions filled incorrectly elsewhere, or that patients won't return for follow-up care. "A patient takes the prescription and keeps reordering until they have a problem," says Steve R. Ali, a Manhattan optometrist. Optometrists complain of the lack of federal or state oversight of mail-order lens companies, which they say have little regard for prescription expiration dates--or don't require prescriptions at all.

Barring more uniform regulation, consumers can't count on getting a great deal from anyone. BUSINESS WEEK contacted six mail-order companies to inquire about ordering a box of six Acuvue lenses. Three of the outfits didn't require a doctor's name or written prescription as long as the lens specifications could be supplied. And prices varied widely, as did membership and mailing fees. The bottom line: None of the mail-order lenses were much cheaper than those ordered from a Manhattan optometrist. Some of them even cost more. Lens-wearer, beware.

By Gail DeGeorge in Miami and Joseph Weber in Philadelphia, with Mark Maremont in Boston and Rochelle Shoretz in New York

54

Banks Bag Profits With Supermarket Branches

By G. BRUCE KNECHT
Staff Reporter of THE WALL STREET JOURNAL.

Cruising the aisles of a Kroger supermarket in Memphis, Tenn., Maria Kittrell is shopping for customers. But instead of offering salami samples, she's selling certificates of deposit.

Ms. Kittrell is an employee of National Commerce Bank, which has a branch in the **Kroger** Co. store. Passing through the frozen-food section without a pause, she explains that it's tough to sell CDs where it's cold. But somewhere between the cookies and the crackers she spots a prospective customer and launches into a rapid-fire sales pitch, detailing everything from interest rates for credit cards to the tax advantages of home-equity loans.

Michelle Gwin, a government tax examiner, is impressed by the credit card's 7.9% rate of interest. "I'm going to fill out an application right now," she says.

There are currently about 2,100 supermarket bank branches in the U.S., up from about 900 in 1990, and their number is growing fast. The reason: As banks are confronted by intensifying competition from mutual funds and other nonbank suppliers of financial services, bankers are concluding that free-standing branches are too expensive to build and operate. Worse still, many of the most desirable customers don't even use branches; they prefer automatic-teller machines.

"Traditional branches still have a role, but supermarkets are where the people are," says John Presley, an executive of National Commerce, a unit of Memphis-based **National Commerce Bancorp.** And Mr. Presley—a cousin and look-alike of Memphis's most famous son, Elvis—believes that making banks competitive will require the same kind of new thinking from bankers that Elvis demanded from record companies.

"Bankers usually want to do business on their own terms," says Frank V. Cahouet, the chairman, president and chief executive officer of **Mellon Bank** Corp., which is opening supermarket branches in Pennsylvania. "But now we have bankers walking in the aisle talking to customers. It's making them think more about merchandising."

Actually, supermarket banking isn't a new idea. Citibank opened several store branches in upstate New York back in the 1960s. But the pioneering efforts failed; waiting for customers to come to them, the branches were relegated to the most unprofitable of financial services: cashing checks.

But today's successful supermarket bankers are aggressively marketing their profitable products. In addition to sending employees into the aisles, National Commerce plants ads throughout stores. In the produce section, so-called talking signs show vegetables juxtaposed with images of financial products. One depicts a head of lettuce and a credit card under the headline "No Fat. No Fee."

The signs work. Ava Petreman bought a $25,000 certificate of deposit after she noticed a sign offering six-month CDs with a 4.5% interest rate, higher than she had seen elsewhere. Presenting her check, the retired telephone saleswoman says, "I noticed the sign this morning, and it is the best rate I've seen."

The bank also uses store public-address systems to plug its products. "Attention Kroger shoppers," one broadcast begins. "Someone in the store has lost $108! By opening a checking account, you can save $108 in monthly service charges for one year. Stop by the National Commerce Bank branch in front of the store and find your $108."

Such tactics impress observers. "More than any other bank, National Commerce has shown that supermarket branches can be more than passive transaction centers," says banking consultant Anat Bird. "They have done it by creating an aggressive sales culture."

Ten years ago, National Commerce was a marginally profitable institution with 21 traditional branches. Unable to expand its retail business, Thomas M. Garrott, the bank's chairman and chief executive, recalls: "Our average customer was 59 years old, and he wasn't borrowing any money."

In his search for a new approach, Mr. Garrott, who joined the bank following a 17-year career as a food wholesaler in 1983, decided to merge his two careers with a move into supermarkets. Opening the first store branch in 1985, the bank now has 49 of them (and at this point just 16 traditional offices). Yesterday, National Commerce announced that it would enter the North Carolina market by opening nine supermarket branches there starting this summer.

Noting that 10,000 to 30,000 people pass through most supermarkets every week, compared with 2,000 to 5,000 for most bank branches, Mr. Garrott believes he has a sure-fire way of taking market share from other banks: "We see our competitors' customers a lot more frequently than they do."

National Commerce's financial results suggest he has a point. Over the past 10 years, the company's earnings per share have grown at a compound rate of 18.3%, better than any other U.S. bank, according to the investment-banking firm of Keefe, Bruyette & Woods. The bank's return on assets catapulted from 0.74% in 1984 to 1.65% last year.

National Commerce has acted as a consultant to almost 100 other banks, helping them to open more than 300 store branches. The most obvious appeal of such branch-

(cont.)

es is their economics: Mr. Presley says 400-square-foot supermarket branches, which cost less than $200,000 to build, break even with just $4 million in deposits. Free-standing branches, which generally have 4,000 square feet and cost at least $800,000 to build, need at least $15 million in deposits to cover costs.

For consumers, a major attraction is convenience. "It takes time to get in and out of a branch," says Mary Irish, a Memphis homemaker. "But I come to the supermarket three to five times a week."

Kroger officials also seem pleased with their resident bankers. Store managers say the bankers are so integrated into stores that customers routinely ask tellers to help them find everything from chicken breasts to dog food. One shopper plopped a large ham on the bank counter and asked a branch manager if she could carve it into thin slices. Says Kroger store manager Mike Sexton: "We consider National Commerce to be part of the store, just like the meat or deli department."

Not only does the bank pay rent for its space (the annual amount ranges from $12,000 to $40,000), but Mr. Sex-ton believes that bank branches enhance the loyalty of his customers and give them another reason to visit the store.

"I'm sure the store benefits," says homemaker Melissa McCall. "I have never walked into a grocery store without buying something."

55

Allen-Edmonds Shoe Tries 'Just-in-Time' Production

But Company Painfully Finds Approach Isn't Perfect Fit for Small Concerns

By Barbara Marsh

Staff Reporter of THE WALL STREET JOURNAL

"Just-in-time" production practices can work wonders for big companies by improving efficiency. But many small firms are still struggling to reap the benefits.

Consider Allen-Edmonds Shoe Corp., a 71-year-old maker of pricey shoes. Three years ago, the Port Washington, Wis., company tried just-in-time methods to speed production, boost customer satisfaction and save money. The result? "It really flopped miserably," says John Stollenwerk, the company's president and biggest shareholder. The manufacturer lost $1 million on the project — and in 1991, resumed doing some things the old way.

Widespread in Japan

Just-in-time practices widespread in Japan and increasingly popular in the U.S., promise to reduce a company's inventory investment and slash production time. Among other things, the just-in-time approach calls for supplying work stations with the precise amount of material needed at the exact time required, thereby eliminating a manufacturer's warehousing of raw materials.

Large companies that dedicate workers and machines to producing items in huge volumes generally derive the greatest efficiencies from just-in-time methods, technology experts say. But small companies with short runs of a variety of products often fail to make such gains. Allen-Edmonds, for instance, makes 41,000 variations of men's and women's shoes in many styles, colors and sizes, and mostly in limited runs. So, the company must keep switching product lines, thereby reducing efficiency.

"It's somewhat difficult for a small company to achieve some of the just-in-time gains of large companies," says Thomas W. Bruett, a partner at Ernst & Young who advised Allen-Edmonds on production techniques.

Like owners of other small, old-line manufacturing firms, Mr. Stollenwerk also had difficulty persuading some of his 325 production workers to accept change. At the outset, Mr. Stollenwerk thought just-in-time concepts could stem his firm's loss of business from retailers unwilling to wait as many as eight weeks for their shoe orders. He sought to slice overall production time by as much as 87% to five days.

His managers grew confident after their initial success with automating the company's main plant in Port Washington. That factory's floor — where shoe soles and uppers are stitched together and finished pairs boxed for shipping — used to be crammed with carts. Workers pushed the carts, stocked with unfinished shoes, between work stations. In 1988, the company virtually eliminated the carts by investing $180,000 in a conveyer that transfers work automatically between stations.

Cut Inventory

The move cut the facility's production inventory of unfinished shoes to 1,200 pairs from 5,000, freeing up nearly $400,000 in capital, company officials say. And production time for a pair of shoes dropped to eight hours from 3½ days. People at the plant "were thrilled. The morale was pretty high," says John Gantner, the company's operations manager.

But it wasn't so easy to get suppliers to go along with just-in-time strategy of matching delivery to need. Suppliers of leather soles did agree to make deliveries weekly, rather than monthly, to Allen-Edmonds.

Worst Defeat

But European tanneries supplying calf-skin hides refused to cooperate. They stuck with their practice of processing huge quantities of hides at once and wouldn't

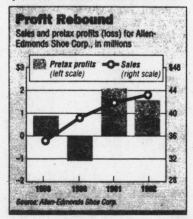

Profit Rebound

Sales and pretax profits (loss) for Allen-Edmonds Shoe Corp., in millions

Pretax profits (left scale) ▪
Sales (right scale) —O—

Source: Allen-Edmonds Shoe Corp.

handle small batches to meet the weekly needs of a small customer, Mr. Stollenwerk says. A bigger customer would have wielded much more power, of course. As a result, Allen-Edmonds still has more than $1 million tied up in monthly inventories of hides.

The just-in-time campaign sustained its worst defeat, however, at the company's Lake Church plant, six miles from the main factory. In a 32,000-square-foot building smelling of hides and leather finishers, workers cut pieces from hides, then sewed them together to make uppers. Seamstresses, paid by piecework, labor intensely. To keep up her pace, one half-seated woman even hurls her body back and forth between her work pile and her machine.

In 1990, managers rearranged this factory's floor in hopes of reducing the number of unfinished shoes. Figuring that such items spent too much time on the two conveyers, the officials removed one conveyer. The production inventory of uncompleted shoes fell dramatically.

But efficiency *dropped*. Mr. Stollenwerk puts much of the blame on his decision to substitute hourly wages for the company's piecework pay system — a change he considered integral to his just-in-time strategy. "We wanted to see if we could create a new culture," he explains.

Just-in-time theory encourages production workers to focus on quality and teamwork, experts say. Piecework, on the other hand, centers workers' attention on handling individual jobs as fast as possible. Going off piecework "might work great in Japan and southern Illinois, but it didn't work great here. [Our] people needed the discipline that the piecework system gives to them," Mr. Stollenwerk explains.

As productivity plummeted, Allen-Edmonds workers complained about co-workers slacking off. Jacqueline Summers, who makes $9 to $10 an hour, stitching wingtips and other pieces, says she observed "more breaks, more laughing, more giggling." A stitcher must pay attention, she insists, because "you see the same shoe all day long in a nine-hour day, and your eyes can eventually cross."

Reinstated Piecework

Finally, after the company lost $1 million in 1990, it reinstated piecework at Lake

(cont.)

Church. Mr. Stollenwerk's managers put more unfinished items back on the factory floor so workers would have more to do. And the executive compromised on his original goal of cutting the company's total production time to five days, settling for two to three weeks instead.

Mr. Stollenwerk says productivity shot back up and in 1991, the company became profitable again. The just-in-time program did save Allen-Edmonds $3.5 million in inventory overhead. The modest improvement in his production time also has helped to retain retailing customers, he adds.

But he grumbles that efficiency experts have yet to come up with a just-in-time solution for small manufacturers, which often require more limited production runs than their bigger rivals.

Some Allen-Edmonds workers long for such a solution, too, because they liked the hourly wage system. Luella Ansay, a 55-year-old stitcher, says that a nine-hour shift of piecework is hard. "Five years ago, I could push it out like you wouldn't believe. But the years go on and you just can't."

56

High tech puts them back on track

Efficiency fuels comeback; bids stream in for Santa Fe

By Earle Eldridge
USA TODAY

WILLOW SPRINGS, ILL. — Hustling inside the control tower at Santa Fe Railway's new rail yard here, Sean Shelton pauses, clicks on the mike of a two-way radio and barks commands to truck drivers below.

"Who needs add-ons?" he yells, his voice booming through the cabs of trucks.

"Go ahead," a voice crackles on the radio.

"This is for Block 8, Track 14. CFSK2307, BNZ236871, UPS2846604," Shelton says.

Within seconds, a driver wheels his rig in front of semi-trailer CFSK2307, hooks it up and rushes toward a freight train stretching a mile in the rail yard.

As he unhitches the trailer, a monstrous orange crane growls open its claws, grabs the 53-foot trailer, lifts it and places it on the train. From parking space to train in less than five minutes.

"Good job," Shelton tells his crew. "Now let's kick it over to the next train."

The future of railroading is unfolding here at Santa Fe's new $73 million Willow Springs yard. The 269-acre yard is one example of how railroads are successfully coupling technology, greater efficiency and marketing to rebuild a once-floundering industry. Just 15 years ago, railroads were being written off as clumsy dinosaurs in a world of convenient truck delivery and quick air service.

Today, they're coming back strong. So strong that Santa Fe Pacific, parent of Santa Fe Railway, has been in the center of a battle of bids and counterbids the past month for control of the USA's seventh-largest railroad. Union Pacific launched a hostile takeover bid for Santa Fe Oct. 5, after Burlington Northern proposed a friendly merger. Sunday, Union Pacific raised its bid to $3.8 billion, topping Burlington's $3.2 billion offer. The winner will become the USA's largest railroad company, beating CSX Transportation.

What's behind the boom? Efficiency.

The USA's railroads are hauling the same amount of freight but with fewer cars, fewer employees, and on less track. They're much more efficient--and profitable.

Railroads can haul the same amount of goods on fewer cars because they double stack containers, carrying two on one rail car. These containers, which are like a semi-truck trailer without wheels, can be delivered by ship, rail or truck. Railroads also are hauling more semi-truck trailers than in the past, which means freight doesn't have to be unloaded between the train and truck. Cranes, like the one at Santa Fe's Willow Springs yard, just lift the loaded trailers--wheels and all--and put them on the rail car.

The result: Railroads are shipping more goods more efficiently. The amount of freight, measured by revenue per ton-mile, is up 33% from 828 million in 1983 to 1.1 billion in 1993. Santa Fe — a leader in trailer hauling — has seen its operating income nearly double in three years to $318 million in 1993.

"Once it was cheaper for a truck to deliver across country," says Robert Krebs, CEO of Santa Fe Pacific. "Now we can do it faster and cheaper."

Demand for double-stacking containers on rail cars is so great that rail tunnels across the country are being expanded. For the first time in decades, tunnels are being built. A $190 million tunnel between Canada and the USA is under construction for the Canadian National Railways at Port Huron, Mich.

Demand for locomotives is so great that construction company Morrison Knudsen has gotten into the engine-building business. Last month, in an alliance with Caterpillar, it delivered the USA's first 5,000-horsepower locomotive, becoming a player in a business long dominated by General Electric and General Motors.

And demand is so great that railroads can't find enough workers. Just three years ago, railroads could call on almost 5,000 laid-off workers. Today, they can't find enough train engineers, conductors and support personnel.

What led to this?

▶ **Deregulation.** The Staggers Rail Act of 1980 did for railroads what deregulation did for airlines. It sparked competition and drove down rates for customers. Before Staggers, it was illegal for a railroad to promise a rebate on late deliveries because it skirted mandatory pricing rules. Now railroads can compete on prices, which is forcing them to be more efficient. "You have to be the low-cost producer. You have to have competitive prices to stay in this business," says Krebs.

> **"Once it was cheaper for a truck to deliver across country. Now we can do it faster and cheaper."**
>
> **— Robert Krebs, Chief Executive, Santa Fe Pacific**

▶ **Expansion.** Because of lower rail prices, more trucking companies are shipping trailers across country by rail, instead of driving them. This so-called "intermodal" shipping is cheaper than paying drivers for long hauls. It costs roughly 50 cents per mile to haul a trailer by train vs. $1 per mile by truck. Last year, trains hauled more than 7 million trailers and containers, vs. 4.5 million in 1984. This year, that number should top 8 million.

Railroads are scrambling to build and remodel rail yards to handle increased intermodal traffic. In May, Union Pacific opened the first phase of a 500-acre, $58 million rail yard in Livonia, La., that will handle 1,500 rail cars. Two weeks ago, Conrail opened a $15 million yard in Toledo, Ohio, to handle shipments of automobiles.

▶ **A strong economy.** As the economy has grown and demand for products increased, rail shipments have increased,

(cont.)

too. Higher demand for low sulfur coal, which burns cleaner than traditional coal, and demand for new cars and trucks also has helped rail traffic. Every 24 hours, 100 trains, each with at least 100 rail cars, pass through Gibbon, Neb., a major junction for Union Pacific's trains traveling across country. Many of them come from coal mines in Wyoming's Powder River basin. Merchandise traffic — which includes autos, auto parts, wood products, food, chemicals and fertilizer — is also up, according to Steve Lewins, an analyst with Gruntal & Co..

►**Technology.** Railroads are leaner, more efficient and safer these days, thanks to computers and high-tech communications systems. It once took 85 people, including dispatchers and signal people, to send a train across country. Today, it takes 20. The five-person train crew is down to two. The caboose is history, replaced by a box transmitting information electronically to the engineer.

Railroads have installed sensors about every 30 miles along their tracks to send computer information to the main dispatch office. Reader sensors identify every rail car. And hotbox sensors provide safety information when, for instance, equipment is dragging the tracks or brakes get overheated.

And coming: electronic brakes on freight cars that will help a train reduce speed in less time and cut turnaround time.

Twenty years ago, railroads gave customers a rough estimate of when a train would leave and an even rougher estimate of when it would arrive. The usual promise was "sometime Tuesday," says Tom White, of the Association of American Railroads.

Now, some railroads have on-time delivery rates of 90% or better.

Railroads have become so time-sensitive that automakers use trains to deliver parts to the factory door in as little as two hours before the part is needed on the assembly line.

Overnight delivery services, such as United Parcel Service, ship many of their semitrailers across country. In fact, Santa Fe's Willow Springs yard primarily will serve a $150 million UPS shipping facility, its largest in the country, scheduled to open in the spring next door to the rail yard.

Santa Fe finds itself in the midst of this rebirth. Its Corwith rail yard in nearby Chicago was so busy with intermodal traffic that the company had to open its Willow Springs facility early to ease the load.

Shelton, the operations manager at Willow Springs, calls his job a daily chess game. He can coordinate loading and unloading a 60-car train in two hours instead of the several hours, or days, it once took. Santa Fe promises that if it gets a trailer an hour and 45 minutes before departure, it will make the train.

And while the railroad relies on computers, telephones, video cameras and two-way radios to get trailers on and off a train, Shelton loads praise on his crew.

"I have to stroke their egos quite a bit," he says. "But they get the job done."

57

CAN EUROPE DELIVER?

UPS's push into Europe has highlighted the shortcomings of the local service sector

By Dana Milbank

RICHMOND, England—The Brown Shirts are on the march again in Europe. But this time, they come from Atlanta.

United Parcel Service of America Inc., the shipping giant, has charged into Europe over the past seven years, spending $1 billion to buy 16 delivery businesses. It has put its brown uniforms on 25,000 Europeans and sprayed its brown paint on 10,000 delivery trucks. Virtually overnight, "Big Brown" has become the largest delivery company in Europe.

As with much else on the Continent, though, the browning of Europe hasn't gone exactly as planned. Some of the surprises UPS ran into: indignation in France, when drivers were told they couldn't have wine with lunch; protests in Britain, when drivers' dogs were banned from delivery trucks; dismay in Spain, when it was found that the brown UPS trucks resembled the local hearses; and shock in Germany, when brown shirts were required for the first time since 1945.

Moreover, a deep recession delayed profit hopes—once pegged for 1994—to 1996, while a maze of tax, currency, labor and legal regulations belied Europe's claim to being a free market. UPS also has had trouble integrating its European businesses and imposing its American ways on local managers, several of whom have quit. UPS's overseas losses last year totaled $267 million—analysts believe its cumulative red ink will reach $1 billion before profits begin—as volume fell "substantially" below forecasts.

So why is UPS—along with many other U.S. businesses in the service sector—bothering?

Because in many ways, Europe is still virgin territory for service companies. Europe's goods-transport industry, for example, now accounts for only $73 billion of business annually (the figure is expected to hit $154 billion in six years). That compares with $374 billion a year currently in the U.S. Despite its profit setback, UPS Europe expects revenue—which hit $1.2 billion in 1993—to grow by 15% to 20% a year here. And it has already outlasted rival **Federal Express** Corp., which has largely retreated from Europe.

"If we could have known the challenges back in '86, I'm not sure we would have made the same decisions," says Theodore T. Gradolf, the American head of UPS's European-business development. "But now that we've weathered the problems, we're more convinced than ever. We're here for the long haul."

And so are a full range of U.S. service companies, from **Fidelity Investments** to **AT&T** Corp. to **Domino's Pizza** Inc.

Good News for Europe

Such moves into Europe are potentially good news for the Europeans, offering a possible economic boost and perhaps a way to reduce the European Union's 11% unemployment rate. While services represent some 54% of gross domestic product in the U.S. economy—and more than 72% of employment—services in Europe account for only about 48% of GDP and 65% of employment. That leaves room for growth in Europe.

"Services are really the only way to go," says Michael Hodges, a political economist at the London School of Economics.

Whether this potential will ever be realized, however, is far from certain. Hampering the spread of services and service-related jobs in Europe is the Continent's reluctance to part with its traditional ways of doing business—in particular, its state-owned monopolies and rigid work practices. The work force here resists part-time work, and claims stronger employment protection and higher nonwage costs than workers in the U.S. Without more-flexible labor practices, says Dr. Hodges, "it will be very difficult to see massive expansion of service industries."

In addition, European governments are wary of building up the service sector, in part because many service companies tend to bring with them low-wage jobs. European politicians, says Peter Daniels, director of the University of Birmingham's Service

Sector Research Unit, see manufacturing as "the engine of economic change" and services as "parasites." The EU governments may outdo one another with tax breaks for factories, but they won't give a pfennig for a UPS sorting center.

That's only part of what American companies must contend with as they try to crack the market. In addition to finding labor inflexible and immobile, they discover that currency, language and cultural differences—despite a good deal of talk and some tentative moves toward European unity—continue to split markets and prevent companies from building economies of scale. "Natural growth is so much easier in the States," says Julian Arkell, a service consultant to the EU based in Annecy, France. Because of the intra-European cultural and economic barriers, he explains, "an innovative product developed in one country is slow to take off in another."

Even so, Europe's underdeveloped service industries give American companies great potential. Though some Europeans, including **British Telecommunications** PLC and **Reuters Holdings** PLC, have expanded through Europe as rapidly as the Americans, the local competitors tend to be small and parochial. The standards of service, like the techniques for providing it, are well below American levels. What's more, U.S. service companies—because of their size, their American customer base and their experience in the more competitive U.S. market—have an edge over European rivals.

"Being a U.S. company with strong U.S. roots, we are head and shoulders above the ones who just come from Europe," says Geoffrey Carroll, the Brussels-based head of northern European operations for Electronic Data Systems, a **General Motors** Corp. subsidiary. "They really can't support a customer outside a certain country. If we take what we're doing in the U.S. and what we've learned in the U.S., we have more expertise at best practices."

Manpower Inc., the Milwaukee-based employment company, virtually created the temporary-help business in Europe. Here for decades, it is the largest such company and derives more than 40% of its world-wide revenue from Europe. Though U.S. service providers remain ahead in Europe, says Manpower President Mitchell Fromstein, "I think the gap is closing, and one of the things closing the gap is multinational companies."

In Europe, Manpower must contend with a host of barriers it doesn't face at home: expensive, government-mandated benefits; long vacations and maternity leaves; and tough restrictions on firing workers or employing temporary help. (Until recently, temps were illegal in Italy and Greece.) But the disadvantages for Manpower are outweighed by the weaker competition here.

Because of the company's U.S. ties, "we've been able to see trends and structure the business to meet those trends," says Lillian Bennett, chairman of Manpower's U.K. division. For example, Manpower made a huge investment in information-technology training 12 years ago; its U.K. rivals are only now beginning to do the same. And after being

pushed by the U.S. and Japan, Manpower's European offices joined the "total quality" movement in 1978--long before the craze hit Europe.

UPS's move to Europe was defensive: It didn't want to lose business from U.S. customers shipping overseas. It entered the market in 1976, with a German business it started from scratch. But with Memphis, Tenn.-based **Federal Express**, **DHL Worldwide Express** of Brussels and **TNT Express Worldwide** of Australia rushing into Europe, UPS decided to move more quickly and went on its buying spree. It now handles half a million packages a day here.

At its sorting center in Isleworth, near London's Heathrow Airport, the operation looks no different from one in Louisville, Ky. At 7 a.m. on a recent morning, its 44 brown trucks are being loaded by men in crisp brown uniforms using conveyer belts and computerized scanners. This morning, the operation is shipping some 4,500 packages-- including multivitamins to Nigeria; leather from New Jersey to Birmingham, England; an excavation machine from Japan to Israel; and blenders from the Netherlands to St. Albans, a suburb of London.

But while UPS operations may look the same in Europe, the company--like Manpower and the rest--faces problems that may be less common or even nonexistent in the U.S.: truck restrictions on weekends and holidays, low bridges and tunnels, widely varying weight regulations, terrible traffic and, in some places, limited highway systems and primitive airports with night curfews. And there are paper obstacles as well: Though most European nations belong to the free-trading European Economic Area, goods leaving the EU must be accompanied by a "single administrative document"--which, ironically, has eight parts. Even within the EU, large shippers must still report their shipments to the Brussels bureaucracy.

The 12 EU nations have nine different value-added tax rates among them, ranging from 15% to 25%, each in a different currency and all charged on international transport. This means that a customer in Liege, Belgium, for example, could be within minutes of a UPS center across the border in Germany. But the customer must call Brussels for a pickup, because it couldn't reclaim the VAT if it paid for the shipment in German marks rather than Belgian francs.

All this bureaucracy adds nearly 30% to UPS's costs, a fact that helps to explain why its shipping prices here are about 30% higher than in the U.S. That's better than before customs disappeared within Europe, when costs were 30% higher still because of border delays. Nevertheless, says Tony Walford, UPS Europe's logistics manager, "it's a hell of a long way from a single market."

119

(cont.)

Perhaps most frustrating of all are Europe's rigid labor laws. In the U.S., UPS relies on many part-time workers and uses temporary layoffs if business is slow. Europeans resist part-time work, and some countries forbid temporary layoffs. So when UPS Europe's business plunges during vacation time in August, its workers are paid to twiddle their thumbs; UPS's workers in Germany, meanwhile, get six weeks of vacation. "It's a fixed-cost operation," says Terry L. Gantt, the company's U.K. operations director. "It's a lot more planning at longer range."

This requires innovation. In Italy, where nonwage costs add 40% to the labor bill, UPS gets around the requirement by hiring self-employed drivers. Each owns his own vehicle and signs a contract in which he agrees to paint it brown and wear the brown uniform. When angry French workers blocked some of the country's highways last year in a national protest, UPS arranged to ship its packages to Spain by ferry. During a German national strike in 1992, UPS moved its air hub from Cologne to London for two nights.

Moving to Europe has also forced the 87-year-old company to re-examine its roots and business style. Its European workers, for instance, didn't understand why it cared so much about having them shave their beards, shine their shoes and wash the trucks each day. The company also couldn't find a way to translate "United Parcel Service" into foreign languages while still keeping the UPS initials. Its name recognition was virtually zero. "We couldn't say, 'Here we are, we're UPS—give us the packages, please,'" says Mr. Walford, the logistics manager. When the company tried to order stationery in London, the printer hadn't heard of UPS and said the $18 billion-a-year multinational would have to pay in cash.

So UPS started fresh. It translated its sales and training materials into 12 languages. In non-English-speaking countries, it called itself simply UPS. After realizing that its traditional method of charging by weight was causing it to get stuck hauling bulky guitars and hoola-hoops, UPS quickly switched to the European method of charging by volume. It concentrated on the business-to-business market, which it figured would be easier to crack, and it launched a heavy campaign of television, print and outdoor advertising. In four years, UPS says, its "unprompted" brand awareness has grown to 40% from 5%.

But while being an American service company here requires adjustments, it also gives UPS an advantage. From its experience delivering nearly three billion packages a year, UPS has developed a system that is far more efficient than any in Europe. And because it made its name in the highly developed and competitive U.S. market, UPS had mastered shipping techniques that hadn't even occurred to European companies.

Hubs and Spokes

When UPS bought Carryfast of the U.K. in 1992, for example, the British company had no computers, no hub-and-spoke system, trucks that were too big for the job and an inefficient delivery record. "Handling packages was hand-to-hand combat," says Mr. Gantt, the U.K. operations director. UPS, by contrast, had been using the hub-and-spoke system since 1960 and was fully automated. In two years, UPS has improved Carryfast's productivity by 20% while increasing its international business.

To transfer its ways to the U.K., the company spent $9 million on new Mercedes trucks, all of them equipped with skylights, special cabin doors and lips on the interior shelves so that packages wouldn't shift around—just like its trucks in the U.S. Each driver now follows a "loop," with each street assigned a sequence number by industrial engineers working on computers. The Europeans have also learned to swallow some of the American-style customer-service mentality, accompanied by baffling abbreviations. UPS introduced OJS (on-the-job supervision) and required marketers to maintain a detailed MOP (master operating plan) for each VLM (very large multinational).

Many of UPS's European competitors are in the minor leagues. While guaranteed next-day delivery has been a fixture in the U.S. for 20 years, it didn't exist in Italy and Spain until UPS introduced the service in the past year or so. Greece still doesn't have that service. UPS's electronic scanner, which enables customers to track packages with a computer, was another new wrinkle in southern Europe.

UPS also found that its European competitors, traditionally tied to only one country, have been slow to take advantage of the common market. Europe's shippers are fragmented: While the U.S. package market is dominated by UPS and the U.S. Postal Service, the top eight companies in Europe control only 32% of the market; UPS, the leader, has a share of only a few percentage points. Europeans also shy away from offering a full range of services, limiting themselves either to express-mail documents or heavy packages. "The funny thing about the European companies is they have more cultural barriers than American companies," says Mr. Walford.

That was the experience at **Courtaulds Textiles** PLC in Britain. Its Gossard unit, a bra maker, had to rely on several carriers to get its goods to Europe. Some would take packages, others would take documents, and not all would serve every country. UPS offered Gossard one-stop shopping. It also threw in its computer tracking system and shipped its bras to East Asia. Gossard dropped the others for UPS. The competitors "provide only what they want to provide," says John Brown, Gossard's export administration manager.

Deep Pockets

But UPS's chief advantage as a U.S. company is its parent company's deep pockets and customer list of American multinationals. Unlike Federal Express, which pulled the plug on its European operations in 1992, amid losses and disappointing growth rates, UPS, which isn't publicly traded, was able to take a longer view. It also found a friendly reception from the U.S. companies already in Europe.

In the past, GM's after-market business relied on warehouses in each country and local trucking companies to ship its goods. But when Europe's internal customs operations were dismantled, GM decided to integrate its warehouses for pan-European distribution, and the national shippers couldn't keep pace.

After ruling out the smaller companies, GM narrowed its choice to UPS, DHL and TNT. But the Australian and Belgian companies couldn't match their American competitor's service and technology. "Being American, they really have the focus on the customer," says Stephan Freichel, logistics manager for GM's after-market business. "As long as the American company has that strong service focus and that integrated approach, they've definitely got a sustainable competitive advantage."

To keep its American customers, UPS now offers services in Europe it doesn't even have at home. The company opened a warehouse in the Netherlands for its customers to use. For one U.S. electronics customer, UPS actually assembles mobile phones after collecting parts from around the world. UPS even handles repairs for Samsonite's luggage in Europe.

Courting its compatriots pays off. Of UPS's largest customers in Europe, 30% are U.S. multinationals. Most of them were UPS customers from the States. Says Mr. Walford, "We come from the same club." ▦

MR. MILBANK IS A STAFF REPORTER IN THE WALL STREET JOURNAL'S LONDON BUREAU.

58

Firm takes season rush in stride

By Ellen Neuborne
USA TODAY

PORTLAND, Maine — Beth Lucas never thought she'd be using her brand-new degree in Japanese to sell Wicked Good Slippers.

But Lucas, 22, works the second shift at L.L. Bean, where her language skills are critical. She's a phone rep in the catalog's fast-growing international division. And this evening, she's helping a customer from Osaka, Japan, buy $3,000 of merchandise.

The caller orders more than 60 items, ranging from a Scotch Plaid Shirt to a black-and-gold dog bed monogrammed with the name "Cha Cha." And Wicked Good slippers — suede leather outer soles with plush lining.

The conversation is entirely in Japanese, sprinkled with a few untranslatable words such as "backordered" and "Gore-Tex." Half-an-hour later, Lucas is done. "That's typical," she says of the length and price of the order. "I think he was putting in the orders for everyone in his office."

By the time she finishes speaking, her phone rings again.

International is just one of the hot spots at L.L. Bean this time of year. In December, when 25% of the year's $890 million business will get done, the phone staff triples to more than 3,000; incoming calls can top 150,000 a day, and 200 packages a minute stream off conveyor belts.

Amid this frenzy, Bean employees are under strict orders to convey nothing but calm and competence to the customers.

Even in case of a fire drill, posted signs instruct phone reps to obey the drill, return to phones and apologize for the delay.

Christmas is coming. You may be panicked, but don't worry. Everything here is under control.

Behind the scenes at L.L. Bean, you can see just how much work and logistical gymnastics go into making you feel that way, no matter what language you speak, where you are calling from, or how close to Christmas you place your order.

Nowhere is that more obvious than here in the main phone center in Portland. In the shell of what used to be a Woolworth store, up to 800 phone reps at a time work the front lines.

Most calls come in Monday mornings. (Monday, Dec. 6, was the year's biggest day with 156,437 calls.) The room hums with the murmur and tap-tapping of reps at their keyboards.

Every inch of space in the center is pressed into service this time of year: training classrooms, the conference room.

A group known as the "Break Team" moves through the maze of partitions to take over as other reps go on break. The average phone rep takes 100 calls a day.

At station S-13224, three-year veteran Debbie Auclair demonstrates her calming skills. A woman on the phone from Berlin, Conn., has been told the item she wants — a Northwoods Flannel Shirt, Size XL, in teal, is backordered.

"Oh no ... oh dear." The caller is at a loss.

"Now, it's coming in, but that might be close for Christmas," Auclair says in a low, sweet voice.

"Yes. You guys are so good about delivery I thought I could wait till the last minute," the caller says.

"Oh yes, I understand. Well, several other colors are available in the Northwoods Flannel Shirt, in the size you want. I have red-and-black available. I show white-and-black."

"Hmmm. ... I do like the red-and-black."

"That's a good color," reassures Auclair.

The caller is relieved. "Good, I'll take the red-and-black."

Tone of voice is key, Auclair says. "You have to keep a light, sense of humor in your tone. That relaxes the customer. You don't ever want them to be nervous about their order."

On the next call, a woman from Franklin, Mass., orders five items, three to be sent to in-laws in Chicago, in two separate boxes. Auclair handles the order and hangs up before tackling the extra computer task of arranging appropriate gift boxes.

"I could have done this part while she was still on the phone, but that would have taken extra time," she says. "A caller gets nervous if things are taking a while, if they hear too much silence on the line. They start to worry."

Across the parking lot is the international division, a much smaller but growing part of 81-year-old L.L. Bean. International will make up 10% to 13% of company revenue this year. That's doubled from last year. L.L. Bean has opened two stores in Japan since 1992 and plans a third in 1994.

The 200 reps here use the same equipment — headsets and terminals connected to a mainframe computer — plus a few tricks of the international trade.

John Olson's work area is peppered with dictionaries: *500 French Verbs; Webster's Compact Japanese Dictionary;* a folder listing exchange rates and duties of a dozen countries.

"When this phone rings it could be anyone," Olson explains.

It could be royalty. The bulletin board boasts a recent fax order from Britain's Prince Andrew. Among his items: a burgundy Chamois shirt. The address in italic at the top of the form: *Andrew, Duke of York, Buckingham Palace, London.*

Key to working here: being able to say "Please turn on your fax machine" in Japanese. Japan makes up 70% of L.L. Bean's international business. Nearly a third is handled by fax.

Fourteen languages are spoken here; 11 reps speak Japanese. For the rest, international manager Bob Schmidt has the fax phrase in phonetic Japanese posted on a pillar in the room.

Once the orders are taken, the computer zaps them 20 miles to Freeport and the 625,000 square-foot distribution center.

This center is so well known for its efficiency that L.L. Bean receives hundreds of requests for tours every year.

"They want to know the secret. They want to know where is the secret Bean dust we sprinkle on everyone to get it right," says Scott Bryant, vice president of customer satisfaction.

Here is the entire inventory of L.L. Bean — as many as 10 million items during this busy time of year.

L.L. Bean estimates "pickers" — employees who walk the maze of shelves fetching items — put in 12 miles a day.

During the holiday season, 5 million orders will be filled from this center, most shipped the day they're received. A computer tracks each one. After it's picked, it's sent to one of more than 100 packers, wrapped in paper or cardboard, addressed with a coded label and sent to a conveyor belt.

Packages then go to Federal Express, which as of this year is L.L. Bean's primary delivery company. Last Monday, the distribution center had its biggest shipping day: 160,000 packages left the loading docks, 20,000 more than last year's record.

(cont.)

Amid the crush, what's the No. 1 thing customer satisfaction chief Bryant worries about between now and the Big Day?

Snow. A couple of feet from a good Maine blizzard could keep phone reps from getting to work and trap the trucks.

"I do watch the Weather Channel," says Bryant. "And I wor-

"I do watch the Weather Channel," says Bryant. "And I worry a lot."

59

JAPAN BEGINS TO OPEN THE DOOR TO FOREIGNERS, A LITTLE

Notoriously tight distribution system shifts with the times.

By Dave Barrager

It's a long way from Japan to Arkansas. But for years, Springdale, Ark.-based Tyson Foods has been bringing in its biggest customers from Japan, one at a time, to tour its facilities, taste new products Tyson is developing and offer advice. It's only one part of the food company's strategy for cracking the notoriously difficult Japanese market.

"We have R&D staff specifically assigned to developing products for Japan," Tyson chairman Don Tyson said. The company has developed a series of products for Japan. And it maintains daily contact with Tokyo.

"It's a long-term time frame," Tyson said. But, "once a Japanese company commits, normally, you've get a customer for the long term."

It's taken 15 years. But Tyson, which entered the market focusing on food service, has made it. And recent changes point to the conclusion that Japan's notorious *keiretsu* system may be opening up a little more to companies wishing to enter the market.

In a meeting last month of the Tokyo Chamber of Commerce (TCCI) and the American Chamber of Commerce, the TCCI beat the drum for a new objective to bring more products tailored for specific niche markets to store shelves--a shift from the usual mass-market, me-too products. For American producers, it means more opportunity to get into store shelves in Japan. The Japanese government, for its part, is hoping niche products will lure Japanese consumers back into stores. After the buying binge in the 1980s and the economic downturn of the '90s, Japanese consumers have grown more reluctant to buy, and--equally worrying to retailers--adopted a blase "seen it, done it" attitude to products.

The niche-product switch is one of several reasons for guarded optimism for American companies. *Teiban*, the old system under which retailers reviewed new-product proposals twice a year with its wholesalers, is

shifting, too.

Japanese chains traditionally have used the sessions, in March and September, to make decisions from whether or not to carry a product to how many stores to stock it in.

"Now stores use POS computer tracking systems to check product performance from month to month," said Larry Davis Blagg, managing director of Market Makers Inc., a marketing and sales consulting firm specializing in market development programs for consumer and agricultural products. "If something's not selling, they drop it and take on a new product." Convenience stores are also developing their own wholesale systems to make sure they have the "products they want when they want them," Blagg said.

Michael V. Aylott, president of Marion Merrell Dow K.K., said that where in the past it took 140 wholesalers to achieve nationwide distribution, new laws governing the pharmaceutical industry make it possible to achieve 95% market penetration with just 20 wholesalers.

Comparative ads, price competition and discount shopping--anathema in Japan a few years ago--have surfaced as attention-getting lures to hook the reluctant Japanese consumer. Big retailers such as Daiei, Jusco and Seiyu are promoting their house-brand products. Retailers and wholesalers, while, as always, averse to risk, are seeking out cheaper sources of proven products. The result is expected to help foreign firms that want to enter the market.

Getting product distribution in Japan has always been far from simple. The country's distribution structure is dominated by the *keiretsu*, a deep-rooted system of powerful interlinked business groups, based on capital investment, contractual relationship or some combination of the two.

Foreign marketers who approach big *keiretsu*-linked retailers are told to take their product to a wholesaler.

The wholesaler provides advantages that foreign firms can't provide: the back-room inventory that stores in cramped Tokyo don't have, delivery of even one or two items a day, and assistance with inventory counting and special sales efforts.

Over 70% of food sales to retailers pass through the keiretsu-dominant import/wholesale network.

"There can be no question the economic dominance of the Big Six is greater than before the war," said Rikkyo University economics professor Yoshinari Maruyama in "The Big Six Horizontal Keiretsu" in *Japan Quarterly* last year.

The system, as one American businessman puts it, "encourages large makers to get larger and prevents small ones from getting bigger." Large companies can parlay their brand image to gain access to importers, to create a formidable presence. Large foreign companies also can more easily afford to have their own office and staff in Japan, giving them an advantage in marketing the product, since they don't have to leave everything to a *keiretsu* importer or wholesaler who may lack the imagination and savvy to present the product most effectively.

The result leaves smaller foreign companies, like their small, Japanese counterparts, at a disadvantage trying to woo retail outlets committed to giant makers and wholesalers.

The *keiretsu* have had an enormous impact on the market. They have inveighed against competitive techniques such as negative or comparative advertising, sales promotions that might start a price war, and against introducing products that upset the neighborhood market "harmony."

Companies that did not meet the standard were not taken in, or--if they transgressed once in--dropped or had their price slashed. A very low price, in the Japanese consumer mind, meant low quality.

Beyond those barriers, were Japan's government regulations. Foreign firms, including those well-established in Japan, need numerous approvals and licenses from various agencies to be able to offer full product lines from fixed retail outlets.

Japanese regulations restrict sales incentives such as discounts and premiums offered to consumers, distributors and retailers--practices essential to product introductions in the U.S.

The retail environment has been equally restrictive. It used to take up to 10 years to get government approval to open a large store. Revisions in the Large-Scale Retail Store Law (LSRSL) have removed some of the obstacles--but the process is still slow compared to the U.S. A law passed by the Japanese Diet in May 1992 requires that applications for new stores be approved or rejected within one year.

Still, marketers and consultants say that the most important requirements for breaking the market are initiative and creativity--in considerable amounts. Market Makers' Blagg cites Ore-Ida foods. The first wholesaler "said the package was too big and the product was too salty for Japan," he said. So the American team went to supermarkets, and asked them to recommend wholesalers "they wanted to use." Market Makers and Ore-Ida went to the wholesalers the supermarkets recommended, "building up to 11 of them, who in turn built up the distribution."

Ore-Ida's sales grew from 30,000 cases a year to 1 million cases a year within four years, with the shift in strategy.

The California Raisin Advisory Board formed its own export trading company three years ago as a cooperative effort by all industry members to market a single brand in Japan. In three years, the California ZUN Raisin brand has seen its share of market grow from zero to 38%.

Ken Barnum, division manager, import sales division, Nippon Polaroid Corp., recommends foreign firms circumvent *keiretsu* dominance by forging links with midsize wholesalers. Polaroid followed that route 30 years ago.

Barnum said that midsize Japanese wholesalers are "more like U.S. wholesalers in that they don't make and sell their own private-label products." They have bilingual staff, send faxes in English and do considerable business in such markets as Hong Kong and Singapore.

To Don Tyson, though, the key is still listening to the market and responding. "They had a demand for exact sizing that the American market didn't have, so we had to put in additional machinery and people," Tyson said.

The company sells a range of products from its mainstay chicken to shrimp, pork, beef and tortillas (Tyson is a major supplier to Mexican restaurants in Japan). It's expanding into processed and frozen processed foods.

"They systematically established a firm presence," Blagg said. "Then they custom-made products for the food-service industry in Japan. Gave them exactly what they wanted."

Tyson said, "Tell yourself you're going to stay awhile. A lot of the success we've had has come because we've been here awhile. We know the people. They've been to Arkansas."

Dave Barrager is a Tokyo-based journalist who covers business issues.

Reprinted from the August 2, 1993 issue of *Brandweek.* © 1993 ASM Communications, Inc. Used with permission from *Brandweek.*

60

Retail Combat

Warehouse-Club War Leaves Few Standing, And They Are Bruised

Wal-Mart and Price-Costco Survive Bitter U.S. Clash, Will Resume It in Mexico

An Intense Game of Chicken

By Bob Ortega
Staff Reporter of The Wall Street Journal

Anyone who doubts what a cutthroat business discount retailing has become need only look at the world of warehouse clubs today.

In a war of attrition stretching from Maine to Mexicali, the operators of the sprawling warehouse stores have just seen their numbers whittled mercilessly from eight to three — or only two if counting just those chains that operate nationwide. The struggle was capped two weeks ago when Kmart Corp., worn down by competition that left scant room for profits, gave up on the business and agreed to sell most of its remaining outlets to Wal-Mart Stores Inc.

But now the survivors — Wal-Mart's Sam's Club, plus a merged Price Co. and Costco and the regional B.J.'s chain — face new challenges. Though they have knocked off several rivals, they did so partly by constantly attacking the others on their own turf, and as a result now find themselves overbuilt in many markets and still having to struggle head-to-head in many places. Worse, they must search for new revenue streams to revive a suddenly flagging growth in the industry.

No Holds Barred

Wal-Mart emerges as one clear, if battered, winner of the warehouse-club wars. And a close look at the battle helps explain the methods Wal-Mart uses to stay atop the retail world — among them remorseless price-slashing, an in-your-face strategy of building or relocating stores to compete directly with interlopers, and sometimes hiring away rivals' employees to get an edge in local markets. In the end, the industry's acknowledged low-cost operator uses its size and market clout to bleed rivals dry.

"When Sam's senses weakness, they've always been very aggressive," says Linda T. Kristiansen, an analyst for Wertheim Schroder & Co., alluding to Wal-Mart's recent purchase of Pace warehouse stores

from Kmart, along with its coveted membership list. "Pace was a weakened operator and Sam's just gave them the kick to finish them off."

For most of the 19 years since Price Co. founder Sol Price opened the first warehouse club, rival chains spread quickly through virgin territory. The concept was simple: Members, mostly small businesses, would pay annual dues of $25 to $50 for the privilege of buying goods in bulk at deep discounts from cavernous, low-overhead stores. By 1991, the industry had become a behemoth with yearly sales of $26.3 billion and a growth rate of 36%.

But most markets could support only a small number of the huge stores, and the major competitors continued to expand aggressively. Inevitably, they began to butt heads in major markets, in ways that sometimes seemed to defy logic. After Pace opened Puerto Rico's first warehouse club, in Bayamon, Sam's opened the second warehouse club on the island — also in Bayamon. "There are plenty of other cities in Puerto Rico," notes Bruce Quinnell, chief financial officer of Pace. "It was not a coincidence."

Meanwhile, in tiny El Centro, Calif., Sam's, Pace and Costco Wholesale Corp. all opened stores within months of each other last year. "In an area with a population base of 75,000," says Thomas Vander Ark, former vice president of strategic planning and marketing for Pace, "nobody flinched." Likewise, Costco invaded Pace's turf in Anchorage, Alaska, by building not one but two stores; Pace retaliated with another new store this year, giving the Alaskan city of 250,000 as many warehouse stores as Denver, a city six times its size, had in 1991.

"It was just a billion-dollar game of chicken," Mr. Vander Ark says.

Sons of Sam's

And in retailing, nobody plays that game better than Wal-Mart. The Bentonville, Ark., company simply won't yield to competitors, even if it means building Sam's Clubs that take sales from other Sam's stores in the area. Retail consultant Peter Monash estimates that Sam's Club cannibalizes itself in 45% of its markets in quest of a dominant market share.

Pace used the same strategy to drive Costco out of Tampa, Fla., says Dan Doerflein, Pace's former senior vice president of merchandising. But it didn't have the staying power to make the strategy work against Sam's in Atlanta. "We weren't successful, because Sam's came in anyway with a large number of warehouses," he recalls, and had the deep pockets and patience to absorb losses for as long as necessary.

As soon as it arrived, Sam's started slashing prices. Pace concluded that its foe had sliced its gross profit margins in that market to below 6%, from the more

usual 9%, says Mr. Vander Ark. Sam's could afford it, because it was pulling huge amounts of money out of Dallas and Houston, where its hold on the market was uncontested. Sam's Clubs in Texas had higher prices, with sales cracking $100 million a year per store, more than double the national average for Sam's Clubs.

So Pace decided to invade those markets, convinced it could make a profit and force Wal-Mart to slash margins there. "It was a defensive move for us," says Charles Steinbrueck, former Pace chief executive.

It was also a big mistake.

"We thought we'd found some geographic voids" in the market, Mr. Steinbrueck says, "so we could be sure not to locate near a Sam's." But Sam's, which already had six clubs in the Dallas area, promptly added several more. As it found out where Pace was building clubs, Sam's even relocated stores to go toe-to-toe with the invader.

Likewise, Price's first store in north Dallas was tough to spot from the nearby expressway because drivers' views were blocked by a huge billboard directing them to the nearby — and brand new — Sam's Club, or, as the billboard put it in a pointed appeal to Texas chauvinism, "the original Texas club." The Price Club outlet lasted 15 months, closing in September.

Mr. Steinbrueck says Pace, at great cost, succeeded in driving down Sam's Clubs' margins, but didn't carve out its own profitable niche. Mr. Doerflein, the former Pace merchandising executive, says that "new [Pace] management, in an effort to protect its resources for other markets, chose to bail out." Mr. Doerflein believes the stores would have been profitable in four or five years, but he concedes that Sam's "had 200 other locations where their margins stayed up, margins they could use to subsidize other locations."

But the battle proved costly even to the winners. Take sales at stores open a year or more. At Sam's Club, such sales had grown 19% in the first half of fiscal 1991, gained only 12% in the first half of fiscal 1992 and then dropped 2% in the first half of fiscal 1993. At Costco, the comparable-sales gains slid from 19% to 11% to 4%; Price went from a 2.6% gain to a 3.6% rise to a drop of 5.9%.

Elsewhere, the battle took on other dimensions. A new Sam's Club in Colorado Springs, Colo., for example, promptly hired as its manager the assistant manager of a nearby Pace Club. "He knew all the members, the prices, our cost structure, our strategy — everything," says Mr. Vander Ark, who acknowledges that in other cases, Pace did the same thing. Sam's quickly made inroads on the Pace store, and lured away some big-spending business members, he says.

"The 'to die for' information was a competitor's membership list," Mr.

(cont.)

Vander Ark adds. He maintains that all the chains looked for sources for that information. Herb Zarkin, president and chief executive officer of Waban Inc., the Natick, Mass., operator of the regional, 49-unit B.J.'s Wholesale Club chain, says that on several occasions people B.J.'s hired from competitors offered to bring membership lists with them—though he says B.J.'s has always responded that "we don't want it."

People in the industry also accuse each other of using underhanded tactics to steal customers. Pace CFO Mr. Quinnell says that after Kmart initially sold 14 Pace warehouse clubs to Wal-Mart last May, for example, there was a rash of Wal-Mart marketers targeting members of remaining Pace clubs, "telling them they ought to sign up with them because we'd soon be going out of business."

But, as with other gripes—charges that Wal-Mart mischaracterized competitor's prices in ads, for example — "when we complained, it stopped," Mr. Quinnell says. "I don't think it was a corporate philosophy so much as aggressive managers trying to win." Don Shinkle, Wal-Mart's vice president of corporate affairs, says allegations that Wal-Mart used such tactics are "preposterous." He adds, "We don't conduct business that way."

One persistent gripe is that Sam's Club engages in predatory pricing. Echoing charges made in a recent Arkansas state-court suit, Waban's Mr. Zarkin asserts that Sam's regularly sells items below its cost "in hopes of driving you out of business." Wal-Mart is currently appealing a judgment in the case awarding three Conway, Ark., pharmacies $290,407 in damages.

In Wal-Mart's Sam's Club in Delran, N.J., Mr. Zarkin contends, the company began selling bulk packages of candy bars such as M&Ms and Mars bars at what he believes was a loss. "We went into the Sam's and bought thousands of dollars of candy and sold them ourselves at the price we paid until they got the message," he says. Whenever Sam's sells below cost near a B.J.'s, he says, "we send people over to buy them out, and then sell the merchandise at their price." A spokesman says Wal-Mart sometimes sells below cost, but not with the intent to drive competitors out of business.

The warehouse-club feeding frenzy has also included plenty of real-estate intrigue. Since the first club into a market has a competitive edge — who wants to shell out more dues for the privilege of shopping at another store with the same stuff? — getting to a prime location first is a matter of urgency. "It wasn't uncommon for several of us to helicopter in to the same intersection on the same day, and all be competing with the landowner for the same piece of dirt," says Mr. Vander Ark.

In Paramus, N.J., Mr. Zarkin of B.J.'s bid what he considered a "more than fair price" for a site that had some traffic problems (no left turn out of the parking lot), only to be outbid mightily by Pace. He thinks Pace often bid too much, while Wal-Mart, among others, has been more prudent.

That doesn't mean doing a deal is easy. In negotiations for sites, "Wal-Mart just grinds you and grinds you down, until I was surprised I was still more than three feet tall," says William Buettner, a vice president for Denver-based developer Antonoff Miller Properties Inc. It haggled with Wal-Mart for five months over a piece of land in Billings, Mont. "They don't know they've got the best deal they can get until they're tap-dancing on your tombstone," Mr. Buettner says.

Frustrated, Mr. Buettner cajoled a bid on the site out of Costco. Then, he says, at a charity event one of Antonoff Miller's owners "casually" mentioned the Wal-Mart talks to a Pace acquaintance. Just days before the Wal-Mart deal was to be signed, Pace rushed in with a better offer for the development rights, which Antonoff Miller accepted. While he won't reveal the amount, he says Pace paid half-again what the site would have leased for under normal circumstances.

Wal-Mart executives were livid, Mr. Buettner says: "I'd have the life expectancy of a second lieutenant in combat if I went into Bentonville today."

As it happened, Pace backed out when it discovered Costco had acquired a lot across the street, on which it could build sooner because the lot needed less work.

Wal-Mart soon exacted its revenge. After a business fronting for Costco signed an agreement to acquire a lot in Great Falls, Mont., according to a suit filed in state court there by Costco, the owner repudiated the agreement, rejected the company's $10,000 check for earnest money and conveyed the lot to Wal-Mart. Wal-Mart broke ground on a Sam's Club the next day — a day that dawned at eight degrees above zero.

Costco's suit accuses Wal-Mart of unlawful interference with its contract. Wal-Mart declines comment because the matter is in court. The property owner, William G. Shull, didn't return phone calls.

Eventually, Pace faltered. A battle like this calls for subsidizing low prices in new cities with profits from markets where one is dominant, but Pace had few such markets. The Kmart unit also couldn't match Sam's distribution system, which gets reordered goods to stores in as little as 24 hours.

In May, Kmart sold 14 Pace stores to Wal-Mart. In June, Price and Costco said they would merge (into what's now Price-Costco Inc.). On Nov. 2, Wal-Mart agreed to buy 91 more Pace stores. That leaves Kmart with 22 Pace stores, which it plans to close on Dec. 24.

As the battlefield smoke clears with Sam's Club and the new Price-Costco left standing, analysts expect some easing of the competition in most cities. But there will be no peace in the huge Southern California market. It was long a Price stronghold, but Wal-Mart has parachuted in by buying Pace's 21 stores there. Now both Wal-Mart and Price-Costco are building several more.

Both national chains also have plunged into the wide-open Mexican market. They are ringing up strong sales from clubs in Mexico City and laying plans to blitz the rest of the country.

Price-Costco, meanwhile, is experimenting with mini-warehouses for small markets. And Wal-Mart is setting up a data-processing system that will allow it to grant credit for the first time, seeking an edge with the relatively untapped market of government and big-company procurement.

Today, Price-Costco has 210 warehouse stores and Sam's has 382. Mr. Steinbrueck, the former Pace CEO, thinks the ultimate advantage remains Wal-Mart's, simply because it keeps its costs so low. "Price-Costco took a major step by combining," he said, "but Sam's is still a step up."

61

IT'S GETTING CROWDED ON LINE

CompuServe, Prodigy, and America Online get ready to face aggressive newcomers such as Microsoft

By the end of the year, some 2.3 million American families are expected to bring home a new personal computer. This will make the 1994 holiday season the most joyous ever for PC makers. It should also warm the hearts of executives at CompuServe, Prodigy, and America Online, because recorded on the hard drives of most of those PCs will be software for logging into on-line services. It's a new twist on the gift that keeps on giving: Thousands of new subscribers will pay month after month to browse news, engage in on-line chats, shop, and swap E-mail.

But a happy holiday may be followed by a sobering new year. While the big three of consumer on-line services have done the spadework to cultivate the market and are beginning to enjoy the rewards, none has a truly dominant position. CompuServe, the venerable pioneer, has nearly 2.4 million subscribers worldwide, but most of them are professional or business accounts. Prodigy, a joint venture of IBM and Sears, Roebuck & Co., has 2 million subscribers but is still running up losses. And while AOL has doubled to over 1 million subscribers this year, it's still a distant third.

"TOO EXPENSIVE." Now, all three are scrambling—cutting prices, adding features, dressing up their appearance, and generally getting ready for a rougher road ahead. Why? Only 20% of the U.S. households that have PCs use on-line services, estimates Odyssey, a San Francisco market researcher. "The playing field is open to competition," says Odyssey President Nick Donatiello.

And the competition is coming, big time. Next year, PC industry superpower Microsoft Corp. is expected to launch its first on-line service, which is being developed under the code name Marvel. The company isn't saying much, but one software executive who has seen a proto-

type says: "Marvel is going to be very competitive." Because it's written for the powerful new Microsoft Windows 95 operating system, which should be out next year, Marvel will let consumers download a file while continuing to browse, for example. And on-line rivals fear Microsoft will undercut them on price. "Generically speaking, on-line services are probably too expensive today," says Nathan Myhrvold, senior vice-president of Microsoft's Advanced Technology Group. "Assuming we do something, our prices will reflect that view."

Microsoft also has a potentially overwhelming advantage: It can build Marvel into Windows 95. In fact, software developers say some test copies already have a Marvel button. Some 6 million PC owners are expected to adopt Windows 95 in the first year, and rivals fear they'll automatically use Marvel. "Distribution channels and the advantages [Microsoft] has there are something to be concerned about," says Barry Berkov, vice-president of CompuServe Information Service, based in Columbus, Ohio. "We'll be out there with others to push for a level playing field," he says.

Microsoft isn't the only new player. Ziff-Davis Publishing Co. is getting ready to launch Interchange, an on-line service under development for more than two years. Ziff, which publishes a string of computer publications, including *PC Magazine*, is focusing on delivering magazines on line, a hot growth area for the three leaders lately. Its initial partners include Digital Ink, a subsidiary of Washington Post Co., and Cowles Media Co.

THE NET THREAT. Unlike the other services, says Michael Kollowich, president of Ziff-Davis Interactive, Interchange from the outset will let publishers display all the text and graphics from their printed products. Word of mouth for Interchange has been so strong that the company already has requests from 77,000 people to sign up for it.

Interchange could become a major player quickly, depending on what happens to the parent company. The Ziff family has put the entire company up for sale, but the nascent on-line service could be sold separately. "Interchange itself is

a very sought-after business," says Kollowich. One possible bidder is billionaire Paul Allen, a co-founder of Microsoft. Previously, Allen had sought a major stake in AOL but was stuck at 24.9% by the company's poison-pill antitakeover provision. He has since sold all his AOL holdings, and his multimedia publishing startup, Starwave Corp., is already working with Interchange to develop a sports-oriented section of the service. Kollowich's only comment: "Interchange will be in new hands shortly."

Another force to contend with could be Apple Computer Inc. The PC maker launched its eWorld service last June. But despite rave reviews for its entertaining and accessible cityscape metaphor for navigating the network, the system has not generated much traffic and only has about 50,000 subscribers. One big hang-up is that it only works with Apple Macintosh computers. But by year-end, every new Mac will have eWorld software built in, and next year, Apple plans a version for IBM-compatible PCs.

Of course, the biggest threat to the on-line empires is the Internet, a quasi-public network of computer networks reaching 20 million people worldwide. Hundreds of thousands of people are joining every month, and scores of start-ups are creating software and services to make the Net almost as easy to use as its commercial cousins.

Feeling the heat, the commercial services are scurrying to expand their connections to the Internet beyond basic E-mail. They're adding access to the Internet's bulletin boards, on-line libraries, and World Wide Web—a sub-network of computers that can dole out information in slick, graphical "pages."

So the big three keep retooling. Last month, Prodigy announced a new basic service: $9.95 a month for five hours of use. That's the same offer AOL makes. For the old $14.95 price, subscribers get unlimited use of any service except the newly added chat lines, the Eaasy Sabre airline-reservation system, and daytime access to Dow Jones News Service. This month, Prodigy plans to offer the service to Canadians as well as a World Wide Web site for Internet users. By

(cont.)

mid-1995, the company says it will deliver software to take full advantage of Windows graphics.

Meanwhile, AOL has announced its own price cut. As of Jan. 1, the company will slash hourly fees—what a customer pays after exhausting the five-hour monthly limit—by 16%, to $2.95 per hour. And to attract owners of new multimedia PCs, AOL on Oct. 24 began shipping new software that uses photos and sounds to guide cybernauts around the system. The company, based in Vienna, Va., is also adding more content and publications such as BUSINESS WEEK.

Even CompuServe, the grandfather of all on-line services, is spiffing up its act. The 15-year-old service has a new software release with "hyperlinks" that let subscribers click on a highlighted word to jump to another part of the service. In addition, it is adding magazines, including *Forbes* and a bunch of Time Inc. publications. It also is producing a multimedia CD-ROM to teach consumers the basics of CompuServe and sign them up for the service. The disk will come bundled with some multimedia computers and upgrade kits.

All these efforts should make cyberspace a friendlier place for consumers. But with the new rivals looming, it may never again feel homey for the big three.
By Paul M. Eng in New York, with bureau reports

The On-line Scoreboard

COMPANY	STRATEGY/FEATURES
AMERICA ONLINE	Has scheduled a 16% price cut for Jan. 1 to make the service more competitive. Strategic alliances with media companies have helped to double its membership base.
APPLE eWORLD	Its radically different interface uses buildings to create the atmosphere of a virtual town. So far, there's not much content behind the pretty face, and it's limited to the smaller Macintosh audience.
COMPUSERVE	Will try to leverage its huge database of information and vast international network to woo new subscribers.
ZIFF-DAVIS INTERCHANGE	Ziff is a household name among PC owners who read its magazines. In development for the past two years, Interchange is expected to go live by yearend.
MICROSOFT MARVEL	The much-rumored service that will supposedly come as part of the new Windows 95 operating system next year. Analysts speculate the service will start small, offering mostly product support.
PRODIGY	Has cut prices and added features such as real-time "chat" and magazines such as *Newsweek*. A new interface closer to the "look and feel" of the Windows operating system is due out by next year.

DATA: COMPANY REPORTS, BUSINESS WEEK

Reprinted from the November 7, 1994 issue of *Business Week* by special permission, copyright © 1994 by McGraw-Hill, Inc.

62

Marketers Shouldn't Give Up on Wholesalers Just Yet

By Bill Wyman

Food-industry observers were taken by surprise when the results of an Arthur Andersen study of the wholesale channel were released earlier this year. The study found wholesalers supply about 56% of total food-industry sales—a figure that's held steady for the past decade. The experts expected it would be lower. Direct shipments, meanwhile, were just 44% of the total.

Brand marketers should take notice. Many packaged-goods companies openly prefer to avoid working with wholesalers, and have all but convinced themselves that they need only be concerned about direct shipments to the top 10 chains. They complain that wholesalers make 34% of their profits from "inside margin" accrued from practices manufacturers are trying to banish, like forward buying, diverting and slotting fees. It's said that the wholesale system is cumbersome, complicated and uncomfortable to deal with compared to ER and other revolutions in distribution that are in the offing. To boot, the independent stores served by wholesalers are said to be a shrinking market.

I think wholesalers—a $230 billion industry—will remain a powerful force in food distribution. Moreover, I think they could be an outstanding opportunity for manufacturers. Sales to supermarkets by wholesalers have increased 5.6% a year over the past 10 years, compared to total retail store sales growth of 5%. Two of the top five direct buying accounts are wholesalers (SuperValu and Fleming). Every indication is that wholesalers have no intention of being plowed under by changing trade practices (though they *will* be forced to scramble to catch up with the changes in the manufacturer-retailer relationship).

Bill Wyman is a partner in Silvermine Group, a Westport, Conn., consulting firm.

What's essential is to make wholesalers a contributor to system efficiency. It's a tall order. But it's attainable. There's no reason why wholesalers must be a more expensive way of doing business. Keep in mind that wholesalers' warehouse and transportation expenses total about 1.9% of net retail sales, comparing favorably to 2.56% for self-distributing chains. The trouble spot is easy to spot. It's the inside

They still account for 56% of food-industry sales, and—with many companies focused on direct-to-store sales—they're an opportunity.

margin. If that 34% were reduced, the cost of doing buisness with wholesalers and chains would be about the same.

Maximizing the effectiveness of the wholesale channel will require efforts by all parties. Wholesalers, for example, could create new profit centers through more effective negotiations with manufacturers, charging more at retail and implementing new pricing structures that put a premium on slow-moving items while discounting the fast movers.

Wholesalers might also earn fees by reducing delivery costs via DSD, cross-docking or continuous replenishment programs. They also could provide consolidation services that combine non-competitive products into full truckloads or ship slower moving products on a geographic basis. With the proper investments in new technologies, and an innovative outlook, wholesalers can find a lot of ways to add value to their services.

Delivering the right goods to the right stores at the right cost through better

management of distribution and information networks is one step. Wholesalers also must become more involved in creating category management, by market pricing strategies and consumer micromarketing programs. Wholesalers account for only 19% of manufacturer alliances and 12% of category management programs. Wholesalers need support from manufacturers if this is to change, and it is in the best interest of manufacturers to provide the necessary help.

Manufacturers could commit higher levels of talent and resources to the wholesale system. The typical sales manager in wholesale has three to five years experience today, v. 10-15 years in the direct channel. Some confectionary manufacturers have begun to put more sophisticated talent and programs against wholesaler-supplied accounts, but most categories are unattended.

Even the most powerful brands are feeling competitive heat these days. The impetus for smaller manufacturers is still more urgent. Pushed from play in large chains by larger manufacturers' category management, strategic alliances and "partnering" activities, and pressured further by premium private label and ebbing consumer loyalties, secondary brands' best hope for growth and survival may be through wholesalers. Through the wholesale system, they can stand out from the crowd, and make headway against larger competitors whose full attentions are focused on direct chain accounts.

With brands under siege, and everyone pouring energy into finding new competitive advantages, manufacturers literally cannot afford to overlook the potential of the wholesale channel. ■

Reprinted from the July 5, 1993 issue of *Brandweek,* © 1993 ASM Communications, Inc. Used with permission from *Brandweek.*

Promotion

63

Cow-ering From Dairy Products: Lactose Intolerance Marketing

The malady of the '90s, or a creation of Madison Ave?

By Judith Schwartz

No less an authority on trendiness than *Rolling Stone* has pronounced lactose intolerance the hot disorder of the '90s. But the companies that are marketing products to what suddenly became a $100 million market are out to prove it's no fad.

Virtually unknown five years ago, the lactose-intolerant condition is said to affect 50 million Americans.

The cause of the stomach discomfort some people feel after eating dairy products is low levels of the enzyme lactase, which is needed to digest the milk sugar, or lactose, found in dairy products. One remedy is to avoid dairy products altogether. But those sufferers loathe to renounce ice cream, pizza, or milkshakes can drink specially-treated milk or take an enzyme-based product along with dairy foods.

The story of the lactose intolerance category is a story of what happens when medicine and marketing converge. An ailment is "discovered" by the scientific community, and then an industry arises to address it. Doctors can recommend products to patients whose digestive troubles seem related to dairy intake. And the manufacturers have a lineup of endorsers from the medical and nutrition establishment.

The two leading products in the burgeoning enzyme market are Sterling Winthrop's Dairy Ease, and Lactaid, sold by a Johnson & Johnson subsidiary. According to LNA, Sterling Winthrop spent around $400,000 advertising Dairy Ease in 1993, while Johnson & Johnson put better than $7 million behind Lactaid milk, and caplets.

Still, much of the marketing effort has been in the form of public relations campaigns. Both companies offer information to the public, through 800 numbers and brochures, and have encouraged untold features in the media: health stories (on digestive ailments, food allergies vs. intolerance, the importance of calcium in the diet, etc.) and seasonal pieces with themes like "July is National Ice Cream month."

"Education will always be a cornerstone in this category," said Christopher Kilbane, manager of marketing communications for Sterling Winthrop in New York, which launched Dairy Ease in 1990. "Millions of consumers were suffering without knowing why, and the medical community didn't have much awareness either."

Critics, however, contend that the "education" campaign has been too effective, creating a "faddist fear" of dairy products that is unfounded.

Apparently, the lactose-intolerance backlash has begun.

And, the industry remains unfazed.

"The controversy was mainly focused on the prevalence issue," said Lori Katz, a spokeswoman for Lactaid. "Whether it's 30 million people or 50 million people who are lactose intolerant, that's still a lot of people."

The 50 million figure comes from the National Digestive Diseases Information Clearinghouse, which is part of the National Institutes of Health.

> **Virtually unknown five years ago, lactose-intolerance is said to affect 50 million. The market has grown to $100 million.**

Certainly, more people are buying products targeted to the lactose intolerant. The enzyme products, classified as a subgroup of the antacid category, generated $34.8 million in the 12 months ending January 1994, according to Towne-Oller, a subsidiary of Information Resources Inc. Lactaid led with a 62.8% share, followed by Dairy Ease at 29.9%, Thompson Medical's Lactogest at 2.5%, and private label brands with 4.4%. Overall, the caetegory dipped 1% last year, which could suggest a maturation of the market, or that consumers are shifting their allengiance to the treated milk products.

Information Resources reported that both Dairy Ease and Lactaid milk products showed double-digit increases in the past year, and sales are more than twice that of the enzyme supplements.

The supplements, which can be taken before or with a meal containing dairy foods, come in several forms: caplets, gel capsules, and chewable tablets. There are also liquid drops to be added to milk. Prices can vary according to outlet, but relief from dairy intolerance does not come cheap. A typical price is upwards of $6 for a package of 36 caplets or tablets. Sterling Winthrop considers its leading seller, the chewable tablet—which its chief competitor doesn't make—a marketing advantage.

"Many people who are lactose intolerant but don't know it have been taking chewable antacids, like Tums," said Kilbane. "One of the most difficult things in marketing is to create a behavior change. With our chewable product, the consumer doesn't have to alter behavior."

There's also the convenience issue of chewables: you don't have to take them with water. The tablets are designed to be mildly sweet, and to dissolve quickly, so as not to have an impact on food.

The rapidly-growing health food store market is getting into the lactose intolerance act.

"People who shop in health food stores tend to be more sophisticated about nutrition and food supplements and are likely to be loyal to a particular brand," said Jeff Hilton, vp of Nature's Way, Springville, Utah.

"The development of digestive enzyme products came out of the health food market," said Hilton. "The basic formulas are all every similar."

Solgar, a major natural vitamin brand, introduced Lactase 3500 last spring.

This product does have a point of differentiation: at 3500 Federal Chemical Code units of enzyme per tablet, it is strong enough so that one tablet should suffice.

"It's had nice, steady growth," said Rand Skolnick, ceo of Solgar Vitamin Company. Compared to mainstream consumer product companies, he said, "We don't make it look as pretty, but that

allows us to leave out a lot of artificial ingredients."

Consumers become aware of products like Solgar's through point of purchase displays, but largely through retailers, said Skolnick.

Lactose intolerance is widespread; 75% of all blacks, Jews, Native and Hispanic Americans have it. Among Asian Americans it's higher: 90%.

The industry leaders have done large-scale advertising. In "The Lactaid Challenge" campaign, Lactaid invites consumers to call 1-800-HELP-KIT for a free test kit, information and samples to determine if they are lactose intolerant. The "Challenge," which has been running more than a year, has been promoted though TV ads and public relations.

Dairy Ease has run television commercials emphasizing how its products "open up a whole new world."

One ad features a man who drives an ice cream truck who, until he discovered Dairy Ease, could never eat the treats he sold.

Television is great for building awareness out of the gate, but print is a better vehicle for the category since it is a complicated message," said Sterling Winthrop's Kilbane.

He added that free-standing inserts or the sides of milk cartons have also been used as print media.

Targeting the media isn't easy. While lactose intolerance is widespread, 75% of all African Americans, Jews, Native Americans and Hispanic Americans have the problem, according to the National Digestive Diseases Information Clearinghouse. Among Asian Americans the number is yet higher: 90%.

Rates are also high among the elderly, since the body's lactase production tends

to decrease with age. These figures are significant since, due to immigration and demographic patterns, many of these groups are expected to increase in population in the coming years.

The treated milk products are sold in quart containers along with other milk in the refrigerated section and are available in whole, skim and nonfat forms. Because the milk is distributed nationally from a single manufacturing source, it's cooked at ultra-high temperatures for a longer shelf life. This makes for an added product benefit.

"We regard the 45- to 60-day shelf life as an advantage, because if there's one lactose intolerant person in a family of five, it doesn't have to be replaced as often," said Kilbane.

Dairy Ease and Lactaid plan to extend their lines to other treated dairy products, including cottage cheese and ice cream, but these are yet to be announced. Dean Foods in Franklin Park, Ill., a licensee for Dairy Ease's milk products, makes a fresh milk product, Easy 2%, under its own label.

"We thought a fresh product would have greater appeal, especially in the Chicago area, which has large African American and Hispanic populations," said Dave Rotunno, director of marketing and administration for Dean Foods.

Easy 2% is distributed in Illinois, Wisconsin and parts of Indiana, Michigan and Iowa.

Dean Foods tested different versions and found that the 2% milk packaged in quarts was most widely accepted by the mainstream. The price is comparable to milk.

"We found people were willing to pay a little more, but not a lot more," said Rotunno.

The company introduced Easy 2% five years ago, and put a lot of effort into public relations and education, largely through health care professionals.

"We have a small number of very loyal consumers who drink milk now because of us, but it's no more than 3% to 4% of our total milk sales," said Rotunno. "We thought it might get higher than that."

The milk and enzyme products are potentially a boon to the dairy industry, be-

(cont.)

cause they enable many who otherwise couldn't to consume milk products. The Dairy Council of Wisconsin, focusing on nutritional education, has developed a 12-minute video called "Getting Along with Milk."

"Most lactose intolerance is self-diagnosed," said Joann Heppes, vp-marketing for the Dairy Council. "Therefore, a lot of people think they can't eat certain foods when they can. Hard or aged cheeses, for example, have little lactose in it."

With new questions about the nutritional value of milk and concerns about bovine growth hormone, consumers may be increasingly looking for "alternative" dairy products rather than ways to incorporate dairy into their diets. The real growth area, then, may be in milk substitutes.

Protein Technology International, a subsidiary of Ralston Purina, St. Louis, makes Isolated Soy Protein for many food products and is now testing First Alternative, a soy-based milk substitute in Arizona, with its large elderly, Native American, and Hispanic American populations, for a test market. It's packaged in quart and half-gallon containers and sold next to milk in the dairy case. First Alternative is formulated to have the nutritional benefits of milk, without lactose, and be lower in fat and cholesterol.

Soy-based milk substitutes represent 1% of milk sales. But you'll see increasing claims of "non-animal protein products."

"There's lots of research coming out on the beneficial effects of soy on chronic diseases such as heart disease and prostate, breast and colon cancer," said John Grady, First Alternative's Brand Manager.

"People who buy these products are sophisticated about the health and nutritional issues. They scan ingredients, almost as though they were buying a medical product. Mainstream consumers are looking for healthful products. This is not the soy of the '70s, with tofu and all that. This is the soy of the '90s."

Soy-based milk substitutes now represent about 1% of all milk sales. As the health issues start coming through, "It will increasingly help us to be able to say: this is a non-animal protein product," said Grady.

Soy "milks" sold through health food and ethnic specialty stores, and increasingly supermarkets, are growing at a rate of 20% a year and approaching $100 million in sales, said Peter Goldbitz, president of Soyatech, in Bar Harbor, Maine, and a leading consultant in soy foods.

That's despite the high price, which usually runs about three or four times the cost of milk.

Some of the top brands include Edensoy made by Eden Foods in Clinton, Mich.; West Brae in Commerce, Calif.; and Vitasoy in Brisbane, Calif.

"These products appeal to people who are lactose intolerant as well as vegetarians, people who want to limit fat or cholesterol and those who choose not to eat dairy products and animal proteins," said Goldbitz.

"And now, the bovine growth hormone issue means one more strike against dairy for those who have been sitting on the fence." ∎

Reprinted from the May 2, 1994 issue of *Brandweek*, © 1994 ASM Communications, Inc. Used with permission from *Brandweek*.

First Advertorials; Now Advernewscasts

By Laura Bird

Staff Reporter of The Wall Street Journal

What's news?

It's hard to tell sometimes these days as advertiser-produced video news releases—not long ago considered oddities — are increasingly turning up on television news programs. These "news" stories — often perky pieces about recently made commercials—are shrewdly produced by publicists so that stations can seamlessly air them as though they were genuine news, rather than the advertising they are.

The videos seldom mention the ad agency that made them because that would decrease their chances of getting on the air. "To the media,  it would be obvious that an agency person has a self-serving interest," explains video producer Robert Chang.

In promoting a recent commercial for Frito-Lay's Doritos Tortilla Thins, Mr. Chang put together behind-the-scenes footage of the shoot, a complete version of the commercial and interviews with a Frito-Lay executive and the Doritos endorser, comedian Chevy Chase.

Mr. Chang interviewed Mr. Chase, asking questions like this: "This is your first commercial. Are you enjoying your work?" But the producer doesn't appear on the tape, and his voice isn't heard; instead, his questions were written on a blank screen so that local stations had the option of dubbing in the voice of their own reporters as if they had interviewed the star themselves.

During this year's Super Bowl, Frito-Lay, a unit of PepsiCo Inc., spent $1.6 million to air two commercials for Lay's potato chips. That was a steep price to reach the 133.4 million viewers who watched the game. The company got a far better deal in the week before the game. Frito-Lay racked up an estimated 729.5 million viewer impressions with the same two commercials — and spent a pittance doing it, thanks to television reporters who aired 1,734 stories about the new ads, using the footage supplied by Frito-Lay.

An Author Gets a Plug

Publicists also create the appearance of bona fide news by interviewing "independent" experts. In 1992, Frito interviewed Ken Auletta, author of a 1991 book on the networks, for a publicity video it produced about Frito's "Doritos Zaptime" ambush of the Super Bowl half-time show. Mr. Auletta said on camera that he thought "Zaptime" was a great idea; he wasn't paid to say so, but his book, displayed on camera during the interview, got a free plug.

Mr. Auletta says he agreed to appear in the Frito video the way he would have granted the producers permission to quote from his book. "It was like doing a TV news interview, only I knew that it wasn't," Mr. Auletta says. "Viewers should know what is news and what is an advertisement. . . . My hope is that I didn't unwittingly contribute to the blurring of the line."

The closer video publicists come to recreating the look of real news, the likelier they are to get their videotape on the air. "You need to give TV stations an interesting vehicle," says Lindsay Schnebly, manager of publicity at Disneyland.

The Walt Disney Co. theme park has a full-time staff devoted to creating video news releases. It produces some of the most-used stories in the industry — for example, features about Elizabeth Taylor's 60th-birthday party at Disneyland and the existence of a cow adorned with a spot in the shape of Mickey Mouse.

Counting Eyeballs

Advertisers go to elaborate lengths to calculate how much their PR plugs would have cost had they aired as paid ads. Toward that end, Medialink, a satellite distributor of video releases, counts up the stations that use the releases and the eyeballs they reach. Pepsi-Cola put out video news footage on the making of a commercial starring Shaquille O'Neal; it was seen by 40.6 million viewers, according to Medialink estimates.

Video produced by Pepsi even shows up in stories that aren't, strictly speaking, about ads. Pepsi provided footage to stations covering the hypodermic-needle hoax this summer, including well-aired tape of a woman caught on a store video camera tampering with a Pepsi can.

Pepsi wasn't so forthcoming when TV reporters requested video of Pepsi endorser Michael Jackson for stories about allegations that he sexually abused a young boy. "We don't think it serves Michael or Pepsi to extend that story," a Pepsi spokesman notes, adding that the marketer also didn't provide footage of endorsers Madonna or Mike Tyson when they ran into PR trouble.

Finding a Lost Child

Indeed, the essence of video news releases is upbeat, and what could be better grist than finding a lost child? L.A. Gear Inc. sent TV news departments a video release it had produced about seven-year-old Jessica Little, who got lost at night in a field in Ripley, Tenn. Two hundred rescuers found her by following the lights on her L.A. Twilights sneakers.

L.A. Gear dispatched Perri Pharris Productions, a video PR firm, to re-enact the tame adventure 72 hours after it happened. "Kids say they have a lot of fun with the lights," noted "reporter" Tony Perri (a Perri Pharris partner) on the tape he produced. "All Jessica's dad can say is he's glad he brought them home."

L.A. Gear declines to say how many stations aired the Jessica Little story, but a company executive crows, "It got picked up everywhere. Face it, it was a commercial for L.A. Gear." Says Mr. Perri: "There's a big difference between hearing about a product from a pitchman and from your trusted local anchorman."

But it is the narrowing of that distance that is raising questions about ethics and news judgment in the television industry. Marvin Kalb, director of Harvard University's Shorenstein Barone Center on Press Politics, says stories about trends on Madison Avenue might be news. But the making of a commercial? "Most of the time, it isn't," he says, noting that viewers are deceived when stations use canned tape "as a substitute for news, alleging it is reality when it's actually an ad concept."

For their part, broadcasters maintain there is nothing wrong with using outsiders' footage when the source is named on screen. "The high road has moved," says Jerry Nachman, former vice president of news for network-owned stations at General Electric Co.'s NBC unit. "The ethical issue becomes: What does the viewer know?"

It is an issue that doesn't concern many stations, however. In a recent survey conducted by A.C. Nielsen Co., every one of the 92 stations surveyed said they use video news releases, or snippets from them, on the air, but only 55% "always" identify the source.

The Internet snares more businesses

Firms plug in to pitch products, solve problems

By Paul Wiseman
USA TODAY

In San Francisco, Joe Boxer Corp. uses it to reach potential customers for its colorful boxer shorts.

In western Michigan, tiny auto industry supplier Greenville Tool and Die uses it to retrieve software that keeps its computer-aided manufacturing system running.

In Mountain View, Calif., Alberto's nightclub uses it to let people see the Latin and African groups that are scheduled to play there, and listen to their music, too. In Washington, the trendy Red Sage restaurant uses it to show a menu of Southwestern cuisine to hungry travelers in cyberspace.

Across the USA, thousands of companies are tapping into the mother of all computer networks — the Internet — to find job candidates, communicate with customers, work out technical problems and peddle their wares. For many businesses, the Internet is the Information Highway without the wait. They aren't patiently holding out for two, three or four years until cable TV operators or phone companies start delivering information on demand over high-capacity TV cables or fiber-optic wires. They're instead using the Internet — a web of 30,000 computer networks that dates back to when Neil Armstrong walked on the moon. The Internet was designed as a decentralized communications link that couldn't be destroyed in a nuclear attack. It has long been the province of academics and researchers (*An Internet primer*, 2B).

But the Internet has evolved into "big business these days," says Gail Grant, resident Internet expert at computer giant Digital Equipment. Already, at least 60 firms have sprung up, offering companies Internet marketing advice. Having an Internet address is rapidly becoming a requirement for doing business, especially in high-tech circles. Government Technology Services realized how important the Internet had become when a "fair number of customers started asking, 'What's your Internet address?'" says Frank Slovenec, president of the Chantilly, Va., company, which buys computer systems for federal agencies.

Until recently, the Internet wasn't easy for anybody but techies to use; finding your way around required typing arcane computer commands. But new technology has made using the Internet simpler. The biggest breakthrough: Mosaic, software developed last year at the University of Illinois' National Center for Supercomputing Applications. Mosaic was developed after Swiss researchers came up with the World Wide Web, a system that allows you to move smoothly across the Internet, jumping from one document to another. Mosaic lets you browse through the World Wide Web, using a mouse to point and click your way to information that interests you. Mosaic also allows users to see moving pictures and hear sounds over the Internet.

The more accessible this global network becomes, the more people use it. Corporate USA couldn't ignore a growing market of 20 million people, many of whom conveniently identify their interests by joining Internet "newsgroups" on everything from science fiction to cats. No wonder commercial use of the Internet is rocketing. As of January, nearly 568,000 computers registered to commercial users were connected to the Internet, up 63% from a year earlier, according to Mark Lottor of Network Wizards, a Menlo Park, Calif., computer hardware and software company. And that figure undoubtedly undercounts businesses on the Internet because not all of them are registered as commercial users. Some are registered, for instance, as "organizations," a category that includes government agencies and other non-commercial enterprises.

There are some drawbacks to the Internet. Security from electronic eavesdroppers and thieves isn't airtight, though it's improving. And would-be marketers run the risk of violating "Net:quette" — the unwritten code of conduct of a somewhat prickly Internet culture — and being "flamed," or bombarded with hundreds of angry electronic messages.

That's not stopping businesses.

A closer look at the network

Everybody's buzzing about the Internet. Businesses are logging on. Bookstore shelves are groaning under the weight of books on how to get onto the Internet and maneuver through it. Consumer on-line services are scrambling to provide their customers access. But lots of people still don't know what all the fuss is about.

Just what is the Internet anyway?

It's a global web of 30,000 computer networks, at least 2.2 million computers and 20 million people in more than 70 countries. Get on the Internet — enter cyberspace, the invisible realm of on-line computer networks and services — and you can tap thousands of databases and chat electronically with experts worldwide on countless subjects. Thanks to new developments, you can even see moving pictures and listen to sounds over the Internet if you have access to sophisticated hardware and software.

Who runs Internet? And how did it get started?

No one really runs the Internet; it's kind of a cooperative. The Internet Society, a non-profit group in Reston, Va., promotes the use of the Internet. What became the Internet was established by the Defense Department in 1969 to connect the Pentagon with defense researchers in academia and business. The idea: have a decentralized communications network that could keep running if even part of it were wiped out by nuclear attack. In 1986, the National Science Foundation spurred non-defense use of the Internet by creating a special network — NSFNet, sometimes called the backbone of the Internet — connecting five new supercomputing centers across the country. Universities nationwide started plugging into NSFNet. By the late 1980s, students at many universities got Internet access when they registered for classes. As new technology has made it easier to use, more individuals and businesses have latched onto the Internet.

Who pays for the Internet?

Tax dollars, funneled through the National Science Foundation and some other government agencies such as NASA, have financed a big chunk of the Internet. Universities and research organizations also pay to maintain their sections. Companies, organizations and individuals who want direct access to the Internet must pay access providers to hook them up.

How do I get on the Internet?

If you have a personal computer and a modem, you can get connected to the Internet for as little as $15 a month. For companies needing high-speed access, there are more expensive options, running from hundreds to thousands of dollars a month. For a free list of Internet access providers, you can call InterNIC Information Services at 1-800-444-4345.

"It's inevitable the Internet will become a commercial vehicle," says Nicholas Graham, CEO at Joe Boxer.

The Red Sage, for instance, runs pictures of some of its dishes on the Internet; a waiter's voice describes them as a string quartet plays in the background. The waiter "was waiting on guests recently and they recognized his voice from the Internet," says Robert Green, the restaurant's beverage manager and resident Internet expert.

Joe Boxer dropped its toll-free phone number three months ago and started relying strictly on the Internet to reach customers. "We've had thousands and thousands of responses," Graham says.

In Clemson, S.C., Mighty Dog Designs markets T-shirts over the Internet. In Los Gatos, Calif., Nine Lives Quality Consignment Clothing makes its ever-changing inventory available on-line and offers to send e-mail messages to customers when new items arrive in their size.

On-line marketing is just one way companies use the Internet. But most companies use it for more mundane tasks such as sending messages and moving data — tasks usually done now by phone or fax machine. Those tasks "are not glamorous. But they're the meat and potatoes of the Net," says consultant Michael Bauer of The Internet Group, a Pittsburgh consulting firm.

Just talk to Greenville Tool and Die. Before the firm started using the Internet about a year and a half ago, employees would have software problems fixed the old-fashioned way. They'd alert their software company in Boston with a phone call, then send a package of computer tapes overnight — and wait for the response. Solving the problem might take several days. Now, communicating electronically, software glitches can be fixed in hours.

One night, Greenville Tool employees sent an e-mail SOS over the Internet directly to the man who wrote the program that was giving them problems — even though he was in New Zealand. The long-distance solution came back the next morning. "It's amazing," says John

> **"It's inevitable the Internet will become a commercial vehicle."**
> — **Nicholas Graham, chief executive at Joe Boxer**

Latva, system manager at Greenville Tool.

Alberto's, the nightclub in Mountain View, Calif., sends information about its specialty — music from Latin America and Africa — to Internet newsgroups connected to those topics. It also lets Internet browsers listen to musical groups scheduled to play there. It works. On June 1, Alberto's announced over the Internet that Brazilian stars Gilberto Gil and Caetano Veloso would be playing there June 26. "By June 2, we had 200 tickets sold," says club owner Alberto Martin. Alberto's didn't advertise in newspapers until a couple of weeks later. Martin says the club has such a loyal following on the Internet that "people who flame us get flamed worse."

But it seems almost inevitable that commercial use of the Internet will continue to grow. Mary Cronin, author of *Doing Business on the Internet*, says she is constantly approached by people who read her book on Internet business opportunities. She felt a little uneasy when someone walked up at a recent Internet conference and, she says, told her: "I bought your book, and I decided to give up what I'm doing to become an Internet entrepreneur."

Looking for Mr. Plumber

WHEN YOU SELL FAUCETS, YOU NEED TO REACH THE TRADE;

AND THE TRADE, IT SEEMS, CAN BE FOUND WATCHING ESPN

Little did Delta Faucet know that its entitlement sponsorship of ESPN's Saturday college football telecast would come with bench support from Chris Berman and Dick Vitale, two of the network's most visible sportscasters.

The country's largest faucet manufacturer, Delta Faucet had just gone through its first title sponsorship of ESPN's halftime report during college hoops games. Doing so had provided a cost-effective way for a moderate-sized advertiser to land a high-visibility sponsorship without breaking the bank.

It wasn't so easy getting there, as the editorial side of ESPN had its reservations about commercial infringement on its programming. "Whenever you begin something like this, there's some concern over the amount of advertising" on the programming, says Tom Talbert, vp/associate media director at Lintas:Campbell-Ewald. "There was some sensitivity in that regard."

Once the debate was settled, Talbert—along with his boss, executive vp/executive media director Bob Gervason, media supervisor Page Sakelaris and media planner Mary Ellen Sierzenga—and Ted Andrusz, the ESPN account executive in Detroit handling Delta, concurred that the next logical step was to bring the client into another entitlement. This time it was the "Delta Faucet Halftime Report" on ESPN's Saturday night college football games that ran from Sept. 4 through Nov. 7 last fall.

In addition to two spots in each game, the entitlement included the following: a 30-second spot within the report, a billboard ("This halftime report is brought to you by the Delta Faucet Company. Delta, the way water is brought to life."), on-screen identification via a logo that appeared over the shoulder of the host, and numerous mentions during the first half of the game. "They were looking for an event vehicle so they could develop a franchise," notes Andrusz. "They hit upon sports as a way to do that."

The identification with ESPN in prime time gave Delta Faucet the ruboff it needed. "It provided a lot of the ingredients we were looking for," says Talbert, who notes that Lintas:Campbell-Ewald has had the Delta Faucet account since 1990. "ESPN's a very merchandisable network. When you're on ESPN, they know how to find it."

The entitlement served two purposes: it provided a level of awareness to consumers of the Delta brand name and it sought to reach the contractors, hardware stores and plumbers who install the faucets.

"We knew this would be a terrific consumer vehicle, but we needed to let the trade know" first and foremost, says Talbert. Enter Berman et al., who gave the buy a serious dose of extra-curricular support.

Berman chipped in to Delta's effort by penning a letter Delta sent out to its trade contacts apprising them of the sponsorship and its duration. Berman's letter was sent along with a football emblazoned with both the Delta and ESPN logos, promising that "With this [football] in hand, you'll be catching the long bomb just like Andre 'Bad Moon' Rison!"

Vitale, who has a penchant for gab, hosted a seven-minute sales videotape produced by Lintas for Delta that also got sent out to the trade. He didn't stop there. "Being the entrepreneur he is, Vitale mentioned Delta Faucet on radio shows he was on," notes ESPN's Andrusz. Vitale also delivered a speech at Delta's annual sales meeting last November, giving away copies of his book to the attendees. Other ESPN personalities lent themselves to Delta as well. ESPN commentator Roy Firestone spoke at the National Association of Plumbing, Heating and Cooling Contractors convention last October, no doubt regaling the attendees with his best plumbing jokes. And former college football coach turned commentator Lee Corso spoke at Delta's employee appreciation day in March.

Talbert says feedback about the campaign from Delta Faucet's suppliers has been positive, as awareness of the entitlement was high. But probably no one expected football fans' awareness of the deal to be high. Andrusz says that a few particularly avid fans were spotted holding up homemade signs mentioning Delta Faucet's halftime report. "This thing took on a life of its own," notes Andrusz, with a hint of surprise in his voice.

Fans weren't the only ones spurred on by Delta's activity; the competition was too. "It certainly got the attention of others," says Andrusz, noting that companies like Moen and Price-Pfister have since expressed interest. "Anytime you have a success, the competition starts to take an interest." ∎

The DEATH and REBIRTH of the SALESMAN

Today's customers want solutions, and companies are remaking their sales forces to satisfy them. But total quality goals and sales quotas still clash. ■ *by Jaclyn Fierman*

I sold systems that people didn't want, didn't need, and couldn't afford.
—Bill Gardner, 23-year IBM veteran, now retired.

NOT SO long ago, many salespeople might have regarded Gardner's admission as the mark of a colleague at the top of his game, one so skilled he could persuade people to act against their own interests. Today, his dubious achievement is more likely to be seen as embarrassing, unenlightened, counterproductive, and even, under some new compensation systems, a shortcut to a smaller bonus. Merely pushing metal, as IBM insiders say, or slamming boxes, as Xerox salesmen daintily describe the act of closing a copier deal, won't carry a sales force in the Nineties. Companies now measure success not just by units sold but also by the far more rigorous yardstick of customer satisfaction. As vendors ranging from Hallmark Cards to Marshall Industries—and even IBM—have discovered, if you anticipate what your customers need and then deliver it beyond their expectations, order flow takes care of itself.

As more managers awake to the challenge, old stereotypes are fading faster than Willy Loman's smile and shoeshine. Forget the mythic lone-wolf sales ace; today's trend-setting salespeople tend to work in teams. The traditional sample case? It's more likely to hold spreadsheets than widgets, and the person hauling it around probably regards herself as a problem solver, not a vendor. These days you don't "sell to" people, you

REPORTER ASSOCIATE *Ani Hadjian*

THE NEW SALESMAN

■ **Today's best salespeople see themselves as problem solvers, not vendors.**

■ **They gauge success not just by sales volume but also by customer satisfaction.**

■ **To reinforce that view, companies are increasingly making customer satisfaction an element in salespeople's pay.**

■ **Despite the new attitudes, selling requires the same mix of grit and persistence that it always has.**

"partner with" them. At the rhetorical frontier of the new sales force, even the word "salesman" is frowned upon; the preferred title is "relationship manager."

Let's admit that the rebirth of the salesman in corporate America remains a work in progress. Not all companies or all salespeople will adapt equally well to the extra training and teamwork that today's more cerebral sales approach requires. Moreover, as long as salespeople work on commission—as they do in virtually every major company today—the rhetoric of total cus-

tomer satisfaction will inevitably clash with the reality of sales targets. "Come quota time, you still reach for the low-hanging fruit," says Robert Rodin, CEO of electronics distributor Marshall Industries in El Monte, California, one of the few companies to have eliminated commissions.

That said, companies that dismiss the new, more collaborative sales methods as a fad are likely to slip behind. Today's demanding buyers are running out of patience with mere product pushers, whether at the new-car showroom, on the floor of a department store, or in the corporate conference room. Jon Gorney, head of information services and operations at Cleveland's National City Corp., captures the mood in speaking of one of his chief vendors: "I don't want IBM coming in here anymore and telling me they have some whiz-bang technology unless they can tell me exactly how it will help my business."

As it happens, IBM knows better than most the dollars-and-cents argument for a more customer-conscious sales approach. Robert LaBant, senior vice president in charge of Big Blue's North American sales and marketing, says every percentage-point variation in customer satisfaction scores translates into a gain or loss of $500 million in sales over five years. What's more, he says, developing new business costs Big Blue three to five times as much as maintaining the old. Says LaBant: "We used to be focused on moving products and were paid on the basis of which ones we sold—$500 for this, $1,000 for that. It was critical that we turn that around."

IF EVER there was a business that cried out for a new way of selling it's that of moving cars from the showroom floor to the driveways of America. The familiar but widely despised old approach is known among automotive historians as the Hull-Dobbs method, after Memphis dealers Horace Hull and James Dobbs, who reputedly created it following World War II. In the old Hull-Dobbs drill, customers exist to be manipulated—first by the salesman, who negotiates the ostensibly final price, then by the sales manager and finance manager, who each in succession try to bump you to a higher price.

Car buyers are fed up. A survey by J.D. Power & Associates found that only 35% felt well treated by their dealers last year, down from 40% a decade ago. Just 26% of buyers rated the integrity of their dealers excellent or very good in 1983; by last year, that figure had dropped to 21%. "People feel beaten up by the process," says Jack Pohanka, owner of 13 import and domestic franchises in the suburbs of Washington, D.C. "You think you got a good deal until you walk out the door. The salesmen are inside doing high fives, and the customer is lying out on the street."

Enter Saturn and its original, no-dicker sticker system. As everyone knows by now, the price you pay for a Saturn is the one on the sticker (between $9,995 and $18,675, depending on model and features). But that's only part of the package. Buy a Saturn and you buy the company's commitment to your satisfaction. A ritual reinforces the promise. When you pick up your new car, an entire team gathers around you, including a representative from service, sales, parts, and reception. They let out a cheer, snap your picture, and hand you the keys. Corny? Maybe, but last year Saturn scored third in a J.D. Power customer satisfaction study, just behind Lexus and Infiniti, which cost up to five times as much.

A fervent convert to the Saturn gospel is Jack Pohanka. One of 180 Saturn dealers in the U.S., Pohanka has seen firsthand the method's effect on customer loyalty and salesmen's morale, and he has extended Saturn-like practices to all his other franchises. "You have to let people walk out the door and not harass them," he says. "That way they may come back or refer a friend to you." Take your car in for body work to any Pohanka dealership and you will get it back vacuumed, washed, and even polished. "Our goal," says Pohanka, "is to exceed customer expectations."

Transforming combative salesmen to customer servants required what Pohanka calls "Saturnization." Every one of his 465 employees, including mechanics and recep-

tionists, went off-site for three days of classroom exercises and physical challenges, similar to the training that Saturn requires of all its dealers. The high point of the cultural remake was the familiar "trust fall"— a backward leap off a 12-foot stepladder into the arms of fellow workers.

Pohanka contends that postfall salesmen no longer compete with each other and so don't hesitate to refer customers to one another if a different Pohanka franchise would better meet a buyer's needs. He points to a 25% jump in sales at the company in the first five months of the year, twice the national rate for cars and small trucks. For his sales staff, the new system translates not only to higher commissions but also to a better frame of mind. Says his Saturn general sales manager Brian Jamison: "I was planning to get out of this business. I couldn't stand all the games we played with customers. This way feels a lot better."

Saturn and Saturn disciples like Pohanka reformed their sales methods to exploit a screamingly obvious market opportunity; for IBM a sales force remake was simply a matter of survival. The company has cut its cost of selling by close to $1.5 billion in the past two years. Its worldwide sales and marketing team, now 70,000 strong, is close to half the size it was in 1990.

Those who survived are part of a new operation that is a cross between a consulting business and a conventional sales operation. Big Blue now encourages buyers to shop for salesmen before they shop for products. Gorney of National City Corp., a superregional bank (assets: $30 billion), handpicked Don Parker as his sales representative after interviewing a half dozen IBM candidates. Says Gorney: "I wanted this person to be a member of my team." An engineer by training, Parker maintains an office at National City, and Gorney has sought his help to drive down the bank's costs of delivering services within the bank and to retail customers in the branches.

Consultants obviously need a more sophisticated set of skills than metal pushers, and IBM has not stinted on their training. For the 300 people like Parker who head client teams, the company has developed a voluntary yearlong certification program. The classroom component consists of a three-week stint at Harvard: one week devoted to general business knowledge, one to consulting, and one to the industry they specialize in serving. For the rest of the year, enrollees work on case studies and then write a thesis on their particular customer. Harvard professors grade the papers. So far, 28 IBM employees have received the certification, along with a

raise. (Parker is in the midst of writing his thesis on National City.) Those who fail can keep trying.

In their new role as purveyors of solutions rather than products, IBM's sales teams don't always recommend Big Blue's merchandise. About a third of the equipment IBM installs is made by DEC and other competitors. Says senior vice president LaBant: "In the Eighties we never would have recommended another company's product because all we were paid to do was install Blue boxes."

LIKE IBM, Fletcher Music Centers in Clearwater, Florida, understands that the key to winning and keeping customers is to figure out what they need, sometimes before they figure it out themselves. A few years ago Fletcher was struggling along with other dealers in the moribund business of selling organs. "There is no natural market for organs," says Fletcher president John Riley, 42. "No one goes to a mall to shop for one." But after conducting focus groups with its main clientele, senior citizens who retire to Florida, Fletcher realized that what these people wanted wasn't so much a musical instrument as companionship.

Today Fletcher drums up business by positioning a "meet 'em and greet 'em" salesman at the keyboard within earshot of elderly mall patrons. "What's your favorite song?" he'll ask. And to the peels of *Chattanooga Choo Choo*, he'll begin his line of patter: "Where ya from? You just moved here? Do you play the organ at all? Ever seen one like this? It's specially designed for someone just like you with no musical background. Come on inside and try it out."

Once inside, the prospect is treated to a pitch heavy with subtext: Buy from us because we can help enliven your retirement years. Whether the customer springs for the $500 used model or the $47,000 top of the line, free weekly group lessons--good for a lifetime--come with the package. Says Riley: "We've seen a fair share of romances develop at these lessons."

Then there are the small details that show elderly customers how much Fletcher cares about their needs: large type on the keys and outsize knobs that arthritic fingers can easily manipulate. Says Sherman Wantz, 75, who just bought his fourth Fletcher organ: "They know how to treat elderly people without making them feel like children. They appeal to a desire in older people to continue accomplishing things in their lives." Such satisfaction is music to

Fletcher's ears. Pretax profits reached $3.5 million last year on sales of $24 million.

Building durable customer relationships is one thing when you're hawking mainframes, cars, or organs; it's a rather different story when you're pushing a product as short-lived as a greeting card. That's why the sales force at Hallmark Cards, the world's largest greeting card company, concentrates on pleasing retailers. Says Al Summy, a vice president of sales and service for cards sold through large merchandisers like Target, Kmart, and A&P: "We're not selling *to* the retailer, we're selling *through* the retailer. We look at the retailer as a pipeline to the hands of consumers." Anything his salespeople can do to make Hallmark products more profitable for retailers, he figures, will ultimately benefit Hallmark.

As a result, Hallmark is reorganizing its entire sales and marketing operation into specialized teams designed to work effectively with product managers at major retailers. In the old days—less than 24 months ago—Hallmark sold pretty much the same mix of cards to every store. Now, using data derived from bar codes at the checkout counter and laptops that supply merchandising information from Hallmark headquarters, salespeople can tailor displays and promotions to a retailer's demographics.

James River Corp., which sells toilet tissue, napkins, Dixie cups, and the like, also understands that when it puts its head together with its retailers', both sides benefit. Specifically, James River shares proprietary marketing information with its customers that enables them to sell more paper products. For instance, it told its West Coast client, Lucky Stores, how often shoppers generally buy paper goods and which items they tend to buy together. Lucky has since reshelved all its paper products and managed to win market share in the category from competing stores.

James River has reorganized the way it calls on customers. Previously, three or more salespeople would approach a company like Lucky Stores: one with plates, one with cups, and one with toilet paper. If all three secured orders, Lucky was obliged to buy three full truckloads, one for each product, to get the lowest price from James River. Today, a unified team from James River will sell Lucky Stores one truckload with a mix of paper products at the lowest price.

At James River, as at Hallmark and IBM, building a sales force for the Nineties has meant a thorough rethinking of a salesperson's job. But an important aspect of managing a sales team hasn't changed much: how you motivate flesh-and-blood salespeople. It remains the same idiosyncratic blend of financial incentive, inspiration, and cajolery it always was. After all, sales is a tough job. Says Larry Chonko, marketing professor at Baylor University in Waco, Texas: "You still need fire in your belly, you still get rejected four out of five times, and you still need energy to get up in the morning and say, 'I can do it,' even if you sold nothing yesterday."

One of the more visible motivators in the game today is Frank Pacetta, 40, who is something of a folk hero at Xerox for having turned around the company's flagging Cleveland and Columbus, Ohio, sales teams. Pacetta has also become a minor media presence of late, thanks to a profile in the *Wall Street Journal*; a major role in *The Force*, a new book about Xerox salesmen by David Dorsey; and the publication of his own manual for sales managers, *Don't Fire Them, Fire Them Up* (reviewed in Books & Ideas).

Pacetta uses a hyperbolic mix of praise and shame to inspire his team of 70 reps in Columbus. For his winners, Pacetta holds testimonial dinners, dispenses effusive hugs, and has them ring a ship captain's bell at the completion of a deal. Weak performers can expect a month-long visit on their desk from an ugly troll doll Pacetta swiped from his son. Salespeople who aren't sufficiently fired up after three consecutive visits from the troll are fired—the title of Pacetta's book notwithstanding.

Sales, Pacetta style, boils down to three simple steps: Identify the customer, make sure your product fits the customer's requirements, and ask for the sale. To minimize resistance on step three, Pacetta recommends the "presell," which he likens to a conversation he might have had when convincing his wife, Julie, to marry him:

"Julie: 'I don't like the way you dress, I don't think you make enough money, and you drive like a maniac.'

Frank: 'If I let you pick out my suits, if I double my income, and if I promise never to exceed the posted speed limits—will you marry me then?'"

In marked contrast to Pacetta's freneticism stands another master of sales motivation, 140-year-old Southwestern Co., America's oldest extant door-to-door sales company. It peddles Bibles and Bible study guides to millions of families, and its Nashville boot camp turns its young sales trainees, mostly college kids on summer vacation, into some of the most dogged salespeople in the country. How's this for a drill? After a week of classroom training, the graduates fan out to assigned territories across the country and settle down to work—up to six days a week, 13 hours a day. Southwestern salesmen ring as many as 65 doorbells a day to make 30 demonstrations, each lasting 20 minutes. Sticking to that schedule, they can expect to close one to three sales a day, enough to earn over $5,500 their first summer. The company, which is privately held, rings up over $100 million a year in revenues.

Don't discount Southwestern as an anachronism. The company's working alumni, well over 100,000 of them, have carried their skills to places like IBM, Xerox, Procter & Gamble, and Wall Street and in many cases are leading the sales revolution going on today. Says alum Marty Fridson, 41, who runs high-yield securities research at Merrill Lynch: "There's nothing magical about sales. You want to be truthful and present a credible story so people will want to do business with you in the future. To sell effectively, you need to present the facts, list your supporting arguments, and learn all the nonverbal cues your customer gives while you're making your presentation."

With one element of sales motivation—how they pay their salespeople—many companies believe they can improve on tradition. IBM, for example, is following a budding trend to base compensation partly on customer satisfaction. Salesman Don Parker says that 45% of the variable component of his paycheck depends on how Jon Gorney at National City Corp. rates him. If Gorney is pleased with the way Parker has helped him meet the bank's business objectives, Parker says that he stands to make "a lot more this year than ever before."

At Hallmark, too, customers get a say in how well some salesmen are paid. In a pilot project, about 100 employees have taken a 15% cut in base pay and made that portion of their income variable, based on retail sales of Hallmark products. If results are good, those salesmen stand to make more than 15%. The point, of course, is to encourage these workers to focus on helping retailers do their job better.

Electronics distributor Marshall Industries has taken this thinking to the next logical step and eliminated commissions altogether. Marshall's 600 salespeople earn a straight salary, with a bonus opportunity of up to 20% more based on pretax corporate profits. In the latest fiscal year, with sales over $800 million, the bonus was 10%.

Marshall CEO Robert Rodin overhauled the compensation system when he realized the distortions that quotas and commissions were creating in the system. "How can you say you're pursuing excellence if you give away TV sets to your top salespeople? Customers got their parts ahead of time so the salesmen could get their prizes.

(cont.)

But guess what? Those customers wanted on-time delivery, not early delivery."

Rodin says his people hoarded inventory in their cars in case they needed it. And in the mad rush to meet monthly quotas, salesmen shipped "anything that wasn't nailed down, to any customer on our list, regardless of their credit standing." The mania strained the shipping department's ability to complete orders accurately: "You can imagine what bleary-eyed warehouse people do at two in the morning."

Rega Plaster, 32, a top Marshall saleswoman, worried at first when Rodin took away commissions: "I wondered where my motivation would come from." She says she was pleasantly surprised at her response: "Within a month, it was like being able to breathe again. This takes the sliminess out of selling. Now I can spend time with smaller accounts and nurture them, and I can do it with a clear mind and conscience." Sales at her Milwaukee branch have risen from a monthly average of $850,000 last year to over $2 million.

FOR ALL the hype and half measures, salespeople in the Nineties can make the world a better marketplace. Any inefficiencies wholesalers and retailers squeeze out of the supply chain will benefit consumers by keeping a lid on prices. And smart solutions from any corner have a far-reaching payoff. At the very least, the new ethos may herald the decline of in-your-face salesmen who sell things people don't want, don't need, and can't afford. ◼

68

Toyota Calling

In Japan's Car Market, Big Three Face Rivals Who Go Door-to-Door

Sales Forces That Cultivate Relationships Play Role In the Trade Imbalance

Winning Over a Housewife

By VALERIE REITMAN
Staff Reporter of THE WALL STREET JOURNAL

TOKYO — Eiko Shiraishi neither needs nor wants a new car. The Tokyo housewife has never set foot in an auto dealership, kicked a tire or taken a test drive.

So how does she end up with a $30,000 gleaming silver Toyota in her driveway?

Chalk up another sale for Hiroyuki Saito, a door to-door salesman who peddles cars the way the Avon Lady sometimes still hawks cosmetics. Mr. Saito is one reason America's trade deficit with Japan is so large, and so intractable.

Japanese cars may be high-tech, but Japanese salesmanship is curiously old-fashioned. As many as half the cars sold in Japan are peddled by door-to-door salesmen, according to the Japan Automobile Dealers Association. Such sales tactics, coupled with high-quality vehicles, stack the odds against the Big Three's U.S.-made cars' ever making more than a dent in

Hiroyuki Saito

the Japanese market — even if all the trade barriers they huff and puff about crumble away.

Says the head of General Motors Japan, J. Michael Durrie: "There isn't any silver bullet that would make it easier to sell products in this very competitive, very expensive marketplace."

Cars are again at center stage of the U.S.-Japan relationship. Roughly two-thirds of the U.S.'s $59 billion bilateral trade deficit is auto-related, and the deficit keeps widening. It grew nearly 3% last month.

With the clock ticking toward Friday's U.S.-set deadline for imposing trade sanc-

tions, a thorny issue remains unresolved: U.S. negotiators want the Japanese to assure that substantially more auto dealerships in Japan will stock American vehicles. The Japanese say they can't force private dealerships to stock products they don't want to carry. Yesterday, the Japanese offered a compromise "dealership-matchmaking" process to identify dealerships that might be interested in carrying foreign cars.

Deeper Problems

But even stocking the cars might not change much. Making the rounds with the solicitous Mr. Saito strongly suggests that the imbalance in automotive trade is due less to regulation than to relationships. The Americans undoubtedly face hassles in getting cars into Japan, but, Mr. Durrie of the General Motors Corp. unit says, "If that was all we had to deal with, we could cope with it."

To be sure, Detroit is making some progress in Japan, the world's second-largest car market. In the first eight months of this year, U.S. auto exports to Japan have nearly doubled from a year earlier. But, at just 22,543 vehicles, they still represent fewer than 1% of the total sold in Japan. Moreover, Honda Motor Co. alone has done more to lift American exports to Japan than the U.S. Big Three combined; it exported 29,000 made-in-Ohio Accords and Civics during the same period.

Instead of tariffs — there aren't any — the Big Three face armies of car-pushers such as Mr. Saito. Toyota Motor Corp. alone has more than 100,000 door-to-door salespeople in a country the size of California; that's half as many as the entire sales force in the U.S. for all kinds of cars. It is also what puts Toyota so far ahead of its 8 Japanese rivals, who peddle cars the same way. Toyota sells two of every five cars in Japan — and virtually every white-collar Toyota executive begins his career by selling cars.

Sales Force Strong

"Toyota's sales force is so strong they just blow everybody else off the face of the earth," says Keith Donaldson, an auto analyst at Salomon Brothers Asia Ltd., whose Tokyo home gets bombarded by car salesmen.

Toyota's itinerant dealers drum up demand literally by walking the extra mile. "We must go outside and, just like a fighter plane, hit the customers," says Mario Sasakura, a spokesman for the giant Tokyo dealership that employs Mr. Saito and 1,300 other salesmen at 79 outlets.

Many Japanese car buyers never go into a dealership. Though the outlets are about as ubiquitous in Tokyo as delicatessens in Manhattan, they serve primarily as bases for the sales armies pounding the pavement. Pitches are made and contracts are signed in peoples' living rooms — a genuine home-shopping network.

Serious and ever-polite — but with an easy laugh — Mr. Saito has often knocked on each of the 3,000 doors in his turf in southwest Tokyo. His black book contains details on the 370 customers to whom he has sold cars; many are repeat customers circled in red. The son of a Toyota parts designer, Mr. Saito started out knocking on about 100 doors a day after graduating from college, but no longer needs to visit so many now that he has developed a regular clientele. He sells about seven cars a month and earns some $70,000 a year, mostly from salary and only little from commissions.

Looking dapper in a navy blue Italian-cut suit and gold silk tie, Mr. Saito knows precisely how to time his pitches: just before the customer's car turns three years old or every two years thereafter. That's when the owner faces an expensive government inspection system, known as the *shaken*, in which replacement of several parts is mandatory.

Mr. Saito also has a special target: the housewife. He plots his visits around her schedule — and the "small window of opportunity" when she is likely to have a few moments to spare: not too early in the morning when she's getting the kids ready for school or doing household chores, not too late in the afternoon when she's headed to the market or fixing dinner. "Once I'm disliked by the housewife," he confides, "the sales activity will end miserably."

In Mrs. Shiraishi's case, Mr. Saito came by with brochures, then drove back with the dealership's Mark II model. He returned with it on the weekend when her husband was on hand to give the final approval. When her new car came in — complete with the lace seat covers that nearly every buyer in Japan orders — Mr. Saito personally delivered it to her house and drove her trade-in back to the dealership.

"At first, I had no intention of buying a new car," Mrs. Shiraishi says, "but Mr. Saito is very good at proposing reasons why I should change" — namely, the $1,600 shaken she faced.

Longstanding Custom

The long-term relationships between dealer and customer are, in essence, mini-*keiretsu*, the Japanese system of doing business with those they know and trust. Extensive face-to-face meetings first establish trust in virtually all fields, long before business is even broached. Even Japan's huge banks drum up deposits by going door-to-door when corporations dole out semiannual bonuses to employees.

The relationships don't end with a sale. Mr. Saito maintains constant contact with customers. There are calls after a purchase to inquire how the car is running, handwritten greeting cards and special invitations for low-cost oil changes and dealer events. Beginning in the 1950s,

(cont.)

Toyota set up driving schools in big cities to help people obtain licenses — and new Toyotas. All this diligence also brings in crucial intelligence and introductions to customers' friends who might be interested in a new car.

Because most new customers are introduced by a previous buyer, buying a Toyota in Japan is like joining a fraternity. Once in the family, many never consider leaving — nor would their personal salesmen give them much opportunity. Just ask Mrs. Shiraishi: "I'm very loyal to Toyota, so there was no choice."

On his rounds on this sweltering day, Mr. Saito knows he is in enemy territory, but he stops anyway at a house with a Toyota sedan parked in front. This is a customer of his former boss, "a good salesman," who now is working for a neighboring Toyota dealership that split off from Mr. Saito's. Bowing half-a-dozen times during a brief conversation, Mr. Saito apologizes for bothering the housewife. He strikes out. "We already have a strong relationship with another Toyota dealer," she explains, referring to his former boss.

Some Courtesy Calls

Then it's on to pay a few courtesy calls on regular customers who have sent other buyers his way, including the client who just replaced his two-year-old, 12,000-mile car with another Mark II sedan — the third Mark II that he has bought from Mr. Saito in about six years. "They didn't really say they wanted one, but I know they like new cars," he says.

Once, when Mr. Saito arrived at a house and realized that both he and a Nissan salesman had been summoned at the same time, Mr. Saito fled. "I try to avoid con-

flict," he says. He followed up later, though, and ultimately clinched the sale.

Not surprisingly, some Japanese think the door-to-door car dealer is a relic. Japan's longest-ever recession has cut car sales for four years in a row. Some 40% of the dealers are bleeding red ink, their association says. Walk-in sales at dealerships have been edging up as fewer women are home to answer the door and customers seek out the latest new fad, sport-utility vehicles.

Ford Motor Co., the most aggressive of the Big Three in Japan, is trying to pull in customers the American way: mounting a media and advertising blitz aimed at enticing would-be buyers into the showroom.

Ford dealers say they don't knock on doors unsolicited, terming that tactic inefficient and costly. But trying to do things differently in Japan can be frustrating. "We need to come up with some ideas to sell more cars without door-to-door sales, but the reality is that we haven't come up with any," says Nobumasa Ogura, a Ford dealership manager in Tokyo. Several Ford dealers do visit customers who have stopped by the showroom, however.

But even some Ford dealers think that success in Japan means doing things the Japanese way, starting with offering high-enough quality to match Japanese rivals. In Japan, a country rich in public transportation, how a car drives is less important than how it looks. Cars are more like ornaments, to be washed and polished constantly but used only occasionally.

Yasutaka Ohata, manager of a Nissan dealership that now also sells Fords in Tokyo, points to a sporty black Mustang convertible on his showroom floor. He grimaces at a five-millimeter gap at the top

of the driver's-side door that tapers to just three millimeters, scratchy plastic edges inside the passenger compartment, and rough surfaces inside the hood top and glove compartment. "You wouldn't find these on a Japanese car," he says. "Americans believe these kinds of things don't affect driving, but Japanese are very picky about small imperfections."

Tetsuhiko Nakamura, managing director of Ford's largest dealership, notes another problem. He says he has difficulty keeping replacement parts in stock. Getting replacement bumpers can take weeks. During this excruciatingly hot summer, Mr. Nakamura says, many customers complained because they couldn't obtain parts for their air-conditioning systems. It is precisely this replacement-parts problem that Japanese dealers cited in a recent survey as a reason for not stocking foreign autos.

Meanwhile, the door-to-door competition is getting even tougher. Japan's manufacturers are shifting factory workers— idled amid weak domestic demand and a shift of production overseas — onto the streets. Some 3,000 Nissan Motor Co. workers, for example, are now making sales calls rather than assembling cars.

"It would be great if we could just wait with an open mouth for customers to come in and feed us," says Mr. Sasakura, the spokesman for Mr. Saito's dealership, where just 20% of the sales are to walk-in customers. "But times are tight, and I don't foresee that happening soon."

69

Star-Struck

A Satellite TV System Is Quickly Moving Asia Into the Global Village

Millions Now Watch CNN, U.S. Soaps and 'Lifestyles Of the Rich and Famous'

Governments Lose Control

By Marcus W. Brauchli
Staff Reporter of The Wall Street Journal

CALCUTTA, India — K.K. Dutta has dropped by his sister-in-law's apartment to watch a little Sunday-evening television. "Relief from the monotony," he shrugs.

And what relief it is in this hot, congested city of rickshaws and ramshackle buildings. A commercial for a miniseries based on Sydney Sheldon's steamy novel "Rage of Angels" fades into the glitzy opening of "Lifestyles of the Rich and Famous." Within moments, Mr. Dutta, a 42-year-old tobacco salesman, is gawking at a million-dollar, 40-foot, pink Mercedes-Benz convertible limousine.

"Wow!" Mr. Dutta exclaims. "That life is entirely different. In Calcutta, we spend half our time on transport — but just getting ourselves around." During a segment on actress Birgit Nilsson, Mr. Dutta zaps "Lifestyles" in favor of a cricket match between Pakistan and the West Indies.

Revolutionary Change

Mr. Dutta's choices symbolize a revolution in the way millions of Asians see the world and lead their lives. At the beginning of the 1990s, heavy-handed, state-run television dominated Asia. Viewers saw little programming from the rest of the world. Few knew how the world saw them.

Today, Asia has joined the global village. In less than two years, satellite television — an unnecessary complication in much of cable-connected North America and a commercial minefield in Europe — has transformed the Eastern Hemisphere. A torrent of news, sports, music and soap operas is loosening government controls over the media and spawning spinoff industries ranging from program-guide publishing to small cable systems. Viewers are changing habits, and once-staid advertisers are revamping strategies. Even fashion flickers to the tube: One New Delhi tailor sells copies of a popular music-TV personality's outfits.

"Our ability to control becomes less and less as we go along," frets George Yeo, the straight-laced minister of arts and information in multicultural Singapore, one of the few places battling to limit satellite TV's access. But even the tiny city-state can't stop it; Mr. Yeo notes that a planned cable-TV system will carry the satellite programs already changing lives elsewhere in the region.

How It All Began

Behind that revolution is a big Hong Kong company that latched onto the ideas of an American entrepreneur. Michael Johnson, a 43-year-old New York native, was so convinced of satellite TV's potential in Asia that he personally took an option to buy a satellite. Arguing that freely broadcasted TV was the ideal advertising format for Asia's increasingly affluent consumers, he persuaded Hutchison Whampoa Ltd. and its cautious billionaire chairman, Li Ka-shing, to sponsor the venture. "Asia was wide open," Mr. Johnson says.

The satellite, AsiaSat I, reached geostationary orbit in April 1990. A year later, HutchVision Ltd., a $300 million joint venture between Hutchison and Mr. Li's family, began beaming TV to 38 countries with a combined population of 2.7 billion. Mr. Johnson is serving as an adviser.

Today, its Satellite Television Asia Region Ltd. (or Star) network can be seen from Japan to Jordan. Satellite dishes costing as little as a few hundred dollars have sprouted in middle- and upper-class neighborhoods. As of February, Star estimated that at least 11.3 million households, or about 45 million viewers, could tune in — quadruple its estimate last June.

They Got Their MTV

Asia is Star-struck. An NBC News crew, on assignment with Burma's Karen insurgents in the jungles along the Thai border, noticed a satellite dish set up near a mess tent. At first, they thought it was a communications apparatus. Then, they heard music. Inside the tent, the guerrillas were glued to MTV.

The government-in-exile of the Dalai Lama, Tibet's god-king, tunes in to Star. So does Khun Sa, the drug warlord who keeps heroin flowing from Southeast Asia.

In China, a government survey shows that at least 4.8 million homes — as many as 25 million people — can receive Star, making China Star's biggest single market. In archrival Taiwan, nearly two million homes get Star, and half tune to their favorite show, the American police serial, "Hill Street Blues."

The network's programming is mainly in English: news supplied by British Broadcasting Corp.; an Asian version of Viacom International Inc.'s MTV music channel; sports on a channel produced in conjunction with Denver's Prime Network; TV programs from the U.S., Britain and Australia on an entertainment channel

known as Star Plus; and Mandarin-language programs on its Chinese Channel — some of them popular, to Star's surprise, among people who don't speak Chinese.

"The penetration has completely exceeded our expectations," says Julian Mounter, Star's chief executive. The network doesn't disclose financial results, but industry insiders say revenue far exceeds programming costs; in January, Star booked more advertising than in all 1992, the insiders say. It has also struck a chord with viewers. The network gets 1,000 requests a day for facsimiles of its program guide; many of those Star sends out are reprinted and sold by the recipients.

Nowhere, though, has Star's impact been more apparent than in India. Many of India's 880 million people understand English. That makes Star's international programming highly attractive to the 3.3 million households that receive it.

"Before, the rest of the world was just a fantasy, and now it's real," says Devraj Kapoor, a 34-year-old airline-ticket agent who says he never liked Doordarshan, India's state TV network. Adds Madhu Jain, an editor at India Today, a newsmagazine: "Star gives you the feel of ringside seats on what's happening culturally."

Conversations in tea lounges of New Delhi hotels often turn on three titillating soap operas aired nightly on Star Plus: "Riviera," "The Bold and the Beautiful" and "Santa Barbara." Ms. Jain and other critics ascribe their popularity to similarities with Indian films. "It's the same escapism: rich, beautiful people having torrid love affairs," she says. But Star's soaps go further than those of Doordarshan, which prohibits kissing scenes.

Lure of Real News

The BBC also has a huge Indian following. After Hindu extremists demolished a mosque in Ayodhya, a city about 250 miles east of New Delhi, last December, setting off riots, Doordarshan barred images of the mosque attack. The BBC, by contrast, had live reports, and its share of Star households hovered at 8% around the clock — double normal levels — and stayed there for a week.

Those ratings slipped only when Prime Sports began covering a cricket match between India and South Africa. Such events have won Star a lot of loyalty. It launched Prime Sports in August 1991, just a month after Doordarshan abruptly truncated the finals of the Wimbledon tennis championship to carry the daily news. Pointedly, Star's first sports offering was 110 hours of coverage of the U.S. Open tennis tournament.

Thousands of entrepreneurs such as Jasbir Singh Kohli, a 43-year-old retired army major, make sure fans can see such events. In just a few years, according to an association he heads, India's home-grown cable networks have expanded into a $100 million-a-year industry.

From his apartment in a south New Delhi neighborhood, Mr. Kohli runs a cable network with 1,000 subscribers who pay an average of $5 a month — in an area where incomes run between $100 and $250 a month. One satellite dish is perched on the balcony of his modest apartment, and two more are on the roof. His front room is jammed with electronic gear, including two videotape players he uses to supplement his satellite offerings with films.

"When I started two years ago, absolutely nobody was doing this," Mr. Kohli says, as he pops a Hindi movie, "Where Is Such Love?", into a videotape player. "Now, there is not an inch of a place in Delhi not covered by cable. There's not a colony, not a slum, not a village."

Getting the Other Side

To stay ahead of competitors, he keeps adding equipment. Now he can pull in Cable News Network as well as a government channel from neighboring Pakistan. "It's anti-Indian, no doubt about it, but I say, let the people see it," he says. "The average man is an educated man. He wants to see every side of the story."

Easy access to such information vexes Doordarshan. The state TV company, notorious for dreary dramas and tightly controlled news programs, has a second channel in India's four biggest metropolitan areas: New Delhi, Bombay, Calcutta and Madras. It now airs "Dallas" — evidence, one Doordarshan executive says, that "we are in tune with change."

It can't afford not to be. Although it still dominates Indian TV with a 40-million household audience and annual ad revenue of about $120 million, its market has been eaten away by Star, which charges only about $1,500 for a 30-second prime-time spot, compared with at least $10,000 on Doordarshan. In March, Doordarshan announced plans to set up three satellite channels of its own — news, sports and entertainment. One problem: Viewers will have to angle their dishes away from the Star signal. "We're facing a big challenge," the executive concedes.

Star's popularity has inspired other competitors, too. Since last October, a Hindi-language channel has piggybacked on Star's appeal — and its satellite. The channel, known as Zee TV, is owned by Asia Today Ltd., a vehicle of several Indian and foreign investors, including the Anglo-French financier, Sir James Goldsmith. It looks like a good investment. In its first year, Zee expects to earn $5 million; in its second year, $20 million. "We have audiences everywhere, [we can reach] the villages where people don't speak English," says Subhash Chandra, Zee TV's 42-year-old chairman.

Dealing With Taboos

Like Star, Zee deals more frankly with taboos such as divorce than state TV does. One result is a debate in India's press over the "cultural invasion." Moreover, in a society that strongly emphasizes education, many parents decry satellite TV as a distraction for children. "I personally like to think our style of living and culture is so far different from what children see on Star that people won't adapt to it," says Sujata Gupta, a 33-year-old high-school teacher in Calcutta.

Mr. Kohli says parents shouldn't worry, but his words aren't reassuring. "I consider this all education," the entrepreneur says, waving his hand at a TV monitor. Besides, he adds: "Everyone knows the ultimate aim of adolescence is to have sex. So what is the harm of letting them show how to do it better? A year ago, I might not talk openly to my children of sex or AIDS. But if they are ignorant, what are you accomplishing?"

Star is acutely afraid of offending viewers — not surprising, since half the countries it reaches are Islamic. MTV in Asia didn't show Madonna's controversial "Erotica" video, for example, though its U.S. sister network did. "It's not in our best interests to come in and offend anybody," a spokesman says. "We want as many eyeballs as we can get."

Besides, youngsters like Star's homogenizing effect — especially MTV. Whitney Houston's "Bodyguard" album sold 800,000 copies in South Korea, a sign of the network's cross-cultural clout in Asia. "Thanks to MTV," one Indian girl told Star, "I can wear a miniskirt to a disco."

In a ritzy Calcutta hotel, several teenagers loiter about, hoping for a glimpse of Danny McGill or Sophiya Haque, the hosts of MTV's prime-time Indian shows, who are in town to shoot an MTV Weekend. Suddenly, Mr. McGill appears in the lobby, back from a helicopter trip to a nearby tiger preserve, and heads for his room. "He's so gorgeous," shouts 17-year-old Joanne Madeira, as she scampers off to intercept him.

New Kinds of Advertising

Such enthusiasm is inspiring new kinds of advertising on Star. Seeing the modern graphics on MTV, many Indian advertisements have adopted a new, more hip look. Jumpin' Mango, an Indian fruit drink, is pushed on MTV with quick graphics and pop music. More staid Godrej Soaps Ltd. uses Star to pitch expensive products to an upscale market — a new niche in Indian advertising. Multinationals, such as Nike and Sony, also are experimenting on Star, airing unified campaigns, in which they show the same commercial in all markets, and image campaigns, in which they try to build brand awareness.

Adjusting to Star has been tough on some advertisers. Products aren't the same in all of Star's countries: Pakistani consumers thought they were getting fake Le Sancy soap because the bars that the manufacturer, Unilever SA, advertised on Star were shaped differently from those on sale in Pakistan. And some products, such as Sony's video cameras, aren't available in some markets.

But advertisers are intrigued and astonished by Star's reach. "We can advertise a product in Thailand and have it reach a remote Indian audience," says Irfan Khan, a general manager at Hindustan Lever Ltd., a Unilever affiliate in India.

Just how remote is evident in the Indian Himalayan town of Dharmsala. A Buddhist monk, two Indian boys and a couple of tourists sit on benches in a shack with a dirt floor. They have paid the equivalent of 13 cents to see a videotaped movie but are watching a Levis commercial on MTV while waiting for the film to begin.

"Everybody likes to see Star, maybe better than movies," says the video shack's 18-year-old operator, Rishi Abrol. Then, he confides in a whisper, "It's not real."

Not real?

"No," he says, "this is only tape. I get it from my friend. He gets Star. But one day I will get Star, too."

70

Avon Calling, By Fax, Phone and Infomercial

By Seema Nayyar

Avon's current advertising campaign calls the company "the smartest shop in town." To Wall Street, the nation's largest direct seller of beauty aids is also shaping up to be the smartest stock pick in cosmetics.

In less than five years, chairman James Preston and a new management team have realigned the balance sheet, rationalized the product mix and raised profit margins. And they have reduced company debt from $1.1 billion to $215 million to boot. It's no wonder that Avon's finding itself in Wall Street's favor once again. With domestic cost-cutting and gross-margin improvement in a strengthening economy, Salomon Bros. analyst Diana Temple describes Avon as her "top cosmetics pick."

"Avon has learned to fine-tune its merchandising mix to appeal to value-conscious consumers," Temple said in a recent industry report.

There's no denying that in the mid-1980s Avon was a troubled company saddled by increased costs and misguided leadership. By 1988 there was also no denying the company was working toward changing that. It hired advertising agency FCB/Leber Katz in 1990, began running print ads with an 800 number in 1991, and started stuffing mailboxes with Avon catalogues last spring. Also last April, it launched the "Four Ways to Be Beautiful" campaign, which provided consumers with four choices for ordering Avon products: by phone, fax, catalogue or representative. And this month it introduced its first network TV advertising in four years, vowing to nearly quadruple its U.S. advertising budget from $9 million in 1992 to $34 million this year.

Just two weeks ago Avon began testing a 30-minute infomercial, hosted by actress Linda Gray, in six cities. This spring it will unveil a new print campaign, one that focuses more on products.

"Infomercials are the next logical step for a direct-marketing company like ours," said Gail Blanke, senior vice president of advertising and communications. "Women have heard it all in terms of products and promises. You have to speak to them in a straightforward, clear way. If you can't do that, you can't compete in this decade."

Given its turnaround, Avon is proving it can compete. And Preston's marketing team is proving to be have an outstanding makeup. Sales for 1992 are estimated at $3.8 billion, according to Temple of Salomon Bros. There's no doubt that much of the growth comes from international markets, where sales are up nearly 12%. But Avon is holding its own in the more mature U.S. market, squeezing out about a 2% sales increase in 1992.

Internationally, the company is experimenting with selling merchandise directly through "beauty boutiques," or specialty shops, while tightening its hold on markets via a $70 million advertising campaign—double last year's.

In the U.S., the focus continues to be on strengthening ties to the consumer and sharpening the Avon image.

"We want to be a consumer-driven company," Blanke said. "There was a point when we would rate ourselves by how many reps we had. Now we're grading ourselves based on the number of satisfied customers we have."

To that effect, there's no question that the 800 number has been a positive move for the company. Women would buy Avon products if they could get to a rep, the company found. So in the service-oriented 1990s, the 800 number and the use of catalogues was a natural evolution. One month after mailing the catalogues and providing consumers with a toll-free number in the print cam-

(cont.)

paign, inquiries jumped from 9,000 a month to 90,000.

"In the 1980s we increased our spending but didn't see an impact on the bottom line because the customer didn't have access to our products," said Nancy Glaser, vice president of advertising and public relations. "We needed to reestablish ourselves with the consumer, put her in control and get her what she wanted."

These days that means marketing quality products at a reasonable price. Emphasis lately has been on the skin-care line, especially on Anew, which the company claims reduces wrinkles. In 1992, its initial year, the product generated nearly $70 million in sales. This fall the company plans a renewed emphasis on color cosmetics by giving the line a more upscale positioning.

It is also forging into new demographic groups, looking for ways to segment the market. It recently gave two marketing directors—Miriam Muley and Sonia Sanchez-Green—additional responsibilities. Muley is pushing Avon into the African-American market while Green is doing the same in the Hispanic sector.

But Avon's not in the clear just yet. The company still needs to better define its image, said John Grace, senior vice president at Gerstman + Meyers, a brand identity firm in New York. "Avon has a problem with brand confusion," he said. "They have to come to grips with what is Avon: a brand, a super-brand or a parent company."

They'll also eventually have to take the next step into the mass market, Grace said. "It's a difficult decision because it takes control away from the company and puts it in

Announcing four ways to be beautiful.

AVON

Avon has revamped its print ads, gone on network TV and nearly quadrupled its budget. Infomercials are "the next logical step," said Gail Blanke, senior vice president of advertising and communications. "You have to speak to women in a straightforward, clear way. If you can't do that, you can't compete."

the hands of the retailer," he said. "But that's where the customers shop, and that's where they ultimately need to be."

Still, Avon's problems these days are a far cry from their troubles during the 1980s, when almost nothing was being invested into the company's core beauty business. These days, Avon's "ladies" are ready to get to work by phone, fax, mail or the traditional door-to-door. ∎

Minorities Play the Hero in More TV Ads As Clients Discover Multicultural Sells

By Leon E. Wynter
Staff Reporter of The Wall Street Journal

Schick's latest television commercial stars the typical American man. Only this man has several faces — Asian, Caucasian and African-American — dissolving into each other in front of the shaving mirror.

The ad represents a transformation in more ways than one. Until recently, minorities' roles in mainstream TV ads were pretty predictable. Black celebrities like Ray Charles and Michael Jordan were cast as themselves. But if minorities didn't have household names, they were usually behind typewriters or airline counters.

As the Schick commercial shows, that's changing. While Hispanics and Asians still have relatively few leading roles, blacks are increasingly the stars in television commercials, portraying characters — including high-powered executives — that used to be off limits for people of color. They are even breaking into personal-product advertising, long seen as too sensitive for non-whites.

For many advertisers, the rationale for casting blacks goes well beyond the symbolic. Schick, says David McSpadden, the company's account executive at J. Walter Thompson, just wanted to be "truer to the marketplace and truer to younger people's perception that they are living in a multicultural world." The ad uses a special effect known as "morphing" that seamlessly blends the races on screen. "We saw immediate sales growth when we introduced it," says Mr. McSpadden. "As a group, the characters seem approachable and likable."

Why has it taken so long? BBDO Vice President Doug Alligood says that the advertising industry tends to be more conservative and risk averse than most people believe. "We're dealing with other people's money. . . . It's the client that sets the tone," says Mr. Alligood, who is black and supervises research on minority and other niche markets.

What has taken the clients so long? "In the early days certain assumptions were made," Mr. Alligood says, "like you cannot show a black person in a superior position because you will offend Southern whites, and that you offend blacks if they're shown as subservient." The safest course, he says, was not to show blacks at all. "There was no research," Mr. Alligood adds. "It was blind prejudice."

The impetus to cast minorities in leading roles in commercials also comes from a new understanding among advertisers that whites and minorities can be reached by the same ads. Pepsi, for example, is making a fundamental "mind shift" to "stop thinking about ethnic marketing as peripheral and think about it as the core business," says marketing chief Jeff Campbell. He points out that a third of Pepsi's young consumers are black and Hispanic. Pepsi eliminated its separate ethnic marketing department last year, and in August it dismissed its black and Hispanic ad agencies to concentrate its limited ethnic TV advertising with BBDO. "At the end of the day we need one image for the product that is powerful for everybody," says Pepsi account executive Jeff Mordos of BBDO.

This year a BBDO diet Pepsi commercial placed the popular, black "Uh Huh Girls" on a beach in bikinis, where they were approached by two white males, breaking the taboo against suggesting interracial sexual attraction. Fruit of the Loom took a similar leap into intimate territory when it put black boxer Riddick Bowe in his underwear in one of its national ads this year.

Federal Express recently featured a black female executive beating out her white male adversaries in a conference-call showdown over a high-stakes deal. The woman was modeled after a real Fedex manager who is black.

Bob Miller, Fedex's marketing vice president, notes that women—often minority women — frequently make a company's decision about which package service to use. The Fedex commercial is intended to appeal to women who aspire to have more control in the workplace, he says.

"These commercials are performing better than any we've done in the last 10 years," Mr. Miller says. "We just think about the market. Those are our customers — real people in real situations. That's how they dress, and that's how they look."

The new look in ads is also aimed at another constituency: employees. Companies committed to attracting a diverse work force want to project that image in their advertising. Fedex prescreens each ad for 90,000 employees on its in-house cable-TV system and solicits feedback. And **Xerox** is running an ad depicting a black woman as an assertive, problem-solving Xerox salesperson. "It's very important for any service company that employees see their reflection and are proud of the way the company is shown on TV," says Michael Kirby, director of world-wide strategic advertising for Xerox.

An ad for **USAir** features a black woman executive on her way to deliver an important speech. While most business passengers are white males, a world-class airline should project American diversity, says Patricia Dewey, USAir senior director for advertising and sales promotion. "Not only will we perhaps get more minority revenue," Ms. Dewey says, "we'll get more loyalty from the general population because that is what they want to see."

Of course, there are still many TV ads that slight or ignore blacks. A tourism ad for Aruba, for example, depicts a white couple frolicking on a beach, with non-whites barely visible in the background. The island is predominantly non-white. "Hey, whose island is this anyway," the man asks. The answer: "Aruba, an island all your own." Marcial F. Ibarra, director of the Aruba Tourist Authority in North America, says that race wasn't an issue in the ad. "I'm aiming to fill my rooms. If the whites do it, then go for the whites," he says. "I'm scared to change that."

And few companies followed **Levi Strauss**'s lead in the mid-1980s, when it aired documentary-style commercials showing people of different races as equals, wearing its 501 Jeans. "People were shocked by the realism because most advertising at that time was story-scripted blondes on the beach playing volleyball," recalls Levi's manager of corporate marketing, Dan Chew.

Advertisers still feel much more comfortable casting blacks than other minorities in TV ads. Asians are seen as a fast growing, but still tiny, market. Hispanic marketing is still driven by Spanish language media. Advertisers are wary about depicting the "typical" Hispanic in English-language ads. "When you're dealing with blacks vs. whites it's very obvious. With Hispanics it's a little trickier," says Mr. Mordos. "Often we cast Hispanics, but in a commercial with quick cuts it can be very hard to see," he adds.

Hiring the right exec tough in E. Europe

Agencies find locals lack experience, foreigners lack language skills

By Laurel Wentz

WANTED: Managing director, 10 years Western advertising experience; fluent in Polish, Hungarian, Czech; entrepreneur, international client handler, new-business dynamo.

This is the dream person international agencies want to develop their business in Eastern Europe, but it's mission impossible for them and their headhunters.

There are plenty of local Eastern Europeans who want to run agencies. But many of them don't understand the needs of the multinational clients that spurred the agencies to open in Budapest, Prague and Warsaw in the first place.

Conversely, there are enough Western agency executives willing to move to Eastern Europe, but they lack language skills and knowledge of the local culture.

"There's a dilemma," said Isabel Bird, managing director of Bird & Co., a London-based executive search consultancy. "How do you find someone who can run a Kellogg's [account] who can also go and win business locally from the telephone company?"

In a recent international job search stipulating Polish language ability, Ms. Bird could find only one person, and he didn't want the job.

When international agency networks started opening in Eastern Europe about three years ago, they teamed up with local agencies or people. But many of these marriages have broken up for a variety of reasons.

Local managers who worked in the ad industry under a Communist regime often were too authoritarian or couldn't deal with multinational clients.

A few agencies have found the ideal bilingual international managers right in their own networks.

Mark Jezewski, 48, will become deputy area manager of the McCann-Erickson Eastern Europe division, based in Vienna, on April 1 and is likely to add Budapest and Prague later. Describing himself as London-born but "100% Polish," Mr. Jezewski's parents fled Poland during World War II to settle in London, where he grew up speaking Polish.

Mr. Jezewski moved to Hamburg from London 2½ years ago to sort out problems on McCann's Unilever business as a director. Now he will be the first to supervise Eastern Europe on a full-time basis for McCann.

"With my Polish background, I was a natural to consider for the job," he said. "We're beginning to learn how much talent there is [in Poland], but it's incredibly raw. We have to get standards up to the level multinational clients expect."

Similarly, Czech-born Josef Havelka, now 41, was an account *(continues on next page)*

(cont.)

director at Leo Burnett in Berlin, who returned to Prague 2½ years ago for the first time since fleeing at 16 from the 1968 Soviet invasion of Czechoslovakia.

"It's an incredible advantage to know the language," said Mr. Havelka, now managing director of Leo Burnett Prague. "It's much harder for an expatriate manager. You never have a deeper understanding of the words. [And local managers] are missing a specific advertising background."

Last year, Mr. Havelka played a key role in setting up a local Association of Advertising Agencies and became its president.

Ogilvy & Mather, McCann and other agencies are looking for executives with similar profiles to head their Prague offices.

"We're looking, but it's not the easiest thing to do; they're in very high demand," said McCann's Prague media director, Nike Mikes, herself of Czech-American descent. "Sometimes Czechs think nothing is possible. Sometimes Westerners think everything is possible. It's just being able to understand both cultures."

For Doris Walczyk, returning to Poland after moving to the U.S. at age 7 is proving the opportunity of a lifetime. At 27, she is managing director and a shareholder in BBDO Warsaw, which hired her away from the local Young & Rubicam office in October.

In addition to handling eight international accounts, Ms. Walczyk is mounting a new-business drive in a market where Polish companies are used to hiring an ad agency for a specific assignment, not an overall account.

"They're not used to planning long term," she said, "but I think this year will see a huge change in the attitude of Polish companies."

McCann's Mr. Jezewski said: "International work is our bread and butter, but every agency will need to have local business, too."

When Hortex, a Polish frozen juice and vegetable company, was seeking an agency late last year to make a TV spot, Ms. Walczyk not

> "It's much harder for an expatriate manager. You never have a deeper understanding of the words. [And local managers] are missing a specific advertising background."

only won the pitch but convinced Hortex that it would be more profitable in the long run to develop a marketing strategy. So far, her agency has made separate juice and vegetable commercials, done print ads and helped with distribution.

When Saatchi & Saatchi Advertising Worldwide entered Eastern Europe three years ago, the company wanted to hire managers with a combination of Western skills and the appropriate Eastern European language. Saatchi was able to do that in only one of three main markets.

Saatchi discovered Imre Kovats, a Hungarian who moved to Austria in 1956 and who was running his own communications agency in Vienna. Mr. Kovats was dispatched to be Saatchi's chief executive in Budapest.

In Czechoslovakia and Poland, Saatchi hired Westerners to teach young local staffs, said Simon Good, Saatchi's London-based corporate development director.

Y&R is sifting through local candidates for a new managing director in Budapest but is having trouble finding a Hungarian with the right credentials.

"How can someone claim to have been an advertising manager for a company for 10 years [under the Communist system] when there was no advertising?" asked Joseph Antos, Y&R Vienna's chairman and regional director for Eastern Europe. "The whole former east bloc was a very simple system—there was no competition."

The Y&R vacancy arose with

the departure of Ildiko Takacs, who became managing director in 1989 after working her way up to marketing head of Hungarian department store chain Skala, Y&R's joint venture partner.

Ms. Takacs allegedly was reluctant to accept supervision from Y&R's regional headquarters in Vienna and last year insisted on pitching independently for a big account to handle advertising for the 1996 Hungarian World Expo. The business ended up going to Y&R's Vienna office. Ms. Takacs later resigned.

"She built a lot, she changed a lot, but at the end of the day, we were faced with the fact that Ildiko was trained in a different system," Mr. Antos said. Some Eastern European managers "are not used to a kind of open society, open partnerships or allowing open discussions."

With ad spending in Eastern Europe forecast to top $1 billion this year for the first time, according to Initiative Media, the window of opportunity for executives combining Western experience with Eastern European roots will only be open for a few years, until local managers become fully trained in Western ways.

In the meantime, Adam Zak, managing director of executive search consultancy Adams & Associates International, Barrington, Ill., is combing Europe, North America and Australia for a managing director/country manager for a U.S. agency about to open a Warsaw office.

He said candidates should have seven to 10 years in the ad industry, excellent leadership and management skills, international experience, fluency in Polish, and the ability to serve Western clients and win Polish consumer goods and services business. □

Ann Marsh and Ken Kasriel contributed to this story.

73

From Witches to Anorexics, Critical Eyes Scrutinize Ads for Political Correctness

By KEVIN GOLDMAN
Staff Reporter of THE WALL STREET JOURNAL

True tales from the files of the PC Squad:

Stylish ads for **Calvin Klein** apparel, featuring waif model Kate Moss, come under attack from Boycott Anorexic Marketing, a special-interest group in Boston that called for a Klein boycott.

Coca-Cola is criticized for "reverse sexism" because a diet Coke commercial shows a group of women ogling a beefy construction worker as he strips off his T-shirt.

And a public service spot from **Aetna Life & Casualty** for a measles vaccine, an ad that depicts a wicked witch with green skin and a chin wart, sparked curses last year from a "witches' rights group," Aetna says.

These are indeed challenging times for Madison Avenue. To attract attention, advertising must be creative and stand out from the pack. Yet in this sensitive environment, advertisers fear they will unwittingly draw the attention of the Politically Correct Squad, those special-interest groups that call for product boycotts when they deem ads to be offensive. An organization called the National Stigma Clearinghouse in New York, for example, monitors advertising for possible offensiveness to anyone with any type of mental illness.

"Utter a word. Write a piece of ad copy. There's at least one group of people you will offend," says Lawrence R. Ricciardi, president of **RJR Nabisco**, in a speech he is scheduled to deliver today to the Advertising Women of New York.

Although the world won't end because of "boring advertising," Mr. Ricciardi says, "Your clients are going to have fewer options at their disposal to sell their products creatively if you have to be careful not to offend every single perceived interest group. Can we marketers be creative in the midst of all this political correctness? Well, we probably can survive, but if society continues to move to the extreme, it sure won't be fun for people in advertising."

Such a rallying cry doesn't impress Ira Zimmerman, advocacy chairman of the National Stuttering Project in San Francisco, founded in 1977. His group, which he says has 4,000 members, protested **Nike** ads that starred the cartoon character Porky Pig. "We feel Porky Pig is always shown as a victim," says Mr. Zimmerman. "For 60 years, stuttering has been used for comic relief in Porky Pig cartoons. Perhaps that is the reason children continue to be teased for stuttering. We want respect, and Nike and other advertisers aren't being helpful."

Predictably, no advertiser says it means to offend anyone. Still, some advertisers, such as **Grand Metropolitan**'s Burger King, have withdrawn or modified ads. Others, like Calvin Klein and Nike, ignore the protests.

Duncan Pollock, an executive vice president at **Ammirati & Puris**, which created the Aetna ad, says an agency's mission is to "come up with the best ads you can. Then, we think about the politically correct implications. However, the important thing is to try to connect with people in as human a way as possible. You can't worry about every special-interest group in America, or else you would be immobilized and unable to do anything."

Companies these days must look at their advertising through one more filtering process, says Stephen A. Greyser, professor of marketing at the Harvard Business School. "Just as in the last 15 years [when] advertisers have had to look through a legal lens in relation to their claims in ads, companies now have to look through a politically correct sensitive lens."

By nature, he adds, political special-interest groups don't laugh very much, and, "The ripple effect of a lot of activist groups protesting is causing us to lose a national sense of humor."

Indeed, Mr. Ricciardi says RJR Nabisco drew fire several years ago from a teachers' organization that didn't appreciate how the profession was depicted in an ad for the company's Chips Ahoy! cookie. The commercial showed an instructor droning on about the solar system; when his back was turned, the class erupted into a party. Despite the teachers' protest, says Mr. Ricciardi, the ad wasn't killed.

Similarly, Aetna has continued to run its "witch" ad. "We try to be sensitive to all concerns," says Kevin Malloy, Aetna's director of advertising. "This is a very strong advertisement. And we're using the universally known images of myths and fables."

Other ads that the PC police have blown the whistle on in recent years:

● A **Nynex** spot was criticized by animal-rights activists because it showed a rabbit colored with blue dye.

● A Burger King commercial stirred controversy because it showed a mother teaching her grown son to memorize and recite the company's ad slogan to get a discount meal. After people with learning disabilities objected, the ad was pulled.

● A commercial for Black Flag insecticide was altered after a veterans' group protested the playing of taps over dead bugs.

● The Alliance for the Mentally Ill of New York State picketed a Daffy's discount clothing store because of a billboard showing an empty straitjacket with the headline, "If you're paying over $100 for a dress shirt, may we suggest a jacket to go with it?"

Mr. Ricciardi says he is "certain [some of the protesting groups'] intentions are sincere. Some of their concerns are legitimate." But he adds, "We're focusing on our own 'isms' to such an extent that we're in jeopardy of wrecking the ideal that led tens of millions of people to come to this country in the first place."

He believes most consumers have a sense of humor and are tired of bland "advertising that's good for you. They want to be treated like adults who can and do make their own decisions."

Price

74

HOW TO ESCAPE A
PRICE WAR

You can't win simply by slashing prices or whittling costs. The way to rise above the battle is by reconceiving the way your company does business.

by Andrew E. Serwer

NOTHING LAYS WASTE to a business landscape like a price war. Engaging your competitors in a pricing battle will likely savage your company and scar your industry for years to come. The casualty list can be appalling. Customer loyalty? Dead. Profits? Imploding. Planning? Up in smoke. Given the massed armies of capital and capacity that most competitors command today, there's less hope than ever of winning a price war. Endure maybe, but walk away whistling "Dixie"? Brother, you're dreaming.

Learn the new set of rules. Rule one: Price wars, a fact of life in businesses such as airlines, tobacco, and long-distance telephone service, are likely to spread to other industries in this era of ultracompetitiveness. Differentiating your product is far more difficult (try differentiating a phone call). So is the tactic of becoming the lowest-cost producer by just chipping away at your existing cost structure, since every company is aiming to be the No. 1 cheapo.

The only way to vanquish desperate, deep-pocketed, dumb-money competitors is to reconceive the way you do business or, to use a coming phrase, reframe it. The handful of companies that have won their battles—from far-flung fronts such as pet food, PCs, and medical products—offer an invaluable set of battle plans for doing business in the 1990s. They've fashioned premium products where none existed, picked up cost advantages through vertical integration, partnered with suppliers, unearthed cheap raw materials unavailable to rivals, or identified new forms of distribution.

"Only the company that breaks out of the box to fight, wins," says Gary Stibel, president of the New England Consulting Group. That means rethinking your work process like H.J. Heinz and reinventing how your customers buy your products the way retailer Best Buy did. Think you're in a commodity business? Think again and turn a generic ugly duckling into a value-added

swan, as mortgage banker Arbor National did. Or emulate carpetmaker Shaw Industries, which pieced together market share and then integrated vertically, creating a power position in its industry. Revolutionize your product and forge alliances as Becton Dickinson has. Or find a profitable niche like Tri-Star Computer, even in an industry that is commoditizing rapidly.

Haven t heard the drums of price war beating in your industry? Don t be surprised if you do soon. Reason: The root causes of these conflicts are still with us and aren't about to abate. Capacity utilization, while rising in many businesses, is still below peak levels. For instance, in food processing, capacity is holding steady near 80%, almost six percentage points below historical highs. The aluminum market, which is swamped with global capacity, is also running at about 80% capacity, more than nine percentage points off its historical average. Meanwhile, those reengineers cranking up productivity down at the old plant are in effect adding to capacity.

Though the Federal Reserve has knocked up short-term interest rates to keep the nation's pace of economic growth in check, most companies, particularly on the consumer side of the economy, are hard pressed to raise prices one iota. Retailers struggle with disinflation as consumers play How Low Can You Go with discounters, warehouse clubs, and category killers; the killers in turn point their price guns at suppliers.

Some businesses are particularly susceptible to price wars. According to Jon Mark, a director of Bain & Co. in Boston, a market with a high percentage of low-end product--ice cream, say--is in the danger zone. The worse-positioned company is one that sells mostly cheap goods in a market dominated by low-end product, since getting the edge in that situation is most difficult. "That's when it's time to completely rethink your

strategy," says Mark. "Your best move would be either to trump or dump the business."

War is also likely in industries where the price gap between brand-name goods and private labels is huge, such as the almost 70% difference in crackers and over 45% in cookies. Companies in industries with little or no barriers to entry are also vulnerable, as well as those with easy sources of cheap capital. Note the falling fees in credit cards.

How bad can a price war be? Awful. Devastating. Take tobacco. In April of last year, Philip Morris cut the price of Marlboros 40 cents a pack, to about $1.80. RJR wheezed and matched the cut. By the end of the year domestic operating profits for the two companies plummeted for the first time ever. How Far? Far. From $2.1 billion to $1.2 billion for RJR and from $5.2 billion to $2.8 billion for the Marlboro Man. Philip Morris stock dropped from about $64 a share before the markdown to the $50-a-share neighborhood, which translates to a $12 billion loss in market capitalization.

Philip Morris is claiming victory. True, Marlboro's market share is now 27.3%, compared with 22.1% last March, while the share of RJR's Winston brand has inched up from 5.9% to 6.2%. But is that the best scorecard? Domestic operating income in Philip Morris's tobacco business in the first quarter fell about 25%, from $1 billion last year to $769 million this year. Shareholders probably aren't in the mood to break out the champagne quite yet.

The flaw in Philip Morris's plan, and many like it, is that you can't—presto!—offset lower prices with higher volume. Elasticity of demand won't stretch far enough to pull you back. According to work done by McKinsey consultants Mike Marn and Bob Garda, the typical S&P 1,000 company would need a 12% increase in sales volume to offset a 3% price cut. That's because variable costs that come along with increased

REPORTER ASSOCIATE *Ricardo Sookdeo*

volume drag down profits (see table). Typically, unit cost won't fall until sales increase about 20%. In fact, Marn says, a price cut of 3% usually produces only a 5% to 6% increase in volume. Take Philip Morris again. It cut prices 18%. The company says unit volume climbed 12.5% in the first quarter of this year. But remember its profits fell 25%. A strategy goes up in smoke.

A price war can hurt a business for years, because it encourages customers to focus only on a product's pricetag, not its value or benefits. And consumers remember the rock bottom. When airlines cut the round-trip fare between New York and Los Angeles to $199 in the summer of 1992, in the minds of consumers they established a new benchmark price, and there it remains.

And contrary to that old saw, price wars usually don't "shake out" an industry. In businesses with mega-assets, such as airlines, food, and packaged goods, capacity never goes away. It often seeks Chapter 11 and emerges with lower costs, particularly in the airline industry. Other troubled companies sell off factories cheap to an entrepreneur who then waltzes in with a minuscule ROI threshold.

Most price wars could be avoided. Many begin by accident, through a misreading of a competitor's moves or a misjudgment of the marketplace. "One price war in industrial electrical products started when an industry trade journal mistakenly inflated the total market volume number by 15%," says McKinsey consultant Marn. "The four major players all thought they lost market share and dropped prices to recover what was never really lost."

Fully understanding your competitors' motives is critical. Except in industries like PCs where prices are constantly falling because of cheaper technology, price cuts are often temporary and targeted at specific markets or customers, or they're made to move excess inventory. Slashing prices seems like good defense, but the strategy can easily scorch the earth.

H.J. Heinz's Pet Products Co., which makes 9-Lives cat food, tried cuts. It also tried raising prices, and that didn't work either. The company finally yanked itself out of the cat food fight by completely rebuilding its business around advantages unique to its strategic position.

YOU THINK pricing is bad in your business, howl about this: Since 1984 Heinz has had to cut by 22% the price to the retailer of a case of 9-Lives, from $6.77 to $5.25, as competitors Nestlé, Quaker, Mars, and Grand Metropolitan tried to scratch each other's market share out. No wonder 9-Lives' Morris gets a little grumpy sometimes. Fed up with the downward spiral, Heinz bucked the trend in 1991 and jacked up prices.

"It was a disaster," says Heinz's Pet Products chief Bill Johnson, 45. "None of our competitors followed suit and our market share dropped precipitously"—like from 23% to 15%.

That's when Johnson, the confident son of former Cincinnati Bengals coach "Tiger" Johnson, realized he had to refigure his business. "We decided to run pet foods assuming the price war would never end," he says. To do so he turned the pricing equation on its head. "Instead of calculating out what it cost to make cat food and price accordingly, we asked ourselves what did consumers want to pay," Johnson explains. His team decided that today's finicky customers would pay between 25 cents and 33 cents per 5 1/2-ounce can, tops. Johnson then went to work rationalizing processes to hit that target. Step one was identifying his company's competitive advantages, to wit, strong brand equity, cheap materials in the form of excess tuna from Heinz's StarKist operations-which goes into more than 15% of Pet Foods' products-and some proprietary manufacturing processes. "Step two," says Johnson, "was a draconian reduction of cost."

Johnson closed eight plants and centralized operations at the company's factory in Bloomsburg, Pennsylvania, expanded from 250,000 square feet to a million today. Though the plant has a stench that could make a sanitation man blanch, it's highly efficient. Output has climbed from about three million cases annually in 1987 to 65 million. High-speed lines whiz 1,500 cans per minute down the line to where super-slicers and choppers work the meat. "We've taken about 30% of the operating cost out of the process," says plant manager Colin Corbett, who's on the prowl to save another 20%.

Heinz also integrated vertically and partnered with suppliers. Steel for the cans, which are fabricated in Bloomsburg, comes from a Heinz finishing plant in Weirton, West Virginia. Poultry supplier Tyson has an addition to a processing plant near Richmond dedicated to Heinz.

The reframing will boost profits at Heinz's cat food business to $55 million this year, up from $41 million two years ago, according to Wall Street analysts. Case volume is growing 5% to 6% per year and operating margins have climbed past 13%—terrific in this industry—at least a 20% improvement. Market share is above 25% and rising.

Today pricing has stabilized, and while competitors have matched Heinz's prices, few are making good money. One, Alpo, is on the ropes. Says Steve Galbraith, a packaged-goods analyst with Sanford C. Bernstein: "Heinz now has one of the most profitable pet food operations in the business." Today Johnson's operations are a shining star in Heinz's otherwise not-so-stellar portfolio of brands. Says Galbraith: "Pet food should be a paradigm for the rest of the company."

You have to be a masochist to work in consumer electronics retailing, where the price wars never end. Neither does the resultant bloodletting. Last year alone Michigan's Highland Superstores, a would-be national chain, collapsed into Chapter 11 and was liquidated. Another national pretender, Silo, was sold to Fretter, a competitor also headquartered in Michigan. Both Fretter and McDuff, which is a part of Tandy Corp., retrenched and shuttered over 20% of their stores. That leaves industry leader Circuit City and upstart Best Buy looking like the last two cars in a demolition derby. Both will survive, but right now Best Buy appears to have the fewest dents.

Best Buy's strategy to win the bash? Figure out what customers don't want and eliminate same, along with the accompanying costs. "We realized that low prices are just a first step, a given, in this business," says Best Buy CEO Richard Schulze, 53. "We knew our prices had to match the discounters', but we also knew we had to offer something different." After a round of focus groups and surveys, Schulze pinpointed what customers disliked most about consumer electronics stores. No. 1: pushy, commissioned salespeople steering them to high-margin items. No. 2: multiple checkout points. "We said, 'OK, we'll get rid of both,'" says Schulze.

Today Best Buy could be called "Den Depot." Its 150-plus stores, which range from 28,000 to 45,000 square feet, are set up like miniwarehouses with merchandise stacked on industrial shelving. Customers load items themselves into oversized shopping carts. Salaried salespeople don't poke or prod—though they are very available to answer questions—and the jumbo checkout area looks like a Toys "R" Us. Unlike those darkly lit Mr. McCool stereo shops, Best Buys are bright and "friendly, like a supermarket," says Schulze, a calm, self-made Minnesotan. Almost half of Best Buy customers and salespeople are women.

The company is remixing its product lines too, to make itself less of a target in the electronics wars. Whereas four years ago 60% of sales came from consumer electronics, now only 38% do. Today, CDs—top price $11.99—and home office products make up 47% of revenues, both faster growing categories.

The result? Best Buy's per store revenue has doubled in three years, to $23 million. Same-store sales climbed 19% last year, and Ursula Moran of Sanford C. Bernstein looks for annual earnings gains of over 20% for the next four years. Best Buy stores average more than 500 transactions a day at $115, vs. about 190 per day at $250 for Circuit City. Simple math. Circuit City, long the industry leader, does have some numbers in its favor: a gross margin near 27%, or more than ten percentage points higher than Best Buy's. But that gross is under siege in cities like Atlanta, where Best Buy recently opened six stores, forcing Circuit to lower prices. Circuit City's net margins have been falling while Best Buy's have been climbing. "Competing on price ultimately gets you nowhere," says Schulze. "You can say you're cheaper, but cheaper than whom, and for how long?"

THAT'S EXACTLY the problem for mortgage bankers. They sell money—what else could matter in that category except price? It's no wonder then that their business is almost constantly in a state of warfare, particularly when rates head up and demand slows. The last clear-out in the late 1980s knocked out or badly clipped nearly every company in the industry—Commonwealth Mortgage and Citifed Financial, for example.

Another fire sale may be at hand. Though mortgage origination hit a record $1 trillion last year, rising rates will probably keep volume under $800 billion this year. Price competition is already heating up and margins are contracting.

Yet Arbor National Mortgage, a midsize company in Uniondale, New York, will likely have another banner year. "We never sell products based on price," says Nancy Boles, Arbor's senior vice president of marketing. "We focus on niche products, repackaging plain-vanilla mortgages, and relationships with the community."

Differentiation in mortgages? Sure. For instance, Arbor will lend to consumers with poor credit ratings. But unlike competitors such as the Money Store or Champion, which price their products assuming a high default rate, Arbor does extensive appraisal work on potential customers' finances, and as a result suffers fewer losses.

Another tactic: Arbor takes a standard Fannie Mae mortgage and repackages it into the Arbor Home Bridal Registry. Couples register with Arbor instead of a department store so friends and families can contribute to the newlyweds' first home. "Running the registry is a lot of work, so we aren't as concerned with getting couples to register as we are in getting inquiries about purchasing a first home," says Boles. "Only three dozen couples have actually registered, but we've had over 5,000 couples call to ask about the service. Their names are now in our database. We hope to have them as customers someday." Arbor also holds mortgage seminars for real estate brokers, accountants, and consumers. And the company plants a tree for customers who want one, either in their yard or in a public forest.

Sensitivity is smart marketing. Arbor's

revenues have jumped over threefold since 1991, to $60 million. Net income has climbed even more, to $7.7 million last year, and Wall Street analysts look for $12 million this year. The delinquency ratio is 1.8%, one of the lowest in the business. Says Gareth Plank, a mortgage banking analyst with Mabon Securities: "Arbor excels at staying above the fray."

Drive 90 miles north out of Atlanta to Dalton, Georgia, where 80% of the nation's carpet is made, and ask Robert Shaw, 62, CEO of Shaw Industries, about pricing. "The carpet business has been overexpanded for a decade," he drawls. "Prices have been dropping for years." Carpet wholesales today for about $5.90 a yard, down from $6.40 in 1989. All the more amazing that Shaw's profits have grown from $22 million, to $100 million, in a decade. How'd he do that?

The answer is domination. Shaw loves gaining market share almost as much as he loves golf, and he's built his own golf course. His motto might be: "Control enough of the market and you can ride out the roughest times. Grow big enough so that your costs fall, and pricing be damned." Since 1984, Shaw has expanded his market share from less than 5% to over 30% today and growing. In the all-important builders' residential segment he's above 40%.

By investing in new technologies and constantly refitting his plants, Shaw has made inefficient foes pay the ultimate price. When competitors like Salem Carpets and the car-

LATEST REPORTS FROM THE PRICE FRONT

PRODUCTS	PLAYERS	PRICING SITUATION	PROGNOSIS
AIRLINES	American, Delta, Northwest, USAir	Regular dogfights send prices crashing about every week. Summer fares fell 30% recently.	Lots of bruised bottom lines in industry.
CIGARETTES	Philip Morris, RJR Nabisco	A 40-cents-a-pack price cut on Marlboro last year burned up billions in market value for Philip Morris.	RJR raised prices by 5 cents a pack on Camel, pointing the way out of the pricing desert.
COMPUTER DISK DRIVES	Conner Peripherals, Quantum, Seagate	Wars forced prices to retreat some 30% last year.	Increasing PC sales to the rescue.
DIAPERS	Kimberly-Clark, Procter & Gamble	Five percent to 15% decline on various brands since last year.	P&G revamps and goes to war.
FROZEN DINNERS	ConAgra, Heinz, Kraft General Foods, Stouffer	Prices dropped 5%; weapons included buy-one, get-one-free offers.	Slim returns for Lean Cuisine and Weight Watchers.
LAPAROSCOPIC SURGERY TOOLS	J&J's Ethicon, U.S. Surgical	Sharp cut in prices, 25% since last year.	Intense competition from newer player lowers U.S. Surgical market share.
PCs	Apple, Compaq, Dell, IBM	Prices have been falling about 8% every three months.	Affordability has pushed demand way up in the home market, but profits get chipped.
SODA	Coca-Cola, PepsiCo	Prices dropped an average 2% last year.	Market share remains the same.
SOFTWARE	Borland, Lotus, Microsoft	In the "suite wars," companies have discounted prices over 60% by bundling software.	Microsoft is leading, but Lotus is gaining with attractive value.
VAGINAL YEAST INFECTION TREATMENTS	Miles, Ortho/J&J, Schering-Plough	Drug went over the counter. Prices shrank by 20%.	Good news for over 13 million American women who suffer every year.

FORTUNE TABLE

(cont.)

pet divisions of West Point–Pepperell and Armstrong World didn't match him, he bought them. The incremental share begat economies of scale, which begat fatter operating margins—8.5% pretax, just about the best in the business. Only three large players remain: Shaw, Mohawk Industries, and the private Beaulieu Group. Shaw is now twice the size of Mohawk, its nearest domestic competitor.

Shaw is turning to increased vertical integration to gain even more control of his destiny. "We want to be involved with as much of the process of making and selling carpet as is practical," he says. "That way we're in charge of costs." The company expanded its polypropylene extrusion capacity so that it now produces 25% of the fiber it uses to make carpet.

On the consumer end of the product, Shaw just launched a program to brand lines of carpet. Branding is, of course, a classic way to turn away from competition on price. In fact, competitor Mohawk is similarly attempting to market its MBA line of carpet. Shaw's Trustmark program requires carpet retailers to commit 50% of their floor space and pay $22,000 for the initial privilege, and then $7,000 in annual fees. In return, Shaw spends $30 million on a national ad campaign, plus in-store displays and promotion, training, sales, and financing help.

Shaw hopes to attract consumers to Trustmark with clear, easy-to-read labels that translate carpetese like *twist, face weight,* and *density* into English. The labels also rate the quality of the rug. Shaw's plan is simple: become the dominant brand in the minds of retailers and consumers. Says textile analyst John Baugh with Wheat First in Richmond: "They say loyalty in this business is about a penny a yard. Shaw may just change that."

A S ALWAYS, one way to exit a price war is to innovate. Take Becton Dickinson's hypodermic needles. The company produces over a billion each year, at a paltry dime apiece worth over $100 million in sales. Prices have been flat to down over the past decade. During one particularly painful period in the late 1980s, a Japanese competitor began selling its wares for 7 cents a unit. In other words, you wouldn't want to be stuck in the needle business. Then Becton Dickinson got together with Baxter International, which had developed InterLink, a needleless needle.

The point to remember is that the needles doctors stick in your arm account for about 50% of the market. The other half are used to hook up intravenous lines to other IVs, which is where the Baxter-Becton team made its mark. InterLink looks like a regular syringe except the needle is replaced by a hard piece of tapered plastic tubing that ends in a blunt tip. Baxter created a new type of plastic-and-rubber seal that could be punctured and then would reseal around such a plastic spike. Baxter asked Becton to produce the spike.

Hospitals gladly pay more for InterLink because the pointless needles lower the risk of accidental needle sticks. Last year health care workers reported about one million sticks, costing hospitals upwards of $400 per incident in lost time and paperwork, excluding any legal or long-term health costs. "That's the attraction," says Gary Cohen, a marketing VP with Becton Dickinson. "Even though InterLink needles cost about 25 cents, hospitals save money."

InterLink sales revenues could exceed Becton Dickinson's traditional needle sales this year, with only 30% of the domestic market tapped and the overseas markets still to conquer. The company's needle division, once puttering along with low single-digit growth, is now bounding ahead in the low double digits and gaining market share on rival American Home Products.

No business has more rampant price competition than computers. The price of an average personal computer has declined from about $5,000 in 1984 to less than $2,000 today and is still dropping. If you're a consumer, clap your hands. If you're a manufacturer, weep.

So What's a PC maker to do? In supercompetitive industries, carving out an impenetrable niche is a matter of life or death. One of the breathing: Tri-Star Computer, a private company in Phoenix making CAD workstations. Tri-Star positions its $4,000 machines underneath the $20,000 workstations sold by Sun, IBM, and Apple, but above generic, toaster-oven PC's.

Originally a maker of general-purpose high-performance machines, Tri-Star noticed that most were bought by architects and engineers, so it filled in that niche. Tri-Star delivers value to power users by buying more high-end components than the big boys, so it gets a price break on more sophisticated parts. The company passes those savings on to customers. Tri-Star always includes high-end features as standard. When most PC makers offer a 14-inch monitor, Tri-Star sells a 17-incher. "With a price break we could sell it for only $400 more than the 14-inch one; our competitors price it at $800 more," says Mike Martin, Tri-Star's head of marketing.

"We occupy a slice of the market that's too small for the big boys," says Martin. "Plus we're too nimble. We keep our inventory small so we can continuously upgrade our machines." It's dangerous territory. Just like in real-life battles, losers in price wars sometimes perish. "It's treacherous all right," says Martin. "We recently watched four competitors just in the Phoenix area go out of business."

It doesn't seem that long ago when companies prided themselves on having the highest prices in their category. A high price carried cachet. Now it's often a liability, a target. Just ask BMW or American Express or MGM Grand Air. Look for the pressure to continue. Consumers demand it, and even an improving U.S. economy will not be of much help. Because somewhere out there a competitor is going to want your market share in the worst way. But remember, there is no worse way to respond than to go to war. Think bigger, think differently.   F

REMAKING
of a
Legend?

By Fara Warner

Eight years ago, Acura drove into America and changed the luxury car market forever. In 1995, Honda's upscale division, with executive vice president Richard Thomas at the wheel, will shake up the category again, aping its competitors by dropping the name Vigor on its midsize car for a system where models are identified by numbers. The numbered strategy under consideration for the entire lineup after 1996 is designed to cure Acura's biggest marketing hurdle--selling relatively low-priced cars like the Integra through a luxury car division.

Welcome to the new "Brand Acura."

"Our long-range equity must be in Acura," said Stephen Cushman, president of Cush Automotive in Escondido, Calif. and vice chairman of the Acura dealer council.

"The short-term conversion from Legend or Integra will be a challenge. But if you have to give it up for the better of Acura, so be it."

Presently, dealers are debating the alpha-numeric system that would wipe out more than a $600 million investment in names like Legend. If approved, it will first appear on the car replacing the Vigor in February 1995, but dealers voted recently to keep the Legend name through 1996.

The makeover doesn't stop there. During the next two years, many of America's 288 Acura dealerships will be transformed into posh, upscale car salons with the requisite wood and marble found in competing show-rooms.

Welcome to the new Acura dealership.

On the showroom floor of the "new" Acura dealer, four cars will compete against luxury makes ranging in price from $16,000 to $50,000, including a 1996 "mystery" car being built exclusively for the U.S. market in Honda's East Liberty, Ohio, plant. That car will get a number not a name and be priced between the Integra and Vigor. The angular $72,500 NSX sports car will take a backseat to a new Legend flagship car. Each car

will be covered by AcuraCare, a long-term service contract now being tested in California.

Welcome to the new Acura.

Honda's stab at luxury is only eight years old, but is being reborn out of desperate times. As it stands, Acura is stalled. While Mercedes and every other competing luxury-car brand has been redefined in the past three years, Acura has stood still. Customers have noticed. Or rather, they haven't. Acura sales plummeted from 142,000 units in 1991 to 108,000 last year, even as its younger Japanese rivals Toyota's Lexus and Nissan's Infiniti, surged to their highest sales levels. The rejuvenated Europeans came back with a vengeance and even Cadillac showed signs of life.

"Acura clearly has had better days," said J.D. Power & Associates' Thad Malesh. "They were the first kids on the block, but when the competition came in, they just folded." Nonetheless, Malesh is forecasting 1995 sales climbing to 131,000 units.

Until the entire Brand Acura concept is in place in 1996, Thomas hopes to at least tread water, even without any new products this year. He'll be down to just two volume products because the 1994 Vigor is expected to sell out long before the new car arrives.

Thomas, who's predicting that sales will jump to 115,000 this year, is betting an overall stronger car market will help, along with heavily subsidized leases and other incentives. Acura also is looking at a used-car lease program for the near future.

Thomas, a self-proclaimed "old sales guy," was brought in by Honda in February 1993 to get Acura back into the cutthroat luxury car war it started with Acura's 1986 rollout. The 55-year-old former high school auto shop teacher previously headed Honda's parts division and lacks experience with luxury makes. His first car industry job was with Toyota and he spent two years at Volvo in the 1970s as the national service operations manager. Because of his lack of luxury expertise, some industry watchers say Thomas is not the man to turn around Acura. Automotive analysts like John Casesa of Wertheim Schroder question his ability to even connect with the people who buy his cars. "Rich Thomas might not be the kind of guy who impresses Acura customers," Casesa says. Maybe. Even Thomas would admit he's a sales and service gearhead who doesn't really understand the appeal of L.A.-based Ketchum Advertising's Integra commercials, which feature dog cartoons, Hot Wheels tracks and now the kitschy Game of Life spots. But one thing Thomas doesn't lack is determination. He finished his bachelor's degree in vocational education through 10 years of night school. But at Acura, he's been slow to reveal just how he'll make the brand a legend again.

Acura's challenge for the 21st century is not that distant from its mission in 1986--to change the way Americans perceive Japanese cars. At the time of its introduction, most Americans thought of Japanese cars as "rice-grinders," good on gas, low on luxury.

Along came the $20,000 Legend. Offering quality, performance and luxury with a price tag far below the European luxury brands, American car buyers responded. In its first year, Acura sold 52,000 cars, most of them Legends. By 1987, sales shot up to 109,000. By the time Lexus and Infiniti entered the luxury market in 1989, Acura was at full throttle with 142,000 units and some of the highest customer satisfaction numbers in the industry. That was Acura's last great year.

With a strengthening yen and a lot of hubris on the part of Acura, sticker prices started to rise at a rapid rate. The Legend went from $30,000 to $35,000 in about a year. A fully loaded Legend now comes in at almost $40,000--twice the price of the original model. The sporty Integra went from $12,000 to $15,000 in about a year. Now a top-of-the-line Integra rings in at $19,000.

Acura's original value/luxury play disintegrated to the point where it felt compelled to tell prospective buyers that "some things are worth the price." Dealers demeaned that campaign by labeling them the "Chanel" ads.

"We kicked that around a long time before we went

with it," Thomas said. "We have a really fine car, but we had to tell people it's going to cost you more than you remember." The Legend is still a value compared to a $50,000 Lexus and well-outfitted Infiniti Q45 at $45,000, but Acura has chosen not to go head-to-head in a marketing war with its higher-priced Japanese competitors.

That is supposed to change under "Brand Acura," which will attempt to persuade Americans that Acura is a brand worthy of competing against the Lexus gold standard. Ketchum will begin working on the new branding campaign long before the Vigor replacement shows up at dealers. Not even Thomas knows what Brand Acura marketing will look like. Still, they've got almost a year to create it, with help from a new 24-

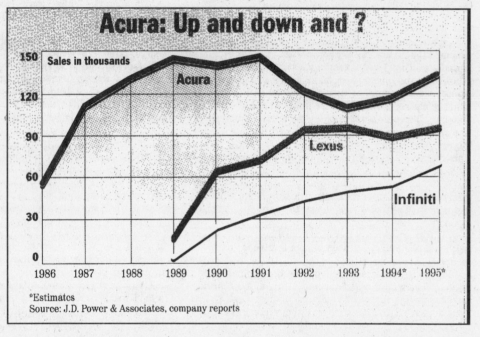

*Estimates
Source: J.D. Power & Associates, company reports

member marketing department brought in under Thomas that will take over many of the duties previously handled by Ketchum. Thomas declined to spell out how much of the marketing work would be brought in-house.

A look at the rationale behind the much-maligned "Some things are worth the price" campaign for the Legend offers insight into how Acura will position the overall brand.

"Acura is known by sports aficionados who know Acura means performance. Now we need to get them to pay $40,000 for a luxury car," said Ketchum's creative director Bill Stenton, who admits he still has to rationalize the "Chanel" campaign to a lot of people. The Legend campaign, with its Greek columns, flowing draperies and lyrical music, was supposed to achieve overall Acura brand positioning. But with the introduction of a $15,000 Integra last year "some things are worth the price" obviously didn't work. The difference is

(cont.)

best spelled out in how Integra's buyers compare to Legend buyers. Integra consumers, almost half of them female, have a household income of $57,000 and watch a lot of MTV. By contrast, Legend buyers are 66% male with incomes of $113,000. The watch *60 Minutes.*

"With Legend, they are trying for an aura of prestige to justify the price," said luxury car analyst Susan Jacobs with Jacobs & Associates in Little Falls, N.J. "But that goes against the flow of luxury dynamics right now with BMW and Mercedes moving prices and image down."

But Stenton sticks by all his campaigns. "Acura is complex," Stenton conceded. "It has been my hope that there's a brand subtext with all the campaigns--that anything Acura attacks they will ace."

Thomas would like to believe that as he embarks on the most radical changes in Acura's history.

Public acceptance of the new numbering system will be the first clear signal that Acura has successfully rebranded itself. Some dealers are still in the dark about exactly what the "alpha-numeric" system will be, so there's no early sign whether people will go for this.

And analysts like Casesa and Malesh hadn't heard of the numbering system. "Acura had gone from the leading edge to buried in the pack with no clear signal as to what it was going to do," Malesh said. "This rebranding is a good sign. But whatever they do they must execute well."

Thomas is laying the groundwork for the rebranding program this year with dealer programs like the cosmetic touches and new training, all tactics very much in fashion in the luxury car industry. His challenge will be doing it better than anyone else or risk falling behind once again. "They can do ownership experience as well as anyone," said consultant Jacobs. "If they do it well, they'll outperform many of the Europeans."

Thomas is initiating more profitable dealer programs like the AcuraCare warranty, along with a used car lease program and refurbishing old dealerships.

After setting the benchmark for customer and dealer satisfaction in its early years, Acura has dropped behind Lexus and Saturn. In the 1993 J.D. Power customer satisfaction index Acura fell to eighth behind even Audi and Cadillac. In dealer satisfaction, based on how dealers perceive the franchise, it didn't even rank above average. Most of the dealer dissatisfaction came because sales plummeted and profits went with the slide. Nonetheless, Cushman and a growing number of dealers are happy with what Acura and Thomas are doing.

"This is a totally new awakening in the car business. Of all the brands I sell, Acura is the most open about its problems," said Cushman, who owns Mazda, Honda and Isuzu dealerships.

While refurbishing dealerships may seem purely cosmetic, it's all port of the grander scheme of making Acura luxurious, not *techy.* "When you walk into a Lexus showroom you feel like you're in a fancy boutique," analyst Casesa says. "There's no hard sell. It's like a family of owners. Acura doesn't do that."

In 1986, Acura used its Honda heritage to create a prestige brand with most of the emphasis on perfor-

mance. Currently, the flagship is the high-priced $72,500 NSX sports car. Now the focus is on the brand's prestige.

Dealers also like the input Acura is asking from them. "There used to be a huge veil of secrecy about new products," Cushman said.

But in mid-April, the national dealer council met to discuss the "mystery" car. No dealer will ever talk about the car, except to say they are impressed. But some industry watchers believe it will be a coupe. Acura is positioning it between the Integra and Vigor. Vigor will move up into the Legend price range with the mystery car coming in at the mid-$20,000 range. It will compete directly against near-luxury makes like the Mazda Millenia and Toyota Avalon as well as Lexus ES300. Acura used the dealer input tactic on the 1996 Legend replacement and many came away with a much stronger sense of the company.

But not all dealers are sold on Acura's commitment to change.

"In comparison to BMW, Acura hasn't done that much," said Melissa Thomas, a BMW and Acura dealer in Columbus, Ga. Along with many other dealers, Thomas had called for an agency review, along with changes in leadership more than a year ago.

But Cushman and his dealer-council counterparts say Acura is working on its problems, first with product planning and then better branding.

And it's getting even more competitive. Acura is rebranding itself just as the luxury market goes through an overall redefinition. Jacobs has revised her luxury outlook for 1994 showing 3% decline in sales to around 1.2 million in sales. Malesh predicts Lexus dropping from 94,000 to 88,000 units with the LS400 dropping precipitously.

The reason for conservative estimates is consumers. In the '80s, forecasters could bet on them paying almost anything for luxury. Now there's uncertainty about how their tastes will play out.

"We don't know if it's back to business as usual, or if buyers are going to be as conservative in buying as they have been," said Malesh.

All this uncertainty can play in Acura's favor--if its rebranding strategy succeeds. Even though the true luxury market is hurting, near-luxury brands like Millenia and Avalon are expected to pull more buyers from luxury. "We're not getting competition from just one mark. It's not just Lexus," said Ketchum's Stenton. "We have competition from companies that are non-luxury makes. The category has been glutted. There's going to be redistribution."

Even detractors like analyst Casesa have to admit that its marketing, not quality, that has hurt Acura.

"Acura cars have always been good products," he said. "With a [dealer] environment like Lexus and some strong marketing, this company would be unstoppable."

76

Discount war can be confusing

By James Kim
USA TODAY

Long-distance carriers are using heavy artillery in their exhaustive battle for long-distance callers, and customers are caught in the cross-fire.

AT&T, MCI and Sprint have escalated their marketing war far beyond even the Coke vs. Pepsi level. MCI's big-hit Friends & Family has begotten Friends & Family II. Sprint's The Most program has given rise to The Most II. AT&T has dispatched Whitney Houston to the front lines. In general, the switch-to-us promotions are sexier. The discounts, bigger. The per-minute rewards, like frequent-flier miles, greater. The trash-talking, louder.

"I thought this would be the most competitive year since AT&T was broken up 10 years ago," says Dave Schmieg, head of Sprint's consumer business. "I haven't been disappointed."

AT&T spent about $250 million last year advertising just to home consumers. MCI spent $140 million. Sprint, about $80 million. Coca-Cola, by contrast, spent about $110 million and Pepsi, about $80 million. This year, ad spending by the Big Three long-distance giants is running well ahead of last year's pace.

The advertising blitz — and all the marketing pitches — has fueled a dash to and from the long-distance firms: 40,000 people a day switch carriers.

Phone companies are also preparing to offer information-highway era services soon, including wireless calling and advanced networks to let you send and retrieve voice, text and video programming. Those new services will ensure growth — and, undoubtedly, pack a hefty profit margin.

So winning new customers now is critical in the $30 billion-a-year consumer long-distance business, expected to grow 6% this year.

Andrea J. Vaughn, 29, of Charlotte, N.C, has switched companies about eight times the past few years. Vaughn, who typically runs up a $100-a-month long-distance bill, started with MCI, which she used in college. But then promotion offers came in the mail: AT&T offered a $75 check to switch, which she did. Then MCI called, offering $50 worth of free long-distance time if she switched back. She did. Then AT&T called back ... and so on.

Now, Vaughn is fed up.

"Finally I said, 'This is ridiculous.' You get tired of the phone calls and the sales pitches," she says. "They harass you." She decided to stick with AT&T, and just not think about it any more. "I'll never change again."

All those TV ads grate on some people's nerves.

"It's just insane," says Kelly Seacrist, a public-relations executive in Washington. "Personally, I don't think you can make an informed choice. You keep hearing all these percentages. All you know is what (Sprint pitchwoman) Candice Bergen tells you. And if I hear that Whitney Houston song one more time, I'm going to lose it."

"Just stop already," pleads Mike McCarthy, a work-at-home dad in San Jose, Calif. "It's not worth it to sit through all those ads just to see if I can save a few pennies."

There are indeed more calling plans to choose from than ever before, according to TRAC, a Washington firm that researches the long-distance industry. It keeps data on nearly 30 plans. MCI alone offers residents almost a dozen different calling plans.

Company officials acknowledge that all the promotions can begin to blur.

"People don't want to spend hours figuring it all out," says Angela Dunlap, head of consumer business at MCI. Adds Sprint's Schmieg: "People want us to get the confusion out of the business. We're trying to make things absolutely simple."

Sprint's latest thrust — called Ti-

LONG-DISTANCE OVERLOAD

Multimillion-dollar marketing blitzes by MCI, AT&T and Sprint could be confusing more customers than they are helping. Major plans the phone firms offer:

AT&T
Ad spending $180 million
True USA Savings: A 20% discount if you spend $10-$24.99 per month; 20% discount if you spend $25 to $74.99; 30% if you spend $75 or more.
True Rewards: Plan allows heavy callers to build up frequent flier points, free talk time or cash awards.
60% of long-distance market

MCI
Ad spending $100 million
Friends & Family: Offers 20% discount on calls made to a preset circle of fellow MCI customers.
Friends & Family II/Sure Savings: Offers 40% discount on calls to present circle of MCI customers and 20% discount to caller in circle but not an MCI customer (includes a $3 monthly fee).
Personal Thanks: Offers points toward airline tickets, merchandise and free minutes.
20% of long-distance market

SPRINT
Ad spending $45 million
The Most: 20% discount on most-called number and to all Sprint customers. If most-called number is Sprint customer, the discount is 36%.
The Most II: Discount of 20% if you spend $30 to $74.99 on long-distance calls, 30% if you spend $75 to $149.99, 35% if you spend $150 or more.
Priority Rewards: Points toward airline tickets, merchandise and free talk time.
10% of long-distance market

(cont.)

mebank, launched this month — offers a pared-down pitch: one free minute for every five minutes of long-distance calling.

And though consumer confusion may be high, not everyone gags when they see a phone-company ad. In most homes, "savings is the No. 1 issue," Dunlap says.

Seattle resident Marcy Zelmar, 25, runs up about $100 a month in long-distance calls, and says: "I'll do whatever I can to get the best deal." The ads? "They don't bother me." She's constantly shopping for a plan to beat MCI's Friends & Family, which gives her a discount if she calls within a circle of MCI customers.

But MCI won't let her go easily.

These days, "success means learning to keep people," Schmieg says. The Big Three long-distance firms review customer accounts roughly every three months, and try to put them on the plan that will maximize savings. They'll also offer current customers the same promotion they offer those who switch from other companies.

All three are trying to build a bit of loyalty among customers such as Cyndi Johnson, 51, of Marietta, Ga. Sprint once let her talk free to her mother, who was coping with the death of her husband.

"Let me put it this way," Johnson says. "You could come in here and offer me $5,000 cash, and I still wouldn't switch from Sprint. They're good people."

People more attuned to the bottom line will be surprised to know that, despite the marketing wars, basic long-distance calling rates have *risen* the past several years.

An index of long-distance prices tracked by the Federal Communications Commission rose 9.6% from March 1993 to March 1994. And three times this year, AT&T hiked basic rates, in the 4% to 6% range. Each time, MCI and Sprint followed.

Over time, the rate increases offset the discounts. Look at it this way: If you get a 20% discount on a per-minute rate of, say, $1, you only pay 80 cents. If the rate goes up to $1.25, with a 20% discount, you pay $1.

"I won't call it deceptive," says

Shopping for long-distance

While long-distance ads tout one service's rates over another, more real savings come from matching your calling habits with one of the many plans offered by each carrier. A comparison of costs based on an average mix[1] of 30 long-distance calls (318 minutes) per month:

Standard plan rates:

AT&T Dial-1	$55.77
MCI Dial-1	$55.47
Sprint Standard	$55.77

Discount plans based on calling rate or high volume discounts:

AT&T True USA Savings	$45.07
Sprint Plus	$46.99
Sprint The Most II	$45.07

Discount plan based on time of day you call:

AT&T AnyHour Plan	$39.07
MCI AnyTime	$38.97
Sprint Select E/N/W (w/Day option)	$44.33

Discount based on selected area codes or phone numbers called[2]:

AT&T Simple Savings	$44.41
MCI SureSavings (w/Friends & Family II)	$40.67
Sprint The Most[3]	$45.98

1 — Average mix of 25% of calls during day, 45% in evening, 30% night/weekend
2 — Reflects about 30% intracarrier calls (i.e. calling another MCI customer if you subscribe to MCI) and about 38% of calls to one phone number.
3 — Under Sprint's 50% promotion, you get 50% off all the calls to the person you call the most no matter who their long-distance carrier is. You get an additional 20% off when the person you call the most has Sprint.
All companies have special offers to induce you to switch carriers.

Source: Telecommunications Research & Action Center (TRAC)

phone industry consultant Danny Briere, of TeleChoice: "But talking only about discounts certainly isn't (telling) the whole story."

Obviously, if you're a heavy long-distance caller, the one thing you don't want to do is pay the standard rate. That's like paying suggested retail prices and passing up the discount price.

Price, however, won't be the key factor forever. "They've gone down about as much as they're going to," says Yankee Group analyst Brian Adamik. "The battle is shifting."

Already, long-distance companies are pitching add-on services, such as messaging and special calling cards. Sprint features a card that allows people to speak commands such as "Call home" and a voice-recognition computer does the dialing. All are

planning to roll out 1-500 services, which will give people one number that will "find them" by ringing several locations: home, office, car or portable.

AT&T completed its $11.5 billion purchase of McCaw Cellular Communications this week and plans to offer cellular calling under the AT&T brand within 18 months. One likely tie-in: AT&T probably will award free wireless talk time to its heavy long-distance callers, through its True Rewards program.

"If you have one company offer a lot of those services, I think people will move to that company," Seacrist says. "People want more than to just save a penny."

Reprinted from the September 23, 1994 issue of *USA Today*, Copyright, 1994. Reprinted with permission.

161

77

Currency Waves

Global Money Trends Rattle Shop Windows In Heartland America

Residents of Troy, Ohio, Find Life Is Costly, Complex When the Yen Is Strong

Robots That Ate the Profits

By VALERIE REITMAN
Staff Reporter of THE WALL STREET JOURNAL

TROY, Ohio — When the dollar drops against the yen — as it has by about 15% since the first of the year — shoppers feel it in America's heartland.

At Harris jewelry store here, the same 18-inch strand of cultured pearls that was a standard wedding gift at $899 a few years ago is now out of the reach of many at $3,000. Nikon camera prices have shot up twice already this year at the B-K Photo Products shop across the street. And prices on a Sharp copier at Trojan Business Machines ricocheted three times in one week as the Japanese electronics maker adjusted costs to reflect the stronger yen. "We definitely see the effects," says store co-owner Debbie Enoch.

That Troy, a city of about 19,000 tucked away in southwestern Ohio, should feel the gyrations of faraway currency trades is emblematic of the reach of the global economy. Swings and American flags hang from inviting porches; mom-and-pop stores line Main Street; and Lee's Family Restaurant promotes a $1.99 chicken-gizzard dinner.

And in a place where welcome signs boast that "civic pride is city wide," few residents know the yen-dollar exchange rate; indeed, a few aren't certain whose currency the yen is.

Tough on Photographers

But knowledgeable or not, they are feeling the pinch, because the fewer yen a dollar is worth, the more dollars it takes to pay for a product imported from a yen-based economy.

Jim Witmer, a Troy photographer, has resorted to buying used lenses since prices on Japanese camera equipment have risen so steeply. Consider a new Nikon 300-milli-meter lens at B-K Photo; its price has soared to about $1,000 in recent weeks, though Mr. Witmer considered it expensive at the $750 it was fetching at the beginning of the year. "I feel sorry for students just starting out who need to buy

equipment," he says.

For car shoppers, Japanese models these days average about $2,000 more than comparably equipped American cars, even though the Japanese are trying to temper price increases by cutting costs and moving some manufacturing operations to the U.S.

The greater effect of the currency gyrations, however, is on businesses. Troy's top executives, who closely monitor currency rates, say the dollar's weakness vs. the yen is a mixed bag. For manufacturers who sell abroad, a weak dollar helps out by making their products more affordable for foreigners who wield strong currencies. But to U.S. businesses that import more from Japan than they export, a weak dollar simply makes what they have to buy harder to pay for.

Robo-Costs

Just ask Hobart Brothers Co., whose 2,000 employees make arc-welding equipment in a downtown factory. Hobart has been hammered by the yen's strength, largely because of a four-year-old joint

Nearing 'Parity'
Month-end value of the dollar in Japanese yen

venture with Japan's Yaskawa Electric America Inc. Known as Motoman Inc., the joint entity buys robots from Japan, then adapts them for industrial applications in a factory in nearby Dayton. The Japanese robots bought by the venture are the bulk of its costs. But robot price increases can't easily be passed along to intolerant consumers, who can easily switch to European and American competitors.

Making matters more complicated for Hobart's Motoman are the fluctuations of the currency of Sweden, where its European business was based. The Swedish krona too has plummeted against the yen; the fall precipitously boosted the cost of Motoman's imported Japanese robots there as well. Motoman wound up shedding the Swedish robotics business as a result. "The krona was devaluing to no end, at the time the yen was strengthening against everything else, so it was a double whammy," says Frank Tracy, Hobart's chief financial officer.

Although the dollar's weakness should make American products cheaper and thus more attractive to the Japanese, the effect isn't always felt, at least not immediately. Consider the experience of PMI Food Equipment Group in Troy, which annually exports $8 million worth of commercial dishwashers and food mixers to Japan. Its Japanese distributor has reduced prices only slightly to customers for PMI equipment, though the American products now cost the distributor substantially less. "This is a case where the distributor took advantage," says Joe Arrigo, vice president for PMI, a division of Premark International Inc.

Also avidly following the yen's strength are people like Kay DeWeese, who farms 1,300 acres with her husband and son. Some of the corn and soybeans they grow are exported to Japan. Mrs. DeWeese regularly tracks commodity prices and currency rates via a backyard satellite dish. "We know the dollar has been low against the yen, which normally makes our grain cheaper," Mrs. DeWeese says. But she also knows that the Japanese are having travails of their own, including a recession and a shaky stock market. "We want to see a strong enough [Japanese] economy to be able to buy our grain," she says.

The health of the Japanese economy also concerns many other export-dependent Troy businesses. For example, the strength of Japanese airline companies is key to B.F. Goodrich Co., which employs 700 here. It sells aircraft wheels, brakes and other parts to Japan Airlines and All Nippon Airways.

A representative of the Japan External Trade Organization (Jetro) recently was in town beating the drum for American exports to Japan. Jetro has 20 such representatives in the U.S., all of them dedicated to easing the U.S. trade deficit with Japan, which continues to widen despite the yen's strength. Statistics are sobering: In the first eight months of this year, the deficit was $36.9 billion, compared with $30.4 billion in the year-earlier period. American producers have long complained, of course, that at least part of this gap reflects how difficult the Japanese make it for outsiders to sell in certain markets.

Still, "20 years ago, I was trying to export American machinery to Japan when the exchange rate was 360 yen to the dollar," says Jetro representative Tsuneo Takahasi, recalling the time he worked for a Japanese trading house in New York. That strong dollar made his task very difficult. "Now, any manufacturer here is in a favorable position. The only problem is going to Japan on a visit, where staying is very expensive."

Troy relies on Japanese business for more than just exports. Japanese corporations employ several thousand workers here at plants along Interstate 75. American Matsushita Electronics Corp., a unit of

Japan's Matsushita Electric Industrial, soon will bolster its work force of 600 employees who make picture tubes for Panasonic color television sets. Honda Motor Co. runs a parts-distribution plant, while Gokoh Corp., a maker of cast-iron and aluminum for automobile engines, employs about two dozen at a foundry material shop. Gokoh is one of numerous regional suppliers whose businesses feed Honda's Accord assembly plant in nearby Marysville, Ohio.

The weak dollar also could be a boon for recruiting more Japanese plants to Troy and other American cities. With the strong yen, the U.S. becomes a more attractive place to manufacture. Already, about 50 Japanese executives and their families have settled in Troy. Residents have also conducted several exchanges with a Japanese sister city, Takahashi. Such influence is apparent not only in the Japanese welcome sign gracing Troy's tattered Holiday Inn. The written driver's-license exam is offered in Japanese to make it easier for executives and their wives to take the test.

Some American workers are aware of the global links. Mike Hines, a foreman in PMI's mixer-assembly and shipping plant, knows that at 1:30 each day, a truck picks up the hand-assembled mixers — some up to eight feet tall — to be exported to places such as Japan, the United Arab Emirates, China and Malaysia. And Tommy Morehead, who earns $11.24 an hour as a quality inspector at PMI's dishwasher plant, knows that if the company didn't export 27% of its wares, "there'd be a lot fewer jobs. People think we're so bucolic and rustic and we don't know anything about exports, but we've been exporting since before World War II," he says.

Many others don't know much about the mechanics of global trade and exchange rates. Yet they understand that demand for Japanese products is a factor in driving up the value of the yen (the other principal factor being real interest rates). Take Mark Baughman, a highway laborer who stopped in at Joe Johnson Chevrolet to check on the long-delayed delivery of a pickup truck he had ordered. "If people bought American products, I don't think we'd have near the problems we have today and then our money would mean something," he says.

That "buy-American" sentiment runs deep here in Ohio, despite the thousands of Ohioans who have found work with Japanese corporations. Says Jean Peeples, on her lunch break from her job at Hobart Brothers: "It's nice to be friends, but we don't have to be bosom buddies. I think we ought to keep our stuff here and they ought to keep theirs there. Because one of these days all their stuff is going to be here, and none of ours is going to be there."

But Joe Newman doesn't feel that way. When he was wounded in the Korean War, he became aware of the yen (then 360 to the dollar) while recuperating at a base in Yokosuka, Japan. Today, in his job as a purchasing agent for the Wright Patterson Air Force base, he needs to know exchange rates for purchases of electronics and other Japanese equipment. "I think it's a good thing to be aware of. Sometimes we fail to look around us and just live in our own little cocoon."

78

A Dose of PR

Drug Firms' Lobbying To Defuse Criticism By Clintons Pays Off

They Highlight Their Search For Cures, Change Minds Even in the White House

Crucial Issue: Price Controls

By Rick Wartzman
Staff Reporter of The Wall Street Journal

President Clinton and the first lady kicked off the health-care debate in early 1993 by attacking the pharmaceutical industry for "shocking" prices and "unconscionable" profiteering. The charges rang true to Garnet Coleman, a Texas state legislator and part owner of a Houston ice-cream company.

Then, Bristol-Myers Squibb Co. got his ear.

Invited by the pharmaceutical giant last spring to a breakfast, Mr. Coleman was told that drug-cost controls being sought by the White House could destroy Bristol-Myers's ability to perform research. "They wanted us to know that there was another side to the story," he says. Mr. Coleman was so impressed that he told the company to use his name when contacting his friend and local congressman, Democratic Rep. Craig Washington.

An Extraordinary Campaign

Mr. Coleman's conversion is but one tiny victory in an extraordinary campaign waged by the nation's major drug companies in the 18 months since the Clintons painted them as Special Interest Enemy No. 1. The result: The companies initially fitted by the White House with black hats have succeeded in recasting themselves as good guys — researchers dedicated to improving health care.

While critics call this image oversimplified at best, it has yielded undeniable results. Just last week, for instance, House Majority Leader Richard Gephardt dropped two provisions from his health-care bill that biotechnology firms considered onerous; although aimed at helping one specific segment of the industry, his actions are a boon for almost all drug companies.

The fight is far from over. As Congress continues its historic health-care debate, the pharmaceutical companies are still striving to beat back proposals ranging from Medicare-drug rebates to demands that they give discounts to retail pharmacies. Nonetheless, the $60 billion industry now is clearly in a far better position than it was to fend off many of the cost-containment regulations aimed at it.

"The industry has been effective in getting its message across," says Democratic Rep. Ben Cardin of Maryland, a key player on the House Ways and Means Committee. "They've been persuasive."

Stark Contrast

The drug makers' campaign contrasts starkly with that of the insurance industry, which the Clintons also assailed. When the insurers got blasted, they counterattacked with "Harry and Louise" ads that sharply criticized the president's health-care proposal. But the drug makers decided to accentuate the positive and find areas of cooperation with the administration.

The drug industry's tactics illustrate that there is more than one way to get action in Washington: You can burn bridges, or you can build them — with millions of dollars in lobbying, advertising and public relations.

Over the past year and a half, the lobbying has been relentless. Nine drug-company chief executives have participated in biweekly fly-ins to the capital to make their case. Bristol-Myers alone has dispatched 30 managers to hold some 350 gatherings with community leaders across the country. Members of this health-care task force have also had 230 meetings with members of Congress and their staffs — a deluge that comes on top of the Capitol Hill contacts routinely made by the company's Washington office. Meanwhile, company officials have made their pitch to more than 820 reporters and editors. They have popped up on talk radio, too.

Industry's Position

Asserting that prescription drugs account for just seven cents of every health-care dollar, while saving millions of lives, industry executives say they are being wrongly singled out. And they contend that the industry already is undergoing wrenching change, forcing tens of thousands of layoffs since 1990.

But they beat the drums loudest of all when discussing their scientists' ability to find new cures: Any government attempts to hold down pharmaceutical prices, they argue, will undermine the industry's $14 billion-a-year quest for new drugs — a research effort inevitably accompanied by a high rate of failure.

"If we get 30 minutes, we talk about price controls," says Ray Egan, senior vice president of health policy at Bristol-Myers, based in New York. "If we get 30 seconds, we talk about price controls."

By stressing that it is industry—not the government or academic community—that discovers more than 90% of new drugs, the companies aim to sell the idea "that we are the hope for the future," says Gerald Mossinghoff, the president of the Pharmaceutical Research and Manufacturers of America. The 36-year-old Washington-based trade group added the word "Research" to its name a few months ago.

Critics say the industry is overplaying how tenuous its research base really is. "They've used that line for as long as I can remember," says John Coster, an assistant professor at the University of Minnesota's Prime Institute, which studies the economics of pharmaceuticals, and a former aide to the industry's No. 1 critic, Democratic Sen. David Pryor of Arkansas. "Data continues to show the drug companies are the most profitable industry in the United States. And data shows that they continue to spend more on marketing than on research and development."

Mr. Coster bristles at a chart put out by the industry that makes it look as if drug prices have declined in recent years; in fact, he says, prices are still going up, though not as fast as before.

The companies decided early on to highlight the research theme. The pharmaceutical association, with a $13 million ad budget this year, launched television and print ads in January that feature people with sick relatives urging the industry to keep hunting for possible cures— with no reference to health legislation.

Ads produced independently by some drug companies sing the same song. "Most People Think We Make Medicines. Actually, Our Job Is To *Find* Them," declares one by Glaxo Inc. a subsidiary of London-based Glaxo Holdings PLC. And Pfizer Inc.'s line: "Before we discovered a formula that worked on life-threatening infections, we tested 3,000 that didn't."

"There were other options that were more aggressive," says Lodewijk de Vink, the president of Warner-Lambert Co. of Morris Plains, N.J. But he is convinced that taking a "higher road" has helped lead to "the different attitude you'll now find toward the industry" on Capitol Hill and even at the White House. In a gesture of good faith, the pharmaceutical trade association went so far as to show its first ad to officials at the White House and Democratic National Committee before broadcasting it.

Fence-mending with the administration was badly needed. President Clinton, who zeroed in on the industry's pricing of childhood vaccines, had been told by his closest political advisers that the pharmaceutical industry made a most inviting target: When hammered during the presidential campaign for their greed, these companies had simply continued to raise prices. Making matters worse for the industry, Sen. Pryor is one of the Clintons' closest friends and had chatted with them several times about what he considered the industry's excesses before the president and first lady came to Washington.

(cont.)

Faced with hostile feelings, the pharmaceutical association set out to forge a new relationship. It made sure it was a primary supporter of the White House in the drive to pass the North American Free Trade Agreement. "That was very conscious," acknowledges Mr. Mossinghoff, the trade-group president. "We looked for ways to work with" the administration. Mr. Mossinghoff also notes that American Home Products Corp. Chairman John Stafford played a major role in promoting the Clinton summer-jobs program for youths.

As much as Mr. Mossinghoff's group has done to turn the industry's reputation around, some companies have joined in an even-bigger blitz. Bristol-Myers, Warner-Lambert, Hoffmann-LaRoche Inc., Upjohn Co. and Monsanto Co.'s G.D. Searle unit are all part of a coalition called Rx Partners that has arranged its own "media tours" in 65 cities. Run on about $3.5 million out of Powell Tate, a well-connected firm headed by Jimmy Carter's and Nancy Reagan's former press secretaries, Rx Partners has also held 15 Washington breakfasts at which the companies' business managers and scientists talk with news reporters.

Stepped-up public relations isn't the companies' only remedy. They have dispensed some $6.5 million in political contributions over the past two election cycles, a study from the Center for Public Integrity in Washington shows. In the 1991-92 cycle, six drug companies — Eli Lilly & Co., Pfizer, Schering-Plough Corp., Glaxo, Merck & Co. and Bristol-Myers—and some of their executives were ranked among the top 20 political donors in the entire health sector, according to the Center for Responsive Politics.

The companies have also hired an impressive army of politicians-turned-lobbyists. Former Republican Sen. Paula Hawkins of Florida is working with the pharmaceutical association. Merck has brought on three former Democratic congressmen, Thomas Downey, Dennis Eckart and Doug Walgren. Pfizer has signed up the firms of former Democratic Rep. Ed Jenkins of Georgia and former Republican Rep. Norman Lent of New York. And some of the companies have employed Mudge, Rose, Guthrie, Alexander & Ferdon, a New York law firm that now includes former Gov. Jim Florio of New Jersey, a state where many of them have big operations.

One important factor for the drug industry is that in the past few years, "managed care" programs have started to hold down drug prices, which in the 1980s were surging 8% to 13% annually; now, they are rising at about a 3% pace, in step with inflation overall. This has given industry lobbyists a chance to argue, in effect: We are on good behavior now; don't penalize us for past sins. Another argument is that even expensive drugs are often cost-effective compared with invasive procedures such as surgery.

Part of the industry's success in telling its story comes from the genuine personal appeal of its products. For instance, Glaxo lobbyists say that when they have cited the 20-year development process for Imitrex, an antimigraine drug, lawmakers and staff members have lit up because either they or relatives suffer from migraines.

Similarly, when Irwin Lerner, then chairman of Hoffmann-LaRoche, went on the "Larry King Show" last summer, he pointed out that the company's parent, Roche Holding Ltd. of Switzerland, owns a large stake in Genentech Inc., the biotechnology concern. Mr. King quickly interjected that Genentech makes tissue plasminogen activator, or TPA, a treatment for heart-attack victims that he himself used. "Saved my life," Mr. King said. "Genentech is a terrific company."

To some degree, all large drug companies have benefited from piggybacking on the political popularity of the highly entrepreneurial biotechnology companies, which generally attempt to develop compounds that mimic human proteins that attack disease rather than relying on the drug makers' chemical approach. When drug stocks — especially biotechs — plummeted after the Clintons' initial blast, some legislators were shaken. "It was a wake-up call," says Pam Bailey, head of a coalition of health-care companies opposing price controls.

Rep. Gephardt's move last week, scuttling a potentially intrusive drug-price review commission and dropping a Medicare rebate on biotech drugs, was aimed at winning votes from Democratic Rep. Lynn Schenk of California and other lawmakers from areas with a lot of biotech firms.

Already, some of the Clinton plan's toughest provisions affecting drug makers have been dumped by lawmakers. They have dropped a measure that would have given the Health and Human Services secretary the authority to exclude from the Medicare program those medicines deemed too expensive. Another provision, forcing the companies to give a rebate as part of any new Medicare prescription-drug benefit, has been watered down from a minimum of 17% to a flat 15%.

Still, bitter battles remain. Under the House leadership bill, the Medicare program would be expanded to cover small-business employees and individuals who can't get private insurance. Thus the 15% rebate on drugs would apply to tens of millions more people.

Led by Bristol-Myers, Upjohn, American Home Products and Schering-Plough, the industry is fiercely lobbying to limit the drug benefit—and therefore the rebate—to the low-income elderly. The American Association of Retired Persons, itself a potent force, is opposing the companies on the ground that such a tightly targeted benefit would leave out too many older people who need drug coverage.

The companies also vehemently object to a provision in the Senate leadership bill that would allow the government to single out drugs that would require a physician's prior approval to be eligible for reimbursement under Medicare.

Drug companies themselves could wind up divided over a measure in the House bill that would force them to give retail pharmacies the same discounts that hospitals, health-maintenance organizations and mail-order drug houses get. The retail pharmacists, also a formidable grass-roots lobby, call this "equal access."

The drug companies have dubbed it, more ominously, "unitary pricing" and have been joined in their opposition by a phalanx of allies — from Kaiser Permanente to the International Ladies Garment Workers Union to family-planning clinics—that currently get steep discounts. In recent weeks, top executives of Merck, Glaxo and SmithKline Beecham PLC have all written letters to associates urging them to contact members of Congress about the discounting provision.

Sen. Pryor is hoping this week or next to introduce an amendment to the Senate bill that, like the House legislation, would ensure that discounts are available to retail druggists, a group he describes in glowing terms. "I always knew that if my son got an earache in the middle of the night, I could call up my friend the pharmacist, and he'd open his store and give him some relief," he says.

Overcoming the popular Mr. Pryor won't be easy, partly because not all the drug companies see eye to eye. John Rector, a senior vice president at the National Association of Retail Druggists, says an Upjohn lobbyist recently told him that several big pharmaceutical companies worry that some of their rivals could get an upper hand in the market if the druggists lose on the discounting issue. An Upjohn spokesman says that although such a contact may have taken place, "we have not changed our position" in opposing discounts for retail pharmacists "and we do not intend it to change."

Regardless, some pharmaceutical companies are clearly worried about competitors, such as Merck, that are acquiring so-called pharmaceutical benefit managers, which steer physicians to particular drugs. Pfizer is also among those raising questions about certain Merck proposals. "We have struggled and continue to struggle to stay together on specific points," says Ken Bowler, Pfizer's chief lobbyist.

Despite such strains, the industry has managed to keep from fraying publicly. "We know we cannot succeed unless we

(cont.)

present a united front," says Steve Conafay, chief lobbyist at the pharmaceutical trade association.

So far, the strategy is working. Indeed, even the Clinton administration now sounds more like an industry cheerleader than detractor. "Drugs, properly used, help save lives," says Ira Magaziner, the president's senior adviser on health care. "As an administration, we are positively disposed to the industry. Even though we have had some disagreements, basically we want to be supportive."

Now, the Tables Are Turning

Exports: U.S. firms face dumping claims abroad

THERE'S ONE CATEGORY IN WHICH U.S. companies lead the world: complaints about dumping. Since 1985, the government has launched more than 320 probes into charges that foreigners are hurting U.S. industry by pricing their products too low. When it decides they have, Washington punishes the foreigners by laying on extra duties, raising the U.S. prices of products from Chinese sodium thiosulfate to New Zealand kiwi fruit and Norwegian salmon. But if Americans think that foreigners aren't trading fairly, the feeling is reciprocated. In an increasing number of cases, it's foreigners who complain about dumping—and U.S. exporters who are under attack. Says Jan Woznowski of the General Agreement on Tariffs and Trade: "This is clearly a new tendency . . . this trend will grow."

Last week the trend hit U.S. steelmakers broadside. On Tuesday, a federal ruling found that parts of the U.S. industry had been injured by cheap imports, clearing the way for stiff anti-dumping duties on selected steel products from 16 countries, including Canada. But on Thursday, the U.S. industry's crusade against foreign unfairness skidded to an embarrassed halt. A Canadian tribunal declared that LTV, Worthington Steel and other U.S. companies are dumping their steel north of the border. That ruling will cost jobs in the depressed Monongahela Valley near Pittsburgh: USX Corp.'s Irvin Works faces an extra 19.6 percent duty on every ton it ships to Canada.

Ash act: Canada's is only the latest case in which foreigners have turned the tables by accusing U.S. business of trading unfairly. India created an anti-dumping bureaucracy last year, and promptly assessed $63.54 on each ton of American-made poly-vinyl chloride, which is used to make plastic films and pipes. 3M must pay an extra 20 percent anti-dumping duty on telephone connectors in Mexico. Belgian chemical giant Solvay wants the European Community to put anti-dumping duties on American soda ash, a key ingredient in glass—although three big U.S. soda-ash producers are owned by EC companies, one of them by Solvay itself.

Paradoxically, the spread of anti-dumping actions is a result of the opening of world trade. As countries like Colombia and South Korea lower tariffs and eliminate quotas, import licenses and other barriers, local industries may be overwhelmed by imports. Anti-dumping investigations can be a convenient political tool, allowing a government to demonstrate that it will protect businesses and workers from "unfair" foreign competition. Although most economists consider dumping benign because it lowers prices for consumers, governments are more likely to judge that a high-profile probe covering one industry will stave off pressure to protect other industries. "It's a good sign, not a bad sign, as it tends to mean they're opening their markets," says Washington trade lawyer Terence Stewart.

The political motives behind anti-dumping laws are visible in Mexico, where small businesses complain bitterly that high interest rates and low import barriers have left them unable to compete with goods from Asia. To deflect the criticism, the government launched a sweeping inquiry in April into whether China is dumping products like toys and clothes on the Mexican market. While they investigate, Mexican authorities are requiring Chinese shoe exporters to pay a provisional duty of 1,105 percent—11 times the value of the shoes.

Beer spat: When U.S. exporters face such complaints, they often contend that foreign proceedings are slanted to protect local firms—precisely the complaint importers voice about the American anti-dumping law. G. Heileman Brewing Co. was hit with duties after Canada found its Seattle brewery to be dumping Rainier beer in British Columbia. Is it possible to dump in just one province? Canadian authorities say it is. Washington wants GATT to overturn the ruling, arguing that Canada should consider prices nationwide. While legal proceedings continue, the higher prices U.S. brewers must charge have decimated their 10 percent share of the B.C. market. Says Heileman general counsel Randy Smith: "I don't think we have even 1 percent right now."

Congress, sensitive to business and labor complaints about imports, has opposed efforts to put new limits on anti-dumping laws. But that tune may change now that anti-dumping laws are costing jobs, not just protecting them. Consider Monsanto. In 1991, the European Community found it guilty of dumping U.S.-made sweetener and tacked on a duty of nearly $13 a pound. "Our main competitor does not operate with such a duty leveled against it," says a company spokesman. Soon, Monsanto won't, either. It will cut exports and open a NutraSweet plant in France next month.

MARC LEVINSON

Retail giant's loss may hurt consumers

'We are not willing to pay extra. We want the best price and the best value.

By Ellen Neuborne
USA TODAY

When an Arkansas judge ordered a local Wal-Mart to raise prices, he fired the latest shot in the ongoing battle between the nation's No. 1 retailer and the small businesses struggling to compete.

When the smoke clears, the price of soap in Conway, Ark., could have far-reaching effects on prices nationwide and unleash a new wave of litigation against the nation's biggest retail success story.

Wal-Mart, whose motto is "Always the low price. Always," was found Tuesday to have engaged in predatory pricing — selling products below cost with the intent of putting the competition out of business. The discounter's Conway store has been ordered to stop selling health and beauty products below cost and to pay three local pharmacies a total of $288,000 in damages. Wal-Mart has promised a swift appeal to the state's Supreme Court.

The Conway case spotlights the struggle between the big and powerful Wal-Mart and its mom-and-pop competition. Advocates of the old-fashioned Main Street business district have long complained that Wal-Mart sweeps into small towns, underprices everyone and drives longtime local businesses under. Wal-Mart argues that the best, most-efficient operator wins. Both sides claim to carry the banner for American free enterprise.

In the middle of this battle between Davids and Goliath, is the consumer, who is showing an insatiable appetite for lower and lower prices, and abandoning long-beloved brand names and retailers in favor of the best possible deals. Everyone loves the local mom-and-pop store, but are you willing to go broke for them? asks Howard Davidowitz, retail consultant. "This is a very unsentimental consumer."

This scenario took center stage in Conway, population an estimated 27,800, but it has been played out countless times in small towns all over the country as Wal-Mart has grown from the lone store established by the late Sam Walton in 1950, to nearly 2,000 stores today. Wal-Mart's cost-cutting allows it to lower prices for customers, and the company uses this strategy to add customers.

When Wal-Mart wanted to do that in Conway, it turned to this tried and true strategy. A variety of health and beauty products hit the shelves priced below what Wal-Mart had paid for them wholesale. This is a common practice among retailers, large and small, often called "loss leaders." Supermarkets practice it weekly. And it's perfectly legal.

It's also very popular.

"Coming out of a recession, this consumer is very focused on price," says Craig Terrill, of Kuczmarski and Associates. "After the '80s, consumers have rethought what they consider a good value. And we've seen this in the move away from brands to generic and in the consumer's choice of retailers: We are not willing to pay extra. We want the best price and the best value."

But three independent Conway merchants — Dwayne Goode, owner of American Drugs, Jim Hendrickson, owner of Baker Drug Store, and Tim Benton of Mayflower Family Pharmacy — charged Wal-Mart crossed the line and violated Arkansas' 56-year-old Unfair Practices Law by cutting prices with the intent to drive them out of business.

And the court agreed. Judge David Reynolds gave the following reasons for backing the plaintiffs:

▶ The frequency and large number of Wal-Mart's below-cost sales.

▶ Wal-Mart's stated policy to "meet or beat the competition without regard to cost."

▶ Wal-Mart's below-cost sales are intended "to attract a disproportionate number of customers to Wal-Mart, " the judge wrote.

▶ Wal-Mart's practice of displaying other stores' higher prices next to merchandise in its stores.

▶ The big price discrepancy between Wal-Mart's Conway prices and

(cont.)

Wal-Mart prices in other towns.

"If this decision is allowed to stand, the result will be higher prices not just for Wal-Mart customers but customers of every retail store, large and small, in Arkansas," says Robert Rhoads, Wal-Mart's lawyer.

Retail industry watchers howl that Wal-Mart is not the loser: The consumer has lost this case, they say.

"I don't see how the judge can put the priorities of three bedraggled Arkansas druggists over the millions and millions of people who shop at Wal-Mart every day," says Chris Hoyt, retail consultant at Ryan Management Group. "The beauty of Wal-Mart is that they control their costs and they are able to sell at lower prices than other retailers."

Wal-Mart has long been a leader in using new computer technology to speed distribution and cut costs. It is a fabled hard-ball player with its suppliers, demanding rock-bottom prices. "America is built on companies being the most efficient. To support the little guy who can't keep up, you would have to make a law making everyone just as inefficient as that little guy. That's loony. And that's not America," Davidowitz says. "That's the way Europe went and they have 11% unemployment."

But small businesses and their advocates are claiming victory. It's about time, they argue, that courts took notice of Wal-Mart's steady steamrolling of small businesses. In 1988, Iowa State professor Kenneth Stone published the study "When Wal-Mart Comes to Town," showing local merchants saw business drop 12% after a Wal-Mart opened.

National Federation of Independent Business spokesman Terry Hill says small businesses should see hope in the Conway case. "It is a good thing if courts can protect a free-market economy that includes small businesses," he says. "A small business can return a lot more to a community than a mega-corp. Profits stay in the town instead of going off to company headquarters."

Don Paul, a shoe-store owner in Westford, Mass., also declared victory. He was part of a local coalition which successfully fought Wal-Mart's entry into this town northwest of Boston. "Anything that stops them from putting more small stores out of business is good news," he says. Wal-Mart has been encountering the Westport story in other parts of New England; communities in Vermont are also fighting the discounter's plans to open stores. And they cite the same reasoning as Westford: to protect local small businesses.

Wal-Mart is not the only company facing the predatory-pricing issue. It took a jury in Galveston, Texas, less than three hours on Aug. 10 to find American Airlines innocent of predatory-pricing charges after four weeks of testimony. Jurors never found that American had an "intent" to drive weaker competitors Northwest and Continental out of business with its 1992 money-losing plan to overhaul airfares.

And U.S. companies complain that foreign competitors are "dumping" their goods at unfair low prices in the USA, threatening U.S. jobs. Dumping is an issue of international trade law, so it's a different legal case, but psy-

chologically similar, says Luke Froeb, assistant professor of management at Vanderbilt University. "You do see the U.S. using anti-dumping laws to keep out lower-priced items, just the way the Conway drugstores are using antitrust laws to keep Wal-Mart prices high."

What worries Froeb more is that the Conway case will encourage small businesses to take their battle with Wal-Mart and other competitors to court. Other predatory-pricing cases against Wal-Mart are pending in Pine Bluff, Ark., Pawhuska, Okla., and Cortez, Colo. It's unlikely, Froeb says, that courts will come up with a legal way to settle the conflict between big and small businesses.

"It's a shame that people will devote resources to competing in the legal arena, rather than doing what any business under fire has to do, which is try to lower costs and lower prices and find a niche," he says. "It's kind of a sad commentary on our legal system."

Morrison Cain, legal affairs spokesman for the International Mass Retail Association, also forsees a proliferation of lawsuits.

"Anytime you start awarding money damages, that's an invitation to more of the same," he says. And if that happens, more U.S. consumers will end up with higher prices like Conway, Ark.

"If I lived there, I would be tempted to travel to do my shopping where the prices favor me," Cain says.

81

Frugal public forces firms to hold line

By James Cox
USA TODAY

Sticker shock isn't what it used to be.

Once conditioned to continually paying more for everything they buy, consumers are getting used to another phenomenon: Prices for an extraordinary array of everyday goods and services have been flat or falling for two to three years.

Consumers, in fact, are paying less for diapers, computers, collect telephone calls and motor oil than they did last year at this time. The 1990-1991 recession and today's slow-growth economy have helped keep prices in check. The three months that ended Sept. 30, consumer prices rose at a miserly 1.9% annual rate and wholesale prices fell at a 2.5% annual rate.

But there are new forces at work, too. Prices are bottled up by an increasingly stubborn, never-pay-full-price shopping public that demands value — and by new competitive pressures facing the manufacturers and retailers struggling to deliver it.

"We're in a sort of virtuous, as opposed to vicious, cycle," says economist Donald Ratajczak of Georgia State University. "Consumers won't accept price increases and therefore producers must cut costs, and that means they must restrain wage growth. And that, of course, means consumers won't accept higher prices."

Virtuous or not, the downward pressure on prices has economists and other experts asking themselves whether they are witnessing a long-term phenomenon. One that will change how marketers set prices and how consumers decide what they're willing to pay. One in which a decade of flat or declining prices could be the norm.

"This is not just a temporary change," argues Mike Marn, director of McKinsey & Co.'s subsidiary that does research on prices. "This could be something quite permanent."

The pressure on prices is coming from:

▶ **Consumers.** They are stingier at the supermarket, the hardware store and the shopping mall because they aren't confident the economic recovery is real and lasting.

Their fears about long-term job security are fed by the continuing barrage of layoffs at once-solid giants such as IBM, Procter & Gamble and Kodak. They see their wages stagnating as employers battle to hold the line on pay and shift health-care costs to workers. They see their spending power under attack as big purchases — a car, a home, college expenses — eat up a greater chunk of income.

In addition, baby boomers, whose spending drove much of the expansion of the 1980s, are changing their ways. They are putting new emphasis on thriftiness — paying off credit-card debt, refinancing their homes at lower interest rates, trading down from premium brands to less-expensive ones and socking away, rather than spending, the savings.

The boomers are "downshifting, reining in expensive spending habits from the 1980s," Marn says. "They are slamming into economic realities of having to pay for the education of their children and save for their own retirement. The demographics are such that a huge chunk of the population is hitting the wall very quickly."

In the past, baby boomers wanted premium and super-premium brands and were willing to pay extra for the cachet. Now, boomers are willing to skip the cachet if they can pay less without sacrificing quality — a trade-off made possible by the astonishing improvement in private-label and store-brand goods in nearly every category. The quality gap between premium brands and second-tier brands — on everything from pain relievers to snow tires — has never been smaller.

In supermarkets — where store-brand soups, window cleaners and personal-care products typically sell for 15% to 35% less than premium brands — private-label market share is on the rise. Having nose-dived after it peaked at 16.5% in 1982, it is almost 19% and climbing.

▶ **Marketers and manufacturers.** They know they can no longer count on annual price increases — inflation plus a percentage point or two — to boost profits. One reason: Consumers have too many cheaper alternatives.

Knowing that revenue growth would be negligible, marketers and manufacturers have been trying to protect profit margins and market share by cutting costs. The past four years, they have laid off workers, closed plants, capped wages, consolidated suppliers, curtailed research and development, streamlined distribution and found ways to ease their pension and health-care obligations. Low prices for key raw materials — copper, newsprint, cotton, certain chemicals — have helped their cost-cutting efforts. Oil prices, for example, are at a three-year low.

"This is typically what happens when economic growth is at a stand-still," says Steve Hoch, University of Chicago marketing professor. "Your only real leverage — you can't build profits at a time like this, you can only hope to maintain them — is to sharpen your pencil and figure out how to cut your costs. You can't raise prices."

Another way many corporations have cut costs is by investing in labor-saving technologies and by redesigning manufacturing processes to improve efficiency and quality. The resulting productivity gains have meant lower costs of finished goods. Many consumer-products companies have passed the savings to consumers in the form of dramatically lower prices.

Consider that a three-pack of Hanes men's underwear, which cost $6.99 at retail in 1985, sells for $4.44 to $4.99 now. Today's Hanes briefs contain more cotton, a higher grade and tighter weave of fabric, and a better-fitting waistband. "It's a better product, and you can buy it for a third less," says John Ward, a senior vice president of Sara Lee, Hanes' parent.

In some industries, however, productivity gains have created excess manufacturing capacity. Desperate to absorb the added capacity, many brand-name manufacturers have begun making private-label goods; others have tried to win more market share by boosting production of their branded goods and undercutting rivals by lowering prices.

While improved efficiency on the factory floor and in the office is good, the surplus capacity has created "more and more capable competitors chasing flat or decreasing (consumer) demand," McKinsey & Co.'s Marn says.

The increased competition keeps a lid on prices. "Every executive you talk to tells you that business is more competitive today than it was five years ago," says Jack Grayson, chairman of the non-profit American Productivity and Quality Center. "That's not just talk, it's real."

Grayson cites competition from new or expanding markets such as China, the former U.S.S.R. and Eastern European countries.

▶ **Retailers.** With consumers so bargain-hungry, retailers are under intense pressure to use discounts, rebates and sales to generate customer traffic in their stores.

Some promise to match their competitors' lowest prices. Others have adopted "everyday low prices" policies. Wal-Mart, perhaps the most skillful discounter in U.S. retailing, is opening Sam's Wholesale Clubs for people desperate for even greater savings than they find at a Wal-Mart store.

There also has been the ascendancy of "category killers" — superstores that concentrate on one category of goods and keep prices low two ways: They squeeze their suppliers for volume discounts that smaller retailers can't hope to get, and the high volume of goods they sell allows them to accept thin profit margins. Category killers are now legion: Toys R Us, Home Depot, Circuit City electronics, National Tire Wholesalers, Staples office supplies.

But the reality today is that everyone is a discounter. Some of the classiest names in retailing — Saks Fifth Avenue, Nordstrom, Neiman-Marcus and others — have opened outlet stores. The Gap, which was built on the premise of casual clothes at moderate prices, plans to open Gap Warehouses, where the clothes will be considerably cheaper than at regular Gap stores.

And the numbers reflect the changes: Discounters had 47% of department store revenue five years ago. Today, they have 57%.

Obviously, there are exceptions. The tab for some goods has been going up. Prices for cat litter, baby food and breakfast cereal have gone up considerably this year alone. Many types of health-care costs continue climbing.

And not everyone is as convinced as Marn that we are seeing a fundamental shift that will result in a sustained period of level or falling prices.

"There's nothing revolutionary or secular or systemic going on here. It's tied to (economic) conditions," says Saul Ludwig, research director at Roulston & Co., a Cleveland brokerage firm.

Still, others are believers.

"The days of being cavalier about raising prices on your brands to increase your profits are over," says marketing consultant Al Ries. "Every time you do that, there's going to be a pack of wolves ready to take your business."

Final Final Sale! Stores Unload Buyers' Errors

By Kevin Helliker

Staff Reporter of The Wall Street Journal

Approaching the cashier, Susanne Lemberger can hardly carry all the designer dresses, jackets and shoes she has picked out. But the price is light — about $200. "It almost seems like a mistake," she says.

It is, and **Dillard Department Stores** Inc. is paying for it.

Ms. Lemberger, a real-estate agent, is shopping in what some department-store executives call a repository of mistakes: the Dillard clearance center in Kansas City, Kan. One of the oldest kinds of discount stores, it is the ignoble home of merchandise that failed to sell — even at 50% off — in Dillard Department Stores. At its half-dozen clearance centers, Dillard unloads some merchandise for less than wholesale. The full retail price of Ms. Lemberger's booty exceeded $1,000.

The existence of these centers shows that department-store retailing remains an art — despite predictions that technology would make it a science. Dillard's computer system tracks every purchase and informs company officials which items aren't selling and need promotion and which are selling out and need replenishing. But as yet, computers can't predict consumer tastes.

Not long ago, Dillard bet on an American Film Classics necktie, featuring illustrations from "Gone With the Wind"; on a polka-dot sweatshirt for teenage girls; and on a dark-brown all-cotton Claiborne lady's jacket. Today, dozens — even hundreds—of these items fill the Dillard clearance center in Arlington, Texas.

"This isn't retailing — it's getting some money out of the goods and washing your hands of it," says Sidney Doolittle, a Chicago retail consultant.

That's a fine distinction for customers who find a Ralph Lauren sweater just as handsome at $29.99 as at $165—and who are willing to buy it in August. "It's the only Dillard's I'll shop," says Jeanne Young, a Missouri schoolteacher who drove 40 miles to Kansas to shop at the Dillard clearance center, past full-price Dillards as well as factory-outlet centers.

Few discount stores or factory outlets can beat the clearance centers' prices. On a recent trip, Ms. Young and two companions "bought $2,200 worth of merchandise — I mean names like Ellen Tracy and Liz Claiborne—for $300," she says.

Predicting consumer behavior is the job of retail buyers; for them, clearance centers are halls of shame. "Walking in and seeing those 1,000 green sweaters you bought isn't pleasant," says Kay Winzenried, a Dallas retail consultant whose 17-year career at the Neiman Marcus chain included a stint as buyer.

At Neiman Marcus, whose clearance centers are named Last Call, buyers are required to "visit their mistakes" twice a year, says Ms. Winzenried, adding that any buyer whose goods consistently land there won't survive. But she and others say that any buyer whose choices never enter a clearance center may be buying too little. "Not having what the customer wants is the biggest mistake," Ms. Winzenried says.

Nor should a buyer apologize, she and others say, for taking risks. In an age of complaints about department-store homogeneity, "buyers should be encouraged to seek novelties, and novelty makes the gamble greater," says Stanley Marcus, the former chief executive of Neiman Marcus who advises retailers on buying matters.

Some department stores have developed separate, profitable chains out of clearance items. The 18 Nordstrom Rack stores feature original merchandise along with unsold goods from **Nordstrom** Inc.'s 55 full-price stores. And Boston's Filene's department store gave birth decades ago to a clearance center, Filene's Basement, that is now a separate chain buying mostly from manufacturers.

But while these profit-seeking chains are better stocked and more attractive, true clearance centers may offer the best deals. Problem is, these centers can be hard to find. They receive little advertising and no publicity, if retailers can help it. "We never comment on the clearance centers," says a Dillard spokesman.

Dillard has placed its centers in unattractive sites that it gained as part of acquisitions. The Kansas City store, once a Macy's, sits in a half-abandoned mall, the store itself half closed. The license plates outside indicate that word has spread far beyond Kansas. Savvy shoppers know when to come, for pickings are slim between shipments. "My daughter-in-law works at Dillard and tells me when new stuff is coming," says Ms. Young, the teacher from Missouri.

For the uninformed, the store can be a shock. With no sign out front distinguishing it from any other Dillard, Robert Adoki, a federal-government worker, pulled off the interstate expecting a full-price department store. "What is this?" he asks, entering what resembles a garage sale. "I thought this was a Dillard."

STUCK!

HOW COMPANIES COPE WHEN THEY CAN'T RAISE PRICES

Grandparents love them. So do parents. And kids do look awfully cute running around in their Oshkosh B'Gosh Inc. bib overalls. But in the past few years, the Wisconsin-based maker of high-quality children's clothing has faced increasing price resistance from consumers. To strengthen its ties to retailers, the company is working closely with department stores, helping to pay for new store fixtures and fancier displays. To lower costs, it's overhauling production processes and investing in worker training to become a highly flexible manufacturer. And in an unprecedented action to jump-start sales, Oshkosh will slash prices by 6% to 8% on its entire 1994 spring line of clothes.

It's not just Oshkosh, by gosh. All across the marketplace, companies are snipping away at their price tags. Mercedes-Benz is lowering prices on some luxury cars by almost 15%. Compaq Computer Corp. is slashing prices on its top-of-the-line personal computers by 23%. Borland International Inc. has chopped the list price on its latest Quattro Pro spreadsheet from $495 to $99. Boeing Co. is effectively freezing the prices of its commercial airplanes for the next five years. Says Ron Woodard, executive vice-president of Boeing Commercial Airplane Group: "Our airplanes cost too much."

RETHINK EVERYTHING. It's the Age of Disinflation--and it's creating a business landscape that few of the managers of these companies have seen in their professional lifetimes. The savvier among them aren't just whipping out the markdown pen, though. Like Oshkosh, a growing number of corporations are recognizing that ferocious pricing pressure means that they have to rethink virtually every aspect of how they do business. In this unfamiliar and treacherous terrain, they're having to abandon many of their old, inflation-inspired business habits. To preserve profits and eke out growth, compa-

nies are being forced to come up with radically different corporate strategies, manufacturing techniques, marketing tactics, compensation structures, and approaches to financing.

Battered by worldwide overcapacity, brutal global competition, slow growth, and high unemployment, corporate pricing power has clearly been crumbling. Since 1990, consumer price inflation has fallen from a 5.4% annual rate to its current 2.7% yearly pace. At the same time, producer price inflation is down from 4.9% to 0.5%. It adds up to "a paradigm shift as profound in its significance for disinflation as the oil crisis of 1973 was for inflation," says Peter L. Bernstein, an economic consultant in New York City.

EXPOSED. In the new world of disinflation, cost-cutting is, of course, essential. But by freeing prices of the distortion of inflation, this challenging environment is also restoring prices to their traditional role as economic arbiter: They are the signals that tell companies and individuals how the marketplace truly values the goods they make and the services they sell. The price a company charges is, in turn, the culmination of every decision it has made along the line. Without the cloak of inflation, all those decisions are directly exposed to the ruthless pressures of the marketplace.

A number of companies are beginning to chart some imaginative paths across the new landscape of disinflation. They're redesigning products for ease and speed of manufacture or stripping away costly features that their customers don't value. Many are paring back expensive rebates and discounts in favor of stable, low, everyday prices. They're seeking to gain a bit of shelter from relentless pricing pressure by forging closer links with their customers or accelerating new-product development. They're working to improve productivity not just with layoffs but

by tearing down bureaucratic barriers between departments and investing in high-tech hardware. Over the past 18 months, real equipment spending has increased by 24%, with about two-thirds of the increase concentrated in information technologies. "The management challenge of the 1990s is to reduce costs--and increase the perceived value of the product," observes Arthur L. Kelly, a private investor and director of Deere, BMW, and Nalco Chemical.

Above all, the relentless pressure of disinflation means that companies must constantly review all aspects of their business to make sure they're doing whatever it takes to offer customers high-quality goods at low prices. "We are in a period of low to no inflation that we may live with till the year 2000," says Southwood J. "Woody" Morcott, chairman and chief executive of Toledo-based Dana Corp., a $4.9 billion producer of automotive parts and other industrial products. "That means you have to get productivity improvements forever."

Of course, it may be too early to say that disinflation is here to stay. Inflationary pressures usually ease during slack times, and both the Federal Reserve and bond traders are convinced that inflation will roar back to life as the economy picks up. Many executives see rising prices on the horizon, too, arguing that business costs are being propelled upward by higher taxes, government mandates, and President Clinton's health-care-reform package. No doubt, inflation scares will periodically roil the markets, and there will always be some companies or industries that are able to raise prices. Even now, the 14% decline in the value of the dollar against the Japanese yen is forcing Japanese companies to hike prices in the U.S. on everything from memory chips to cars, which could give domestic rivals in those markets some pricing room.

Still, certain industries, such as

Strategies for Thriving in Disinflationary Times

Target Pricing. Forget traditional cost-plus pricing. Instead, reverse the equation for price-driven costing. Meeting pricing targets means reengineering the corporation to speed up new-product development, simplify design, and reorganize the work flow.

Value Pricing. Coupons, discounts and rebates have gotten out of hand. Cut back on expensive promotions and instead offer stable, low, everyday prices.

Stripping down. Offer cost-conscious customers quality products with fewer bells and whistles at a cheaper price.

Adding Value. Introduce innovative products sold at a modest premium. Back them with a strong merchandising and advertising campaigns.

Getting Close to Customers. Find out what customers really want and give it to them. Use the new information technologies to closely track their needs and your costs.

Going Global. The future is now. It's a way to increase unit volume, and less mature markets offer more pricing flexibility.

---

tires and energy, lived with lower prices through much of the 1980s. By the turn of the decade, gale winds of international competition and deregulation propelled disinflation into a broad array of manufacturing and consumer-goods businesses. What is most striking now is the spread of disinflation to previously immune sectors of the economy, such as legal services and health care. Even in the pharmaceutical industry, which enjoyed the luxury of raising prices at twice the rate of inflation through the 1980s, price-cutting is becoming rampant.

PLENTY OF GOODIES. To be sure, disinflation's spread is far from bad news. It means that consumers won't have to worry about sticker shock every time they pick up a box of detergent. And corporations can count on stable or falling prices for a host of raw materials, parts, services, and labor--not to mention capital costs, which are at their lowest levels

in 25 years.

But inflation was the devil we knew--and the devil that companies had learned to live with. When prices were soaring, hiking revenues and reported profits was as simple as changing a price tag. Pay raises were easy, too. "When you have inflation, it covers up a lot of sins," says Eugene P. Beard, chief financial officer at Interpublic Group of Companies Inc., the advertising-agency holding company.

Disinflation, by contrast, is a much sterner taskmaster. A 1% drop in price will slash operating profits by 12.3% for the average Standard & Poor's 1000 company, assuming that costs and volume remain the same, figures Michael V. Marn, a consultant at McKinsey & Co. To avoid that kind of devastation, a growing number of companies know that they can no longer let their internal processes determine price. Rather, it's price that must determine pro-

cess.

In the traditional approach to pricing, a company comes up with a selling price by adding up its costs, factoring in overruns, and putting an acceptable profit margin on top. These days, such cost-driven pricing is a recipe for too-high prices and a nice wide opening for lower-cost rivals.

That's why some companies are reversing the price equation. At General Motors Corp.'s Cadillac division, for example, marketers begin by setting a target price for a new model. "Then, you say your profit is so much, and you back down into the cost. We never used to do it that way," say Janet Eckhoff, Cadillac's director of marketing and product strategy. "We're backing into the [price] from the customer's perspective now." Her boss, GM Chief Executive Jack Smith, is a big believer in the target-pricing technique.

(cont.)

This seemingly simple shift in pricing philosophy has profound implications for product development, sourcing, manufacturing, and management. For example, target pricing won't work if it takes five to six years to develop and produce a car: Costs, competition, and consumer demand will have shifted too much in half a decade. To set a realistic sales price, the development cycle must be three years or less, as it was with the Neon, Chrysler Corp.'s new $9,000 subcompact. In turn, speeding up the development cycle requires stitching together teams from engineering, design, finance, marketing, and production. It means empowering workers and using lean manufacturing techniques. It means working with suppliers to deliver quality parts. Many of these efforts were already under way as companies strove to improve productivity, quality, and customer responsiveness. But disinflation has made them vastly more urgent.

TEAM EFFORT. Compaq is a case in point. After being battered for several years by low-cost personal-computer rivals, Compaq struck back in 1992. It now builds computers that cost up to 60% less through what it calls "design to price."

Here's how it works: A design team comes up with specifications for a new computer. It sits down with marketing, manufacturing, customer service, purchasing, and other departments. Based on a price target set by marketing and a profit-margin goal from management, the team determines what the costs will have to be. To achieve cost targets, engineers design products with fewer parts, and reuse parts from existing designs. Compaq's factories have been overhauled to crank out products more cheaply. And supplier contracts have been renegotiated, cutting material costs by $212 million in 1992 and $425 million this year.

The first products manufactured under the new pricing system, the Prolinea personal computer and the Contura notebook computer, came out in less than eight months. Since the third quarter of last year, Compaq's sales volume has skyrocketed 64%, and profits have nearly doubled.

Cincinnati Milacron Inc. is another manufacturer that is paying renewed attention to manufacturing during the design process. It now builds machine tools with 30% to 40% fewer parts. On the new Maxim 500, a machining center it introduced last year to replace its T-10, design streamlining reduced the number of fasteners from 2,542 to 709 and cut assembly time from 1,800 hours to 700 hours. Altogether, the approach cut production costs by 36%--and the selling price for the Maxim 500 is the same as it was for the machine it replaced. Plus, the Maxim takes up 60% less floor space, can be installed and started up in two days instead of two weeks, and makes much more rapid changeovers, which sharply increases productivity.

Similar tactics paid off in lower production costs for Milacron's plastic injection-molding machines, which now typically sell at 7% to 9% below list price. "Five years ago, we couldn't be predictable with that [discount]," says Milacron CEO Daniel J. Meyer. "Now, we can not only be profitable, we're gaining market share."

Other companies are seeking to escape pricing pressure by embracing a "value-added" strategy--introducing a new or improved product that can still be sold at a premium price. Intel Corp. has its Pentium microchip, Gillette Co. has its Sensor razor system, and Goodyear Tire & Rubber Co. has its Aquatred, an all-season radial designed to provide better traction on wet roads. The Aquatred costs an average of $90, about 10% more than Goodyear's previous top-of-the-line mass-market tire. Yet the company has sold more than 2 million Aquatreds since its introduction two years ago. Goodyear concentrates on speeding new products to market and backing them with strong merchandising and advertising campaigns once they get there. "If you can have a richer mix, that's as good as a price increase on the power end," says Chief Executive Stanley C. Gault.

QUALITY GENERICS. But selling value may be the toughest marketing job around these days. For one thing, the quality of many generic products, from diapers to cigarettes to drugs,

has dramatically improved in recent years. The inroads of generics forced Philip Morris Cos., for example, to slash prices on its flagship Marlboro brand by 40 cents a pack. With brand loyalty on the wane, it's a challenge for marketers to find the right price gap between a name brand and a low-cost rival. "A brand will carry a premium, but the question is, how much of a premium?" says George J. Bull, Grand Metropolitan PLC's CEO for food operations.

Moreover, consumers now expect low prices even on many value-added products. Emerson Electric Co., an $8.2 billion instruments-and-electronics maker, finds it increasingly difficult to raise prices even on innovative products. "In general," says Emerson CEO Charles F. Knight, "customers see little reason for price increases." Emerson and most other manufacturers, he adds, are sharing whatever cost reductions they get with their customers, putting even more downward pressure on prices.

That has some companies taking virtually the opposite tack from premium pricing: They're stripping down, selling a product at a cheaper price by offering less. It's a tactic Southwest Airlines Co. has exploited to become the most profitable carrier in its industry, and United Airlines Inc. may emulate it by setting up a new low-cost subsidiary to compete against short-haul rivals. Says Robert L. Crandall, chief executive of AMR Corp., parent of American Airlines Inc.: "The market is telling all the traditional airlines that they must compete in a low-cost, low-price world."

Even such a flashy brand marketer as Reebok International Ltd. is stripping down. Its best-known sneaker is the $135 Shaq Attaq, named after Shaquille O'Neal, the popular center for the Orlando Magic Basketball team. But sales of such top-of-the-line sport shoes, after surging for much of the 1980s, have been slowing sharply industrywide. So Reebok plans to launch four different versions of the Shaq Attaq next year, with prices ranging from $60 for a stripped-down sneaker to $130 for a gadget-laden one. It expects to sell most of its shoes in the $50 to $80 range in 1994--about $10 to $15 less than last year's best-selling range.

Another costly tactic that some companies are stripping away is the frenzied rebate and discount strategy they once relied on to lure customers. They're using the savings from eliminating such costly promotional gimmicks to pay for everyday low prices. Consumer giant Procter & Gamble Co., for example, has slashed its promotional spending to help pay for 10% to 25% price cuts on several of its products, including Pampers and Luvs diapers, Liquid Tide detergent, and Folger's coffee. **LEAN TAB, FAT MARGINS.** And on Oct. 4, Burger King Corp. abandoned coupons, discounts, and direct mail as key weapons in the fast-food wars. Instead, it's using everyday low "value pricing" and "combo meal" bargains, much like McDonald's Corp. and Taco Bell before it.

In most markets, Burger King is cutting the price of its croissant-sandwich breakfast combo to $1.99 from $2.47, and its Whopper hamburger with french fries and a drink is down to $2.99 from $3.72. The savings from getting rid of promotions means that the new strategy won't have much of an impact on profit margins in the near term, and higher volumes will eventually show up in better margins, says Sidney J. Feltenstein, Burger King's senior vice-president for marketing.

New information technologies are also helping some companies price better. Data bases and computer networks allow managements to move away from traditional average-pricing techniques. Instead, the new information technologies let companies closely track customer prefer-ences and finely target prices, says McKinsey's Marn. Similarly, new accounting systems, such as activity-based cost accounting, allow managers at Hewlett-Packard, General Electric, and Dana to quantify in depth the costs of production inefficiencies. And having a better handle on production costs encourages smarter pricing.

In industries such as health care, the pressure of disinflation is also driving companies into mergers and alliances that would once have been unthinkable. Consider Merck & Co.'s $6 billion purchase of Medco Containment Services Inc., the country's largest drug discounter. Then there's Columbia Healthcare Corp.'s $5.7 billion acquisition of HCA-Hospital Corp. of America, which will create the nation's largest hospital chain. The purchase fits with Columbia's push to add volume and cut costs in response to price pressures. "Our strategy is focused on believing that prices will come down," says Columbia CEO Richard L. Scott.

Nevertheless, considering the inflation experience of the past three decades or so, does it make sense for companies to go through the turmoil of adapting to a disinflationary world? It certainly seems so, especially as price wars rack industry after industry, from airlines to cigarettes. "We've found the U.S. to be the most price-competitive market in the world," says David de Pury, co-chairman of the board at ABB Asea Brown Boveri Inc., the Swiss-Swedish maker of capital equipment.

The pricing pressures are global, though. Japan is flirting with deflation, as is most of Europe. Worldwide, overcapacity plagues machine tools, chemicals, consumer electron-ics, and computers. Zenith Electronics Corp. figures its prices for VCRs and TVs have dropped more than 3% a year since 1984. Its lost revenue from falling prices tops $2 billion over the past 10 years, says CEO Jerry K. Pearlman.

Continued corporate bloodletting also means that disinflation is likely to be a fact of life for some time. In just the past few weeks alone, Woolworth Corp. said it plans to eliminate 13,000 jobs, four major drug companies reported a total of 11,000 layoffs, and Anheuser-Busch Cos. announced a 1,200 person cut. Overall, employment is about 3.5 million workers below what the job count would be if the U.S. were in a typical post-World War II recovery, according to Stephen S. Roach, economist at Morgan Stanley & Co.

Disinflation, like inflation before it, is taking on a momentum of its own. Pricing pressure leads to more restructurings, and restructurings lead to more disinflation. Every twist in pricing strategies for a low-inflation world ends up reinforcing the disinflation trend.

Today, prices are signaling companies to move beyond the slash-and-burn strategies of cost-cutting and reinvent their organizations to thrive in a world of low inflation. Low everyday prices--with vast everyday implications--are here to stay.

By Christopher Farrell in New York and Zachary Schiller in Cleveland, with Richard A. Melcher in Chicago, Geoffrey Smith in Boston, Peter Burrows in Dallas, Kathleen Kerwin in Detroit, and bureau reports

Marketing Strategies: Planning, Implementation, and Control

84

Policies are high-risk, not practices

Believed to be one of USA's best-run companies

By David Craig
USA TODAY

MAYFIELD VILLAGE, Ohio — Progressive Corp.'s suburban Cleveland offices look more like the headquarters of a Silicon Valley firm than of the USA's seventh-biggest automotive insurer.

Modern art is everywhere. Ceramic cloud sculptures hover above an expansive atrium. Andy Warhol prints line hallways. Even stranger for an industry known for its stuffiness: Virtually everyone is casually attired, several in shorts and T-shirts. Even Chief Executive Peter Lewis frequently dresses down.

The relaxed atmosphere isn't the only thing that makes Progressive so, well, progressive. The 29-year-old company was the first to specialize in insuring high-risk drivers — those whose policies were canceled by mainstream insurers because of traffic tickets, accidents or drunken-driving convictions. Of Progressive's 1.9 million policyholders, 70% are considered high-risk.

Problem drivers aside, some management experts consider Progressive one of the USA's best-run companies. Boston-based management consultant Mike Hammer, author of *Reengineering the Corporation*, considers Progressive a prime example of a corporate success story. "I'm very impressed with the quality of management. Lewis is really an inspirational and visionary person," says Hammer. "Their claim to fame has been high-risk insurance, which most companies avoid like the plague. But they've thrived."

Six years ago, Progressive was stumbling badly. Rival Allstate had passed it as the No. 1 provider of high-risk coverage. And in California, which accounted for 25% of Progressive's earnings, voters passed Proposition 103, an initiative that rolled back insurance rates 20%. Progressive had to refund $51 million to policyholders.

"Ours was a near-death experience," says Chief Financial Officer Bruce Marlow. "It was a massive wake-up call."

Lewis realized sweeping changes were needed. "We had gotten fatheaded. We thought we were as smart as we said we were. We left the door open and Allstate walked in," he says.

For years, lack of competition in the high-risk market — which mainstream auto insurers had long shunned — allowed Progressive to pass higher costs on to customers who had nowhere else to turn. Allstate then began courting the high-risk market — 20% of all drivers — by lowering premiums.

By 1991, Progressive's earnings plunged. Lewis, a lanky 60-year-old known for his love of art and fierce competitive spirit, had already begun ripping apart the company to make it more competitive. Progressive slashed costs — among the industry's highest. Nearly 20% of the workforce was eventually laid off. An unsuccessful foray into the long-distance truckers' insurance market was scuttled.

The California experience also made Lewis realize consumers' growing antagonism toward the insurance business. "People were saying, 'We hate your guts, we're going to kill you and we don't give a damn,' " he says.

Progressive changed the way it provided customer service, figuring if you treat them right, they'll remain clients.

Most auto insurers typically make you file a claim, come to their office, get a couple of repair estimates and take weeks to settle. Progressive offers a 24-hour, mobile claims service. Adjusters go to policyholders' homes or, often, go directly to the scene of an accident. They help locate tow trucks and rental cars. Sometimes they even settle on the damages and write checks on the spot.

"It used to be based more on my convenience when I got out to meet the customer," says Carl Metzger, claims branch manager for Progressive's East Cleveland office. "Now it's the exact opposite. When the claim comes in, it's what the customer wants that counts."

A policyholder is given a Progressive Gold Card that lists the policy number and a 24-hour, toll-free claims number (1-800-AUTO-PRO). About 80% of policyholders are contacted within nine hours after an accident is reported. Half of Progressive claims are settled within two weeks.

"They had to make a concerted effort to make (quicker claims) happen," says Steven Goldstein, spokesman for Insurance Information Institute. "It means they give consumers the benefit of the doubt and aren't fighting over many claims."

That's a wise strategy at a time when service is all that sets many companies apart. "Progressive doesn't do it out of altruism," Hammer says. "They are smart enough to realize the way to succeed is by doing enormous things for the customer."

Among Progressive's biggest changes was transforming corporate culture. The overhaul was extensive, from abolishing dress codes to decentralizing management. Progressive also adopted tactics of total quality management — which establishes teams that have free rein to improve quality and boost efficiency. "We want to get away from the mind-set that the company had to pick between low costs and high quality," Marlow says. "In fact, low costs and high quality are synonymous."

Now, 17 teams hold decision-making responsibilities. One team came up with "gainsharing" — an incentive plan tied to individual and overall corporate performance. It pays bonuses based on profitability, growth and cost-saving efforts.

All of Progressive's 7,000 employees have ample motivation to pitch in. Gainsharing paid $23.4 million in bonuses last year.

Money isn't the only motivator. Fear is too. Progressive doesn't punish failure, but it doesn't put up with incompetence, either. "Lewis has said he's fired more MBAs than the rest of the industry combined," Hammer says.

The efforts have paid off. Earnings have flourished — net income, which hit a seven-year low in 1991, hit a record $267 million in 1993. Progressive shares are up 104% since January 1992, vs. just 2% for the Standard & Poor's index of property and casualty insurers.

Lewis, however, isn't satisfied. Progressive's expenses were among the highest in the industry in 1991, when it spent 32 cents for every $1 of premiums received. This year Progressive expects that amount to drop to around 24 cents, just above the 22-cent industry average. Lewis wants to get that below 20 cents by decade's end.

Lewis sees vast opportunities in an industry that he says is riddled with flaws. "It's a lousy system that needs fundamental and systemic change," he says.

Progressive is stepping up efforts to court more mainstream, low-risk drivers. They've sold low-risk policies in Tampa and Miami for two years and just branched into Cleveland and Houston. Next week, they begin marketing in Orlando, Fla. To boost consumer recognition in those markets, Progressive is offering "Express Quote," which gives consumers rates for Progressive, State Farm, Allstate and regional insurers.

(cont.)

"They are on the cutting edge of the revolution of providing point-of-sale information to the consumer," says Lewis' former Princeton classmate, consumer advocate, Ralph Nader.

Whatever the company comes up with next is likely to keep it ahead of the competition. "Progressive is very aggressively trying to come up with the latest widget," says Rob Gensler, insurance stock analyst at mutual fund giant T. Rowe Price.

85

LOOKING CHIPPER? YOU BET

Famous Amos' star started rising again when it discovered vending machines

By Fara Warner

In 1983, you'd spend $5 a pound for a Famous Amos cookie and probably chomp it down at a gourmet outlet. Ten years later, it only takes a handful of change and a quick glance through a vending machine to nibble on what is now the No. 1 cookie on the vending circuit.

That's how far the company has come since the flamboyant founder Wally Amos sold his trademarked name and cookie brand to the Bass Brothers in 1985. Since then, the company's gone through four owners until last September when it was bought by President Baking Co. of Atlanta, the fourth-largest baking company in United States and best known as the biggest supplier of Girl Scout cookies in the country.

The turnaround for the gourmet cookie came under Keith Lively, who became president and ceo of Famous Amos Chocolate Chip Cookie Corp. in 1988 when it was acquired by the financial firm The Shansby Group.

Lively, a former Nestle marketer, immediatley saw vending as the perfect place for Famous Amos.

"The industry had generally used price to sell the product, but cut the quality," Lively said. "The weird thing is that consumers don't come back if the quality isn't there."

The strategy has boosted the brand to $81.3 million in 1992 sales, almost double 1991's figures.

Vending was the first of a three-pronged strategy to remake Famous Amos, once the height of gourmet, into a viable supermarket brand. Vending machines have gotten the cookies trial, then the products were presented to wholesale clubs and mass merchandisers in big bags at a much lower price for what is still considered a premium brand. Lively also continues to sample the cookies heavily, usually having something in the works three weeks out of a month. Now he's finally ready to embark on his biggest battle—breaking into supermarkets.

"I'd like to see us have our own section in the grocery store," Lively said hopefully. "I think we can create a brand umbrella that will justify that."

Lively was recruited by The Shansby Group to take charge of the struggling company, which had lost much of its panache and brand equity as it passed through numerous financial entities. The Bass Brothers sold it to the Kimmel Group who then sold it to brothers Jeffrey and Ronald Baer. Finally it landed at San Francisco-based Shansby—led by former Shaklee chief Gary Shansby—which then sold it to President for $60.6 million in September 1992.

The pin-striped, button-down Lively never tried to emulate the flamboyant Amos or the financiers who had run the company following Amos' leave-taking. "Clearly, all of them thought they could turn this company around," Lively said. "But they all followed the tactics of the previous owners."

Amos certainly had plans of grandeur. In 1984, he already had 40 retail shops, three wholesale plants and plans to open up another 170 stores in the U.S. and another 30 overseas. But even as he expanded rapidly, Amos cast the company as an upstart, telling the story of how he started the business with just $25,000 and no high school diploma.

Lively's more back-to-basics approach has paid off. The cookie leads in vending, warehouse clubs and mass merchandisers. It's the main cookie supplier to 5,500 Burger Kings. Sales have increased 927% since Lively and his team of executives—including marketers from Kraft General Foods and Life-Savers—took over.

In 1988, the brand was failing miserably, operating at a loss of $2.3 million. Sales had slipped from a high of $9.5 million to $4.5 million.

Lively figured there was hope for the brand if he could remove the historical "gourmet" baggage connected with Famous Amos.

Lively continues to lock horns with Amos, who came back a couple of years ago using his name, his likeness and his voice to push a cookie under the name

(cont.)

Cookie & Chip. "He was even saying 'I'm back'," Lively said. The two groups are still in a litigation battle that Lively expects to be finished by summer. Now Amos is starting another cookie company under the name Uncle Noname, a Hawaiian word for an elderly man in a legend. But it seems more like a cynical word play considering Amos' lawsuits about losing his name.

But Lively is more concerned with moving into supermarkets. Last year, when Shansby sold Famous Amos to President Baking, the idea was that President could add the distribution clout necessary to take Famous Amos beyond the vending machine and cavernous halls of price clubs.

President was already a baking supplier to Famous Amos, which contracts all of its baking. Conversely, Famous Amos offers President expertise in brand names, something the Atlanta-based company hasn't had a strong position in.

Lively knows he's got to offer supermarkets more than the name. He's introducing a new line of cookies this month, featuring a cream-filled cookie like an Oreo. The product will be introduced in vending machines and warehouse clubs first before being tried out in the competitive supermarket aisle.

Still, Lively knows he has to proceed cautiously. Expanding too quickly was Wally Amos's main mistake.

Vending continues to be a main channel for Famous Amos. That's not likely to change even with more distribution in supermarkets. While there's no glamour, advertising or promotion in vending it has two things to offer: a captive audience and a $21 billion-plus category.

Until he brought Famous Amos into the category, Nabisco's Oreos were the No. 1 cookie in vending. Everything else was sold on price, not quality, which left the once-gourmet cookie brand with the perfect opening. "We didn't see a comparable product in vending," Lively said.

Lively took the opposite approach. He priced Famous Amos at 10 or more cents higher than the competition, but the well-known gourmet name got trial. The cookie area of vending is grossly underdeveloped. It only took the Famous Amos chocolate chip variety nine months to nudge Oreos out of its first-place position.

People continuously give Lively anecdotes about how popular the cookies are in vending machines. In one seven-building industrial park, people would go in search of the vending truck because they had run out of cookies before the distributor finished his rounds. "Vending was just such an obvious way for us to broaden consumer trial," he said. "We reached an enormous amount of consumers who then started asking for the cookies at other places—like supermarkets."

The next line of attack was warehouse clubs. There Lively wooed the owners with sampling that goes for three out of four weeks in the month and offered any kind of packaging they wanted. Selling in warehouse clubs also puts Famous Amos on shelves on small markets and delis whose owners often stock their shelves from the warehouse store.

Getting his own place on the big grocery shelves won't be easy. Lively had a difficult enough time moving into supermarkets in the first place. Store shelves already are overcrowded with line extensions like miniaturizations of Oreos, Nutter Butters and Chips Ahoy. Not even Keebler can command its own section in many stores.

"We still plan on retaining a low profile," Lively said. "We don't want to compete with Keebler or Nabisco." But he wouldn't mind take a small bite out of Sunshine. ∎

Reprinted from the April 5, 1993 issue of *Brandweek*, © 1993 ASM Communications, Inc. Used with permission from *Brandweek*.

86

Shoving Back

How H-P Used Tactics Of the Japanese to Beat Them at Their Game

It Hogged Patents, Cut Costs And Pared Prices to Grab Market in Inkjet Printers

Tested on Tortillas and Socks

By STEPHEN KREIDER YODER
Staff Reporter of THE WALL STREET JOURNAL

It was such sweet revenge.

Last year, Hewlett-Packard Co. faced a challenge from NEC Corp. The Japanese giant had plans to attack H-P's hegemony in the burgeoning computer-printer market in time-honored Japanese fashion: by undercutting prices with new, better-designed models. Over a decade ago, the tactic helped other Japanese companies grab the lead from H-P in a business it had pioneered, hand-held calculators.

This time it didn't work. Months before NEC could introduce its inexpensive monochrome inkjet printer, H-P launched an improved color version and slashed prices on its bestselling black-and-white model by 40% over six months. NEC withdrew its entry, now overpriced and uncompetitive, after about four months on the market.

"We were too late," says John McIntyre, then a marketing director at NEC's U.S. unit. "We just didn't have the economies of scale" to compete with H-P.

A few years ago, U.S. companies were ruing Japan's unbeatable speed to market and economies of scale in many industries, and printers were a prime example: Japan made four out of five personal-computer printers that Americans bought in 1985. But now many American and Japanese companies are trading places, a shift confirmed by an annual global survey that reported Tuesday that the U.S. has replaced Japan as the world's most competitive economy for the first time since 1985.

H-P is one of the most dramatic of an increasing number of U.S. take-back stories, in technologies including disk drives, cellular phones, pagers and computer chips. H-P didn't even start making PC printers until 1984, but it is expected to have about $8 billion in printer revenue this year.

Among other things, the H-P story dispels common myths about the relative strengths of the U.S. and Japan, showing how big U.S. companies, under proper leadership, can exploit American creativity while using their huge resources to deploy "Japanese" tactics. H-P used its financial might to invest heavily in a laboratory breakthrough, then kept market share by enforcing rules that are gospel in Japan: Go for mass markets, cut costs, sustain a rapid fire of product variations and price cuts, and target the enemy.

Richard Hackborn, the H-P executive who led the charge, also succeeded because he could do what his Japanese counterparts couldn't: Buck the system. His printer-business teams were in outposts like Boise, Idaho — far from H-P's increasingly bureaucratic Palo Alto, Calif., headquarters — where they were

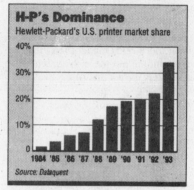

H-P's Dominance
Hewlett-Packard's U.S. printer market share

(bar chart showing values from 0 to 40% for years 1984, '85, '86, '87, '88, '89, '90, '91, '92, '93)

Source: Dataquest

permitted, though sometimes reluctantly, to go their own way.

H-P's other top executives for the most part preached high-profit, high-cost products for niche markets — which is how H-P lost the calculator business. Mr. Hackborn's troops set profit margins below the corporate norm and went for the mass market themselves. They moved fast and defied corporate rules when it meant winning customers.

"If you're going to leverage American culture but compete globally, you need a balance of entrepreneurship and central leverage," says Mr. Hackborn, who retired last year to become an H-P director. "The rugged individualism of cowboy culture alone doesn't work; but to be centrally directed doesn't either, because you lose the tremendous contribution of local innovation and accountability."

Japanese industrialists have often sermonized about U.S. complacency and myopia, but Japanese success, it turns out, can breed the same. H-P kept its huge lead because Japanese manufacturers, flush with success, spent too long squeezing profits out of old technologies and ignored signs that the American market — the bellwether — was rapidly changing.

"H-P understood computers better, it understood American customers better, it got good products to market faster," says Takashi Saito, head of Canon Inc.'s inkjet-

printer business. Japanese makers' culture hindered the kind of quick decision-making needed in the fast-paced U.S. computer market, he says, and as a result, "The market is H-P's garden."

Hewlett Packard's journey to the top of the printer market began with a laboratory accident in 1979 and culminated in a rout of the Japanese beginning in 1992.

When H-P started thinking of entering the printer market, it realized it couldn't unseat the dominant Japanese makers, such as Seiko Epson Corp. and Oki Electric Industry Co., without a technological advance. Japan had a lock on the mass market with low-cost, well-engineered "dot matrix" printers, which form relatively rough letters.

The seeds for the H-P breakthrough had been nurtured by engineers in a converted janitor's closet at a Vancouver, Wash., plant since 1980. The year before, an H-P scientist noticed drops of liquid splattered over his lab bench. He had been testing a thin metal film by zapping it with electricity; when the metal grew hot, liquid trapped underneath began to boil and spurted out. The discovery evolved into the "thermal" inkjet.

Mr. Hackborn saw that inkjet technology had compelling advantages over laser printers for the mass market: It was cheaper, it was more easily adaptable for color printing and no one else had perfected it. The idea of using a jet to spit ink on paper had been around for years, but no one had found a good way to pump the ink through tiny holes.

Richard Hackborn

H-P's first inkjet printer in 1984 was hardly a knockout. It needed special paper, the ink tended to smear and it could print only 96 dots per inch, compared with today's 600 dots. "H-P's first inkjet was terrible quality," says Norio Niwa, president of Epson's U.S. unit. "Our engineers thought that if they announced such a product, they'd lose face."

H-P saw it differently. It had also introduced a successful line of expensive laser printers for corporate customers, but the company believed that ordinary computer users would soon demand higher-quality printouts of text, graphics and photographs. There was a mass market in the making — the kind that H-P had previously blown. To prevent a repeat, H-P had to invest heavily in its low-cost inkjet technology, Mr. Hackborn says, and "learn from the Japanese" by building it into a family of products.

(cont.)

Meanwhile, the Japanese were making mistakes. Canon, which had edged ahead of H-P in patenting early inkjet designs but had agreed to share the patents, chose a complex implementation that would set it years behind. And Epson, the king of dot-matrix printers, ignored warnings of changing consumer tastes.

Executives from Epson's U.S. unit began traveling to Japan around 1985 to tell headquarters that low-budget PC users would soon demand high-quality printers and that Epson should invest more in technologies such as inkjets, says Peter Bergman, a former Epson marketing executive. "Their approach was, 'Who are these Americans to come over and tell me how to build our products?' " he says.

Epson had an inkjet technology of its own, but it was an expensive variation. Besides, says Mr. Niwa, the Epson executive, "Every engineer was looking at dot matrix because we had a big market, big profits, big business, and the technology itself had a long history."

The same kind of mistake could have happened at H-P. Headquarters became increasingly bureaucratic, with product plans requiring many levels of approval. But business units are set up as fiefs, each having great autonomy. "We had the resources of a big company, but we were off on our own," says Richard Belluzzo, who has taken over from Mr. Hackborn. "There wasn't central planning . . ., so we could make decisions really fast."

A Patent Offense

Based on decisions made in the hinterlands, H-P engineers adopted two Japanese tactics: They filed a blizzard of patents to protect their design and frustrate rivals, and embarked on a process of continual improvement to solve the inkjet's problems. They developed print heads that could spit 300 dots an inch and made inks that would stay liquid in the cartridge but dry instantly on plain paper. One engineer tested all types of paper: bonded, construction, toilet — and, for good measure, added sandpaper, tortillas and socks.

In 1988, H-P introduced the Deskjet, the plain-paper printer that would evolve into the model now taking market share away from the Japanese. No rivals loomed, but the line still wasn't meeting sales goals in 1989. It was competing with H-P's own more-costly laser printers. Sales were too low to pay the high costs of research and factories. The inkjet division needed new markets to avert a financial crisis.

That autumn, a group of engineers and managers assembled for a two-day retreat at a lodge on Oregon's Mount Hood. They pored over market-share charts. That, says Richard Snyder, who now heads H-P's PC inkjet business, is "when the lights went on." H-P hadn't targeted the right enemy. Instead of positioning the inkjet as a low-cost alternative to H-P's fancy laser

printers, the managers decided, they should go after the Japanese-dominated dot-matrix market.

Dot matrix, the biggest section of the market, had serious flaws — poor print quality and color. Epson, the No. 1 player, had a soft underbelly: No competitive inkjet and the distraction of an expensive and failing effort to sell a PC. "We said, 'Maybe this is a good time to attack,' " Mr. Snyder says.

H-P did so with the obsessive efficiency of a Japanese company. A week later, H-P teams were wearing "Beat Epson" football jerseys. The company began tracking Epson's market share, studying its marketing practices and public financial data, surveying loyal Epson customers and com-

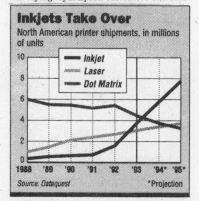

Inkjets Take Over
North American printer shipments, in millions of units

Source: Dataquest   *Projection

piling profiles of Epson's top managers. Engineers tore apart Epson printers for ideas on design and manufacturing, a tactic the Japanese often use.

Among the findings: Epson's marketers got stores to put their printers in the most prominent spots; Epson used price cuts as tactical weapons to fend off challengers; consumers liked Epson machines for their reliability; Epson's printers were built to be manufactured easily. H-P responded, demanding that stores put its inkjet printers alongside Epson's. It tripled its warranty to three years and redesigned printers with manufacturing in mind.

Engineers learned Epson got huge mileage out of a product by creating a broad line consisting of slight variations of the same basic printer. By contrast, "we were taken with the notion at H-P that you had to come up with a whole new platform every time," Mr. Snyder says. Change came hard. In 1990, as H-P was developing a color printer, engineers were set on creating a completely new, full-featured mechanical marvel. Marketers suggested that a simpler, slightly clumsier approach, would be good enough for most consumers.

Tweaking a 'Kludge'

There was a near mutiny among the engineers until a product manager named Judy Thorpe forced them to do telephone

polls of customers. It turned out people were eager for the product the engineers considered a "kludge." H-P learned that "you can tweak your not-so-latest thing and get the latest thing," Ms. Thorpe says. By sticking to the existing platform, H-P was able to get the jump on competitors in the now-booming color-printer market.

By 1992, it became clear to Japanese makers that dot-matrix printers were under assault, with sales falling for the first time as inkjet sales soared.

When the Computer City division of Tandy Corp., the Fort Worth, Texas, company, was preparing to open its first stores in the summer of 1991, it told printer makers that it expected inkjets to be a hot category, says Alan Bush, president of the chain. The Japanese responded that they didn't have anything ready. "We were very astounded," says Mr. Bush. "In the summer of '91, for an inkjet-product line you had your choice: H-P, H-P or H-P."

When Japanese printer makers that had been investing in inkjet research tried to move into the market, they ran into a brick wall: H-P had a lock on many important patents. Citizen Watch Co. found H-P had "covered the bases to make it very difficult for anyone else to get there," says Michael Del Vecchio, senior vice president of Citizen's U.S. unit. Citizen engineers trying to develop print heads learned H-P had some 50 patents covering how ink travels through the head. "It's like being in a maze: You go down this path and suddenly you're into an area that may infringe on their main patents and you have to back up and start over."

This barrier to entry meant competitors lost valuable time. "Every year that went by that we and other people were unsuccessful in reinventing the wheel, [H-P] got a greater and greater lead," says Mr. McIntyre, the former NEC executive.

Then there were H-P's economies of scale, which allowed it to undercut almost anyone else's prices; by the time Canon came out with the first credible competition, H-P had sold millions of printers and had thousands of outlets for its replacement cartridges. And H-P used its experience to make continual improvements in manufacturing. In constant dollars, for example, today's Deskjet costs half as much to make as the 1988 model.

This has allowed H-P to carry out a vital strategy: When a rival attacks, hit back quickly and hard. When Canon was about to introduce a color inkjet printer last year, H-P cut the price of its own version before its rival had even reached the market. The black-and-white printer, priced at $995 in 1988, now lists for $365.

"They've been very good about eating their own young," Mr. McIntyre says.

And consuming the competition as well. H-P now holds 55% of the world market for inkjets. The success in printers, including

183

(cont.)

lasers, has propelled enormous overall growth at H-P, making it one of the two fastest-growing major U.S. multinationals (the other is Motorola Inc.). H-P's other divisions have been transformed by the printer people's mass-market approach and now seek to make the lowest-cost personal and hand-held computers on the market.

H-P's lead in printers could bring even more profits because inkjet mechanisms are finding their way into facsimile machines and color copiers. Sales could explode if, as expected, inkjet becomes the technology of choice inside TV-top printers for interactive-TV services. Printers will "be like toilets," says Mr. Hackborn. "They'll play a central role in the home."

87

Total Customer Service

PHELPS COUNTY BANK'S PRICES ARE HIGH, ITS PRODUCT LINE
IS NOT THE MOST EXTENSIVE, AND YET IT DOMINATES ITS MARKET.
THE SECRET? TURNING EACH EMPLOYEE INTO A PROBLEM SOLVER
FOR CUSTOMERS--AND INTO A KEEN OBSERVER
OF THE BOTTOM LINE.

THE OTHER DAY MY BANK SENT ME ITS catalog. I am not making this up. It was a glossy, full-color booklet trumpeting all the "products" (as the banking industry likes to say) and services I could sign up for: Home-equity credit. International personal banking. Mutual funds. On and on for nearly 60 pages. Little yellow sunbursts ("New!" "Special value!") left the impression that I could probably get it all at a bargain—and that I'd better send in my order right away.

I have a modest suggestion for the people who run my bank, in case they ever ask me, which they haven't.

Folks, forget the glitz. Forget all the different kinds of accounts (four checking, two savings, five "packages") you describe in your catalog. Nobody can tell them apart anyway. Trash the little yellow sunbursts. Trash all the other marketing hype. Instead, take better care of me and all the other customers.

As things stand, I'm likely to go into my branch and find a line six deep, one teller window open, and two other tellers chatting behind "Next Window Please" signs. If I phone for information about refinancing my mortgage, I'm lucky to get a call back a week later. My friend Peggy patronizes the same bank and one day

brought in a check for 200 English pounds. The hapless teller first asked what a pound was. Then—because there was no key for *pound* on her keypad—she grumpily asked Peggy if she could just record it as 200 *dollars*. I remember when people used to refer to their banker, as in, "I'll ask my banker about that." Peggy and I don't have a banker. We have a marketing organization staffed by people who don't know one kind of currency from another.

In light of all that, what I'd like to do is pick up Phelps County Bank, an institution currently headquartered in Rolla, Mo., and move it, intact, to my home-town. Then I could do business with the friendliest, most service-oriented bank I've ever seen. I know, this plan may not be entirely realistic. So I'd at least like other bankers—and other businesspeople—to understand how PCB, as it's known, takes care of its customers, and to see how that approach has brought the little bank startling growth and prosperity, and to appreci-

> 'A bank is just like any other business—only you don't have any worries about cash flow.'
>
> —*Emma Lou Brent*

BY JOHN CASE

(cont.)

ate the fact that PCB's two chief competitors, both affiliated with big bank holding companies and bearing those holding companies' well-known names, have dropped to number two and number three in town while PCB has taken over as top banana.

As they say, there's a lesson here. Maybe a lot of lessons, because it turns out that PCB chief executive Emma Lou Brent had to build a different kind of company before her bank was capable of delivering the level of service that has made it so successful.

ROLLA, MO., SITS IN THE foothills of the Ozarks, a two-hour drive from St. Louis southwest along Interstate 44. It's a modest-size community, pure middle America, set apart from a thousand similar towns only by its lovely surroundings and a University of Missouri campus. Its economy isn't exactly booming, but neither is it depressed. There's a little farming. The university generates some business, as does a modest stream of tourists and retirees. The bank's catchment area—including Rolla, the neighboring town of St. James, and the surrounding countryside—is home to some 35,000. PCB's main office sits on the corner of Eighth and Pine streets, downtown. The building was once a hotel, though by the time the bank was founded, in 1963, it had degenerated into a flophouse. Today it has been reborn, with plush carpets and dark wooden paneling, as befits a thriving financial institution. Thirty-six of PCB's 55 employees work here. The rest staff three other facilities: a branch in St. James, a drive-in bank on the outskirts of Rolla, and a tiny office on the university campus.

The service on which the bank stakes both its reputation and its bottom line makes itself felt in a dozen different ways, routine and not so routine.

The lobby opens five minutes before 9 a.m. and closes five minutes after 3 p.m.—there are no disgruntled customers peering in and looking angrily at their watches. If people knock on the door after closing, customer-service reps have been trained to invite them into a secure room and ask how they can help. Reps have the authority to resolve most customers' complaints on the spot. Mr.

Jones is upset because he lost track of his checkbook balance and now doesn't want to pay the overdraft charge? A rep like Patti Douglas might refund the amount if she thinks it was an honest mistake. Or she might propose splitting it with him.

At the windows, Melanie Boyda and other tellers learn basics that escape tellers at banks like mine. "When you hear the door open, look up," recites Boyda. "If you see somebody looking around, lost, help them. Acknowledge customers. Let them know you know they're there." Tellers, too, can resolve many customer complaints—unless there's a line, in which case they refer them to a customer-service rep. PCB's customer-service creed, displayed on easels in the lobbies and the loan department, reminds tellers (and everyone else) of their commitments. No keeping customers waiting while you finish paperwork. No using "the computer" or "policy" as a reason for not doing something.

In the loan department, lending officers typically sit down with prospective borrowers for most of an hour, just to get to know them, before even beginning on the loan application. The bank's newspaper ads carry lending officers' home phone numbers, as do the officers' business cards. Customers are encouraged to call nights or weekends on urgent matters. House calls of that sort go in both directions. The day I visit, Adolph Mueller at the St. James branch reports closing a recent $150,000 loan—in the evening, at the customers' home. "They both work, and they have three children," explains Mueller matter-of-factly. "So it's a convenience for them."

Service is partly a matter of systems, and PCB monitors its service by sending surveys to new borrowers (after three months) and customers opening new accounts (after six). The surveys alert the bank to bottlenecks ("Would you say that the waiting time, if any, at the bank is acceptable?") and to unmet customer needs (an automated teller machine at the drive-in facility). Service is also a matter of innovation, and PCB employees are forever coming up with new ideas. Patti Douglas, the customer-service rep, has developed a detailed proposal for a program aimed at seniors. Peggy Laun, an assistant in the loan department, has been investigating the possibility of offering electronic tax filing.

But service is also a matter of day-in-and-day-out culture, of people going out of their way to be helpful. Managers know that and make it a point to reinforce behavior that reflects the culture. "Remember when Mary tracked down that guy's Veterans' Administration check that hadn't come in yet?" asks Bonita Prock, senior vice-president in charge of operations, as she and three other managers sit around reminiscing. "She called around and got everything straightened out for him. She even called the telephone company because they were going to cut him off. And Patti--a customer came in that had been duped by somebody over the phone. Before she was done she had talked to the Better Business Bureau in California and gotten those people their money."

Last spring the bank sponsored a promotion dubbed the "You Bet We Can Can-can," with graphics complete with caricatures of staffers doing the cancan, and advertised it all over Rolla. Tell us a story of employees who went out of their way to help you, the bank asked customers. Each month, we'll pick one. The winners--customer and employee--will each get dinner for two.

At banks like my own, such a request would be a joke. When PCB tried it, literally hundreds of responses poured in. A flower-shop owner, short of cash to pay for the repair of a critical piece of cooling equipment, called the bank while the angry repairman waited; Jody Sanders, a PCB loan officer, hand-delivered a small loan to cover the expense. At church one Sunday, an apparel retailer mentioned to Alice Malone, a customer-service rep, that she was having trouble with her credit-card imprinter. "When I got to the bank Monday, there was a new imprinter waiting for me," the retailer reported. A professor at the university got his mortgage approved by PCB before he had even moved to Rolla. Later, he wrote, the bank went to bat for him against an insurance company that had canceled his policy but tried to get its automatic monthly payment anyway.

PCB builds its very mission around that kind of service—"Always give customers more than they expect," preaches CEO Brent—and spares no expense in the pursuit of it. But the business logic is unassailable because service is the one essential ingredient of PCB's profitability. The bank's prices are high. Its interest rate on residential mortgages, for example, may be as much as a full percentage point above the competition's. And its product line isn't the most extensive in town. (Other banks offer items such as mutual funds.) So top-quality service is the only way PCB can keep customers coming in the door.

As for how you build a company capable of delivering that level of service—well, that's something it took Emma Lou Brent several years to learn.

BRENT, KNOWN TO ALL AS EMMY, was born in 1938 on an Arkansas cotton farm. College wasn't in the cards. She married a man who became a high school chemistry teacher; they had two children. As the kids reached school age, in the late 1960s, she looked around for work—something that would allow her time for Scouts and other after-school activities. Phelps County Bank hired her as a part-time relief teller. Soon she was filling in for a variety of employees, staying after work when necessary, learning on the job during the day, studying banking manuals at night. When her children reached junior high she went full-time, taking on more responsibility every year. In 1976 the principal owner, Don Castleman, asked her to become executive vice-president. Six years later he named her CEO.

Maybe because of that up-from-the-bottom history, Brent is an unusual, almost paradoxical, figure. On the one hand, she exhibits confidence bordering on fearlessness, leading her employees to regard her with something close to awe. "She's an aggressive, self-taught, gutsy woman," says one, "and she has led this bank to success." On the other hand, she has a healthy respect for what she doesn't know. She'll tell you of the time she forgot to pay the bank's tax bill, just because she assumed it was due the same day as individual taxes. She remembers learning to say, "I'll get back to you," when the Federal Reserve called with a question she couldn't answer. She felt she'd never succeed unless she

attracted smart people to work with her.

In the early 1980s, of course, running a small bank was a daunting-enough prospect for anyone. "I kept hearing that community banks were not going to be a thing of the future," Brent recalls, the clipped syllables and soft twang of her speech reflecting her roots in the region. "By the year 1995 or 2000, people said, we'd have a banking system like the Canadians'—seven or eight large banks. Banks in places like Rolla would be franchises." She doesn't add, though she might have, that a version of that prediction came true for Rolla's two other commercial banks. Both changed hands during the decade. Both now carry the names of huge statewide bank holding companies, Boatmen's and Mercantile.

Characteristically, Brent had a plan. "I visualized what I thought the community bank of the future would need to look like. It would need to have a whole staff of knowledgeable, intelligent bankers to work with people." Banking wasn't just taking money and making loans—big banks could do that well enough. It was helping people manage their lives, their assets, their businesses. It was providing hands-on personal service, the kind that would let a customer speak proudly of "my banker." Granted, that would be a tall order. The bank would need to attract, keep, and motivate first-rate, customer-oriented people, and somehow build up that culture of service. A second tall order: making money with the plan. Good people don't come cheap. Personal service is costly because it's time-consuming. The bank's prices could be a little higher than the competition's—but in Rolla, Mo., they couldn't be a whole lot higher. To make money with its costly approach, PCB would have to operate with unparalleled bottom-line efficiency.

Brent began with some straightforward moves, the stuff of sound banking and good management. She cleaned up the loan portfolio, taking some losses and tightening up on delinquency. She revamped lending procedures, emphasizing the ability to repay a loan more than the collateral behind it. ("It never did make sense to me to lend $50,000 on a $200,000 farm if the customer couldn't pay back the $50,000.") She let go a couple of people who didn't share her

outlook; she hired people who did. She continually updated the bank's computer system.

But she also took three less-conventional steps, not so much because she had a grand strategy in mind as because they seemed, intuitively, like good ideas. As it turned out, they were the seeds of a company that could realize her vision.

• While looking for some sort of profit-sharing or retirement plan—"to let people know their work was appreciated," she says, and to encourage them to stay with PCB—she heard about employee stock ownership plans, or ESOPs. An ESOP was an appealing device: it could provide employees with a retirement benefit, and it could give Castleman, who owned most of the stock, some liquidity. Brent established a small plan, and the plan bought a little stock. Over time she began to see other possibilities in the ESOP. Maybe ownership would give employees a reason for taking that extra step with customers. And in an industry in which companies were changing hands regularly, employee ownership offered a degree of job security that would surely attract the best people. Bit by bit, the ESOP began buying Castleman out (although he remains chairman).

• Figuring her employees would need training if they were to be "knowledgeable, intelligent bankers," Brent brought in Dale Carnegie instructors and arranged for the American Institute of Banking to offer her employees classes in banking principles. She set up seminars in sales techniques and in problem solving. To make sure everyone was familiar with the services PCB offered, she designed a yearlong in-house training program, in which each department prepared a session for the others. The program culminated in a mock "Jeopardy" game with six employee teams competing and an electric scoreboard tallying the answers. (See "Turning Education into a Game," Managing People, September 1992.)

• Remembering her own days as a teller—and her frustration when management ignored her ideas—Brent began involving the bank's employees in decisions. At first it was mostly informal. But in 1987, when she mapped out PCB's first formal goal-setting meeting, she invited not just managers or the board but the whole staff. ("I said, 'You've gotta be kidding!'" recalls an employee who had recently joined PCB from another bank. "At the other place, the executives would get their computers and leave. Then they'd come back and say, 'This is our plan.'") The goal-setting meetings became regular annual events. Meanwhile, Brent created an ideas program she called the ESOP Challenge. Employees with ideas for improvements of any sort—new products, process improvements, whatever—could write them up and present them to top management. The best idea each month would win its author $100. The best of the year brought a trip for two worth $1,500.

By 1991—nine years after she took over as CEO—those seeds were taking root, and Brent figured it was time to take notice of the "new" PCB. So that fall the bank threw itself a banquet dubbed the Old Settlers Dinner. The managers put on a skit—Brent played Thomas Jefferson, others played Ben Franklin and John Adams—celebrating PCB's independence and declaring war on "megabank" competitors. The upstart's weapon: its commitment to service. The revolutionaries unveiled a "customer-service creed" drafted earlier by a committee of employees and hand-lettered on parchmentlike paper. Everyone signed it. "Each of us has the authority and the responsibility to do what we feel necessary to solve a customer's problem," read one of the document's many declarations. "We are owners of our bank, and customers expect owners to solve problems."

It was a symbolic statement, of course. But there was a distinct reality behind it. Gradually, almost without anyone's realizing the extent of the change, PCB was becoming an unusual kind of company. What made the difference was how Brent's three initiatives evolved over time—and how they turned out to fit so neatly, hand in well-matched glove, with her vision of a service-oriented business.

W HERE OWNERSHIP WAS concerned, Brent's problem was making it real—not just words on paper but something that employees felt and acted on. Thousands of companies have ESOPs, after all, thanks in part to the tax breaks the plans offer. But a re-

tirement plan with a few shares of stock doesn't magically transform employees into owners, and it doesn't keep them on the payroll when another company offers $50 more a week. For Brent's strategy to work, people had to stay at PCB, building up relationships with customers. And they had to care about the level of service the bank offered those customers.

For a while, PCB's ESOP fell into the who-cares category. "The attitude was, It's just a piece of paper and it doesn't mean anything," says operations VP Prock. Even Brent got tired of trying to persuade her staff members that they were really part owners of the bank. "There was a short period of time when I just let it die," she admits. "It was too hard to convince people."

What overcame everyone's skepticism was—no surprise—money.

An ESOP is actually a trust, legally separate from the bank itself. PCB's, a so-called leveraged plan, works like this: The ESOP borrows money to buy stock from Castleman. PCB contributes so much to the ESOP each year, and the ESOP pays down its debt. As it does so, it allocates shares to individuals' accounts.

One way to make this one-step-removed ownership seem real, Brent had read, was to contribute sizable amounts to the ESOP, thus hurrying along the process of debt reduction and stock allocation. In 1986 the bank contributed $50,000 to the ESOP. By 1989, however, the yearly contribution was up to $250,000, and in the past couple of years it has been higher still. Soon big numbers were appearing on individual employees' statements. When a couple of long-timers retired, taking their cash with them, the skeptics watched in amazement. "They saw a couple hundred thousand dollars going out—and they knew only two people had left," says Prock. "It made them realize it's real money."

Real indeed. Right now the ESOP owns virtually all the bank's stock. (It bought the last batch of Castleman's shares last June.) Seven people have ESOP balances in six figures. Many more have balances between $50,000 and $100,000. In another 10 years, the ESOP will have paid for and allocated all its shares—and the bank, presumably, will have continued to grow, thus boosting its share value. At that point an account worth $50,000 today—about the average—should be worth close to

$200,000. For comparison, a typical three-bedroom home in Rolla sells for perhaps $60,000.

PCB enthusiastically broadcasts its employee ownership. Ads and other marketing materials trumpet it. Business cards announce "employee owner" instead of the employee's title. Employees elect a seven-person ESOP committee and send representatives to national employee-ownership conferences. The committee publishes a newsletter called "PCB ESOP Pride."

What lend substance to all the hoopla, however, are the economic underpinnings. Every spring, the bank holds a shareholders' dinner. There's entertainment, good food, maybe a speech or two. But the highlight of the evening, by common consent, is when Brent passes out the sealed envelopes showing individual ESOP balances and projections for the future.

It's a family affair, with spouses as interested as employees. "I barely got to look at mine," says Patti Douglas, grinning as she thinks back on her first dinner. "My husband had it ripped out of my hand!" When they both looked at the numbers, it hit them. "That's when it really came home to me, full-fledged," she adds. "Gee whiz. I'm an *owner* of that bank."

Asked to elaborate, Douglas turns reflective. "If you're just an employee, you know no matter how hard you beat your head against the wall, they may or may not notice. You may or may not get a raise. You may or may not get a promotion. Here, all that gets put aside. *Anything* that I can do for this bank to improve it, to bring in new customers, to increase the bottom line, I benefit from."

Douglas isn't thinking of leaving anytime soon. Aside from the occasional employee who leaves to start a family or accompany a spouse on a move, turnover at the bank is virtually zero.

T RAINING PRESENTED BRENT with a different kind of problem. On the one hand, delivering first-rate service requires no more than a positive attitude and job-specific skills, like knowing what to do when a customer wants to deposit English pounds. Ownership, combined with the banking and business-skill training employees were receiving, thus went far toward producing those intelligent, knowledgeable bankers. On the other hand, service is by definition costly. And unless all the employees were paying as much attention to the bottom line as they were to customers, PCB would service itself right out of existence.

So about a year ago Brent embarked on a program to teach all employees how their bank makes money, and hence what they can do to boost profits and control costs.

New employees get what amounts to basic training—a chart titled "How We Make Each Dollar and How It Is Spent," complete with real figures for the last seven years. Brent walks them through it as part of their orientation, pointing out essential figures. ("It's easy to see that your biggest income producer is your loan portfolio.")

Others have begun more advanced training in the financials. PCB's seven customer-service reps, for example, recently spent part of every Thursday's meeting calculating by hand item after item on the bank's so-called monitoring report. "We could pull them off the computer, but this way we really understand where the numbers come from," one rep explains. The report, a compilation of nearly two dozen ratios used in the industry, provides a detailed snapshot of the bank's performance as a business.

An incentive-compensation plan pays annual bonuses based on six or eight key numbers. The purpose isn't so much to reward or retain people; the ESOP does that, as do salary levels that are 20% to 30% above market rates. Rather, it's to focus attention month by month on crucial variables such as loan delinquency. (A nice touch: the plan was introduced late in 1992, ostensibly for implementation—and first bonus—in 1993. Then management surprised the employees by paying 1992 bonuses anyway.)

Thanks to all the training, people learn to keep a hawkeye on key figures—and to take action if they're headed the wrong way. "We watch deposit totals," says Boyda, the teller. "If they're down, maybe we need to cross-sell a little more." Tellers also watch their overtime hours, knowing that too much overtime cuts into earnings. Customer-service reps, such as Douglas, get monthly reports detailing the accounts they have opened and closed and how much those accounts earned the bank. "If I see that one of my customers has closed an account," she says, "I'll get on the phone and ask if there was anything wrong. We don't want to lose a customer due to dissatisfaction."

PCB makes money by attending to a hundred such details. Traveler's checks and other reimbursables go out for payment immediately. If they don't, says Bonita Prock, someone's likely to holler. ("Do you realize that the $30,000 you could have shipped cost us x dollars a day?") Customer-service reps learn to be generous in refunding service charges to disgruntled customers—but not too generous, because the refunds will reduce the "noninterest income" line of the income statement. "We've gone to the point of breaking down the loans by facility, breaking down the vaults by facility, so each facility can track itself, see where it is and how it compares," explains Prock.

The signs of PCB's success show up in the reports, provided throughout the banking industry, that compare an individual bank with banks of a similar size and situation. In a recent one, PCB's so-called peer banks had per capita personnel costs of $27,340. That was 21% lower than PCB's costs of $34,810, which included payments to the ESOP. Yet PCB's return on assets was 23% higher than that of its peers.

B RENT BEGAN HER EXPERIments with employee involvement in modest-enough fashion, through steps such as inviting everyone to the annual planning meetings. But corporate culture is a dynamic entity—and when fundamentals such as ownership and employees' understanding of the business change, so too does the nature of involvement. Consider PCB's main suggestion program.

Last July Patti Douglas's entry in the monthly competition was her proposal for a seniors program. Hire a program director, she recommended, and develop a comprehensive marketing program to appeal to elderly customers. Offer special checking and savings accounts. Sponsor meetings and seminars to help seniors with financial planning. Set up an advisory board of over-65 people to serve as "ambassadors" in the community. Behind the 12-page proposal lay nearly two years' worth of research. Douglas had dug up demographic statistics. She had compiled information about what every other financial institution in the area offered seniors. She tracked PCB's experience with its existing elderly customers. She costed out her proposal and projected its impact on the bank's bottom line. The week before it was due, she estimates, she spent 27 off-the-clock hours getting it ready.

Douglas's proposal—it won both a monthly and an annual award—was unusual in its level of detail. It was not so unusual in its level of sophistication. Sandy Karr (in loans) and Stella Ravenscraft (in bookkeeping) researched and designed the customer survey that the bank uses to evaluate its service levels. Peggy Laun investigated whether the bank should offer its customers electronic tax filing with the IRS.

Brent and other managers, of course, make the decisions about whether and when to implement the ideas. That doesn't mean the suggestions disappear into a managerial black hole. Proposals often come back to their originators for more research or for modification. This originators often become point people for research and development in the areas they've carved out. Laun, for instance, recommended against offering electronic filing with the IRS in her original proposal. The software, she had learned, was still pretty iffy. But she has since become the bank's clearinghouse for information on the subject and plans now to look at the possibilities once more.

The mechanisms of involvement have undergone an evolution of their own. For a while, PCB had an active committee known as the Problem Busters, charged with untangling bottlenecks and dealing with employee grievances. Over time Brent noticed a funny thing: the committee had less and less to do. Employees were learning to solve problems on their own. They let everyone else know what they had done through the bank's electronic-mail system. Today the Problem Busters mostly track the E-mail messages, watching for recurring issues and occasionally offering a helping hand.

It's hard to quantify exactly how all the innovations proposed and implemented by bank employees have paid off. But Brent keeps a little productivity chart that she likes to look at periodically. It measures the bank's costs and earnings per million dollars of assets per day.

In 1989 PCB's total overhead—a figure that includes all personnel expenses—came to $93 per million dollars of assets per day. Net income was $34. In the first six months of 1993, overhead had fallen to $90. Net income was up to $45.

THE DRAWBACKS OF PCB'S approach are few in number but not zero. Since the bank's employees are human, not every transaction results in a happy customer. ("There was a lady who was pretty unfriendly," reports a college-student customer contacted by *Inc.*) Yet the bank's very emphasis on service leads customers to expect near perfection. "The better we are in service, the better we constantly have to get," says Brent, shaking her head. "When a customer has been referred by someone, they're expecting first-class service from the minute they walk in." Like a manufacturer aiming for zero defects, PCB has little margin for error.

Then. too, not every employee is as gung ho about the ESOP and participatory management as, say, Patti Douglas or Peggy Laun is. Indeed, the system tends to squeeze out people who prefer a job that begins at 9 and ends at 5 and doesn't take too much thinking in between. That process isn't bloodless. Says Brent, "We had situations where employees wouldn't want to do something—but wouldn't want the person next to them to do it, either, for fear they'd look bad." No-

body other than a couple of senior people was asked to leave, but many did: Brent estimates the bank had a 20% turnover in the two and a half years between early 1986 and late 1988. Even today, she adds, new employees can quickly feel lost or left behind. That's why the bank has recently implemented a "buddy system" to shepherd them along.

And yet, what struck me, the days I spent visiting PCB, was how much fun people seemed to have. Several employees mentioned getting together for pizza after work—and racking up a video on the machine down in the lunchroom. The bank's newsletter reads like a high-spirited gossip sheet. ("EMMY BRENT had her whole family with her for her birthday & some birthday it was—she ended up cooking. Haven't they heard of eating out? . . . The big news for SANDY KING concerns her son, Derik, who graduates in May with his M.D. degree. . . .") And Bill Marshall, senior vice-president in charge of loans, told me how his staff gently informed him he'd have to answer the phones for half an hour every Thursday.

"One of the employees came to me and said, 'I've noticed we're all under a lot of stress. Everybody's up to here, and we're going as hard as we can go.' I had been up there saying how great things were--our growth last month was great--and here were these people saying, You're killing us.

"Anyway, they went out and bought a game. It's like charades, and what they decided was, they were going to

play it for half an hour every week. They didn't come to me and say, Would you mind? They said, 'On Thursday mornings, do you have appointments?' And I said no. They said, 'That's great--because you need to answer the phones while we play our game.'"

It was only for a little while, and it was early in the morning, when calls would be few. Even so, there aren't many companies in which the support staff would decide to take time out for a game, then inform the boss he had to play receptionist. "People are always pushing," says Marshall. "They correct their own problems before they get to us--the petty problems just don't appear. People are way past that and are creative. It's difficult to keep up with."

Ultimately, the key to PCB's success may be as simple as that: people are always pushing to do a little more, a little better, stress or no. All of them.

"I always have higher hopes for us than where we are now," says Emma Lou Brent, who set the bank on its present course. "I'm always saying there are so many things I still want to do."

Evidently, she's not the only one who feels that way. ∎

Additional research was provided by Louis Carranza.

88

'Do Call Us': More Companies Install 1-800 Phone Lines

By CARL QUINTANILLA
And RICHARD GIBSON
Staff Reporters of THE WALL STREET JOURNAL

Your chocolate bar tastes funny. Your hot dogs don't smell fresh. Your laundry detergent is missing a measuring scoop. Where do you go to complain?

Try the telephone.

More than two-thirds of manufacturers now offer 1-800 numbers, up from 40% a decade ago, according to a 1992 study by the Society of Consumer Affairs Professionals in Business. And as the war between brand names heats up, more companies are implementing toll-free lines. "It's the cost of doing business these days," says Jeanne Lukas, co-partner of the Loring Partnership, a Minneapolis-based marketing consultant. "Companies have to have a vehicle where people can go."

According to a study by the Technical Assistance Research Programs, a customer-service research firm in Washington, D.C., 86% of consumers believe 800 numbers on packages connote quality products. But companies have another compelling reason to offer their customers a free phone call: "We get immediate feedback on our products," says a spokeswoman for the Starkist Foods division of **H.J. Heinz** Co.

Still, not everyone is a convert. While **Procter & Gamble** Co. prints 800 numbers on nearly all items, food giant **ConAgra** Inc. has them on just a few. **Quaker Oats** Co. is just now phasing in 800 service across the board as it seeks to become what an executive says is "a more consumer-driven company." **Gerber Products** Co. has a 24-hour advice line — staffed with mothers who work part time — but rival **Abbott Laboratories** doesn't print a number on its Similac brand baby formula.

Why the hesitation? For one thing, toll-free hotlines are expensive to staff, some costing millions of dollars a year. And as calls pour in, the pressure to answer phones quickly—and pleasantly— is intense. "If a toll-free number is mismanaged," says Ms. Lukas, "it can be incredibly costly. The customer can actually be dissuaded from using the product."

Furthermore, consumer complaints triple when an 800 number is implemented. Some manufacturers ask, " 'What's the payout?' " says Philip Kotler, a marketing professor at Northwestern University in Evanston, Ill. "For some companies, the costs seem to exceed the value."

Heinz, one of the country's major pack-

Calling the Hotlines: What We Found

COMPANY	WHAT CALLER RECEIVES	COMPANY REPRESENTATIVE'S PHONE MANNER	CALLER'S TIME ON HOLD
SmithKline	Refund	Cheerful	None
Duracell	Coupon	Sympathetic	None
Kraft General Foods	Coupon	Professional	None
Mars Inc.	Refund*	Efficient	None
Nestle SA	Coupon	Efficient	None
Warner-Lambert	Refund*	Efficient	None
Gerber	Coupon	Earnest	30 seconds
Frito-Lay	Refund	Cheerful	1 minute
Mattel	Refund	Professional	3 minutes
Colgate-Palmolive	Coupon	Cheerful	3 mins., 46 secs.
Binney & Smith	Coupon	Cheerful	5 minutes
Dow	Refund	Professional	5 minutes

*Consumer gets refund after product is returned

Illustrations by Rupert Howard

aged-foods concerns, disconnected 800 service for most of its products because of "the expense of maintaining a hotline" and the fact that many of the phone inquiries involved requests for recipes and other product information that could readily be handled by mail. The company continues to have a baby-food line (1-800 USA BABY), however; and consumers with questions about other Heinz products have learned to call that number, knowing they will be transferred to a consumer-affairs expert elsewhere in the company.

Obviously, answering the complaints of unhappy customers all day isn't a fun job. Some callers yell at phone representatives. "It's hard to stay calm sometimes," says one phone representative who requested anonymity. "I've seen [colleagues] just set the phone down and start slamming walls."

Still, leaving a customer's complaint unresolved is dangerous for a company, especially since consumers share their experiences with others. A 1992 study found that callers who had their complaint solved quickly told five people, on average,

about the helpful service. Those who weren't satisfied told nine to 10 people.

But while 800 numbers may enhance a company's image, they're unlikely to help win over new customers. "It's not about new conquests," says John Goodman, president of Technical Assistance Research Programs, in Washington, D.C. "It's about just keeping the customers you've got."

Toll-free service has been around since 1967, according to **American Telephone & Telegraph** Co., which pioneered it but now has more than 500 competitors in the business. The first year there were about seven million 800 calls. Last year, AT&T handled 13 billion, about 21% of the minutes consumed for product and other consumer-service inquiries.

Giant companies like DowBrands L.P., a subsidiary of **Dow Chemical** Co., receive up to a quarter of a million calls a year, and every new product that includes an 800 number increases the workload.

To keep calls down, some companies put 800 numbers only on some of their products — those they think will generate

(cont.)

sufficient consumer questions to justify the expense. **Campbell Soup** Co., for instance, has an 800 number on its Healthy Request line of premium soups but not on its familiar red-label soup cans. The company's Swanson's frozen dinners carry 800 numbers, but its Pepperidge Farm baked goods don't.

At ConAgra, it's up to the product's managers and marketers whether the package has an 800 number. Its Hunt-Wesson division has numbers on new items, such as Wesson cooking spray, but not on Wesson cooking oil. Some Orville Redenbacher popcorn varieties have numbers, others don't.

Celestial Seasonings Inc., the herbal-tea maker, prints 800 numbers on all but its top-10 selling products. "Some companies slap the number right on there, and they don't have the people to back it up," says a spokeswoman for the Boulder, Colo., company. "You're making matters worse."

Some companies have hesitated to use 800 numbers precisely because they feared getting too many calls. For a long time, cereal boxes didn't have 800 numbers because manufacturers thought that kids, reading boxes over breakfast, would reach for the phone.

Such concern wasn't totally unrealistic. **General Mills** Inc. once offered a toll-free chat with the Lucky Charms leprechaun. "The phone company went ballistic," a spokesman says.

Despite the pitfalls, marketing experts praise toll-free lines as a way to give companies a human face. "It's kind of sad that more companies don't maximize the ease with which consumers can reach them," adds Dr. Kotler, the marketing professor. "But if you're going to have a number, it takes a lot of detailing. Some companies just may not want to spend all their time answering phone calls."

89

Quality woes are spreading like a rash

Many recalled vehicles are never brought in for repairs

By James R. Healey
USA TODAY

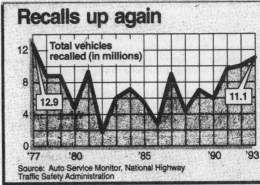

Recalls up again

Total vehicles recalled (in millions)

12.9

11.1

'77 '80 '85 '90 '93

Source: Auto Service Monitor, National Highway Traffic Safety Administration

By J.L. Albert, USA TODAY

Auto recalls are highest in 17 years. Quality problems are delaying the introduction of key models. And government probes of potential defects read like your worst automotive nightmare: Fires, exploding air bags, collapsing seats, out-of-control steering, faulty seat belts.

In fact, federal officials took the dramatic step last week of warning everybody who drives a station wagon, hatchback car, sport-utility vehicle or — especially — a minivan that their tailgates could flop open and eject passengers in a crash. "We recognize the great popularity of minivans and will be working very aggressively to get to the bottom of this issue quickly," Transportation Secretary Federico Peña said as part of the warning.

Even if the government orders a recall, it won't be a cure-all. About one-third of vehicles recalled for safety problems never make it back to the dealership for repairs, according to Auto Service Monitor, a firm that tracks recalls. It estimates that there are close to 20 million cars and trucks wheeling around out there with safety defects.

The unsettling scenario is in sharp contrast to the oft-repeated claim that today's cars and trucks are the best ever. Is there a conspiracy to lie about quality? Are automakers taking short cuts in design and manufacture to keep costs down?

The reassuring consensus: No.

Even industry watchdogs aren't barking. "I don't think you're seeing any corner-cutting. There is an overall improvement in quality. There's no question about that," says Clarence Ditlow, executive director of the Center for Auto Safety. The center, a consumer activist group in Washington, D.C., is unsparing when it believes a car company is to blame.

In fact, the only public sniping is coming from automakers themselves. Ford Motor officials have publicly said they think Chrysler has taken short cuts. That provoked a profane rejoinder from Chrysler President Robert Lutz.

Ford could be jealous. Chrysler is best among Detroit's Big Three at getting out models fast and cheap. It typically spends three years and $1 billion developing a car or truck. Ford, by contrast, spent $1.5 billion and four years on Windstar, a 1995 minivan now arriving at dealerships. And it shelled out a staggering $6 billion on a line of compact sedans, on sale now in Europe as Mondeo, and out this summer in the USA as the Ford Contour and Mercury Mystique.

Chrysler is an easy target. It is heavily advertising a slew of redesigned models, so they are in the spotlight. It developed them using efficient teams, which it also touted. After putting itself under the microscope that way, Chrysler had to recall every one of those high-profile models the past year.

In one case, Chrysler had about the worst luck imaginable. A seat belt buckle failed while its Dodge Ram pickup was undergoing the government's own 35-mph crash tests. That was just one incident, but the feds hardly could overlook it. So the popular pickup is under investigation for seat belt defects.

"You don't like to see these things happen. You wish every vehicle would have a perfect run: No accidents, no injuries, no recalls. But unfortunately that doesn't happen always," says Tom Kowaleski, Chrysler spokesman.

Often a supplier is to blame, not the automaker. It was a faulty ignition part, for instance — not bad design or sloppy assembly — that forced Chrysler to impound and repair all 15,000 of the Neon small cars it had built last month. And it was defective shock absorbers from a supplier that forced Ford to stop the Windstar minivan assembly line two days this month to replace the shocks.

Today's problems respects no brand, price or year. They range from potential seat belt hassles on $8,000 Pontiac LeMans minicars to sticking throttles on $80,000 BMWs.

If automakers aren't getting shoddy, what's causing the recalls, probes and launch delays? A number of things:

▶ **Complexity.** It is the favorite villain. "I don't think there's anybody sitting some place saying, 'Let's design things cheaper.' It's just that you have all the tubes and wires in a car today. Those are the main source of recalls: Wires that get pinched, and fluid tubes that come loose because somebody didn't quite anticipate the amount of vibration," says Noland Harris, head of Auto Service Monitor.

If complexity is, indeed chief culprit, the troubles could get worse. Tightening government rules on safety, pollution and fuel economy are expected to make cars and trucks even more like computers on wheels than they are now.

▶ **Politics.** "The government is perhaps more diligent. Under Reagan and Bush, it wasn't all that interested in recalls and investigations," says Robert Knoll, head of auto testing for *Consumer Reports* magazine, echoing comments by many industry watchers.

Not so, protests Uncle Sam. "It has nothing whatsoever to do with whether the Democrats or the Republicans are in power. I've been running this office for three years, and it is non-partisan. It's based on facts, looked at by career people," insists William Bouehly, associate administrator for enforcement at the National Highway Traffic Safety Administration.

▶ **Increased production.** Automakers are hustling to keep up with zooming demand, and that will mean some gaffes. "Overall quality levels have gone up, and will keep going up. But, that said, boom times put some real pressures on quality," says John Hammond, an expert on manufacturing at auto researcher J. D. Power and Associates. "When plants work over-

(cont.)

time, extra shifts, it makes it hard to keep quality levels up. We expect to see that. . . . It's insidious. You're working one Saturday a month, then three Saturdays a month, then four, then 10 hours a day. It creeps up on the workforce," Hammond says.

▶ **Image polishing.** Toyota's Lexus luxury brand turned a faulty light into a chance to prove how far it would go to please customers — even flying mechanics to far-flung owners to make repairs in their driveways. General Motors' Saturn small-car subsidiary did the same, sending a new seat and an employee to Alaska for one owner, then made ads about it. In the few years since, automakers have tried to spin every product flaw into a chance to crow about their dedication to customer satisfaction.

"The marketplace is increasingly competitive. The only choice a manufacturer has is to take care of problems," says consumer advocate Ditlow. "It's far better to get ahead of the curve, do a voluntary recall and say it's because you want to take care of customers. Better to recall than stonewall."

(cont.)

Quality
How to make it pay

When the "total quality" mantra swept U.S. boardrooms in the 1980s, few companies responded with the fervor and dedication of Varian Associates Inc. The scientific-equipment maker put 1,000 of its managers through a four-day course on quality. The company's Silicon Valley headquarters buzzed with quality-speak. Talk of work teams and cycle times replaced discussion of electrons and X-rays. There was even a mascot, Koala T—a manager who wore a koala costume and roamed Varian's cafeteria handing out homilies about quality.

And it wasn't just buzzwords and bear suits. Varian went about virtually reinventing the way it did business—with what seemed to be stunning results. A unit that makes vacuum systems for computer clean rooms boosted on-time delivery from 42% to 92%. The radiation-equipment-service department ranked No. 1 in its industry for prompt customer visits. The semiconductor unit cut the time it took to put out new designs by 14 days. W. Edwards Deming and J. M. Juran, the famous management consultants and leading prophets of quality, would have been proud.

But while Varian thought it was playing quality by the book, the final chapter didn't feature the happy ending the company expected. Obsessed with meeting production schedules, the staff in that vacuum-equipment unit didn't return customers' phone calls, and the operation ended up losing market share. Radiation-repair people were so rushed to meet deadlines that they left before explaining their work to customers. Sure, Varian could boast about quality. But in 1990, its sales grew by a paltry 3%, to $1.3 billion. And Varian posted a $4.1 million loss after a $32 million profit in 1989. "All of the quality-based charts went up and to the right, but everything else went down," says Richard M. Levy, executive vice-president for quality.

Levy isn't the only one who's dismayed. Countless other managers have heeded the siren song of total quality management, or TQM, only to discover that quality doesn't necessarily pay. At Johnson & Johnson, quality teams for several product lines criss-crossed the country, benchmarking against other companies, but costs skyrocketed. In 1990, Wallace Co. won the Malcolm Baldrige National Quality Award. Two years later, the oil equipment company filed for Chapter 11 as the cost of its quality programs soared and oil prices collapsed.

RALLYING CRY. Of course, the quest for quality doesn't always have unhappy results. Detroit, for instance, finally caught the quality wave in the 1980s, and it's hard not to shudder at the thought of how the Big Three would be faring today if they were still turning out Chevy Citations instead of Saturns. And much of the rest of U.S. industry would be locked out of the game in today's global economy without the quality strides of the past few years.

But at too many companies, it turns out, the push for quality can be as badly misguided as it is well-intended. It can be popular with managers and their consultants, but as at Varian, it can devolve into a mechanistic exercise that proves meaningless to customers. And quality that means little to customers usually doesn't produce a payoff in improved sales, profits, or market share. It's wasted effort and expense.

That's why a growing number of companies and management thinkers are starting to refine the notion. Today's rallying cry: return on quality. Concepts such as better product designs and swifter manufacturing aren't being rejected, but advocates of the new theory are abandoning the narrow statistical benchmarks worshiped by some TQM acolytes. Instead, managers are trying to make sure that the quality they offer is the quality their customers want. And they're starting to use sophisticated financial tools to ensure that quality programs have a payoff. Roland Rust, a Vanderbilt University professor of management and one of ROQ's chief apostles, says executives have to worry about only one thing: "If we're not going to make money off of it, we're not going to do it."

START with an effective quality program. Companies that don't have the basics, such as process and inventory controls and other building blocks, will find a healthy return on quality elusive.

CALCULATE the cost of current quality initiatives. Cost of warranties, problem prevention, and monitoring activities all count. Measure these against the returns for delivering a product or service to the customer.

DETERMINE what key factors retain customers-- and what drives them away. Conduct detailed surveys. Forecast market changes, especially quality and new-product initiatives of competitors.

FOCUS on quality efforts most likely to improve customer satisfaction at a reasonable cost. Figure the link between each dollar spent on quality and its effect on customer retention and market share.

ROLL OUT successful programs after pilot-testing the most promising efforts and cutting the ones that don't have a big impact. Closely monitor results. Build word of mouth by publicizing success stories.

IMPROVE programs continually. Measure results against anticipated gains. Beware of the competition's initiative and don't hesitate to revamp programs accordingly. Quality never rests.

(cont.)

The ROQ revisionism is attracting a growing number of corporate devotees across a wide spectrum of industries. Banking giant NationsBank Corp., for example, now measures every improvement in service, from adding tellers to offering new mortgage products, in terms of added revenue. Telecommunications powerhouse GTE Corp. is looking for quality at reasonable costs. Even companies that were in the vanguard of the 1980s quality push are considering the benefits of ROQ. "We're trying to isolate quality improvements that just don't add any value to the service that is delivered to the customer," says Michael E. Reed, managing director of operations at Federal Express Corp.

For FedEx, a 1990 Baldrige recipient, that has meant rethinking its original quality goals. In its sorting operation, for example, FedEx stressed speed over accuracy. Workers met schedules, but the number of misdirected packages soared as they scrambled to meet deadlines. FedEx eventually fixed most errors, but redirecting each wayward package cost it some $50. Now, the Memphis-based shipper has eased the sorting crunch by investing $100 million in new equipment that routes packages to various destinations.

ROQ is more than just a new twist on an old theme. Many companies believe that applying a bottom-line discipline to quality is crucial at a time when the economy is rebounding and competition is growing. AT&T CEO Robert E. Allen, for example, receives a quarterly report from each of the company's 53 business units that spells out quality improvements and their subsequent financial impact.

RETURN THRESHOLD. Everything from the installation of new technology to methods of improving billing accuracy is held up against an array of financial yardsticks, such as potential sales gains and return on capital. Based on its experience, AT&T has found that when customers perceive improved quality, it shows up in better financial results three months later. "This is the most important thing that AT&T has ever done," Allen told a meeting of top managers the day before his June board presentation.

To win approval from AT&T's top management these days, proponents of any new quality initiative must first demonstrate that the effort will yield at least a 30% drop in defects and a 10% return on investment. Ma Bell used those criteria last year to maintain its supremacy in the toll-free 800-number

market. To reduce service outages--its customers' biggest complaint--AT&T mulled a vast modernization program. But it seemed unlikely that the staggering $1 billion-plus project would net enough new customers to clear the 10% investment-return threshold. Instead, Ma Bell invested $300 million in backup power equipment to guard against failures in its 800-number system. "It isn't the old 'Give me money and I'll fix it' stuff," says Phillip M. Scanlan, a corporate quality officer. "We're taking the cost out of making our system better."

CHASING PRIZES. Of course, quality was always supposed to make bottom-line sense. In the Deming and Juran doctrines, empowered employees would make quicker and more market-based decisions. Faster and better manufacturing processes would lead to improved products and broader market share. That message was popularized by Deming in the 1950s, and it soon became the cornerstone of Japanese management theory. The quality theory emigrated to the U.S. in the 1980s as American companies tried to duplicate the Japanese miracle.

For some of them, including Motorola, Intel, Hewlett-Packard, and General Electric, excellence became the norm. But others among the legions who followed Deming came to confuse process with purpose. Quality devotees grew obsessed with methodology--cost-cutting, defect reduction, quicker cycle times, continual improvement. Before too long, customer concerns seemed to fall by the wayside.

Quality became its own reward. Standards were more important than sales. And companies appeared more interested in chasing prizes than profits. Pleasing the International Standards Organization, which sets European quality standards, became a paramount concern for some companies. Meanwhile, Baldrige wannabes often tripped and fell as they tried to complete an obstacle course of requirements that emphasizes process over proceeds. "There's been an insufficient focus on the aspect of quality improvements that will make the largest contribution to overall financial performance," admits Curt W. Reimann, director of the Baldrige Quality Award.

The new focus on the relationship between quality and financial returns does have its detractors. Critics say it's just a smokescreen behind which

companies are cutting back on their quality efforts. A healthier economy and rising sales may be prompting them to slack off on the costly discipline of TQM. And some companies--Hewlett-Packard among them--argue it's a mistake to take a bean-counter's view of something as fundamental as quality. Yes, HP makes its decisions about quality based on sound business considerations. But that doesn't mean it takes out a calculator every time it launches a quality program. "Saying that this is a quality move and this is what it's worth is like saying, 'What's my left lung worth?'" says Richard LeVitt, director of corporate quality. "Quality is intrinsic to our whole business."

IRONING IT OUT. To its advocates, ROQ is about getting companies back to something that's equally intrinsic to everyone's business: customer focus. Instead of talking about attracting new customers with dazzling statistical displays of quality, ROQ emphasizes customer retention. After all, selling more to existing customers is a cheaper way to build market share than luring business away from competitors. "Customers are an economic asset. They're not on the balance sheet, but they should be," says Claes Fornell, a University of Michigan professor who is a leading ROQ advocate. Extensive surveying, perhaps even inviting customers into design and production processes, helps companies identify the key factors that affect customers' buying decisions.

One company that's looking closely at how and why customers choose to buy is Promus Co., the Memphis-based hotel and gaming company. When it wanted to lure more customers to its Hampton Inns chain, Promus decided to offer guaranteed refunds to any customers dissatisfied with their stays for any reason. Refunds totaled a mere $1.1 million in 1993 for Hampton Inns. But guest surveys showed that the policy was pretty persuasive. Promus reckons the program brought in an additional $11 million in revenue for the Hampton chain last year. An added bonus: higher employee morale. With everyone from maids to front-desk clerks empowered to grant refunds, employee job satisfaction climbed steadily. Turnover at the chain fell to 50% last year, from 117% three years ago.

The refund program also helped Promus identify guests' chief annoyances. One of the biggest complaints at its Embassy Suites Inc. chain was a lack

196

(cont.)

of irons and ironing boards. Promus had always staffed its hotels with service people who spent their entire time ferrying irons from room to room. But no amount of coaching or planning could move the irons fast enough to satisfy demand.

Then, Promus ran some numbers. At a cost of roughly $80, the chain could put a board and iron in every Embassy Suites room. By depreciating the expense over four years, the cost would average some $20 a room--a mere $475,000 per year on the expense side of the ledger. "We have literally no problems now from an area that was one of the largest complaint generators," says Mark C. Wells, Promus' senior vice-president for marketing.

Listening to customers is the easy part. Doing what they want without spending into oblivion can be difficult. After its dispiriting experiences with TQM, Varian has focused on finding less expensive ways to please customers and boost quality. When customers complained about the long time that was needed to set up its radiology equipment at hospitals, the company didn't just send out an army of installers, as it would have in the old days. Varian took its time identifying several hundred possible solutions, ranging from the way it shipped products to how they were installed.

BONDING. In the end, Varian changed many of its procedures. For example, it decided to ship cables in plastic bags rather than the "popcorn" filler it had been using. That saved 30 minutes of cleanup time. The company also redesigned key parts to make them fit together more easily. Varian's customers were delighted. The changes saved 95 hours in setup time, worth as much as $50,000 per order to hospitals. Varian also saved $1.8 million a year. "Everything we do, we do because it makes good business sense," says Levy.

ROQ also means that companies have to learn when not to listen to customers. GTE spent $2 million in 1989 to launch a "customer bonding" program designed to respond to customers who called with complaints or questions about cellular-phone service. But the bonding program raised unrealistic expectations among customers, who suggested that GTE offer everything from on-line yellow pages to psychic hot lines. And a survey found that customers were still likely to cancel after calling to complain. After studying its cellular system, GTE

HOW COMPANIES ARE RETHINKING QUALITY

A growing number of companies are focusing their efforts to improve quality on measures that produce tangible customer benefits while lowering costs or increasing sales. Among them:

AT&T Telecommunications giant measures all quality programs in terms of financial returns. Demands at least 10% return on quality investments.

UPS Instead of stressing prompt delivery at any cost, the company is giving drivers free time to talk with customers. The hand-holding improves customer relations and helps develop sales leads. UPS figures the drivers could produce millions in additional sales.

FEDERAL EXPRESS Rather than just pushing workers to meet strict package-sorting goals, FedEx is investing in sorting equipment. The company hopes to cut down on misdirected packages, which can cost it $50 a piece.

GTE After setting up program to encourage questions and suggestions, GTE found customers who called and complained were also more likely to drop cellular service. GTE upgraded system to stop complaints in the first place.

VARIAN ASSOCIATES The company studied hundreds of different methods to reduce the time it takes to set up its radiology equipment in hospitals. One solution: a different way to package cable equipment that both saved Varian money and speeded up unpacking.

ZEBRA TECHNOLOGIES Introduced a new low-end printer to keep customers happy. But company designed the $1,495 equipment so that it couldn't be upgraded and compete with its high-end product, which sells for $1,995.

DATA: BUSINESS WEEK

decided that what it really needed to do was improve its switching to stop complaints in the first place.

Proponents argue that ROQ tenets can be applied across a company's operations, from personnel policies to product development. Consider tiny Zebra Technologies Corp., a Vernon Hills (Ill.) maker of bar-code printers. Zebra had developed a reputation among customers as a manufacturer of high-quality, top-of-the-line printers. But the company also saw a lot of sales potential in the low-end portion of the marketplace. A low-priced, low-frills printer was a cinch to make. But such a model would pose two risks: It might tarnish Zebra's image of quality with its customers. Worse, it might cannibalize the existing product line.

CHERISHED BELIEFS. The solution? Zebra came up with a no-frills version with a plastic housing that pleased its clients. But it didn't give away the store: It made sure that the stripped-down $1,495 printer couldn't be upgraded, to ensure that it wouldn't compete with its high-end $1,995 model, which is faster and can print on different kinds of materials. The result: The new Stripes printer helped Zebra's sales climb 47% last year, and margins on the new printer match those from Zebra's original line.

Rethinking quality can force some companies to abandon cherished beliefs. United Parcel Service Inc., for example, had always assumed that on-time delivery was the paramount concern of its customers. Everything else came second. Before long, UPS's definition of quality centered almost exclusively on the results of time-and-motion studies. Knowing the average time it took elevator doors to open on a certain city block and figuring how long it took people to answer their doorbells were critical parts of the quality equation. So was pushing drivers to meet exacting schedules. UPS even shaved the corners off delivery-van seats so drivers could slip out of their trucks more easily. All next-day packages had to be delivered the next day by 10:30 in the morning.

The problem was, UPS wasn't asking its customers the right questions. Its surveys barraged clients with queries about whether they were pleased with UPS's delivery time and whether they thought the company could be speedier. When UPS recently began asking broader questions about how it could improve service, it discovered that clients weren't as obsessed with on-time delivery as previously thought.

(cont.)

The biggest surprise to UPS management: Customers wanted more interaction with drivers—the only face-to-face contact any of them had with the company. If drivers were less harried and more willing to chat, customers could get some practical advice on shipping. "We've discovered that the highest-rated element we have is our drivers," says Lawrence E. Farrel, UPS's service-quality manager. "Now, we're viewing drivers as more of an asset than a cost."

In a sharp departure, the company is encouraging its 62,000 delivery drivers to get out of their trucks and visit customers along with salespeople. It also allows drivers and additional 30 minutes a day to spend at their discretion to strengthen ties with customers and perhaps bring in new sales. Delivery quotas are important, but now, UPS is willing to add extra drivers so that others can be freed to spend time with customers. As an added incentive, UPS is paying drivers a small commission for any sales leads they generate. The program has cost UPS $4.2 million in drivers' time so far this year but has generated "tens of millions of dollars" in revenue, says Farrel.

NO PROOF. It may be a while before companies get it right. ROQ measurements can be maddeningly inexact. Among the uncertainties: How much of a return is enough? How fast can a company expect a payoff? "You build evidence, but you can't claim proof," says Eugene Nelson, director of quality-education measurement at Dartmouth-Hitchcock Medical Center in Lebanon, N.H. And the new quality revolution depends heavily on customer surveys, which, as UPS learned, can be misleading if they're not carefully designed and executed.

And there isn't a lot of help out there. Major consulting firms, such as Andersen Consulting, Booz Allen & Hamilton, and Ernst & Young, still deep into their efforts to "reengineer" Corporate America, are just now turning some attention to ROQ. Many management experts believe companies have to rethink their basic operations before addressing return on quality. "If you initiate a quality program with people who are obsolete, you make them very good obsolete people," says Andersen associate partner Leonid Lipchin.

Still, some management thinkers are building thriving businesses as they spread the ROQ gospel. Michigan professor Fornell runs an Ann Arbor consulting firm, Anjoy QSC, that boasts 60 full-time consultants, offices in four countries, and 25 multinational clients that include UPS, Oldsmobile, and IBM Europe. In October, Fornell, the University of Michigan, and the American Society for Quality Control, an association of corporate quality managers, will start publishing a Customer Satisfaction Index that will measure quality improvements in 40 different industries against returns on investment. Fornell has designed a similar system for the government of Sweden, which uses it as an economic indicator. Meanwhile, Vanderbilt's Rust has formed his own consulting firm, Strategic Profit Systems, and is marketing ROQ software that forecasts long-term economic returns from quality improvements.

That eye on financial results keeps quality programs from running amok, ROQ proponents argue. And for the first time since Deming launched the quality imperative, companies can start developing precise tools to measure results. With a well-implemented return-on-quality program, they can get more than a sense of a job well done and the opportunity to spout lofty rhetoric about valuing their customers. They can get the kind of results that they can take to the bank.

By David Greising in Atlanta, with bureau reports

91

Saturn 'Homecoming': Publicity Stunt, Or Triumph of Relationship Marketing?

By John Bissell

When about 44,000 consumers bought tickets to celebrate their ownership of General Motors' Saturn automobile at the car maker's Spring Hill, Tenn., plant in late June, the news media blanketed the nation with stories about it. An additional 100,000 Saturn-ites participated in picnics and parties sponsored locally by their beloved Saturn dealers nationwide, generating still more news coverage on the local level.

Though the media attention was impressive, the Saturn "homecoming" should be less remembered as a publicity stunt than as a milestone of relationship marketing. If you assume that each Saturn owner brought another family member, that means about 70,000 owners of the 700,000 Saturns sold to date, or about 10% of the total, thought enough of their cars to join the festivities. Remarkable.

All this adulation for a sleepy, unimposing and inexpensive car with outdated design and an uncertain future. Saturn's potential for cult status seems inherently lacking. It has none of the "tough guy" appeal of Harley-Davidson or the "sexy" allure of Mustang. Even more incredible is that this coup was hatched by General Motors, that bastion of traditional and conservative marketing. And yet, as David Sholes, ceo of direct response agency Rapp Collins Worldwide put it, "They succeeded in *doing* something we all *want* to do."

How *did* they do it? Don Hudler, vice president of sales, service and marketing for Saturn, said the car's unlikely charisma is not accidental. "If you hadn't already put the pieces in place, the 'homecoming' party wouldn't have worked," he said.

The Saturn phenomenon is not the result of a stand-alone marketing or sales tactic, but a long-term, strategic, customer-oriented, "total business" approach.

Management consultant Bill MacKinnon, GM's personnel vice president during Saturn's formation, explained that every aspect of the subsidiary's development was bottom-up and consumer-focused. "Right from the start, Saturn took a people-oriented, integrated, total business approach that encompassed not only product design and marketing issues, but ostensibly unrelated matters like the manufacturing site selection and human resources issues such as where the UAW fit in," he said.

A hand-picked management team was awarded the latitude to make decisions independent of GM's hidebound culture. It's worth noting that GM has mightily tried, but not succeeded, in retrofitting its existing divisions with Saturn-esque principles (e.g. Oldsmobile). "A piecemeal approach will not work," said MacKinnon.

That the car itself is not as important as the *relationship* Saturn owners have with their dealers is another key factor. This relationship begins at the beginning, with Saturn's "no dicker sticker" policy. "By removing the negotiating process, Saturn immediately transformed the buyer-seller relationship from adversarial to service-oriented," Sholes said. This initial consumer-dealer bond is reinforced throughout the ownership experience and has enabled Saturn to weather difficult times. Most notably, these include a major product recall and strong, new competition from Chrysler's Neon, a less expensive, sportier and fully-featured car.

Perhaps most important, Saturn's brand of "relationship marketing" is working because General Motors has allocated adequate time and money to establish a place in the hearts and minds of consumers. Over the past 10 years, GM has invested over $5 billion, but so far sells only 270,000 Saturns per year. Under ordinary circumstances, GM might be accused of sending good money chasing after bad. The situation may be different for Saturn, however, because GM's investment is in building long-term consumer loyalty from outside GM's established customer base, not quick-hit awareness and trial.

In a recent speech, Peter Mills, ceo of Ross Roy Communications—a Chrysler agency that specializes in relationship marketing—expounded on this critical point of difference. After citing a Bain Corp. statistic that a 5% increase in loyalty results in 60%-80% greater profits, he said, "If 80% of corporate profit comes from customer retention, not acquisition . . . why is it that only about 20% of marketing expenditures are currently targeted against what we could loosely call customer-loyalty marketing?"

Saturn's response was evident at Spring Hill. This otherwise unremarkable product has instilled extraordinary customer loyalty via a "total business" approach to relationship marketing. The Spring Hill experience strongly suggests that the Saturn experiment may be headed for stellar profitability, assuming GM continues its support. ∎

John Bissell is managing partner at Gundersen Partners, a search/management consultant firm based in Detroit and New York.

Reprinted from the August 8, 1994 issue of *Brandweek*, © 1994 ASM Communications, Inc. Used with permission from *Brandweek*.

Ethical Marketing in a Consumer-Oriented World: Appraisal and Challenges

92.

THE GLOBAL VILLAGE FINALLY ARRIVES

The New World Order is a version of the New World writ large: a wide-open frontier of polyglot terms and post national trends.

This is the typical day of a relatively typical soul in today's diversified world. I wake up to the sound of my Japanese clock radio, put on a T shirt sent me by an uncle in Nigeria and walk out into the street, past German cars, to my office. Around me are English-language students from Korea, Switzerland and Argentina—all on this Spanish-named road in this Mediterranean-style town. On TV, I find, the news is in Mandarin; today's baseball game is being broadcast in Korean. For lunch I can walk to a sushi bar, a tandoori palace, a Thai cafe or the newest burrito joint (run by an old Japanese lady). Who am I, I sometimes wonder, the son of Indian parents and a British citizen who spends much of his time in Japan (and is therefore—what else?—an American permanent resident)? And where am I?

I am, as it happens, in Southern California, in a quiet, relatively uninternational town, but I could as easily be in Vancouver or Sydney or London or Hong Kong. All the world's a rainbow coalition, more and more; the whole planet, you might say, is going global. When I fly to Toronto, or Paris, or Singapore, I disembark in a world as hyphenated as the one I left. More and more of the globe looks like America, but an America that is itself looking more and more like the rest of the globe. Los Angeles famously teaches 82 different languages in its schools. In this respect, the city seems only to bear out the old adage that what is in California today is in American tomorrow, and next week around the globe.

In ways that were hardly conceivable even a generation ago, the new world order is a version of the New World writ large: a wide-open frontier of polyglot terms and postnational trends. A common multiculturalism links us all—call it Planet Hollywood, Planet Reebok or the United Colors of Benetton. *Taxi* and *hotel* and *disco* are universal terms now, but so too are *karaoke* and *yoga* and *pizza*. For the gourmet alone, there is tiramisu at the Burger King in Kyoto, echt angel-hair pasta in Saigon and enchiladas on every menu in Nepal.

But deeper than mere goods, it is souls that are mingling. In Brussels, a center of the new "unified Europe," 1 new baby in every 4 is Arab. Whole parts of the Paraguayan capital of Asuncion are largely Korean. And when the prostitutes of Melbourne distributed some pro-condom pamphlets, one of the languages they used was Macedonian. Even Japan, which prides itself on its centuries-old socially engineered uniculture, swarms with Iranian illegals, Western executives, Pakistani laborers and Filipino hostesses.

The global village is defined, as we know, by an international youth culture that takes its cues from American pop culture. Kids in Perth and Prague and New Delhi are all tuning in to *Santa Barbara* on TV, and wriggling into 501 jeans, while singing along to Madonna's latest in English. CNN (which has grown 70-fold in 13 years) now reaches more than 140 countries; an American football championship pits London against Barcelona. As fast as the world comes to America, America goes round the world—but it is an America that is itself multi-tongued and many hued, an America of Amy Tan and Janet Jackson and movies with dialogue in Lakota.

For far more than goods and artifacts, the one great influence being broadcast around the world in greater numbers and at greater speed than ever before is people. What were once clear divisions are now tangles of crossed lines: there are 40,000 "Canadians" resident in Hong Kong, many of whose first language is Cantonese. And with people come customs: while new immigrants from Taiwan and Vietnam and India—some of the so-called Asian Calvinists—import all-American values of hard work and family closeness and entrepreneurial energy to America, America is sending its values of upward mobility and individualism and melting-pot hopefulness to Taipei and Saigon and Bombay.

Values, in fact, travel at the speed of fax; by now, almost half the world's Mormons live outside the U.S. A diversity of one culture quickly becomes a diversity of many: the "typical American" who goes to Japan today may be a third-generation Japanese American, or the son of a Japanese woman married to a California serviceman, or the offspring of a Salvadoran father and an Italian mother from San Francisco. When he goes out with a Japanese woman, more than two cultures are brought into play.

None of this, of course, is new: Chinese silks were all the rage in Rome centuries ago, and Alexandria before the time of Christ was a paradigm of the modern universal city. Not even American eclecticism is new: many a small town has long known Chinese restaurants, Indian doctors and Lebanese grocers. But now all these cultures are crossing at the speed of light. And the rising diversity of the planet is something more than mere cosmopolitanism: it is a fundamental recoloring of the very complexion of societies. Cities like Paris, or Hong Kong, have always had a soigne, international air and served as magnets for exiles and emigres, but now smaller places are multinational too. Marseilles speaks French with a distinctly North African twang. Islamic fundamentalism has one of its strongholds in

Bradford, England. It is the sleepy coastal towns of Queensland, Australia, that print their menus in Japanese.

The dangers this internationalism presents are evident: not for nothing did the Tower of Babel collapse. As national borders fall, tribal alliances, and new manmade divisions, rise up, and the world learns every day terrible new meanings of the word Balkanization. And while some places are wired for international transmission, others (think of Iran or North Korea or Burma) remain as isolated as ever, widening the gap between the haves and the have-nots, or what Alvin Toffler has called the "fast" and the "slow" worlds. Tokyo has more telephones than the whole continent of Africa.

Nonetheless, whether we like it or not, the "transnational" future is upon us: as Kenichi Ohmae, the international economist, suggests with his talk of a "borderless economy," capitalism's allegiances are to products, not places. "Capital is now global," Robert Reich, the Secretary of Labor, has said, pointing out that when an Iowan buys a Pontiac from General Motors, 60% of his money goes to South Korea, Japan, West Germany, Taiwan, Singapore, Britain and Barbados. Culturally we are being re-formed daily by the cadences of world music and world

fiction: where the great Canadian writers of an older generation had names like Frye and Davies and Laurence, now they are called Ondaatje and Mistry and Skvorecky.

As space shrinks, moreover, time accelerates. This hip-hop mishmash is spreading overnight. When my parents were in college, there were all of seven foreigners living in Tibet, a country the size of Western Europe, and in its entire history the country had seen fewer than 2,000 Westerners. Now a Danish student in Lhasa is scarcely more surprising than a Tibetan in Copenhagen. Already a city like Miami is beyond the wildest dreams of 1968; how much more so will its face in 2018 defy our predictions of today?

It would be easy, seeing all this, to say that the world is moving toward the *Raza Cosmica* (Cosmic Race), predicted by the Mexican thinker Jose Vasconcelos in the '20s--a glorious blend of mongrels and mestizos. It may be more relevant to suppose that more and more of the world may come to resemble Hong Kong, a stateless special economic zone full of expats and exiles linked by the lingua franca of English and the global marketplace. Some urbanists already see the world as a grid of 30 or so highly advanced city-regions, or technopoles, all plugged into the same international circuit.

The world will not become America. Anyone who has been to a baseball game in Osaka, or a Pizza Hut in Moscow, knows instantly that she is not in Kansas. But America may still, if only symbolically, be a model for the world. *E Pluribus Unum*, after all, is on the dollar bill. As Federico Mayor Zaragoza, the director-general of UNESCO, has said, "America's main role in the new world order is not as a military superpower, but as a multicultural superpower."

The traditional metaphor for this is that of a mosaic. But Richard Rodriguez, the Mexican-American essayist who is a psalmist for our new hybrid forms, points out that the interaction is more fluid than that, more human, subject to daily revision. "I am Chinese," he says, "because I live in San Francisco, a Chinese city. I became Irish in America. I became Portuguese in America." And even as he announces this new truth, Portuguese women are becoming American, and Irishmen are becoming Portuguese, and Sydney (or is it Toronto?) is thinking to compare itself with the "Chinese city" we know as San Francisco.

93

MANAGING BY VALUES

IS LEVI STRAUSS' APPROACH VISIONARY—OR FLAKY?

Talk, talk, talk. As a black mid-level executive at Levi Strauss & Co. in the early 1980s, that's all Louis Kirtman got from the white men above him in top management. Levi's had long enjoyed a reputation as a socially responsible employer. But that didn't mean much to Kirtman as he watched black executives he thought were highly qualified passed over for plum jobs, while his own career seemed stalled on a lonely plateau. Top management always mouthed diversity, Kirtman says, "but in the end, they chose people they were comfortable with" for key positions.

Fast forward to 1994, and Kirtman is a much happier man. As president of Levi's Britannia Sportswear division, the 48-year-old executive is a step away from joining the company's senior management ranks. Life changed for him in 1985, when senior executives began feeling heavy pressure from above to make "workplace diversity" a reality rather than a topic of conversation. The chief of Levi's then-ailing European division tapped Kirtman to help rescue the unit. The young executive made the most of his opportunity and landed on the fast track. "We started to improve at Levi's," he says, "when we stopped talking about values like diversity and started behaving that way."

Levi Strauss is embarked on a grand social experiment. It is struggling mightily, though not always successfully, to live up to a singular, lofty vision of how to run a modern corporation—a vision set forth by none other than Chairman and Chief Executive Robert D. Haas, the great-great-grandnephew of founder Levi Strauss (page 51). The vision combines traditional liberal idealism with a set of management precepts straight out of the '90s zeitgeist of inclusion and "empowerment." Haas calls it "responsible commercial success." More conservative executives might call it flaky.

Haas believes the corporation should be an ethical creature—an organism capable of both reaping profits and making the world a better place to live. Creating tangible opportunities for minority employees such as Kirtman is only one part of the equation. Haas is out to make each of his workers, from the factory floor on up, feel as if they are an integral part of the making and selling of blue jeans. He wants to ensure that all views on all issues—no matter how controversial—are heard and respected. The chairman won't tolerate harassment of any kind. He won't do business with suppliers who violate Levi's strict standards regarding work environment and ethics. A set of corporate "aspirations," written by top management, is to guide all major decisions.

If many of these goals sound familiar, it's because countless other companies have tried to embrace them to one degree or another. Xerox, Johnson & Johnson, and MCI are all noted for their efforts to promote diversity of background and thought among their workers. Nike, Microsoft, and Federal Express are well known for pushing authority down through the ranks and allowing employees plenty of input when it comes to running the business.

Some companies approach diversity and empowerment as competitive tools. "We don't encourage homogeneity here," says Timothy F. Price, president of business markets at MCI Communications Corp. "The price you pay for conformity is lack of creativity." Others are learning to give ethnic minorities, homosexuals, and women protection and respect out of a late 20th century defensiveness: In an ever more litigious society, they fear being sued.

No company, however, has embraced a values-based strategy the way Levi's has. Sitting in his San Francisco office wearing a pair of pointy-toe boots, a plaid shirt, and stone-washed 501s, Haas explains why: "We are not doing this because it makes us feel good—although it does. We are not doing this because it is politically correct. We are doing this because we believe in the interconnection between liberating the talents of our people and business success."

Haas points to a study issued on May 30 by Gordon Group Inc. for the California Public Employees' Retirement System (CalPERS). Its conclusion: Companies that involve employees more often in decision-making boast stronger market valuations than those that don't. The report suggested that CalPERS might see stock gains by pressuring companies to improve workplace conditions. Says Richard H. Koppes, the pension fund's general counsel: "This is one of the screens we'll use in looking for what companies we target."

Levi's, of course, won't be on Koppes' list. Ever since the $1.6 billion leveraged buyout Haas led in 1985, the world's largest apparel maker has been a private company. CalPERS would probably like a piece, though. Record sales and earnings for five of the past six years culminated in a 36% rise in profits last year, to $492 million on sales of $5.9 billion. And Morgan Stanley & Co. estimates that the stock—94% of which is in Haas family hands—has appreciated 1,300% since the LBO.

But this year, sales have slowed to a crawl, and operating profits will likely decline. A big problem is that Levi's is proving clay-footed when it comes to developing new products and getting goods into its retail outlets. Has the company's emphasis on "values" distracted it from the nuts and bolts of running its business? Haas says no, but plans to spend $500 million starting this summer to restructure Levi's manufacturing, marketing, and distribution systems. He feels the company is in a temporary lull; in the long run, he insists, the cultivation of a

THE CEO AS GURU
LEVI'S HAAS ESPOUSES "RESPONSIBLE COMMERCIAL SUCCESS"

(cont.)

culture devoted to such values as diversity and empowerment will make Levi's all the more responsive in the marketplace.

The jury is still out on that. BUSINESS WEEK had the opportunity to travel within the world of Levi's this spring and glimpse firsthand how Haas's experiment is proceeding. The following set of snapshots provides ample evidence that Haas is a long way from realizing his vision. "We are only a few steps along in our journey," he agrees. "We are far from perfect. We are far from where we want to be. But the goal is out there, and it's worth striving for."

'WHAT'S NEXT, CRYSTALS?'

Margaret P. Lourenco wasn't so sure about this values stuff when she first came to Levi's. A 32-year-old, can't-sit-still financial planner, she left J.P. Morgan & Co. in New York for San Francisco in 1990. She remembers well her reaction when she was first given the "Aspiration Statement," the corporate credo at the center of Haas's values-based strategy. "When I first read it," she recalls, "I said 'Phew, what are we going to have next, crystals?'"

A lot of people have that reaction. Printed on paper made from recycled blue denim, the Aspiration Statement hangs on office and factory walls throughout Levi's. To emphasize its gravity, Haas made sure it was crafted by top management, not the human resources department. At Levi's, one-third of an employee's evaluation is based on "aspirational" behavior: Ignore issues such as diversity and empowerment, and you might not get your raise.

After the button-down atmosphere at Morgan, Lourenco was bemused by the "I'm O.K., you're O.K." nature of Levi's culture. But then she took a chance and politely criticized her boss for what she considered heavy-handed behavior. To her surprise, he agreed and changed his act. "I found that Aspirations isn't about New Age feel-good," she says. "It's about being open and direct. It's about getting rid of hidden agendas."

For his part, F. Warren Hellman worries that all this management-speak risks clogging up the works at Levi's. Doing the right thing is fine, he says, but "there's a danger that this will

WHAT LEVI'S ASPIRES TO

NEW BEHAVIORS

Management must exemplify "directness, openness to influence, commitment to the success of others, and willingness to acknowledge our own contributions to problems."

DIVERSITY

Levi's "values a diverse workforce (age, sex, ethnic group, etc.) at all levels of the organization.... Differing points of view will be sought; diversity will be valued and honestly rewarded, not suppressed."

RECOGNITION

Levi's will "provide greater recognition—both financial and psychic—for individuals and teams that contribute to our success...those who create and innovate and those who continually support day-to-day business requirements."

ETHICAL MANAGEMENT PRACTICES

Management should epitomize "the stated standards of ethical behavior. We must provide clarity about our expectations and must enforce these standards throughout the corporation."

COMMUNICATIONS

Management must be "clear about company, unit, and individual goals and performance. People must know what is expected of them and receive timely, honest feedback...."

EMPOWERMENT

Management must "increase the authority and responsibility of those closest to our products and customers. By actively pushing the responsibility, trust, and recognition into the organization, we can harness and release the capabilities of all our people."

DATA: LEVI STRAUSS & CO.

degrade into a touchy-feely, I-don't-want-to-offend-you, creativity-stifling style of management." Hellman is hardly a disinterested observer. A San Francisco investment banker, he's Bob Haas's distant cousin and a Levi's director.

Don't get the idea that Hellman is not foursquare behind the chairman. Even though he though it was a terrible idea to leave such a potentially lucrative market, he joined the unanimous board

vote to pull $40 million of Levi's business out of China in protest of human-rights violations there. "Basically, we love Bob," Hellman says. "Bob has made a fortune for everyone, and you owe Bob one." Still, he says, "the challenge for Levi's is to be sure that decisions are not just 'nice' decisions, but decisions that are meant to enhance shareholder value."

"I haven't seen the word 'nice' anywhere in the Aspiration Statement," growls Robert D. Rockey Jr., president of Levi Strauss North America. Openness and respect don't equate with niceness, he says. "Honesty is the key." Levi's 360-degree review process, which requires that an employee be evaluated not just by his or her superior but also by subordinates and peers, isn't always pleasant. Rockey says his own evaluation "upset my self-image. I thought I was more caring. I was afraid to be personal." The reviews caused Rockey to loosen up somewhat, to command less, to listen more. But as his fellow workers can attest, the former Navy reserve captain still feels no need to be nice.

'WE'RE NOT A PERFECT COMPANY'

As far as some of the company's customers are concerned, Levi's has been a little too nice to its competition for the past few years. W. Barger Tygart, J.C. Penney Co.'s top merchandiser, finally has his wrinkle-free Dockers. But he had been clamoring for them for a year while Haggar Apparel Co. and Farah Manufacturing Co. soaked up sales in the hottest segment of the men's pants business. "They don't have the flexibility" to move fast on fashion trends, Tygart gripes. Levi's admits that it already has lost at least $200 million in sales by being slow into the wrinkle-free market. This year, the missed opportunity will contribute to Levi's first profit decline since 1988.

It has been a long time since retailers have been happy with Levi's customer support. Good thing the company offers high-quality clothes and a great brand name. "If you weren't Levi's," and executive at California's Mervyn's department stores once told the company, "you'd be gone." Tygart notes that Levi's might take 25 to 30 days just to replenish a standard lot of pants; Haggar or Farah do it in 10.

204

(cont.)

"That's 15 or 20 days when all we're selling is the competing product," Tygart says.

Such problems raise the question of whether Levi's emphasis on values is distracting. Haas insists that is not the case. Levi's, he argues, allowed its product development and customer service in the U.S. to slip because the company had been struggling to keep up with heady growth at home and explosive growth overseas. "We're not a perfect company," he says. "We could be doing a better job in customer service."

Haas believes the problems would be worse if it weren't for the company's free exchange of ideas. "If anything," he says, "I think our values help address the problems because we get more two-way communication." Levi's is counting on communication more than ever as it moves toward a solution: This summer it is heading full bore into a $500 million effort to remake its product-development and distribution systems. Warehouses will be relocated, computer systems will be overhauled, employees will be uprooted--and some of them may lose their jobs. Levi's executives acknowledge this will test the values strategy. "An environment of uncertainty produces a lot of fear," says one. "It's easy to regress to old behaviors in a situation like that."

Not surprisingly, Levi's whole approach to the reengineering is uniquely, well, aspirational. More than 6,000 of the company's 36,000 employees were asked to provide advice on what Levi's should be doing differently. With that input in had, nearly 200 of the company's key managers took over an entire floor of cubicles at Headquarters and spent more than a year planning at a cost of $12 million. The company's Diversity Council, which is a direct link to senior management for groups representing blacks, Asians, Hispanics, gays, and women, also played a role in the decisions made.

The process took much longer and involved far more people than advisers at Anderson Consulting thought wise. But Haas says orienting the organization toward a common goal will prove more efficient in the long run. He sees the Aspiration Statement serving as a mountain climber's rope. "It allows individuals to take risks that they couldn't take if they weren't bound together by a common understanding," he says.

'I'M NOT A 35-YEAR OLD WOMAN'

A diverse workforce, unafraid to volunteer idiosyncratic ideas and opinions, leads to better marketing decisions, insists Daniel M. Chew, Levi's director of corporate marketing. That doesn't mean market research and focus groups can be dispensed with. But an employee base that's more reflective of the customer base can make a company hipper and more responsive, Chew believes.

Long gone are the days when everyone wore the same kind of Levi's. Today, the company sells 200 styles of blue jeans alone. There is no way, Haas says, that top management can stay on top of fashion trends without help from deep within the organization. "I'm not a 35-year-old woman," says Haas. "I'm no hip-hopper. I'm not the target customer."

An example of diversity in action: While the gritty, independent hipsters in Levi's "501 Blues" TV ads have drawn young customers like a strong magnet, they didn't click for Levi's Hispanic employees and customers. "Why is that guy walking down the street alone?" they asked. "Doesn't he have any friends?" Scenes of friends and family would resonate better in their culture, they said, and given that Hispanics buy 50% more Levi's than the average customer, this was important information. So, Levi's launched a fresh series of 501 ads for the Hispanic market that downplayed individuality to emphasize camaraderie instead. Sales in the Hispanic community have been booming.

But even at Levi's, diversity at the top is a troublesome goal. Haas's executive management committee is composed of seven middle-aged white men and one middle-aged white woman. While Haas openly recognizes the disparity between word and deed at the upper echelon, he explains that building talent takes a long time. Levi's has doubled the percentage of minority managers, to 36%, since Haas became CEO in 1984. Women have climbed from 32% of the management ranks to 54% in the same period. In both cases, Levi's vastly outperforms the average U.S. corporation, according to federal labor statistics.

Louis Kirtman, who is Levi's top black executive, says the company still has work to do, but he's happy with the fact Levi's has moved more than a

dozen minorities and women into mezzanine-level management slots. A Hispanic man now runs Levi's South American sourcing operation. Women hear up Levi's operation in Britain and Mexico. When some of the senior managers in their fifties move on, Kirtman says, "you'll see the real change occur."

Of course, all this talk about the importance of diversity is a thorn in the side for some white males at Levi's. Several executives say, though not for attribution, that they've heard plenty of white males grumble about feeling "disempowered" as they try to advance within the corporation. Haas doesn't offer such employees much in the way of solace. For those white males "who focus on self-improvement and their contributions, the chances are good," Haas reflects. "We've eliminated the automatic promotions based on the old-boy network."

'PEER PRESSURE CAN BE BRUTAL'

Salvador Salas is a long way from the old-boy network. Fingertips wrapped in green adhesive tape to prevent cuts and scratches, Salas sews blue-jean waistbands all day at the nonunion Kastrin Street factory in El Paso. If Haas's idealism is running into reality when it comes to white male egos in the executive suite, consider the factory floor. Empowerment and teamwork can be alien, uncomfortable concepts for those who have spent their working lives taking orders.

Salas likes his job, but he's not so sure about the new team system Levi's is introducing in its 27 U.S. sewing plants. Instead of grouping workers by function--all the zipper-sewers in one area, all the belt-loop attachers in another--Levi's has created multitask teams of 20 or 30 workers each. They are responsible for completing individual orders by assembling full pairs of pants, from waist to hem. After 18 months of teamwork in El Paso, turnaround time from order to shipment has dropped from seven days to three. But the workers aren't all getting along.

Under the team system, a worker's incentive pay is tied to team performance. A poor performer or absent worker affects everybody's paycheck. When someone is perceived to be faking sick days or lollygagging on a sewing machine, tempers flare. Says Salas: "Somebody's fooling around, and somebody else calls attention to that, and the first guy will just flip him off." Supervisor Gracie Cortez says that "it gets tough out there." She finds herself intervening to prevent "big fights." Says plant manager Edward Alvarez: "Peer pressure can be vicious and brutal."

Kastrin Street plant workers got two weeks of training before the team system kicked in, part of it devoted to group dynamics. Alvarez allows it "wasn't enough." Since then, 4 of 39 teams have undergone one-day let's-get-along sessions with a private consultant. But even that hasn't done the trick. "We're trying to find a more effective way to do it," Alvarez says.

While most Levi's plants are nonunion, Levi's gets credit--even from the union leaders it does have--for running some of the safest most worker-friendly factories in an industry notorious for abuses. "Here, I can get up and go to the restroom or get a drink when I need to," says rivet setter Emerio Ponce, who has worked for another apparel maker in El Paso. "I wasn't used to that."

Still, critics charge that Levi's pays a lot more attention to workers and training at headquarters than in the factories. Milton Moskowitz, co-author of *The 100 Best Companies to Work For In America*, dropped Levi's from the list in the most recent edition, partly because of what he sees as a double standard. Although Haas has assured, for instance, that the partners of gay employees get health benefits--something that resonates loudest in San Francisco--he has shut down a pants factory in San Antonio in favor of moving the business to low-wage Costa Rica. The decision idled 1,100 workers.

Levi's President Thomas W. Tusher says the company simply had no choice: The San Antonio plant made Dockers, which require twice the labor content of blue jeans. Levi's had to move to a low-wage country to compete on price in what has become a brutal market for casual all-cotton slacks. Other companies make similar decisions every day. But because of Levi's self-conscious reputation as an employer who cares, it opens itself up to plenty of criticism.

Haas's standard reply is that guaranteed employment is not a part of Levi's values system. Such a pledge would be "unwise and dishonest," he says. Still, as the restructuring program goes forward, more dislocations and layoffs are likely. When they come, Bob Haas will have a lot more explaining to do.

'WE DON'T SUPPORT CHILD LABOR'

The simple truth is, living up to a value system as comprehensive as Levi's is hard. It takes hours and hours of work. Today, near the Levi's contractor in Dhaka, Bangladesh, you can see young girls in pigtails, clutching textbooks to their red-and-white school uniforms as they file into class. But not long ago, these same girls—11, 12, 13 years old—toiled full-time as seamstresses, earning $384 a month sewing Dockers casual pants.

In 1992, to square its international sourcing practices with its own ethical code, Levi's began cracking down on child-labor violations by enforcing International Labor Organization standards that bar employment of children under the age of 14. Two Bangladeshi contractors admitted to Levi's that they hired children and agreed to fire them.

They also argued to Levi's officials, however, that the girls and boys provided their families' sole economic support—most of them were the oldest children in large, single-parent families. "We don't support child labor," says Robert H. Dunn, Levi's corporate-communications and community-affairs chief. "But our intention is not to have a devastating effect on families."

Levi's could have ignored its code or it could have canned the kids and forgotten about them. Instead, it worked out a compromise with the contractors: If they continued to pay wages and agreed to hire the children back when they turned 14, Levi's would send them to school and foot the bill for uniforms, books, and tuition.

The deal sounds expensive all the way around. But between the two, Levi's and its contractor have spent just a few thousand dollars. Besides, says Haas, such actions pay dividends in terms of brand image and corporate reputation. Just ask such companies as Wal-Mart Stores and Nike, which have come under fire for their Third World subcontracting practices. "In today's world, a TV exposé on working conditions can undo years of effort to build brand loyalty," says Haas. "Why squander your invest-

ment when, with commitment, reputational problems can be prevented?"

'IT'S A MATTER OF LEADERSHIP'

Bob Haas doesn't have to meet with stock analysts. He feels no pressure from Wall Street for neat, predictable quarterly results. Even the banks that funded his leveraged buyout are off his back: The company's mammoth cash flow has shaved debt to 4.6% of total capital. Would the company behave any differently if it were publicly traded? "It would take a lot more fortitude on the part of Levi's executives," Haas says. But he insists that "this is not a matter of structure, it's a matter of leadership."

Public company or not, Levi's experiment in corporate culture will attract attention and invite criticism. Noted apparel consultant Alan G. Millstein speaks for the many cynics when he says: "The company has the P. C. mindset. The Haases think they talk to God."

Now that enough operational problems have cropped up to slow financial results, Haas has given his critics some ammunition they didn't have before. But he goes out of his way to say that you can't abandon management-science efforts simply because things get tough. Too many managers, he feels, use that as an excuse to hide their "resistance to the idea that the soft sides and hard sides of management can be combined."

It's not so much that they can't be combined but that they may have unintended consequences when they are. Dealing with the surprising, often contradictory results of managing by values may be a manager's toughest task. Many managers are likely to ask themselves: Is it worth the trouble? Many, perhaps, would say "no."

"People are comfortable with the traditional ways of doing business," Haas says. "They might say, 'We aspire to do the things you've done, but we don't have time for it, the stock market wouldn't value it, or we're not as prosperous as Levi Strauss is.'" When it comes to managing by values, Haas has a ways to go to meet his own exacting standard. But he can't be faulted for bowing to what's comfortable.

By Russell Mitchell in San Francisco, with Michael Oneal in New York and bureau reports

94

Rating game is serious at buyers' guide

Magazine's quality testers take to task the products we take for granted

By Katy Kelly
USA TODAY

YONKERS, N.Y. — You don't have to be a rocket scientist to be a good judge of washing machines.

Or maybe you do. Birgit Sauer, Massachusetts Institute of Technology grad and rocket scientist, is paid to do the wash. Before that, she made the coffee. About 4,000 cups. Fortunately, her boss helped.

Sauer is one of 96 *Consumer Reports* scientists devoted to ferreting out flaws in such life necessities as hair dryers and antacids, boom boxes and comfortable shoes. Their work is among the oddest of odd jobs, but their tests are stringent and their attitudes serious.

CR is part of the non-profit Consumers Union, founded in 1936 with the goal of helping buyers sift through advertising hype and get the best product for their money. The magazine, which accepts no freebies and runs no ads, is the personal shopper for 5 million subscribers.

A poor rating can undermine the most popular of products. (In 1988, when *CR* reported the Suzuki Samurai had a tendency to roll over when making sudden swerves, sales went from good to nearly nil.) And a top rating can turn a sleeper into a must-have. (Sales of Saucony running shoes jumped after they scored high in May '92).

The magazine's Operations Committee meets once a year and, with reader and employee input, decides which products to test. Some, like car tests and the commercial airplane air-quality test featured in the August issue, must be done away from home base.

But most trials — many of which take months — are conducted at CU headquarters, a 100,000-square-foot, two-story cement building that houses *CR*'s editorial and technical staff. It's a place where offices look like offices, labs look like prize storage for a TV game show and scientists act like nothing you expect.

Engineer Jim Nanni, a Home Environmental Products Senior Project Leader, is a professional-looking, tie-wearing man. He is flushing sponges down a toilet.

He clocks the time it takes for each to travel through clear plastic pipes and measures how far a single flush will carry the cellulose. When he has flushed enough, he'll know how to test the 30 different models of low water-consumption toilets that surround him.

Baby equipment fills the lab of Recreation & Home Improvement Project Leader Werner Freitag. Stashed to one side are the 18-pound sandbag-and-duct-tape "babies" he plops into swing seats to see if hardware holds.

The 33-year *CR* veteran also tests the durability of some smaller pieces with a "short-distance drop test." An untrained visitor might not recognize that this grown man throwing a rattle on the floor is, in fact, doing the work his job description requires.

There are many less amusing ways to earn a living. CR scientists start at $30,000 a year, and most stay for the long haul. Research panelists (trained civilians who evaluate products such as food and clothing that can be judged only by human beings) don't need a degree. But those working in Foods must be able to name that scent — including chocolate, wintergreen and barbecue sauce — after just one blind whiff. (It's harder than you might think.)

Some panelists are easy to spot. At 10:30 a.m., the first wave of CR walkers takes to the halls for their twice daily 1-mile loop in and around the building. They're professionals "trained in wearing shoes," says Senior Lab Technician Tom Mutchner.

To qualify for the June-to-September project, panelists submitted to a foot inspection. Bunions are an unacceptable sore spot. A stubbed toe or blister will bench a panelist.

Usually, test products are bought at random stores across the USA by one of CR's six full-time and 100 part-time incognito shoppers, but since footwear needs fitting, shoe testers hit the malls. Each bought 15 pairs of specific shoes, paying with cash or personal credit cards to keep the salesperson from guessing the reason for the shoe-buying frenzy.

Après walk, they fill out evaluation forms, sizing up their shoes. In the interest of science, testers wear identical, company-issued socks. "Recently, it's been 99 (degrees). We've been seen around the halls wearing shorts, T-shirts and a pair of black wingtips with black socks," says Mutchner.

"The dad look," adds his colleague, Recreation & Home Improvement Project Leader Maurice Wynn, who is breaking in a pair of test shoes as he works.

Wynn's lab is crowded. A garage door is bolted to the ceiling (a leftover from the garage door-opener test) and structures that appear to be crafted from a giant Erector Set take up much of the floor. CR designed them to test the lasting power of cross-country ski machines, running each for the equivalent of a year's worth of use by ideal people — those who actually work out every day.

Sometimes machines can't do man's work. "For the tennis rackets, we played six hours a week," Wynn says. (Everything "is fun the first time, before you ride 15 bikes up a hill three or four times each.")

But at other times, the work is inspired. Like when Wynn helped create a device to measure heat that gathers under in-use bicycle helmets. The result: an aluminum head that looks like a forerunner of *Star Wars'* C3PO, with a light bulb inside and heat sensors imbedded in the skull. The test "man," which cost the magazine about $4,000 to produce, was something of a hothead until he was modified with a women's bathing cap. "Did you ever fall into a job that feels so right?" Wynn asks.

The guys in the adjoining lab agree. They're opening and emptying cases of motor oil into coded barrels. It will be tested in New York City cabs, fitted with new engines to make the test fair.

Their neighbor, Home Environmental Products Assistant Project Leader Jack Toback, is vacuuming at the speed of light. Literally. Precision vacuuming requires him to keep pace with chaser lights. This is the only way to be sure all test carpets sprinkled with the industry standard "dirt" (10% talcum powder, 90% sand) are cleaned equally.

The machines are tested in a climate-controlled room. "To get consistent results, we maintain it at 70 degrees with 40% humidity," explains Senior Project Leader Frank Iacopelli. The reason: "Humidity will affect how dirt comes off a carpet."

After each vacuum has done its best, the men weigh the machine on a scale and deduct its pre-workout weight. Then, to account for the still-missing dirt, they weigh the carpet and subtract its pre-dirtied weight.

If cleaning for a living isn't your cup of tea, consider sipping something citrus. The CR food testers (some of whom double as shoe testers) are blind-taste-testing orange juice. Dozens and dozens of cups of orange juice. Pity them on margarine days, when they had to test it without any distractions like bread or crackers. Still, says Testing Director of Foods Connie Corbett: "There are some good times, like gift-box chocolates."

It doesn't matter if they like what they chew. Testers aren't asked about preferences but instead rate products on criteria such as intensity of taste and texture. A job perk: They work only three hours a day. More would be detrimental to their palates. To avoid outside influences, they sit in booths resembling library study carrels. Visitors are prohibited. (Your cologne may change the way they perceive their work.) And the air inside the room is pumped out, to prevent stray smells from test kitchens from influencing the judges.

Do these people wear their jobs on their hips? "It's unprofessional to swallow everything," says tester Myra Schutzer. "You can't be fair to the product if you do."

And being fair is how these judges judge themselves.

95

Unjustified Returns Plague Electronics Makers

By Timothy L. O'Brien

Staff Reporter of The Wall Street Journal

OK readers, 'fess up. How many of you have purchased a radar detector for a weekend getaway or a camcorder to videotape a special event and then returned the product for a refund once you've finished using it?

Retailers, tell the truth. A customer returns a cordless telephone, complaining that he couldn't figure out how the darned thing works. If your staff lacks the expertise to help, do you refund your customer's money and ship the phone back to the manufacturer labeled as defective?

If you're in either camp, you have become the nightmare of the nation's consumer-electronics manufacturers. Questionable returns have become the worst problem plaguing the consumer electronics business, according to the Electronic Industries Association, a trade group based in Washington, D.C. A draft of a yearlong study the group plans to release today says the problem is "detrimental to the viability and vitality of the consumer-electronics industry."

Manufacturers say excessive and unwarranted returns force them to repackage and reship perfectly good products, imposing extra costs that squeeze their profits. They say the problem is growing largely because of limitless return policies offered by retail superstores that now dominate consumer-electronics retailing.

While the problem exists for every manufacturer, it is most acute for the many small companies in the field. They often lack the inventory and scale to absorb such recurring costs.

"There is an escalation of problems with returns, and it's frightening," says Jerry Kalov, president of **Cobra Electronics** Corp., a small Chicago maker of cordless telephones and radar detectors. "I think of this as a problem with consumer ethics and retailer ethics."

Only weeks ago, Mr. Kalov says, Cobra received a cordless telephone, returned by a retailer, that was two years old. The retailer had given the customer a complete refund — even though a dog had clearly chewed up the handset.

"Why would a customer return that, why would the retailer accept it, and why should the manufacturer have to accept it back?" asks Mr. Kalov.

Many manufacturers are furious at retailers who, they say, need to crack down on returns. Among other things, today's

Points of No Return

Guidelines from the Electronic Industries Association for consumer electronics retailers and manufacturers to control return problems

RETAILERS
- Improve the training of sales personnel
- Inquire specifically why customers are returning products
- Don't offer refunds on products that have been clearly abused
- Shorten the duration of return policies
- Only mark as defective products that truly are defective
- Communicate return policies to customers

MANUFACTURERS
- Improve the quality of owner's manuals
- Establish telephone lines for direct customer support
- Establish common names for common product features
- Bar-code product serial numbers on all boxes

Nancy Doniger

industry report recommends that retailers make a better effort to determine the reasons for returns and improve the training of sales personnel. It also suggests that manufacturers improve their owners' manuals and establish customer support lines.

"This issue really hits one of my hot buttons," says Robert Shaw, president of **International Jensen** Inc., a Lincolnshire, Ill., maker of audio products. "This problem is driven by the power-retailers out there who haven't recognized how devastating this is to some of their smaller suppliers."

Manufacturers say superstores such as **Wal-Mart Stores** Inc., which pride themselves on courting customers with generous money-back guarantees, are too willing to give refunds on anything that comes back through the door. Retailers generally bear little of the costs of products returned because they're said to be defective.

This, say manufacturers, causes such odd phenomena as the "Super Bowl Problem." This occurs when a large-screen

television set is bought before a Sunday Super Bowl party. On Monday, after the last empty beer can has been thrown out, the set is returned.

Then there is the "Wedding Problem," which occurs when dad buys a camcorder on Friday to record his daughter's Saturday wedding. By Monday, daughter is off on her honeymoon, and dad is getting his money back.

Mr. Shaw estimates that such bogus returns lower his company's earnings by about 25%. He says only about 15% of the products that are returned to his company are defective. Mr. Kalov, who recently brought struggling Cobra back to profitability, says returns are also hurting his earnings.

Another problem brought on by superstores, say manufacturers, is that salespeople aren't as knowledgeable as those who worked for the smaller specialty retailers that superstores have largely replaced. When frustrated customers, confronted with a dizzying array of new electronic gadgets, can't get help learning

(cont.)

how to use them, they dump their purchases back in the retailer's lap.

When these returns show up as "defective" merchandise back at the manufacturer, they are often poorly packed. If any parts are missing, the manufacturers say they have to absorb the return as a loss or try to sell it below cost to a factory outlet. Even if all the components are still in place, the unit has to be spruced up, repackaged and sent back to the retailer — assuming the model hasn't become outmoded. (Some superstores have been known to accept returned merchandise that is four or five years old.)

Some superstores acknowledge that a problem exists with their return policies and say they are sympathetic to the burdens imposed on their vendors. Wal-Mart, based in Bentonville, Ark., says it is experimenting with a new 90-day return policy to make things easier for vendors. The company says it can't describe the terms of its current return policy because it varies across product lines.

Wal-Mart also says its salespeople are knowledgeable about the products they sell. "I can assure you we have the best training in the business," says Don Shinkle, Wal-Mart's vice president for corporate affairs. "Are our salespeople experts? Obviously, no they're not."

Kmart Corp., based in Troy, Mich., says its policy guarantees a full refund, "no questions asked," any time a product is returned no matter how long since the date of purchase. Best Buy Co., an Eden Prairie, Minn., superstore chain that specializes in electronic goods, says it has tightened its return policy on camcorders and radar detectors. The company now has a five-day limit on returns for those products, compared with 30-day limits on other items, and it says that has helped cut down on abuses.

Small manufacturers say they also need the leverage and lobbying capabilities of larger manufacturers to help persuade more retailers to make changes. Thomson Consumer Electronics Inc., a large Indianapolis manufacturer that is a unit of France's Thomson SA, says that bogus returns cost the company "millions and millions of dollars" annually. It says it is negotiating with retailers to help solve the problem.

In the meantime, some smaller players are opening telephone support lines to assist customers. Timothy Johnson, vice president of Phoenix Gold, a Portland, Ore., concern that makes amplifiers for car stereos, says such support lines have helped keep his return rate low.

But Mr. Johnson says the cost of establishing such services will ultimately be passed along to consumers in the form of higher electronics prices, ironically undermining shoppers' efforts to get lower prices in the first place by patronizing superstores.

96.

Libraries of Killers Often Include a Book Or Two From Paladin

* * *

Telling How to Booby-Trap Or Bomb Is Good Business To a Successful Publisher

By ERIK LARSON
Staff Reporter of THE WALL STREET JOURNAL

BOULDER, Colo. — Peder Lund, owner of Paladin Press, a mail-order publisher here, is delighted. He has just learned that the Library of Congress keeps one of his books in its rare-book collection ' r security reasons. "I've got to write that down," he says.

The book, one of many Paladin publishes on everything from making bombs to being a successful hit man, is called "Kill Without Joy." A 500-page how-to guide to homicide, it even offers a few tips on decapitation.

Mr. Lund, 50 years old, is unabashedly candid about his motives and wares. "I prefer to make decisions about publishing based on what we want to publish and what our customers want, rather than acceding to any particular desire for respectability," he says, his chair tipped back, a loaded .357-caliber Magnum revolver resting, as always, on the right-hand surface of his desk. With a gravelly laugh, he adds: "Why bother? It's not on my agenda."

Primers on Violence

At a time when America is struggling with a rising tide of urban violence, Paladin Press enthusiastically peddles primers on the techniques of violence. Its books are well-known to police and federal agents who have found them in the libraries of serial killers and bombers. The L.L. Bean of mayhem, Paladin is the most visible company in a little-known but robust industry often called the "gun aftermarket," which includes scores of small publishers, manufacturers and gun-show exhibitors devoted to peddling murderous know-how of all kinds. That such an industry exists at all demonstrates the power of the First Amendment to protect even advice on how to garrote, stab and burn.

"I've got to give you credit," one satisfied Paladin customer wrote the company. "You offer controversial, often shocking literature that is invaluable to all Americans." He had ordered five books. One, "Improvised Explosives," tells how to build package bombs and booby-trap a door. "It's a pity," the customer wrote, "that all mail-order companies don't follow your example."

Peder Lund

A Wallingford, Pa., parent was less delighted: "Take our son's name off your mailing list *immediately*. You should be *stopped* from sending your publication through the mail to minors."

Mr. Lund and a partner, Robert K. Brown, founded Paladin in 1970, after both had served with the Army's Special Forces in Vietnam. (Mr. Brown left Paladin in 1974 to start Soldier of Fortune magazine, and remains its publisher.) The two took the name Paladin not directly from the character on the classic TV show "Have Gun Will Travel" but from a class of medieval knights who roamed the countryside correcting injustice. But Paladin Press had no great interest in righting wrongs. "The point," Mr. Lund says, "was pure profit."

He won't disclose Paladin's current fiscal results, but the company seems to provide him a comfortable living. He drives a $45,000 Range Rover and spends up to five months a year at a cottage Paladin owns in Britain's Cotswolds. A veteran of three divorces, he lives with a longtime female friend in a mountain home complete with a one-story indoor waterfall.

He has encountered business obstacles executives don't typically face. Printers have refused to print Paladin's books. An answering service refused to take its calls. Two different banks asked Paladin to take its business elsewhere. Magazines and newspapers, including this one, have declined to accept its advertisements.

Not So Ordinary People

Paladin's catalog includes "21 Techniques of Silent Killing"; "Hit Man: A Technical Manual for Independent Contractors," purportedly written by a practicing professional; and "Homemade C-4," a guide to making the powerful explosive.

Such books, while having little influence on normal individuals, tend to draw vulnerable, socially isolated people, says Dr. Park Dietz, a forensic psychiatrist and consultant for the Federal Bureau of Investigation. He often encounters patients who have read Paladin books, including two serial killers responsible for 16 deaths, and finds they tend to incorporate "the world view" of the books. "My concern is not just that one can learn to build a better bomb this way," he says, "but also that through sufficient immersion in this subculture one comes to find a greater need to build the bomb."

Indeed, bomb investigators say they routinely find Paladin books in the possession of bombing suspects. "Hundreds of times," says a bomb expert with the federal Bureau of Alcohol, Tobacco and Firearms.

Bomb-squad members themselves are among Paladin's most motivated customers. Joseph Grubisic, commander of the Chicago police bomb squad, got on the company's mailing list in order to be prepared for bombs made from Paladin recipes. Charles Stumph, commander of the Orange County, Calif., sheriff's bomb squad, looks through every book his squad finds. "Every time I open one up," he says, "it scares me. The majority of people who buy these books have no idea at all what explosives will do."

That the books may pose the gravest danger to their own users is known to the marketers. Mr. Lund acknowledges that the "The Anarchist's Cookbook," published elsewhere but offered in Paladin's catalog, contains flawed recipes for making explosives, but adds: "There are so many copies of that book extant, I don't see how not selling another one is going to be in any way redeeming."

Billy Blann, owner of Desert Publications, El Dorado, Ark., says his company's "The Poor Man's James Bond," also sold by Paladin, is downright dangerous. "Anybody who fools with this stuff," he says, in a profound Arkansas twang, "has got to be a fool."

Publisher, Pragmatist

Still, Paladin continues selling such books. "As a human," Mr. Lund says, "I feel very sorry for anyone who's put through any physical suffering. As a publisher and as a pragmatist, I feel *absolutely* no responsibility for the misuse of information." Just in case, Paladin inserts disclaimers in many of its books warning

(cont.)

the work is for entertainment or information purposes only.

So far no one has sued Paladin over its books. "And I think it would be a travesty of the legal system to do so, don't you?" Mr. Lund says. "Do you sue General Motors because a kid runs over his schoolmate in a stolen car? Do you sue the manufacturer of a hammer because a child picks it up and bashes his little sister's head in? I can't see any clear-thinking person holding someone responsible for conveying information."

Mr. Lund points out that not all his books involve violence. He cites books on military history and handbooks for law-enforcement officers. His customers aren't crooks, he says; they buy his books as a "cathartic," a means of harmlessly working off frustrations with bosses, former wives and intractable institutions by imagining acts of violence and revenge. "I think there are many, many Walter Mittys on our mailing list," he says.

America's free-speech gladiators say the law can't, and shouldn't, halt Paladin's prose. What's the difference, asks Robert Peck, of the American Civil Liberties Union, between a Paladin handbook and a techno-thriller that goes into explicit detail? "The First Amendment makes no distinction between that which is done as literature and that which is done as a how-to book," he says.

Jack Thompson, a Miami lawyer who campaigned against the song "Cop Killer," sees it differently. Most Americans want the likes of Paladin Press "aggressively pursued and prosecuted," he says, "but they've been abandoned because of a lack of will by the government at every level." He adds, "The ACLU has been very successful in convincing an entire generation of prosecutors that you can't do anything about this stuff."

The U.S. Supreme Court sides with Mr. Lund. It has ruled that acts of speech can lose their First Amendment protection only when they are virtually certain to lead a listener or reader to an immediate act of violence. Even some bomb investigators agree that Paladin-type guidebooks shouldn't be banned. "What I'd really like," says Charles Stumph of the Orange County squad, "is for more people to be responsible, whether it's publishers or book retailers or wholesalers, and say 'no, enough's enough.' "

In fact, there are some things Paladin won't publish.

Advice on altitude-sensitive detonation devices, for example. "We don't want to be the scapegoats for an investigation of an airliner coming down," Mr. Lund says.

And explicit books on poisons.

But why these scruples?

"We all have our boundaries, wouldn't you say?" Mr. Lund replies. "Perhaps my boundaries are different from yours. My boundaries are different from many people's."

Reprinted from the January 6, 1993 issue, by permission of *The Wall Street Journal* ©1993 Dow Jones & Company, Inc. All Rights Reserved Worldwide.

212

97

Chlorine-Free Paper Is Clean But Unpopular

By Timothy Aeppel
Staff Reporter of The Wall Street Journal

Louisiana-Pacific Corp. figured industrial customers would be as enthusiastic as environmentalists were when it stopped using chlorine at its sprawling pulp mill in Samoa, Calif.

It figured wrong.

Looking for ways to clean up its waste water, the company eliminated chlorine, which makes paper snowy white, from its bleaching process. That meant that chlorine's byproducts, which include dioxins that accumulate in fish and other creatures, would no longer be dumped into the ocean.

But there are few buyers for the less toxic pulp. Louisiana-Pacific, based in Portland, Ore., says it is selling its "totally chlorine free," or TCF, pulp at a deep loss and recently halted production at the Samoa mill to work off mountains of inventory.

The travails of the Samoa plant underscore the dilemma pulp and paper companies face in the war over chlorine. Because of its highly toxic byproducts, environmental groups are lobbying to ban chlorine from paper mills and other industrial processes. As part of the Clean Water Act, which comes up for renewal before Congress this year, the Clinton administration has proposed a study to see if the use of chlorine should be limited or banned.

Most U.S. papermakers still use some kind of chlorine treatment to whiten their paper. They insist there's no market for the brownish TCF paper. Although none has done detailed market studies, they say consumers expect bright white paper when they flip through a magazine or open an envelope. In addition, making TCF requires costly investments in new technology. A study by International Paper Co. estimates the industry would have to spend $9.6 billion in capital investments to go chlorine-free.

As technology improves, however, TCF paper should start looking more like the competition, and its price will eventually come down. And when this happens, more people will be likely to buy it. "This market is evolving right now," says Peter Sweeney, a marketing official at Cross Pointe Paper, a unit of **Pentair** Corp. in St. Paul, Minn., which is developing TCF paper products.

Cross Pointe started out making pure TCF paper, but then realized that more buyers wanted products that include recycled material. Within the next two months, Mr. Sweeney says, the company will unveil a line of paper that mixes TCF with recycled paper. It is as white as paper made with chlorine and is priced "within 5%" of traditional opaque stock, Mr. Sweeney says.

The company doesn't advertise its paper, but gets calls from environmental groups and companies that have heard about it and want to buy it. "There's a market need," he says, "and we have to identify how large that is." Environmentalists hope that someday, most paper will be both recycled and 100% TCF.

The few companies that buy TCF paper use it primarily for annual reports or environmental brochures to show their pro-green sentiments. "We pay more for it, but we decided it's important to a portion of our readers," says Robert Garth, co-publisher of Scuba Times magazine, a bimonthly for scuba enthusiasts that publishes part of each issue on TCF paper. Mr. Garth figures he pays about 20% more for the paper.

Time magazine's editorial staff, pressured by the environmental activist group Greenpeace, said they would explore using paper bleached without chlorine. But the Time Inc. magazine group refused, noting that going to chlorine-free paper isn't "a corporate policy." Last week, however, Time Inc. announced that all of its magazines would be printed on recycled paper, which can be virtually indistinguishable from new paper, by 1996.

Louisiana-Pacific switched to TCF only after being sued in U.S. District Court by a group of activist surfers and the Environmental Protection Agency for dumping waste water into the ocean. The company could have built a secondary-waste treatment system. "We decided it was cheaper to eliminate the source of the problem than to build the secondary treatment," says Barry Lacter, a company spokesman.

The papermakers' main argument against TCF is that there is a cheaper alternative. Most U.S. mills have switched from using pure chlorine, the chemical element, to a mix of chlorine and chlorine dioxide, a chemical compound made of chlorine and oxygen. Chlorine dioxide reacts differently with pulp, generating fewer dioxins. Mills that shift to 100% chlorine dioxide are even carving a niche for themselves among environmentally aware consumers by labeling products "elemental chlorine free" or ECF.

"We believe dioxin is no longer an issue in the pulp-bleaching process," says Richard Phillips, vice president of technology at **International Paper** Co., the U.S.'s largest paper maker. "Increasing the amount of chlorine dioxide can allow most mills to cut dioxin emissions to nondetectable levels," he says, adding that International Paper achieved that in 1992. (While dioxin is widely believed to be carcinogenic, it is still unclear what level of exposure to it is dangerous to humans.)

Environmentalists say even small amounts of dioxin are unacceptable. "It's the difference between chlorine and chlorine-lite," says Mark Floegel, head of Greenpeace's International Chlorine Campaign. "It's two-thirds less polluting; but it's still stable in the environment — so we're just slowing the rate of accumulation."

Another industry argument is that even green consumers are more eager for recycled paper than TCF. Still, pressure to produce chlorine-free paper is likely to grow. In addition to the Clinton administration's proposed chlorine study, the EPA is re-examining its risk assessment for dioxin — which could also have an effect on chlorine use.

In the U.S., some companies are combining technologies — creating hybrid mills that cut dioxin to a minimum. For example, Stamford, Conn.-based **Champion International** Group uses oxygen — rather than chlorine — in the initial bleaching stage in all its mills. Waste water from this stage is less toxic and thus easier to recycle. Chlorine dioxide is introduced only in later stages of processing.

Meanwhile, back in Samoa, Louisiana-Pacific is facing tough choices. With little domestic demand for its pulp, the company is eyeing other ways to make the business profitable. One option would be to shift from making so-called kraft pulp, used for paper, to producing "fluff" for use in products like disposable diapers. The company may also join forces with a paper maker to produce its own TCF paper products.